ANISHINAUBAE THESAURUS

Anishinaubae Thesaurus

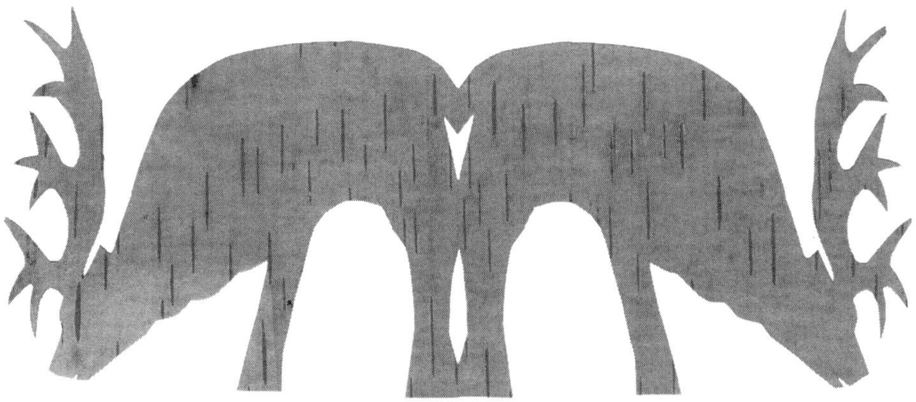

Basil H. Johnston

Michigan State University Press • *East Lansing*

Copyright © 2007 by Basil H. Johnston

♾ The paper used in this publication meets the minimum requirements of ANSI/NISO Z39.48-1992 (R 1997) (Permanence of Paper).

Michigan State University Press
East Lansing, Michigan 48823-5245

Printed and bound in the United States of America.

13 12 11 10 09 08 07 1 2 3 4 5 6 7 8 9 10

LIBRARY OF CONGRESS CATALOGING-IN-PUBLICATION DATA
Johnston, Basil.
Anishinaubae thesaurus / Basil H. Johnston.
p. cm.
ISBN 978-0-87013-753-2 (pbk. : alk. paper)
1. Ojibwa language—Synonyms and antonyms. I. Title.
PM852.J59 2006
497.3—dc22
2006100330

Book and cover design by Sharp Des!gns, Inc., Lansing, MI

The bark cutting of a caribou used on the cover is by Anishinaubae artist Lois Beardslee from a private collection and is used with permission of the artist.

green press INITIATIVE Michigan State University Press is a member of the Green Press Initiative and is committed to developing and encouraging ecologically responsible publishing practices. For more information about the Green Press Initiative and the use of recycled paper in book publishing, please visit *www.greenpressinitiative.org.*

Visit Michigan State University Press on the World Wide Web at *www.msupress.msu.edu*

Contents

Preface

This Anishinaubae thesaurus does not contain the 400,000 or so words that make up the Anishinaubae language. Nor is it intended to set a standard for orthography, though there is an urgent need for such standard. My object is more modest. I have compiled a small but practical thesaurus that will be useful to teachers, translators, interpreters, writers . . . and maybe orthographers.

The number of terms, words, and roots set down in this text approximately correspond to the number of basic terms, words, and roots that an ordinary person would need not only to get by, but also to have command of a large vocabulary.

I was not unmindful of the need for standardization in the spelling in the Anishinaubae language as I put this text together. There are so many orthographers, so many systems, so many dictionaries, but there is nothing, sad to relate, to read. For this mess, universities and the provincial ministries of education are to blame. They have endorsed courses in orthography in Native language teaching programs as if orthography can be mastered by every Joe and Jane. And, still, despite their training, no two of these orthographers are likely to agree on the spellings of words. Likewise, universities dispatch squads of linguists with reams of credits in incomprehensible styles and systems, who nevertheless cannot say the most basic things in a Native language.

One enterprising individual devised a colored system that was supposed to make learning the Anishinaubae language fun and effortless. About the only thing that the beginners learn with this system is how to express themselves in colorful terms and using off-color language. Writers using this system need a case of magic markers to score their meanings and tenses. Another "innovative" linguist pulled a double vowel system out of a hat that, *presto*, was supposed to be uniquely and distinctively Anishinaubae. Alas, the poor e, o, u, and the wretched little consonants were given no such distinction. And what was supposed to have been new and different bears a remarkable resemblance to Finnish orthography. Universities and their scholars ought to know better than to encourage orthographers to set spelling standards that run counter to human literary experience in other cultures and eras, where writers, not "spellers" or grammarians, set orthographic and usage standards. It would have been better had these institutions offered courses in grammar and writing rather than sponsored orthography.

There is good reason to believe that these flawed spelling systems are founded only on the sound. Judging from the spelling and construction of words and expressions in these systems, little thought seems to have been given to sense and sight (appearance), two other factors that should govern orthography. Words represent the ideas, feelings, and wants of a person and, as such, they are more than merely sounds.

It is as a writer in both English and Anishinaubae and as a translator that I came to know something of and to appreciate the construction of Anishinaubae words. As a writer, translator, and teacher I deal with ideas and meanings. Not only am I asked "What does this mean?" but I also ask of myself and others "How can I get my meaning across?" A writer must know how a language works and what its words mean. In order to interpret the Anishinaubae heritage as accurately as possible, I had to learn about its basic structure, usage, and meanings.

For our ancestors to have created a language that is at the same time simple in structure and construction, rich and complex in range and depth of meanings, and musical and moving is extraordinary.

In all, the total number of prefixes, verbs, nouns, and suffixes that make up the basic vocabulary of the Anishinaubae language probably does not exceed 5,000; yet, the ability to combine these many prefixes and suffixes with roots adds an immense number of words to a working vocabulary. A person speaking the Anishinaubae language will need to memorize no more than 700 prefixes, 3,500 roots, and 100 suffixes to be fluent and to be in command of thousands of words.

What I found about this language, as I wrote and translated, is that many, if not most, terms and expressions have three meanings. The first identifies a person, place, thing, idea, or act. The second signifies the origin of the term or expression from its prefixes and roots, and thereby conveys its etymology. The third connotes understandings that refer to some insight, ideal, belief, precept, institution, value, concept, or notion.

The part of speech in the Anishinaubae language that is key to this three-fold function is the prefix. Like adjectives and adverbs, prefixes alter the meanings of root verbs and nouns. The meaning intended will depend upon context and circumstance. Unfortunately, some of these prefixes, as pronounced, sound the same. While it is not difficult to distinguish the meanings of prefixes in the context of speech, this is less clear when they are taken out of this context.

Putting sounds on paper is another thing altogether. Print, writing, is filtered through the eyes, not the ears. Let there be no mistake about that: words, sentences, paragraphs, stories—the whole bit—are meant to be read. The eyes need to be trained to recognize letters and words, just as the ears need to be trained to distinguish sounds. For this reason, spelling standards need to be established. Prefixes that are often pronounced alike need to be given their own spellings to give them their own identities, and to therefore aid recognition. Reading should not be an excruciating exercise in deciphering, but a pleasurable act of extracting meanings, feelings, ideas, images from the written word.

Sense and sight should play as important a role in spelling as sound. Sense gives meaning to sound, while appearance gives distinction to sense. These are the considerations that influenced the spelling that I have offered here.

Format

Anishinaubae Thesaurus is divided into five parts—nouns; adjectives, adverbs, conjunctions, prepositions, and pronouns; suffixes; verbs; and prefixes—that correspond roughly to the structure of the language. (There are additional verb roots listed in a glossary.) Most of these main parts are further subdivided into categories; for example, related nouns are grouped together, and verbs are marshaled according to similarity. The rationale for this format is to enable beginners and others unfamiliar with my spelling system to find words, along with their meanings, more easily than in conventional thesauruses, which presume that users know the language, the spelling, and the etymology. The entries in the undivided chapters are listed in alphabetical order. For each entry, a number of meanings—by no means all—have been set down, along with several examples of usage.

Anishinaubae Thesaurus includes words, terms, and expressions under nouns that other standard Ojibway dictionaries do not list; it includes the only list of prefixes, along with their meanings and examples of usage compiled to date; and it provides the only known compilation of verbs that shows the etymology and definition according to their roots and affixes. The approximately 650 prefixes listed here should be especially useful to translators and writers.

Because words sometimes have several meanings, the divisions in the book are not as clear or tidy as one would hope. To write a complete thesaurus with cross-references was not my object. Still, despite its limitations, the organization and content of this thesaurus should be a much more useful reference to beginners, translators, teachers, and writers than any text currently available.

The Anishinaubae language is, in the main, a verb active voice oriented language. Its principal parts consist of roots, both noun and verb, prefixes, and suffixes. Roots may be compared to nouns that represent general ideas as do may English nouns. To give them sense and specific meanings, prefixes are added to them. When conjoined to noun roots prefixes are like adjectives; when linked to verb roots they are akin to adverbs. A prefix hitched to a suffix that serves as a verbalizer, the new term formed is an infinitive and a noun and a verb in all forms. Noun roots can, in association with a verbalizer, become verbs. The Anishinaubae language is a very versatile language.

Benefits

Anishinaubae Thesaurus is unique. It contains many words, terms, and expressions not found in standard dictionaries. For example, nearly 250 plants, along with the meanings of their names and their and uses, are listed. Topographical features are set down according to the composition of the land, according to the way Anishinaubae people classify landforms. It provides 650 prefixes, along with their meanings and examples of their usage, a feature no other dictionary has. It furnishes both in the independent and root forms for more than 3,000 basic verbs, in a section that also exemplifies the construction of terms and expressions from the conjunction of prefixes and roots.

Anishinaubae Thesaurus is practical. It will serve translators in their work by placing within their reach prefixes and verb roots that will enable them to select the right combination of terms in order to compose words and expressions that are apt, precise, and graceful.

Anishinaubae Thesaurus is easier to use than traditional, conventional dictionaries by virtue of its format. Trees are listed under trees, fish under fish, food preparation under "cook," and operations or functions of the mind under "think." No longer will one have to spend hours in turning over hundreds of pages to find a word that may not even be listed.

Anishinaubae Thesaurus will increase the user's vocabulary, enhance his or her writing, and foster greater precision in usage.

Orthography

I have used the Roman alphabet and the English phonetic system in this outline and other publications as the basis of spelling, in spite of their limitations, to conform to an alphabet and a phonetic system that students are already familiar with, to assist them in their enunciation and pronunciation. But sound is not the sole factor that governs orthography. The word, term, or expression in print is meant for the eye and, as such, must facilitate recognition. Sound, sense, and sight all play a part in dictating the spelling of words.

The orthography needs, as well, to reflect the pace of articulation, not solely the fast pace of Southern Ontario but also the more controlled pace of other speakers from other parts of the Anishinaubae *aki*. Beginners need to hear words and sentences articulated clearly, something that can only be done slowly. Furthermore, the grace and the elegance of the language deserves modulation. For this reason vowels are used.

Many words in the Anishinaubae language have three meanings conferred upon them by prefixes that themselves have a multiplicity of meanings. There is the surface meaning that is at once understood by everyone. Then there is a second meaning given by the prefix and the core term. Third is what may be regarded as a philosophic meaning. Our word for truth or correctness or any of its synonyms is *w'dae'b'wae,* meaning "he or she is telling the truth, is right, is correct, is accurate." From its composition—the prefix *dae,* which means "as far as, inasmuch as, according to," and the root *wae,* a contraction of *waewae,* referring to sound—emerges the second meaning, which gives the sense of a person casting his or her knowledge as far as he or she can. By implication, the person whom is said to be *dae'b'wae* is acknowledged to be telling what he or she knows only insofar as he or she has perceived what he or she is reporting, and only according to his or her command of the language. In other words, the speaker is exercising the highest degree of accuracy possible given what he or she knows. In the third sense the term conveys the philosophic notion that there is no such thing as absolute truth.

But not all words yield the second and third meanings from their construction and usage. Some, like Anishinaubae, Maudjee-kawiss, Pukawiss, Cheeby-aub-oozoo, and Nana'b'oozoo derive their meanings from stories and other contexts.

In the Anishinaubae language the prefixes, suffixes, and core terms, and the need to give affixes that have similar sounds a distinctive appearance, that decide, or ought to decide, orthography. What makes spelling difficult is that the Anishinaubae language is also part tonal and that there are momentary pauses sometimes in the pronunciation of vowels. I have used a dash (-) to indicate this speech characteristic. Except for emphasis, personal pronouns—*neen, keen, ween, neenawind, keenawind, keenwauh, weenawauh*—are contracted in speech. To show this practice, as well as to avoid misunderstandings, I have set down only the first letters of these pronouns, followed by an apostrophe to indicate the letters so left out—*n', k', w', n', k',* and *w'* for I, you (*sing.*), he/she, we, you (*pl.*), and they. *Neenawind* and *keenawind* are first-person pronouns in the plural number. *Neenawind* means *we* but not you, which may refer to one person or several. *Keenawind* means *all of us, no one excepted.*

Negatives, because they may be pronounced either with a long *e* or a short *i*, are troublesome. I have elected to write them using the form yielded by the present indicative, as in *kauween, w'waubussee, noondumaessee,* or *izhausseewuk.*

The main points of departure from other spelling systems are as follows:

- *au* to represent the *a* sound, as in daughter
- *ae* to represent the *e* sound in Ted, both nasal and guttural

- *ee* to represent the long *e,* as in meet
- *i* represents the short *i,* as in pit
- *zh* represents the *zh* sound in measure
- *hn* represents the nasal sound.

In cases where the second consonant of a double consonant should be accentuated, as in double sh's, n's, m's, and k's, I have inserted an *i* to show this trait.

The orthography used in this and other texts is not offered as the final solution, but rather as a start in establishing some form of standardized spelling in our language. Ideas and suggestions to help refine and improve the spelling and simplify it so as to facilitate reading are welcome and invited. Above all, if there are no texts, novels, histories, storybooks, songs, prayers, poems, and dramas to read, there is not much point in developing spellers and orthographic systems.

Nouns

aki *land; earth; soil*

abikimigauh; abi-kummikauh an isthmus
adjiwae-kummik in all the world; everywhere; worldwide; in every quarter of the globe
ae-ishkwau-kummikauk the horizon; the ends of the earth
agaum the shore
agidau-aki uphill
agid-udin uphill; hilltop
ani-geeshk-aubikauh a scarp; an escarpment
assin; assineen; assineek stone(s)
aumini-kaugun(un) spawning grounds
aunikae-ginoon-aeyaung an isthmus
awuss-agaum the other side of the sea, ocean
ayauniko-dunnauh a mountain range
beetoo-ipeeg(oon) pond(s)
gabowau-gawinigun(un) dam(s)
gaugee-idjiwun(un) a falls
geeshk-aubikau-dunnauh a gorge
geewi-ossae-kaun a hunting territory
ginoonaeyaung an isthmus
gummee; gummeen a large body of water; sea(s); ocean(s)
gummeeng at, on, by, in, near the sea
ishkoonigun(un) reserve(s); reservation(s); a remnant; something left over
ishkotae-dunnauh volcano(es)
ishp-aubikau-dunnauh a mountain range
kabaeshiwin; kabaeshiwinun overnight camp(s); stop-over place(s)
kaka-dunnauh a mountain chain
kaukau-ipeekauh a falls
kawaewin; kawaewinun trail(s)
kidu-gaum; kitchi-gaum a continent
Kitchi-Gummeeng a Great Lake; ocean; sea
kitigaun(un) field(s)
kogaediwin; kogaediwinun village(s); park(s); a gathering place
konim(un) dam(s)
maewishkodae; maewishkodaen prairie(s)
maewishkooskaun; maewishkooskaunun meadow(s)
maumeeng downstream
meekun kemauh meekunnuh a road; a trail
metikwauk-aki; metikwauk-akeen forest(s); wood(s)
miniss; minissun island(s)
ministik; ministikoowun island(s) in or at the mouth of a river, usually formed by silt
minitik, minitikoowun an island in or at the mouth of a river, usually formed by silt; islands
Misheen-maukinaukoong North America; the Island of Michillimackinac, Land of The Great Turtle
Mishi-geeshk-aubikau-dunnauh the Grand Canyon
Mishi-Gummeeng a Great Lake; an ocean; a sea; Lake Michigan
mushkeeg-mushkeegoon swamp(s); marsh(es)
naeyaush a point; a peninsula
nanimeeng upstream
naunau-agaum the middle of the sea, ocean
naunauwi-agaum the middle of the sea
nauwitch far out to sea

neess-udin; neessau-aki downhill
niminauwaewigun(un) boat launch(es); harbor(s)
nindo-baun; nindo-baunun well(s)
noopimeeng inland; the hinterland
odaenah; odaenawun a town; a permanent settlement; a place where families collect
odaenauh(n) nation(s)
ogauming; augumin on the opposite, other side of the shore
ondauss-agaum on this side of the sea, ocean
papiko-dunnauh alps
pushkawauk-dauwingauh a desert; a barren, infertile place
pussaun-kaun(un) ditch(es); moat(s); canal(s)
tibaewih the shore
tikip; tikipeen spring(s)
waush; waushun; waudj; waudjun den(s); cave(s)
weequaed; weequaedoon bay(s)
widjiw; widjiwinun mountain(s)
winnigum; winnigumeen portage(s)
zaugeeng a river mouth; a delta; an outlet
zaugigun; zaugiginun small lake(s)
zeepee-kautchigun(un) canal(s)
zeepi kemauh zeebi a river
zhaek-udin a foothill
zheebaunauh; zheebaunaun a narrow; a strait(s)

kummik *earth; soil; land; terrain*

adjiwae-kummik the ends of the world
aedawae-kummik both sides, either side of the earth
ae-iqua-kummik the terminus; the rim; the edge of the earth, land
aenigook-wauk-kummik the entire world
agid-kummik the earth's surface; on the earth
anaum-kummik underground; hell
augawae-kummik the other side, the sheltered side of a height of land
auzhawae-kummik the other side, the side opposite, around the other side of
baeshowae-kummik near, adjacent, adjoining, neighboring lands, territories
beeto-kummik between the tiers of earth, earth's strata
dubussi-kummik a lowland; downstream; a depression; a basin
geewitau-kummik around the land, the earth; all around; on every side
ishpu-kummik the highland; the heights
maegawae-kummik all over; in the midst or center of the land
makatae-kummik black earth, soil
mashkowi-kummik the solid, hard earth, soil
mino-kummik the good, bountiful earth; spring
mishishawae-kummik the wide open plain; exposed, bare earth
misqui-kummik red earth, soil
mittu-kummik bare earth; naked ground
miziwae-kummik everywhere; every quarter of the globe; worldwide; every land; far and wide
mizzu-kummik the earth; the bosom of the earth; the bare ground
Mizzu-kummik-quae Mother Earth
nakae-kummik on this side; here; over this way
nimbunae-kummik one side of the earth
nooki-kummik soft earth, soil
pekae-kummik to one side
piko-kummik hilly land, terrain
pugwood-kummik the hinterland; the back woods; remote lands, territories
pushkawauh-kummik cleared, treeless land, terrain, territory
shawae-kummik the slant of the earth
waub-kummik white earth, soil
waussau-kummik shiny, shimmering land
waussawae-kummik distant, remote, far-off lands, territories
wauwiyae-kummik a round, oval land, territory
zauwau-kummik the brown, copper soil
zoong-kummik the strong, firm earth

aen-kummikauk *topography; geography; landforms; soil; the contour of land; the nature and character of terrain*

ani-baeki-kummikauh the land that slopes; a slope
baeshowae-kummikauh the land that is nearby; nearby land

bauski-kummikauh dry, parched soil
bautae-kummikauh soil that is dry, arid
beeto-kummikauh stratified land
cheecheeng-kummikauh the land, earth that quakes; an earthquake
dazhawae-kummikauh flat land
dupuss-kummikauh the lowland, depression
geezhogitae-kummikauh dry, arid land
makatae-kummikauh dark, black earth, land
mashkowi-kummikauh hard, strong soil, land
maunaud-kummikauh rugged and broken terrain
mino-kummikauh fertile soil; the ground is regular, even
nimbunae-kummikauh canted ground
nipeewi-kummikauh the ground is damp, wet
nook-kummikauh the land, soil is soft
piko-kummikauh hilly, mountainous, irregular land
pissu-kummikauh a basin; dale; dell; ravine; valley
pushkwau-kummikauh exposed, barren, open land
shawae-kummikauh canted land
taetae-kummikauh shaking, trembling land
tautau-kummikauh earthquake; land leveled by a bulldozer
teeteeng-kummikauh a tremor
tootoo-kummikauh an earthquake
waub-kummikauh white earth, clay
waun-kummikauh a hollow, or low place on the surface
waussawae-kummikauh a far off, distant land
wauwiyae-kummikauh mounds, drumlins
weembau-kummikauh the ground that is hollow
ween-idjeesh-kummikauh muddy, grimy soil, earth
zauwau-kummikauh brown soil, earth, land
zhingu-kummikauh flat, plain land
zoong-kummikauh firm, strong land, earth

---

ae-inaubikauk *a metal, rock, ore; the nature, character, form, formation of rocky, mountainous land (from* waubik*—metallic; ferrous; rocky)*

---

ae-inaubikauk the nature, character, form, structure of rocks or mountains
agid-aubikauk kemauh agid-aubik the summit, crown, crest of the mountain, heights, rocks
anim-aubikauh a mound of rocks; a chain of mountains; a ridge
apeet-aubikauh the altitude or height of mountains
baengi-waubikauh moistureless rocks, stones, bluffs, mountains
baesh-aubikauh (baepaesh-aubikauh) striped, streaked rock, stone, mountain
baug-awaubikauh rocky shoals
beessi-aubikauh small stones, rocks
beeto-waubikauh tiered rocks, stones; sedimentary rocks
bimi-n-aubikauh kemauh baemi-n-aubikauk along the edge, lip, rim of a mountain, mesa
book-waubikauh the rocks that are broken, jagged, cracked, smashed
daessi-aubikauh flat rocks, stones; shale; sedimentary rock; a mesa
daushk-aubikauh a crevice, fissure, cleft, fracture in the rock
dupuss-aubikauh low, depressed mountains, rocks
dupuss-aubikauk; dupuss-aubik at the lower level of rock, mountain
geen-aubikauh jagged, sharp rocks, stones
geeshk-aubikauh sheer sided mountains, bluffs, escarpment
ishp-aubikauh lofty mountains, rocks
ishp-aubikauk the heights; somewhere at, near the summit
kauk-aubeekauh a precipice; a sheer drop
kitug-aubikauh mottled, flecked, speckled rock, stone, mountain
maunaud-aubikauh irregular, impassable, difficult, impenetrable mountains, bluffs, rocks
mino-aubikauh convenient, well set mountains, bluffs, rocks
misqawau-bikauh reddish, coppery rock
naeg-waubikauh crevices, nooks, recesses in

the rock, mountain
nipee-waubikauh wet, damp rocks, stones, bluffs, mountains
nishinaud-aubikauh irregular, cluttered rocks, stones
nooki-waubikauh soft, pliant rock, shale, ore
nubug-aubikauh flat, sedimentary rock
piko-d-aubikauh a rocky projection; a mound of rocks
shawae-aubikauh tilted, slanted rock, mountain, peak
shooshawae-aubikauh straight, true, direct, upright rock
waequae-aubikauh the edge of a mountain
waun-aubikauh hollow rocks, stones
wauwiy-aubikauh rounded, oval rocks, stones
weebawau-yaubikauh a mountain pass
weemb-aubikauh the rock, mountain that is hollow; caves and hollows within the rock
zheeb-aubikauh a tunnel, a subterranean passage in the rock, mountain
zhooshki-waubikauh smooth, slippery rock, stone, mountain

---

inudunnauh *the structure, construction, configuration, formation of land; topography of either rock or gravel or clay; altitude, elevation*

---

aedawae-dunnauh on either side, every side of the mountain
agid-dunnauh at the top of the mountain
ani-baek-dunnauh slope, sloping land
ani-dunnauh the mountain chain that bears in such direction
apeeti-dunnauh the elevation, altitude
aupita-dunnauh halfway up the mountainside
auzhawae-dunnauh on the opposite side of the mountain
auzhoo-dunnauh the mountains, inclines, slopes, sides that criss-cross
awuss-idunnauh on the other side of the mountain
awuss-nakae-dunnauh on the other side of the mountain
baepaesh-idunnauh streaked, striped mountains
banaud-idunnauh a craggy mountainside
bimi-dunnauh a parallel mountain ridge
dawa-dunnauh a space between mountains; a valley
dupuss-dunnauh kemauh pussu-dunnauh a valley
geeshkaukae-dunnauh crags
geeshk-dunnauh a precipie
ishpu-dunnauh a highland, height of land (origin of the name Spadina—a street in Toronto)
kaka-dunnauh steep mountain sides
kakau-dunnauh craggy mountains
maegawae-dunnauh amidst the mountains
maud-idunnauh the start of the mountains, hill, slope
nae-dunnauh at the end of the mountain chain
nauwi-dunnauh halfway up or down a hill, mountain
neessau-dunnauh the foothills
ondaus-nakae-dunnauh on this side of the mountain
papiko-dunnauh; piko-dunnauh a mountainous place
saugi-dunnauh a pass leading out
shaek-dunnauh the base of a hill, mountain
zheebau-dunnauh a tunnel through a mountain

---

aen-anidauwingauk *the formation, contour, configuration, cast, feature, composition of sand, sandy soil, land, terrain*

---

anaum-auwingauh a sandy sub-surface
assineehnse-dauwingauh land, ground, soil composed of pebbles, gravel
ba-dauwingauh a sand bar; spit
baebeek-idauwingauh a serpentine ridge; the hummock or spine of land that snakes about
daeti-gawaungiwingauh a sandy beach
dazhawaeg-idauwingauh a level surface of land
geek-idauwingauh eroding land, soil
geeshki-idauwingauh a sand bluff, cliff
goondauwidauwingauh quicksand; the sandy soil that swallows
inin-auwingauh fine sand
ishp-idauwingauh high sand hills, dunes
miniss-aunawingauh islands, sand bars

formed by silt

mino-dauwingauh fair, pleasant soil, ground

mitawun sand

naegow sand

naendawin-auwingauh sandy

obad-auwingauh a sand bar, a spit

obaun-awaungauh a passage between dunes or sand bars

oozhae-idauwingauh a bank of sand; a sand bank

opi-wingauh sandy cliffs, banks

paupaug-idauwingauh solid, packed down ground

piko-dauwingauh hilly, with many dunes, moraines, terrain

pini-dauwingauh; bini-dauwingauh fine sandy soil; origin of the name Penetanguishene—a city in Ontario

shakau-dauwingauh cool and damp sandy soil, terrain

tautaug-idauwingauh flat, level soil, terrain, surface

zhing-dauwingauh sandy flats

zhingi-mik-wauniwungauh a lode of sand, a vein, a ribbon of sand

---

inummoh *(root) the direction of a trail, path, road; the route, course*

---

agaussidae-ummoh a narrow road

agidau-akeewae-ummoh a road leading uphill

akeewaedin-immoh a road leading to the north

akeewaek-immoh a road leading homeward

assineewud-immoh a road constructed of gravel, stone

auzhawae-immoh a road leading to the other side

auzhidae-ummoh a crossroads

baebeekid-ummoh a meandering road, trail

baupaugid-ummoh a well-worn road

chaekauk-immoh the road going into woods

gawaek-ummoh a straight, direct road

ishkawaek-ummoh a winding road

maunaudid-ummoh a broken, irregular road

maungidae-ummoh a wide road

mindaubee-ummoh a road leading down to the water

mino-immoh a pleasant, agreeable, easy for travel road

naeyaush-immoh a road leading to the cape

neessau-akeewae-ummoh a road going downhill

nipeewud-immoh a wet, damp road

nissowauk-immoh the convergence of three trails, roads, routes

pekae-ummoh the road bearing in another direction

shawaek-ummoh a slanted road

tibaewae-immoh a road running along the shore

tik-ummoh a short road or one that cuts across another

zaugauk-immoh a road emerging from a forest, woods

zhaedunnau'd'immoh a road running down to the base of a mountain

zhooshkid-ummoh a slippery road

---

inu-dummauh kemauh ae-'n'dummauk *the nature, form, terrain and character of the bed of a body of water other than a river*

---

anibaek-dummauh the water bed slopes down gently

geeshkeen-dummauh the water bed drops off steeply; a bank

ginoween-dummauh the water is deep

tikoween-dummauh the water bed is shallow

---

inau-gummauh *the form, character, nature, color of a body of water*

---

aehnse-inau-gummauh the body of water with many spills, outlets

aundjigae-gummauh where the body of water changes

aunikae-gummauh the point where one body of water extends into another body of water

baugawau-gummauh a shoaled lake, body of water; the body of water characterized by shoals

beenau-gummauh the body of water that is clean

gaushaugawau-gummauh a body of water with many shoals; a shallow lake

gaussau-gummauh a narrow, small body of water

Gau-wautae-gummauh a glistening body of water; Kawartha, Ontario
gawau-gummauh a stagnant body of water
geezhoo-gummauh a warm body of water
ginoo-gummauh a long body of water
Ginozhae-gummauh Pike Lake
Kaugigae-gummauh Everlasting Lake; waters
Kiniw-gummauh Eagle Lake, Ontario
maetau-gummauh the confluence of two bodies of water, rivers
Mauttau-gummauh the source of or the point where the body of water commences; Mattawa, Ontario
mishi-gummauh an immense, great body of water
misqawau-gummauh a reddish body of water
nigowi-gummauh the body of water whose bottom and shores consist of sand
Niminau-gummauh a harbor; a place where ships, boats are beached and launched; Tobermory, Ontario
Pukawau-gummauh the land around the body of water that is hilly; Golden Lake, Ontario
tikau-gummauh a cool body of water
Timi-gummauh a deep body of water; Timagami, Ontario
waugau-gummauh an angled body of water
Waushau-gummauh a clear body of water; Washago, Ontario
Waussau-gummauh the bright, shiny body of water; Georgian Bay
Waussawau-gummauh the body of water that reflects the light of torches; Lac du Flambeau, Wisconsin
Wauwiyae-gummauh an oval body of water, round; Round Lake, Ontario
Weemb-awaewae-gummauh Echo Lake
weeni-gummauh a dirty body of water
Widjiw-gummauh Mountain Lake, Ontario
Wiyaeshkawau-gummauh an angled, curved body of water; Curve Lake, Ontario
zauguni-gummauh an outlet
zaugunitau-gummauh the body of water that serves as an outlet
zhaeng-gummauh a body of water clear of ice
zheebau-gummauh; zheeboo-gummauh the narrows between two bodies of water
zhingau-gummauh a body of water overflowing its banks
Zhooni-au-gummauh silver waters, Lake Simcoe, Ontario

---

ini-ipeeyauh *the quality of bodies of water*

---

anee-ipeeyauh; aumi-ipeeyauh the overflow of waters
beetoo-ipeeyauh waters layered (warm and cold)
ikoo-ipeeyauh the depth of waters
iskau-ipeeyauh the seepage of waters into the ground
meewi-ipeeyauh a river overflowing its banks
naeyaukoo-ipeeyauh the rise of waters inundating a small point of land
nauzh-ipeeyauh receding waters
ween-ipeeyauh brackish waters

---

ae-inaushkauk *waves; breakers; surf; swell; billows; the nature, character and quality of waves*

---

abeed-aushkauh approaching waves
anim-aushkauh the waves going in the opposite direction
an-waushkauh the waves are dying down, quietening
apeet-aushkauh the rate of the speed of billows during the wavy period
aubid-aushkauh ever wavy
aubood-aushkauh curling, twisting waves
aund-aushkauh the swell resumes
bae-waushkauh a slight surf
baug-waushkauh waves breaking on a shoal, reef
bauzhid-aushkauh breaking over a dock or break water
beetae-waushkauh the breakers froth and foam
bigum-aushkauh the arriving billows
boon-aushkauh the waves die down
booz-aushkauh the breakers enter the boat
dupuss-aushkauh low waves
gazhee-aushkauh fast-moving waves
gotaumig-waushkauh the waves are frightening, huge, furious
ishp-aushkauh the waves are high, big waves

mamaud-aushkauh the waters begin to churn
maudaugumm-aushkauh waves begin to form
maud-aushkauh it begins to get wavy
maung-aushkauh the waves are big
medawae-aushkauh the surf can be heard
nishinaud-aushkauh the swell is irregular
ond-aushkauh the source of the billows
pagid-aushkauh the breakers pound the shore
pugusk-aushkauh the waves slap on some surface
soossawae-aushkauh the spray of waves
titabi-aushkauh curling, rolling waves
waub-aushkauh white-capped waves
wauss-aushkauh glistening waves
zaum-aushkauh a heavy sea; billowy
zhae-aushkauh reversing waves

---

ae-tigawauyauh kemauh tigawaeyauh *the character, nature, form, direction, structure of a river bed, river valley, river, waterway, water course, channel*

---

ani-tigawaeyauh the course and direction of the river bed, channel
aubumau-tigawaeyauh the river, channel; a meandering river bed
baebeeski-tigawaeyauh a winding river, channel, river bed
baugawau-tigawaeyauh the water bed, channel rife with reefs, sandbars, shoals, flats
bimi-tigawaeyauh the watercourse, river bed, channel winding by
ishki-tigawaeyauh a curving, bending river, channel, river bed
min-itigawaeyauh; minis-itigawaeyauh the river having many islands created by silt along its course or at its mouth
neengadawi-tigawaeyauh the river, channel that divides, or splits into two
ondji-tigawaeyauh the watercourse's, river bed's source
pissiki-tigawaeyauh the watercourse, channel, river bed that circles back
teemi-tigawaeyauh a deep watercourse, river, channel, river bed
waebi-tigawaeyauh the river, channel, river bed that narrows
wawaushki-tigawaeyauh a serpentine, meandering river, channel
waweeshikiwi-tigawaeyauh a meandering river, channel, river bed
weebawau-tigawaeyauh a river gorge

---

aen-idjiwung *the flow of a river; the current; the character, nature, quality, rate of flow or current of a river, stream*

---

abau-idjiwun; obau-idjiwun flow through a narrow channel
abee-idjiwun flow and ebb; a tide
ae-izhi-idjiwung the direction, pace, character, nature of a flow of water
agidau-idjiwun the highlands; a divide; a water table; uplands; headwaters
agik-idjiwun whirlpools; eddies at the bottom of rapids
akiko-idjiwun the violent swirl of waters at the foot of rapids
ani-idjiwun the river flowing in that direction
aubumoo-idjiwun whirlpools
aum-idjiwun an overflow, spillover
auyauboo-idjiwun whirlpools
baedi-idjiwun a slow moving current
baekau-idjiwun a slow, peaceful current
baugawau-idjiwun rapids
bauzhidji-idjiwun an overflow, spillover
bawitigoo-idjiwun rapids
beeto-idjiwun an underwater current
bimi-idjiwun a current flowing by
cheegau-idjiwun near the stream or the current or the rapids
daushk-idjiwun the river divides in two
gaugee-idjiwun a current flowing over a ledge of a rock to form a falls
gausk-waewae-idjiwun the stream that creates a murmuring, bubbling sound as it flows
gaussi-idjiwun a narrow stream
Gawaek-awaek-idjiwun the current that flows back and forth; Little Current, Ontario
gawaek-idjiwun the current flowing in the right direction
gazhee-idjiwun a fast current

Gazheeskau-idjiwun a fast-flowing river; Swift Current, Saskatchewan
geek-idjiwun the flow of a stream over a ledge, edge
Geeshkau-piko-idjiwun a steep waterfall; Bobcaygeon, Ontario
geesk-aubik-idjiwun a waterfalls, over a cliff
Ginoowau-idjiwun it flows over a great distance; Long Rapids, Ontario
Goodjee-idjiwun convergence of water near the outlet; the merging of waters; Couchiching, Ontario
ini-idjiwun flowing in a certain manner
izhi-idjiwun flowing at a certain pace, mode, in a particular direction
kakau-piko-idjiwun a steep waterfall
kaudaeyau-gummi-idjiwun the division of a river into two branches
kaukau-ipee-idjiwun a river tumbling over a series of ledges, one almost below the other
mashkoowi-idjiwun a strong current
minitigo-idjiwun a current flowing among and between islands created by silt
mino-idjiwun a good, salutary current
mook-idjiwun emergence of a stream, river
mooshkidji-idjiwun flowing to capacity
nakaewae-idjiwun the stream fading from sight
nana-eedjiwun a river backup caused by blockage downstream
nauwau-idjiwun the middle of a stream
neessau-idjiwun the lowland; downriver; the outlet
neezaun-idjiwun a dangerous current
nisso-idjiwun a three-channeled river; the division of a river into three branches
obau-idjiwun a current flowing through a narrow channel
ondji-idjiwun [identifies] the river's source
oombi-idjiwun the water bubbles, boils, foams up
pagidau-idjiwun where a stream casts, hurls itself, as on a shore, wharf
payaugoo-idjiwun the current flowing over shallows
peendji-idjiwun the current flowing into, inside
piko-idjiwun the current flowing over a hump, prominence
pissikaub-idjiwun flowing in reverse
tikum-idjiwun a crosscurrent
waubau-idjiwun the current flowing so rapidly that its surface appears white
waubishki-idjiwun the current froths and foams white as it flows
zaugidau-ipee-idjiwun it streams out
zaugidji-idjiwun the current flows out
zaum-idjiwun the current overflows, flows too far
zhae-idjiwun the current backs up
zhaekau-idjiwun the foot of the rapids; where the rapid, rough flow changes into a regular current
zheebaup-idjiwun a current flowing through, as through a gorge or a tunnel
zheebau-piko-idjiwun a current flowing through a narrow passage and over a projection
zheebau-tigo-idjiwun a current flowing between islands; a channel
zheebauyau-idjiwun the stream that flows through a passage, as through a pipe
zhingau-idjiwun the river that spreads as it overflows its banks

inaukawauh *the character, nature of a forest*

bim-aukawauh it is forested along the way
cheegi-aukawauh near the forest
dupuss-aukawauh a forest of short, stunted, underdeveloped trees
gabo-waukawauh a thickly wooded forest
ishp-aukawauh a forest consisting of towering trees
makatae-waukawauh a dark, black forest
maum-aukawauh an uneven, tangled forest
oshki-waukawauh a new stand of trees
pushki-waukawauh a forest denuded of leaves, composed of dead trees; a cleared out forest
waub-aukawauh a stand of hardwood
weebawae-yaukawauh an avenue between trees
zheeb-aukawauh a sparsely treed forest; a thinned out forest
zheeba-waussae-yaukawauh a thinly treed forest; sparsely treed, enabling a person to

see farther than would be usual
zhingob-aukawauh a stand of balsam, fir
zug-aukawauh a dense, impenetrable forest

metig(ook) *trees*

akauwauhnsh(eek) juniper(s)
baupaushkigizigae-gunauk(ook) elder(s)
baupaushkizigae-gunauk-meen(uk) elderberry, elderberries
baupauss-pigiw(uk) balsam(s)
begaessaun-meeni-gauwuhnsh(eek) a plum tree
begaunauk-meeni-gauwuhnsh(eek) walnut tree(s)
bookidoosh-gauwuhnsh(eek) pear tree(s)
gawaunduk(ook) spruce(s)
geeshkaunduk(ook); geezhig(uk) a cedar
gibwaumaewish(uk); gibwaumeesh(uk) hazelnut tree(s)
gozig-wauko-meeni-autik(ook) a pear tree
inin-aunduk(ook) spruce(s)
inin-autik(ook) maple tree(s)
kaugaug-maewish(eek) kemauh kaugaug-meesh(uk) hemlock(s)
kaugaug-meen a sumac fruit
kaugaug-meen-gauwuhnsh(eek) sumac(s)
kaugaug-meesh(uk) hemlock(s)
keegundauk(ook) cypress(es)
mamaundau-metig(ook) lilac(s)
meenaus-gauwuhnsh(eek) hawthorn(s)
metig-meen(uk) acorn(s)
metig-meesh(uk) kemauh metig-maewish(eek) a red oak tree
metig-waubauk(ook) hickory tree(s); the source for bows
mishee-meen(uk) apple(s)
mishee-meeni-gauwuhnsh(eek) apple tree(s)
mishi-meesh(uk) kemauh mish-maewish(uk) a white oak
misqwau-beeg-meen-gauwuhnsh(eek) a dog-wood (tree)
misqwau-wauk(ook) red cedar(s)
mooninoohnse(uk) an ironwood
mushkeeg-wautik(ook) tamarack(s)
neep(eek) elm(s)
niteemish(uk) white ash
okikaehnse(uk) black spruce
okikaehnse(uk) jack pine
paukawangaemauk(ook) red pine(s)
peepeegiwunaushk(ook) elder(s)
peepeegiwunaushk-meen(uk) elderberry, elderberries
pegaessaun-gauwuhnsh(eek) plum tree(s)
pegaun-koo-meen(uk) hazelnut(s)
pegaun-koomeesh(uk) hazelnut tree(s)
quae-meesh(uk) kemauh quae-maewish(uk) cherry tree(s)
soossawae-meen(uk) choke cherry, cherries
soossawae-meeni-gauwuhnsh(eek); soos-sawae-meesh(uk) kemauh; soossawae-maewish(uk) a choke cherry tree(s)
waedoop-(ikook) alder(s)
weegoob-maewish(uk); weegoob(eek) a basswood
weegwauss(uk) birch(es) (origin of *weegwaum* —birch-bark lodge(s))
weenisik(ook) yellow birch(es)
weessigauk(ook) black ash(es) (the source of splints for baskets)
zaudee(k) poplar(s); aspen(s)
zeezigoob-maewish(uk) kemauh; zeezi-goob-meesh(uk) willow(s)
zhawae-meesh(uk) beech(es)
zheeg-maewish(uk) soft maple(s)
zhigaug-meesh(uk) kemauh zhigaug-maewish(uk) bluebeech(es)
zhingob(eek) a fern; fir; balsam
zhingwauk(ook) pine(s)
zhingwaukokoonauk(ook) pine cone(s)

ae-izhi-igiwaut metigook *parts of a tree*

aung-sug(ook) driftwood; dried stick(s)
baenaundug(ook) deciduous tree(s)
baugun-autik(ook) a lightning-struck tree or limb
beewigugun(un) chip(s)
cheebik(un) kemauh cheebikaehn(un) root(s)
kaewuhnzh(un) underbrush
kaugauwaundug(ook) evergreens
keeshk-inukut a stump
kikud(ook) stump(s)
kitowaun(uk) log(s)
maun-sug(ook) a hard wood
meenkaun(un) seed(s)
mishee-wautik(ook) dead tree(s)
mishi (missun) firewood

naukunushk(ook) ferns
neebeesh(un) a leaf, leaves
nook-autik(ook) kemauh nookushk-autik(ook) a soft wood
nugaek(ook) bark
odudjigawae vein-like markings on bark
pikwaukoot(oon) a knob on a tree, knobs on trees
tikwun(un) limb(s)
wunukizit the crest of a tree
zaegawaebimauk(ook) tree(s) with horizontal branches
zaug-bug(ook) leaf shoot(s)
zaug-meen(uk) bud(s)
zugutaegin tinder; punk
zuzugaukawauh swail

inaundaewin *color; shade; hue; tint*

makataewauh black, dark, etc.
misqwauh red, maroon, carmine, crimson, etc.
waubishkauh white, pale, wan, ashen, etc.
w'makataewizih he/she who is black, dark, etc.
w'misqwauzih he/she who is red, carmine, crimson, etc.
w'waubishkizih he/she who is white, pale, wan, ashen, etc.
w'zauwizih he/she who is gold, yellow, brown, copper, amber, etc.
w'zhauwishkoozih he/she who is green, blue, purple, indigo
zauwauh gold, yellow, brown, copper, amber, etc.
zhauwishkwauh green, blue, purple, indigo
zhooniauh silver, crystal, lustrous, gleaming. *Note:* To form words that refer to color with greater precision than the basic terms listed above, the suffix *inaundae* (usually contracted to *aundae*) is appended to other words and terms.
booz-aundae dark, darker
meen-aundae blueberry colored
mushkeeg-meen-aundae cranberry colored
nigik-inaundae grey, like the color of an otter
odae-meen-aundae strawberry colored
zhoo-meen-aundae grape colored (at any stage)

kabik-issaewin *time*

abi-boong wintertime
bim-audiziwin a life
dasso-geeziss each, every month
geeziss the sun
kabae-eehn a long time; ages; decades
maumindjitch the last time; once more; one more chance
neebin summer; the season of bounty
neebing in the summer, summertime
neezh-geeziss two months
ningo-abi-boon (beboon) one winter for one year
ningo-geeziss one month (there are thirteen months in the Anishinaubae year; it corresponds to the lunar year and to the number of a woman's menstrual periods)
ningo-kikinoonoowin one year
tikwaukih autumn; the cool season (from *tik-auyauh*—it is chilly)
tikwaukik in the fall, autumn
zeegwun spring; the flow of sap
zeegwung in the spring, spingtime

geezissook *months*

Manitou-geeziss January
Numaebini-geeziss February
Onaubini-geeziss March
Baubauk-inutae-geeziss April
Waubugonae-geeziss May
Odaemini-geeziss June
Meen-geeziss July
Misquo-meeni-geezis August
Mino-meeni-geezis September
Bunaukawae-geezis October
Kishkudini-geezis November
Manitou-geezissoohnse December

geezhigutoon *the days of the week*

Ishkawau-anamie-geezhig Monday; the day after the praying day
Neezh-geezhig Tuesday; the second day
Aupitoo-issae; Zoozaep-geeshig Wednesday; midway; Joseph's day
Neewi-geezhig Thursday; the fourth day
Nauni-geezhig; Auzhidae-autiko-geeshig Friday; the fifth day; the cross day
Nawautau-geezhig Saturday; the suspension

of labor day
Anami-ae-geezhig Sunday; the praying day

aen-geezhiguk *the day's phases*

abeed-aubun dawn; daybreak
awuss-naugoh the day before yesterday
awuss-waubung the day after tomorrow
bidjeenaugoh yesterday
geezhig(utoon) (igoon) day(s)
geezhiguk during the day
geezhigut day
ishkawau-nauwiquae afternoon
kigizhaeb morning
kigizhaebauwigut morning
naukishih evening
naukishik during the evening
nauwiquae noon, midday
nikeewigud dusk
noongoom now; today
oongauzheeguk now; today
waubun dawn
waubung tomorrow

aen-igoon
dasso-igoon a certain number of days
neezhi-dunnuh-neewi-igoonugizit on the 24th of . . .
neezh-igoon two days
nisso-igoon three days
nisso-igoonugizit on the third [day] of . . .

ae-izhiwaebuk *the weather*

ae-inaumidaek the barometric pressure
ae-inaumidukawaeng the forecast deduced from the signs
ae-inauniquok the formation of clouds
aen-geezhiguk the sort of weather conditions prevailing on a particular day
anim-akeekauh it is thundering
aubowaumigut; aubowauh it is mild, loosening up
bigum-ut the storm is arriving
cheecheeng-kummikauh an earthquake
dagoon-ipeessauh a rainbow
gimiwun it is raining
gizhautaemigut; gizhautae it is hot
gizhinaumidae it is sultry
kissinaumigut; kissinauh it is cold
madookud it is damp, dewy
mino-geezhigut it is a fine day
mizhu-quot it is clear
mukwumee-ipeessauh it is freezing rain, sleet
nawautin it is calm
neessikaudut the weather is unsettled, is unravelling, inclement
ningawaugun a rainbow
ningawaun-quot it is overcast
nipeewun; nipeewut it is wet
nitcheewut it is boisterous weather, very stormy
noodin it is windy
pishibaubee-aunimut a whirlwind
pishibaubeewoh swirling, drifting snow
pishibau-ipeessid-ossaemigut kemauh; pishibau-ipeessid-ossae a tornado
tiki-ayaumigut it is cool, chilly
tootoo-kummikauh a tremor
waussimoh it is lightning
wauwautae it is lightning
wauwautum it is lightning
zaessaegiwun hail
zoongipoh; zoogipoh it is snowing

gimiwunoowin *rain; the quality and character of rain*

ipeessauh *the nature, form, character of rainfall*

ani-ipeessauh the rain that is on its way
animau-ipeessauh the rain that is departing
apeetchi-ipeessauh the rain that falls at a certain rate
aubidji-ipeessauh perpetual rain
aundji-ipeessauh returning rain; raining anew
autae-ipeessauh the end of the rain
awun-ipeessauh a drizzle attended by fog; mist
baekauh-ipeessauh quiet rain
beessi-ipeessauh small raindrops
beewi-ipeessauh small raindrops
bigum-ipeessauh the rain arrives
bimi-ipeessauh the rain goes by
boon-ipeessauh the rain stops
boozi-ipeessauh the rain gets in

dani-ipeessauh it is raining in a certain place
gauski-ipeessauh a drumming, murmuring rain
gawaetaun-ipeessauh the rain is overwhelming, frightening
geezhoowi-ipeessauh the rain is warm
inauss-ipeessauh rains in one's face
ishkwau-ipeessauh the rain stops
izhi-ipeessauh it rains in such a way
kinigawi-ipeessauh the mix of hail and rain
maudjee-ipeessauh it begins to rain
maung-ipeessauh large rain drops
medawae-ipeessauh the rain can be heard
mino-ipeessauh a beneficial rain
mukwoomee-ipeessauh sleet, freezing rain
nanawaudji-ipeessauh it rains for nothing; does little good
noondae-ipeessauh it rains at an inopportune time
pishibau-ipeessauh a tornado
pizhunzhaewi-ipeessauh lashing, whipping rain
pungi-ipeessauh rain drops
tautawi-ipeessauh it rains at intervals
tik-ipeessauh the rain is cold
titibau-ipeessauh a tornado with rain or a water-spout
zaum-ipeessauh there is too much rain
zeeseegi-ipeessauh a deluge; sheets of rain

---

ae-inau-goonugauk; goon-igoonugauwin *the nature, character, quality of snow; the fall of snow*

---

apeetau-goonugauh the snow that is of a certain depth
asa-goonugauh hard packed snow
augawauss-goonugauh the snow that forms an obstruction preventing passage
baupau-goonugauh the snow that is packed down
beenau-goonugauh the snow that is clean
bimau-goonugauh a snow ridge
chaugau-goonugauh the snow that is all gone
dawau-goonugauh a space, a passage between snow fields
dupussau-goonugauh the snow that is shallow
gaupau-goonugauh the crust is brittle
gaupau-goonutae the crust is brittle
goonikauh-goonugauh there is much snow
ishpau-goonugauh the snow is deep
kikaudau-goonugauh chilling snow
maemi-meen-unutae particles of snow remaining on the ground
mashkowau-goonugauh hard snow
maumeekawau-goonugauh unbelievably deep snow
mitau-goonugauh the bare snow
mitau-inutae the snow is all gone; the ground is bare
mitchi-inutae the snow is all gone; the ground is bare
ningawau-goonugauh the snow buries an object from sight; the snow melts
ning-inutae the snow is melting
nookau-goonugauh the snow is soft
nookawauyauh the snow is soft
onaubunutae the snow is hard; a crust
pikodaug-goonugauh snow dunes
shakau-goonugauh the snow is cold, wet
showau-goonugauh slush
waedaeyauh the snow is hard; a crust
waussau-goonugauh the snow is dazzling
weembau-goonugauh there are hollows within the surface of the snow
weenau-goonugauh the snow is dirty
zhooshau-goonugauh the snow is slippery
zhooshkawau-goonugauh the snow is slippery

---

ipoo *the manner, character, nature, quality of a snowfall*

---

abeedj-ipoh the snow is coming
anawau-ipoh it stops snowing
aussimi-ipoh it snows directly in one's face; to head into a snowfall
autae-ipoh it stops snowing
baedji-ipoh it is snowing gently, quietly
beessi-ipoh it is snowing small flakes
beewi-ipoh it is snowing small flakes
bimi-ipoh it is snowing
boon-ipoh it stops snowing
gazhee-ipoh the snow falls fast
ishkwau-ipoh it stops snowing
maudji-ipoh it starts to snow
maung-ipoh it is snowing large flakes

nipeewi-ipoh it is wet snow
noondae-ipoh it snows too soon; at an inopportune time
shagi-ipoh wet snow that melts as it falls to the ground
tautiwig-ipoh it snows at intervals
zaum-ipoh it is snowing too much
zoog-ipoh it snows
zoong-ipoh it snows

---

inoodiniwin *the direction, nature and character of a wind*

---

akeewaedin the north wind or the "go home" wind
pungishimo-inoodin the west wind or the "setting" wind
waubun-inoodin the east wind or the "dawn" wind
zhauwun-inoodin the south wind or the "blue" wind

---

ae-inaunimutiwin *nature and character of the wind*

---

anaun; anaum; inaun; inaum *air; oxygen*

---

abeed-aunimut the wind is coming
apeet-aunimut the rate, velocity of a wind
aubid-aunimut it is always windy
aund-aunimut the wind starts again
autae-aunimut the wind dies out
beemisko-aunimut the wind twists, turns
bigum-aunimut the wind arises; arrives
bim-aunimut the wind blows by, nearby
boon-aunimut the wind dies down
cheegi-aunimut the wind blows close by
gaund-aunimut the wind springs up
gausk-aunimut the wind murmurs
gawaek-aunimut the wind changes direction
gaweeshk-waunimut the wind whistles
gazhee-aunimut the wind is strong, fierce
gizhau-aunimut the wind is warm
mashkow-aunimut the wind is strong
maud-aunimut the wind starts up
medawae-aunimut the wind sounds, echoes
mino-aunimut the wind is pleasant, favorable
nawautin-aunimut the wind has stopped; it is calm
oomb-aunimut the wind rises
oond-aunimut the origin, source of the wind
ozaum-aunimut the wind is excessive
peend-aunimut the wind blows in
pidik-waewae-aunimut the wind roars and rumbles
tik-aunimut the wind is cool
titibee-aunimut a whirlwind
weessig-aunimut the wind stings
zaeg-aunimut a frightful wind
zaug-aunimut the wind blows out

---

geezhig *the sky; firmament*

---

abi-boon-geezhig winter sky
aedae-geezhig; aedawae-geezhig both sides of the sky
anung(ook) star(s)
aupita-geezhig half the sky
awuss-geezhig the far side of the sky
beetoo-geezhig between the skies
begonae-geezhig a hole in the sky
Cheeby-meekunnuh the Milky Way
cheengwun a meteor
geewitau-geezhig around the sky
geezhigoong in the sky
geezis(ook) the sun(s)
ishkotae-geezhig fiery sky
kaugigae-geezhig everlasting sky
kineu-geezhig eagle sky
mayauwi-geezhig in the middle of the sky
misheewi-geezhig the sky; the vault of heaven; the entire sky, space
miskwi-geezhig red sky
miziwae-geezhig in every quarter of the sky
neebini-geezhig summer sky
neegaun-geezhig leading sky
nimbunae-geezhig one side of the sky
ogimau-geezhig chief sky
ondaussi-geezhig on this side of the sky
shawae-geezhig sloping sky
waubi-geezhig white sky; eastern sky
waukae-geezhig clear sky
waussi-noodae aurora borealis
zauwa-geezhig yellow sky
zhauboo-geezhig through the sky
zhauwuno-geezhig southern sky; blue sky

ae-inauniquok *a cloud; the nature, shape, character, color of clouds*

abeed-auniquot coming cloud
anim-auniquot the clouds that are departing; clouds scudding away
animkee-auniquot thunder cloud(s)
aubood-auniquot curling cloud
auniquot a cloud
awun-quot foggy cloud
awuss-auniquot the other side of the clouds
baepaesh-auniquot striped clouds
beeg-wauniquot broken clouds
bigum-auniquot arriving clouds
dupuss-auniquot low cloud(s)
gidjig-auniquot cirrus clouds; thin stripped clouds
ishkotae-auniquot fire cloud
ishp-auniquot high, lofty clouds
kaugigae-auniquot forever cloud
kineu-auniquot eagle cloud
kitug-auniquot mottled cloud(s)
maegawae-auniquot enveloped, enshrouded by clouds
makatae-auniquot dark, black clouds
maud-auniquot clouds begin to form
mayau-auniquot clouds veiled in the very middle
mishee-mino-auniquot great good cloud
misqawi-auniquot red cloud
mizhu-auniquot cloudless; clear of clouds
nauzh-auniquot lowering cloud
ningaw-auniquot overcast
waubun-iquot white cloud; morning cloud
wauss-auniquot shiny cloud
zauw-auniquot yellow cloud(s)
zhaubo-wauniquot; zheeb-auniquot; zhee-bau-auniquot through clouds
zhauwano-quot southern cloud

Anishinaebaek *North American Indians; natives; First Nations people*

Anishi-naubae(k) either Spontaneous Being(s) or The Good Being(s)—most likely The Good Beings, to correspond to the understanding that humans generally mean well
Assinee-Bawaun(uk) Assiniboine(s)
Ayauch-ininih(ininiwuk) Blackfeet
Bawaun(uk) Dakota(s) (*lit.* to roast)
Boodawae-autumee(k) Pottawatomi—a branch of the Anishinaubae Nation, whose name refers to their function as Keepers of the Fire
Bunigo-Bunigook Delaware(s)
D'ishkawau-gummeek the dwellers at the last great lake to the east
Dazhi-ishkawau-gummee(k) the so-called Algonquins, who call themselves Maumee-ininiwuk
gayaut-ishinaubae(k) an aboriginal
Maedaut-ishinaubae(k) a North American Indian other than Anishinaubae
Maeyug-ishinaubae(k) a North American Indian other than Anishinaubae
Maumee(k) the name the so-called Algonquins call themselves
Mino-meenae(k) the Menominee; The Good Seed or The Wild Rice People
Mishi-zaugee(k) the Mississaugi(s); The Dwellers at the Large Mouth of a River—a branch of the Anishinaubae Nation
Mushkeegoohn(uk) the Cree; Dwellers of the Muskeg
Naudowae(k) any one of the Six Nations; They Who Fetch
Ningik-gabow(uk) the abridged form of this name—The Kickapoo—means Standing like Otters; why they were called that, no one knows
Ojibwae(k) a slightly derogatory Cree term for the Anishinaubae, whose speech sounded slurred to them—Those Who Stammer and Stutter (this and Chippewa are used in the names of many fine hotels and watering holes)
Ottauwau(k) a branch of the Anishinaubae Nation whose name may derive from their use of a river reed called the Ottauwuhnshk in their mattings and partitions, or from *odauwae* (*odjauwau*), meaning the grant of right to pass through Anishinaubae territory to nonresidents upon payment of a toll (toll collectors were warriors who arranged their hair in a roach style)
Waubun-akee(k) the Abenaki; People of the Dawn

Weenipeego(ok) the Winnebago; The Dirty Water People; a recreational vehicle
Y'ae-oshkut-ishinaubae(k) aboriginal(s)
Zaugunukeehn(k) Sauks—a branch of the Anishinaubae Nation whose name means Dwellers at the Mouth of a River
Zhauwuno(ok) Shawnee(s)—a nation related to the Anishinaubae; The People of the South

ogimaubuneek *some former chiefs*

Aehnssaehnse Little Shell, a chief in Wisconsin around 1800; a family on Christian Island, Ontario
Aumoohnse Little Bee
Aundaeg-weeyauss Crow Flesh; a chief in the Sault Ste. Marie area around the 1670s
Baebeezig-indibae Curly Head
Beedud Coming Storm
Begonae-geezhig Hole in the Sky (or Day) or Perforated Cedar; the Pleiades
Buzwa Reverberation, a chief around the 1650s; a family in the Spanish River area, Ontario
Chechauk A Crane; the name of a family living in the New Credit First Nation Reserve, Ontario; many in North Western Ontario
Ginae-beeg Snake
Keeshkimun Kingfisher, a chief in Wisconsin around 1800
Kinoshaemaeg Pike (from *gin-oshae-maeg*—long-bodied fish), a chief from the Keweenaw area in Northern Michigan, who was also known as Mino-waewae—Mellifluous—for his eloquence; a family on the Wikwemikong First Nation band list in Ontario
Kitchi-Cheemaun [Lorenzo] Big Canoe, a chief at Georgina Island, Ontario (preferred The Big Kiss as the interpretation of the family name)
Kitchi-Ojibway Big Ojibway (so named for his massive size and height, around 7 feet); war chief in the Wisconsin-Michigan area around 1790s
Kitchi-Waubezhaeshi Great Marten (from *kitchi*—big; *waub*—white; *ozhaeshih*—body), a war chief around the 1760s;
Kitug-bizheu Mottled Lynx
Makatae-benaessi Blackbird, a war chief; a family on the Walpole Island First Nation, Ontario
Makatae-Kaikaik Black Hawk, a man of the Sauk and Fox people celebrated for his resistance to U.S. armed forces and to settler encroachment, who was hunted down as a common criminal
Misheekaehnse Little Turtle
Misqaw-auniquot Red Cloud
Miziwae-pigoh All Ribs, a medicine man who dreamed of and foretold the coming of the White People
Mongozid Loon's Foot (from *maung-ozid*—loon's foot), led resistance to White expansion in the Midwest in the 1750s
Moskokomaun Red Knife; a family registered on the Muncey First Nation rolls, Ontario
Mukwoh Bear, a chief in the Midwest
Naewaush Gliding Down and In as Do Some Birds, a chief in the 1800s from the Owen Sound area who took part in the defence of Canada at Queenston Heights, Ontario, in 1812, beating back the Yankee invaders
Naudawae-quae Iroquois Woman, a chief in southern Michigan
Neegaun-geezhig Leading, or First Day
Neegaun-ub Sitting in Front; a chief in the 1850s
Noodin Wind, a chief in the Michigan-Wisconsin area around the 1850s
Odjitumo Red Squirrel
Oshki-bug New Leaf. (translated as Flat Mouth by scholars, though there is no way that Flat Mouth can be derived from *oshki*—new; *bug*—leaf), a chief in Wisconsin around 1800
Pawis Herring (Pawis is a mistransliteration of *kaewiss*—herring), a family belongs to the Shawanaga First Nation, Ontario
Peguis Sparrow Hawk (from *peepeeguis*—sparrow hawk; a shrill voiced high pitched shriek), a chief in Southern Manitoba around 1812
Pigaegun Rib
Pontiac a man who led the First Nations' resistance to the westward expansion of the

colonial invaders and planned the siege of Fort Detroit, 1763; a man who saw the loss of land, equality, freedom, independence and the cultural and spiritual heritage of his people if they did not resist expansion and contain it (the name may come from *punt-eeyauk*, a term referring to the point where a basket's rim meets and joins, or from *gabod-eeyauk*—impassable woods)

Shawae-Geezhig Sloping Sky, or Leaning Cedar

Waub-Chechauk White Crane

Waub-odjeeg White Fisher, chief of Wisconsin and Michigan, 1750–1790

Wazhushk-kun Muskrat Liver

Weegibaehnse Little Root, a young woman who led a party of survivors ravaged by smallpox away from their contaminated village to safety and on to survival

Wibokemigad Commencement of an Event, a patriot who supported Pontiac in espousing resistance and laying siege to Fort Detroit to check White expansion in 1763; a family that belongs to the Wikwemikong First Nation in Ontario

Zauwau-indib Yellowhead, a hunter-fisherman who took up the war club to resist White expansion and encroachment

Zauwi-kaik Brown Hawk

Zhaedaewish Old Pelican, a Sault Ste. Marie Anishinaubae chief around 1670

Zhauwuno South

Zhingob Evergreen

Zhingwaub-assin Magic Stone, a Sault Ste. Marie Anishinaubae who lived around the 1670s

Zhingwauk Pine, a family man who took up weapons to defend his country and heritage against the invader in the war against the Americans in 1812 (he and other native leaders, with their forces, contributed at least as much, if not more than General Brock did in repelling the invaders; a family that resides in Kitigaun-zeepeeng [Garden River] in Ontario

Zoong-Kummik Strong Earth, a warrior who rose to prominence in the 1800s

manitou(wuk) *spirit(s); sprite(s); incorporeal being(s); deity, deities; God(s); supernatural being(s); essence; substance; mystery, mysteries; properties; attributes; the unseen; intangible reality*

Abi-boon kemauh; Abi-boon-kae kemauh; Abi-boon-aubae Winter or Winter-maker, one of the muses. Abi-boon kemauh/Abi-boon-kae presides over winter, snow, hardship, and sickness, and generates winds, storms, cold, and blizzards.

Ae-pungishimook The West, one of the muses who dwells in the land of the Setting Sun. Ae-pungishimook ravished Winonah four times, fathering Maudjee-kawiss, Pukawiss, Cheeby-aub-oozoo, and Nana'b'oozoo.

Animikee-benaessih(wuk) kemauh, Ishkotae benaessih(wuk), and **Animakee(k)** The Thunderbirds, Firebirds, Thunders. These are the safeguardians of Mother Earth's well-being, generating warmth and rain to cleanse and fertilize her and to give drink to her children. Also known as grandfathers, they remind human beings to pay their dues and respects to the manitous and to the ancestors.

Cheeby-aub-oozoo the third son of Ae-pungishimook and Winonah. A mystic and musician, Cheeby-aub-oozoo obtained the drum for the Anishinaubae people and established the traditions of dream quests, music, changing, composition, communication with the manitous, and sacred rituals.

Daebaudjimoot The Raconteur, Storyteller. Daebaudjimoot was a friend of N'okomiss, Nana'b'oozoo's grandmother, and a tutor to Nana'b'oozoo. He began the practice and tradition of storytelling in the Anishinaubae culture. He was a teacher, instructor, and safeguardian of the historical and cultural heritage of the nation. People were fond of listening to Daebaudjimoot but they seldom took him seriously.

Gawaessind The Feared (from *gotaudjiwin*—fear). Gawaessind was a bully who singled out and abused the Paueehnssiwuk (little people; elves), who in the end assassinated him.

Geeziss; Keeziss Father Sun, a symbol of Kitchi-Manitou, The Creator

Kitchi-Manitou God, The Creator, The Great Mystery

Kizhae-Manitou The Respected, Revered Mystery, another term for The Creator

Maemaegawaehnse(ssiwuk) Little Strangers, Those Who Speak an Alien Language. These little manitous, who dwell in the woods, are the safeguardians of children.

Maudjee-kawiss the first son of Ae-pungishimook and Winonah. Preceding his brothers into life and the world, and obliged to care for his younger brother, Maudjee-kawiss exemplified the nature and character of leadership. In adulthood he was at the forefront in providing for the needs of communities and protection for his people. He was a man of action and deed who inspired his followers and neighbors. On one of his trips abroad he brought back the idea of a wampum sash on which to record the people's deeds.

Misheen-maukinauk kemauh mikinauk The Giant Turtle lent its back to Spirit Woman as a place where she could give birth to her children; for its service to the manitou and humanity, it was appointed messenger between humans and the manitous, between generations, present and future.

Mishi-bizheu The Great Lynx, a manitou of the underworld, who dwells in waters, in rapids, at the edge of falls and below, and is the nemesis of Nana'b'oozoo and humans

Mizauwaubeekum(ook/oowuk) little manitous, who dwell on mountainsides and rocky heights. The name derives from the gold, copper, and pyrite imbedded in rocks.

Muzzu-kummik-Quae Mother Earth. By breathing the breath of life into the clutch of soil that Geezhigo-quae had etched around the rim of the Giant Turtle's shell, causing it to swell and grow into a continent, she infused into the earth the attributes of motherhood: nourishment, clothing, shelter, healing, teaching, and instilling a sense of beauty and goodness

Nana'b'oozoo the youngest son of Ae-pungishimook and Winonah. Nana'b'oozoo is the archhuman; he means well, but more often than not, he fails because his appetites get the better of him and overcome his higher nature. When he succeeds it is by chance rather than skill or design; it is akin to a miracle. Nana'b'oozoo represents the ordinary human being in his or her daily struggle to discharge his or her duties toward the manitous, neighbors, kin, family, and Mother Earth. Like many human beings, Nana'b'oozoo blunders and bumbles along.

Nauneediss a patron of good health

nebau-naubae(wuk) a male siren, half-man, half-fish performs the same functions as does the mermaid

nebau-naubae-quae(wuk) a mermaid. Both mermen and mermaids are akin to sirens who lure their victims into their clutches and then bear them to their dwelling places at the bottom of the sea, where they transform them into half-fish, half-woman beings.

N'okomiss; N'oko Winonah's mother is the symbol of all grandmothers in their role as the pre-eminent teachers and safeguardians of the cultural and spiritual heritage of the people.

pau cchnssiwuk little manitous who reside on the shores of lakes and banks of rivers. As sentinels, their purpose is to warn humans of the presence of sirens.

Pauguk The Flying Skeleton. As a human being, Pauguk coveted his brother's wife because of a misperception that she was fond of him. To possess the young woman, Pauguk murdered his brother. As a result, the manitous of the Underworld, and of the Upper World, and the Cheebyuk of the Land of Souls, horrified by the heinousness of the deed, refused to accept him, so Pauguk became an outcast, unwanted, exiled into a region midway between the Sun and Planet of Ice.

Pukawiss the second of Ae-pungishimook

and Winonah's sons. Pukawiss (*lit.* cut off; disowned) was so named because the father, unable to persuade the boy to abandon his frivolous pastimes and to attend to life's more fundamental and practical skills, gradually disowned his son. What the father did not know was that his son was a dramatist, a performer, who interpreted in form of dance what he perceived in order to amuse and instruct. To coax him to marriage, women made costumes that Pukawiss wore in his performances. He is the patron of festivals, dramas, dances, and style.

Waubun The Dawn that Originates in the East; one of the four muses. This manitou symbolizes youth, hope, dreams, vision, and regeneration. Waubun is constantly in struggle with Ae-pungishimook—old age, death, infirmity, wisdom.

Weendigo The Giant Cannibal. Weendigo lusted for human flesh. But no matter how much it ate, it never satisfied its hunger. Instead, it grew in size with each meal so that its hunger remained in proportion to its mass. The Weendigo symbolizes the character of human appetites which, when indulged, only stimulates them into demanding ever greater indulgence until they take control of reason, common sense, and the person.

Winonah a young woman, ravished by Ae-pungishimook, as age ravishes youth. By physical union with the young woman, Ae-pungishimook conferred on Winonah manitou attributes that enabled her to bear their four sons four generations apart.

Zhauwundaessih The South, one of the muses. Depicted as a woman, Zhauwundaessih represents growth, birth, bounty, beauty, goodness.

---

manitou-kaewin *invocation of the manitous; spiritual exercises*

---

anami-aewin(un) chants with words uttered to the accompaniment of a small drum; petitions to the manitous abiding in the heavens for guidance and strength in the quest for rectitude and in the discharge of one's duties

bawaudjigaewin kemauh pawaudjigaewin dream; dream quest. Men and women who needed supernatural intercession to learn something went to a secluded retreat where the manitous were known to abide, a dreamer's place, and there invoked the manitous to come to appear to them in dream, the realm of the manitous.

cheeby-akeeng the Realm of Soul-Spirits, the next world, an abode of peace, tranquility

cheeby-autik a grave marker on which is inscribed upsidedown the deceased's totem (*doodaem*)

cheeby-inaukaewin the Feast of the Dead. Neighbors and kin are invited to a feast, usually in midautumn, where places and bowls are set for deceased family members as well as the living. Throughout the evening and night neighbors visit neighbors, eating the food offerings and telling stories about their departed ones.

cheeby-indoowigaun an enclosure constructed and erected over a grave

cheeby-kaun a grave yard, or a crypt

cheeby-kunnuh the Path of Soul-Spirits. It is believed that the passage of a soul-spirit from the Land of the Living to the Realm of Soul-Spirits takes four days

cheessi-akee-ininih; cheessi-akee quae a mystic; one who has such a close kinship with the manitous that he or she can summon them to him in a specially constructed structure which they cause to vibrate as they address the mystic in an ancient language (*lit.* shaker/mover of the earth)

cheessi-gummig the structure in which the *cheessi-akee-ininih* or *cheessi-akee-quae* performs the Shake the Earth Ceremony.

kookoogaupigun the bridge that spans the river separating the Realm of the Soul-Spirits from the present

madoodizoon (Madootizaun) a purification, often referred to as the sweat lodge

makataekaewin the blackening of one's face as a sign of propitiation during vigil prior to participation in a ceremony

manitou-kauzoowin any act, rite, ritual

or ceremony in which the manitous are invoked

mauz-aubindumoowin a dream or vision in which the message or the image is unclear or incomplete—other and still further dreams and visions are required to clarify or complete the message or the image

medae-megis the symbol of the *megis* was adopted by the Medaewaewin (a society) as an emblem signifying a rebirth in the moral order

Medaewaewin a society of medicine men and women dedicated to the study of the curative properties and attributes of plants, healing, and the relationship between living and upright life (walking in balance), and well-being. The term may be derived from *mino odae-aewin*—good hearted, or from *medaewaewin*—sound. The latter sense may come from the practice of communicating with the manitous by means of the drum, whose resonance carried their petitions to the manitous that dwelt at the very ends of the universe. In some communities there were four grades or orders of membership; in others, eight.

medae-waeyaun the medicine pouch carried by members of the Medaewaewin

medae-wautik a cedar post within the interior of the *medae-wigaun* symbolizing the Tree of Life, cut live and then taken down at the termination of the ceremonies

medae-wigaun the Medaewaewin lodge, a long house in which the society conducts its ceremonies and meetings

medawaewae-igun; daewae-igun a drum used in private and in public ceremonies to communicate with and to invoke the manitous

megis a small shell that appeared in the sky above the village of a band of Anishinaubaek during their sojourn on the east coast. The presence of the shell was interpreted as a sign that the band was to return to its homeland that was granted to them by Kitchi-Manitou.

ningik the otter, a patron of the Medaewaewin. According to legend, the otter retrieved and delivered the snake root as a medicine from the bottom of the sea to Nana'b'oozoo through dream.

oshkaubaewiss kemauh Kaubaewiss a bearer and keeper of the sacred pipe. These safeguardians were especially appointed.

pakatae-kaewin fasting, abstaining, "making hunger." Prior to the vision or dream quest or undertaking a ceremony that involved the manitous, a man or woman fasted for four days.

pauwauwaewin revelation; an awakening; a vision by which a person gains an understanding of matters that had previously been obscure

pawaugun a pipe. The Pipe of Peace, a sacred instrument, said to have been presented by Ae-pungishimook to his son Nana'b'oozoo after their battle as a symbol of reconciliation, peace, goodwill. It is smoked to initiate ceremonies and important meetings.

waubuno a fully accredited member of the Medaewaewin who, it is said, assisted men and women who sought success in love or in hunting. The members of the Society of Dawn conducted their ceremonies at daybreak, hence the name.

waussae-yaubundumoowin the vision, whole, complete, clear. Youths began their vision quests around their twelfth year, and its receipt marked initiation into adulthood.

weekaun; n'eekaun brother; the term by which members of the Medaewaewin refer to one another

zaug-mauh a term used by the members of the Medaewaewin to refer to nonmembers, "outsiders"

zheesheegwun a rattle made from a turtle's shell and used in ceremonies to dispel illwill and evil

---

megooshaewin *a festival, celebration, ceremony, ritual*

Animoosh The White Dog Sacrifice. At the end of the Mino-waeziwin, the war dance, a little white dog is killed. Its liver is extracted and sliced and given to the warriors raw.

Cheeby-inaukaewin a feast of the dead observed annually in the autumn

Kaugaugeehn Kemauh Kaugaugisheehn Festival of the Raven

Mino-waeziwin the so-called war dance. Actually, it was an enactment of previous triumphs in pre-figuration of what the raiders meant to do to the enemy.

Oshki-nitaugaewin the first kill ceremony. This feast was conducted on the occasion of a youthful hunter's first kill of an animal or a bird that was edible, such as a squirrel, groundhog, porcupine, rabbit or a partridge.

Pagidinigaewin the wake, the vigil, and the funeral conducted over a four day period

Wauweendaussoowin the naming ceremony

Zauzau-keewaewin; Zauzaukeewaetchigun triumphant war cries;. The Painted Pole Festival. Following a successful raid, the returning triumphant warriors were tendered a feast and festival at which they re-created their victories in act and by war-cries, while their booty was suspended from a painted pole.

Anishinaubae-neemiwinum *Anishinaubae dances*

Note: These performances are more like ballet in style and purpose than ordinary dances. The performances are meant to dramatize some event, happening, story, or even dream. Only a few can be given here.

Begoosaendjigae-wigauwin the Begging Dance

Maemaengawauhwinugauwin the Butterfly Dance—now called The Fancy Shawl Dance

Maewishkodae-binae-igauwin a Prairie Chicken Dance; a mating dance

Nindo-binikaewigauwin a dance performed on the night before warriors set out on a raid

Pawaugun-igauwin the Dance of the Sacred Pipe

Quae-neemiwin a woman's dance

Wauwiyae-beekitchigun-agauwin the Hoop Dance

Zaussau-keewaewin a victory dance performed after a successful raid

---

doodaemiwiwin *totems*

ogimauwiwin *leadership*

chejauk a crane

kaikaik a hawk

kauyaushk a seagull

kineu a bald-headed eagle

makatae-zheeb a brant

maung a loon

peepeegizaehnse a sparrow hawk

gizhaudauwissoowin *safe guardianship*

bizheu a lynx

mukwoh; nokah a bear

myeengun a wolf

gautawaewauwissoowin *providing the necessities*

addik a caribou

amik a beaver

moozoo a moose

waub-ozhaesh a marten

wauwaushkaeshih a deer

wazhushk a muskrat

kikinoomaugaewin *teaching*

addik-maeg a whitefish

gin-ozhae a pike

mizyh a catfish

numae a sturgeon

numaebin a sucker

naundiwiwaewin *healing*

maukinauk kemauh mikinauk a turtle

mizundumoh a blackwater snake

muk-akee a frog

nebaunaubae; nebaunaubae-quae a merman, mermaid

nigik an otter

zheesheegawae kemauh maedawaehnwae a rattle snake

---

inoodaewiziwin *family relationships*

Note: Some of the terms in this section cannot stand or exist alone but must be adjoined to a possessive pronoun to bestow on them sense. To reflect practice and usage the first letter of the pronoun that accompanies the term is included—*n'* for *neen* (my); *k'* for *keen* (your), *keenwauh* (yours), or *keenawind* (ours); *w'* for *ween* or *weenwauh* (his, hers, its, their).

abi-anoodjeehn; abi-anoodjeehnuk a child, children; a habitué; one who remains and lingers in one place

akiwaehnzee; akiwaehnzeewuk an old man, men

akiweewizaehnse; akiweewizaehnssuk boy(s)

aunikoo-ipidjigun(uk) a great grandchild, children; a bond between generations

daessinauh; daessinauk single male virgin(s)

daessinau-quae; daessinau-quaek single female virgin(s)

daunissikaun a stepdaughter

gae-kikauhn; gae-kikauhnuk elder(s) (from *w'kikauh*—to age)

gauwizid; gauwizidjik orphan(s) (from *w'geewizih*—adrift; at a loss; disoriented)

geegaung; geegaungook virgin(s); spinster(s)

geeminee-idjaugun(uk) a child conceived on the sly—as in the back seat of a car or recreational vehicle—and born out of wedlock

ininih; ininiwuk a man, men

inoodaewiziwin a totemic family

ishkawae-idjaugun(uk) the last born

kaetizid; k'aetizidjik elder(s) (from *kitiz-iwin*—old age)

kawisskaun a stepson

k'd'aung-ozhaen; k'd'aung-ozhaehnuk your female cousin(s) (a term only females use)

k'd'ozh; k'd'ozhuk your nephew(s)

k'd'ozheem-quae; k'd'ozheem-quaek your niece(s)

k'dawaemauh; k'dawaemauk your sister(s) (a term only males use)

k'doodaem; k'doodaemuk your totemic emblem, family

k'missaehn; k'missaehnuk your older sister(s)

k'needjauniss; k'needjaunissuk your child, children

k'neegee-igook your parents (natural or foster)

k'ningooniss your son-in-law

k'suyaehn; k'suyaehnuk your older brother(s)

k'weedigik;k'weedigikook your sister(s) (a term only females use)

k'weetauwiss; k'weetauwissuk your male cousin(s) (a male speaking)

k'zhiniss your father-in-law

k'zigoossis your mother-in-law

maudjee-kawiss the eldest son; the starting son

maudjee-quaewiss the eldest daughter; the starting daughter

mindemoyaehn; mindemoyaehnuk an old woman, women

naubae; naubaek male(s); human being(s)

nawaendaugun(uk); nawaemaugun(uk) cousin(s); relative(s); kin

n'bimi-gaedaugun(uk) my neighbor(s)

n'd'aunikaen-mishoomiss(uk) my great grandfather(s)

n'd'aunikaen-ookomiss(uk) my great grandmother(s)

n'd'auniss; n'd'aunissuk my daughter(s); one who warms a heart, comforts

n'd'ogeem my mother (from *w'neegi-auwis-soh*—to raise, bring up)

n'doodaem my totemic emblem, family

n'doodoom my mother (only children use the term)

n'eedjauniss(uk) my child, children

need'ozhaun(uk) my cousin(s); people of the same stock

n'eetauwiss(uk) my brother(s)-in-law

n'gushih my mother

nim; weenimoon brother-in-law; sister-in-law

ningot-odaewiziwin a family; a single family

nitam-ozhaun(uk) the firstborn

n'kawiss; n'kawissuk my son(s)

n'kitizeem; n'kitizeemuk my elder(s)

n'mishoomaehn; n'mishoomaehnuk my uncle(s); my father's brothers

n'mishoomiss(uk) my grandfather(s)

n'nim; n'nimuk my sister(s)-in-law (only males use the term)

n'nozhaehnsh aunt (maternal)

n'ookomiss(uk); n'oko my grandmother(s) (*n'oko* is used by the western Chippewa and the Cree)

n'osse my father

n'ozhae-ishaehnse; n'ozhae-ishaehnssuk my grandchild, grandchildren

n'sheemaehn; n'sheemaehnuk my younger brother(s), sister(s)
n'sim; n'simuk my daughter(s)-in-law
n'weekauniss; n'weekaunissuk my brother(s)
n'zhishaehn; n'zhishaehnuk my uncle(s); my mother's brothers
n'zigoos my aunt (paternal)
oshki-nawae; oshki-nawaek a young man, men; new cheek(s)
oshki-neegi-quae; oshki-neegi-quaek a young woman, women
ossekaun a stepfather
quae; quaewuk a woman, women
quaezaehnse; quaezaehnssuk girl(s)
waebinigun; waebinigunuk deserted person(s)
wae-ogeemikaun a stepmother
weedigaemaugun a spouse; a friend, companion
weedjeewaugun a spouse; a friend, companion
weewun a derogatory term for spouse
yaubae; yaubaek female animal(s)
zae-zeekizid; zae-zeekizidjik the eldest
zheegauh; zheegauk widower(s)

Anishinaubae-anookeewin(un) *vocation(s); calling(s); occupation(s)*

---

anoodaugun(uk) hireling(s); delegate(s); employee(s); representative(s)
cheesi-akee-ininih (ininiwuk) gayae; cheesi-akeewiss(uk) the person who can cause the earth to move, shake, tremble; a medium who communicates with the manitous and who in turn receives messages from the supernatural
gautawaenawae-quae(k) nurse(s); health care worker(s)
mashki-akee-ininih (ininiwuk) a medicine man; male doctor(s)
mashki-akee-quae(k) a medicine woman; female doctor(s)
matchi-gawaehnish a rake; scoundrel; rogue; villain; rascal; cad; hooligan; felon; renegade; rat
mazhinawae; mazhinawaek a messenger; herald(s); a chief and council's courier who delivers messages and news
Medaewae-ininih (ininiwuk) a male member of the Medaewaewin, a medicine, healing society
Medaewae-quae(k) a female member of the Medaewaewin
minissinoh; minissinook warrior(s)
ogimauh; ogimauk a chief; a leader; a person who counts many followers, supporter(s)
okaubaewiss(uk); oshkaubaewiss(uk) pipe-bearer(s); carrier(s)
waubunoh; waubunoowuk a member of the Waubuno Society, a medicine-healing society that usually conducted its meetings at dawn

---

anookeewinun *some occupations*

---

anamie-ininih(wuk) a clergyman, clergymen,, priest(s); rabbi(s); pastor(s)
anamie-quae(wuk) nun(s)
anoodaugun(uk) employee(s); hireling(s); deputy, deputies, delegate(s), aide(s), etc.
anookeetaugun(uk) employee(s); servant(s); hireling(s); laborer(s); etc.
aunikoo-inootchigae-ininih(wuk) male translator(s), interpreter(s)
aunikoo-inootchigae-quae(wuk) female translator(s), interpreter(s)
autae-tchigae-ininih(wuk) male firefighter(s)
autae-tchigae-quae(wuk) female firefighter(s)
auttissookae-wininih(wuk), -quae(wuk) racon-teur(s); story-teller(s)
baupinooz-waugun(uk) clown(s)
beewaubikookae-ininih(wuk), -quae(wuk) steel worker(s); foundry worker(s), etc.
cheebaukawae-ininih(wuk), -quae(wuk) cook(s)
dubauk-inigae-ininih(wuk), -quae(wuk) judge(s); magistrate(s)
gaga-nootumaugae-ininih(wuk),-quae(wuk) lawyer(s); advocate(s); spokesman, spokeswoman
gageemoo-zaubundjigae-inninih(wuk), -quae(wuk) a spy, spies
gautawaenawae-quae(wuk) nurse(s)
gazeebeeg-inigae-ininih(wuk), -quae(wuk) launderer(s)
geegitoo-ininih(wuk), -quae(wuk) councillor(s)
geegoohn-kae-ininih(wuk), -quae(wuk)

fisher-man, fishermen; fisherwoman, fisher-women
geewi-ossae-ininih(wuk), -quae(wuk) hunter(s)
iko-zaubundjigae-ininih(wuk), -quae(wuk) seer(s); oracle(s); diviner(s), etc.
inaugummi-issitchigae-ininih(wuk), -quae(wuk) brewer(s)
izhi-beegae-ininih(wuk), -quae(wuk) writer(s)
kiki-noomaugae-ininih(wuk), -quae(wuk) teacher(s); instructor(s)
kishki-gawausso-ininih(wuk), -quae(wuk) tailor(s)
kitigae-ininih(wuk), -quae(wuk) farmer(s)
makatae-ikoonayae(k) priest(s); a mission-ary, missionaries
mashki-akee-ininih(wuk), -quae(wuk) doctor(s)
mauwindoo-gindaussee-ininih(wuk), -quae(wuk) accountant(s)
mazin-ibeegae-ininih(wuk), -quae(wuk) artist(s)
mazin-ikoodjigae-ininih(wuk), -quae(wuk) sculptor(s)
medawaewae-itchigae-ininih(wuk), -quae(wuk) musician(s)
metigwauk-akee-ininih(wuk) lumberjack(s)
minissinoh(wuk) warrior(s)
naeshinaudji-pugizood(jik) go-go dancer(s)
naup-qawaun-sheehn(wuk) sailor(s)
neeb-akee-ininih(wuk), -quae(wuk) medicine man, medicine men; medicine woman, medicine women
neegae-ininih(wuk), -quae(wuk) trapper(s)
ningo-akee-ininih(wuk), -quae(wuk) under-taker(s)
odauwae-ininih(wuk), -quae(wuk) a sales-man, salesmen; a saleswoman, saleswomen
shoossi-igugae-ininih(wuk), -quae(wuk) painter(s)
tikoonawae-ininih(wuk), -quae(wuk) police officer(s)
tikoonigae-ininih(wuk), -quae(wuk) police officer(s)
zeeg-inigae-ininih(wuk), -quae(wuk) bar-tender(s)
zhimaugunish(uk) soldier(s)

weeyoogiziwin; inau-weeyoowigiziwin

the anatomy; the shape or form of a body

adaup-agidigawaun(un) knee-cap(s)
agidik(ook) knee(s)
anik(un) arm(s)
atiss navel(s); belly-button(s)
atiss-waeyaub(een) nerve(s)
aumikun(un) jaw(s); jaw-bone(s)
aunikoogunaun a joint
aunkae-kunaegun(un) joint(s)
babeewaugaewin(un) small limb(s)
bausae-eeginaun marrow
bawaum(un) thigh(s)
beegoogunaun(un) ankle(s)
bikwun(un) back(s)
bikwun-aeyaub(een) spinal cord(s)
bimidauk-inaugun(un) collar-bone(s)
binauk-inindj(een) finger(s)
chechauk(oon) a soul; a principle of life
cheecheegoom(uk) wart(s)
cheeshidut(un) muscle(s); tendon(s); liga-ment(s)
cheetudum(un) sinew(s)
chibooway an aura spirit (*poss.* origin of Ojibway) (*also* chiboowim)
chingiwuneekun(un) thigh bone(s)
daekooswun(un) kidney(s)
daengawy(un) face(s)
daenigoom(un) nostril(s)
daeniniw(un) tongue(s)
daunibeen(un) nape(s) of the neck
deeyaush(un) posterior(s); rump(s); buttock(s)
dinimaungun(un) shoulder(s)
doodoosh(uk) breast(s)
doon(un) mouth(s)
doondun(un) heel(s)
dooskwun(un) elbow(s)
gaukaewindjigun(un) gristle(s); cartilage(s)
gauzhug(uk) gullet(s)
gibowin(un) abdomen(s)
goondaugun(un) throat(s)
goondaushk-waeyaub(een) windpipe(s)
goondaushkwy(oon) a gullet
goondaushkwyh(oon) windpipe(s)
indib(un) head(s)
inindj(een) hand(s)
ishkeehnzhig(oon) eye(s)

ishkunhsh(een) nail(s)
ishkunigun(un) gum(s)
itigoozee(n) kidney(s)
jauhnsh(un) nose(s)
jeet(een) female sex organ(s)
kakauwaundjigun(un) cartilage(s); gristle(s)
kaud(un) leg(s)
kaudaegun(un) shin(s); shin bone(s)
kaugaugee(n); kaugaugim(oon) uvula(e)
kaukigun(un) chest(s)
kidin(un) female sex organ(s)
kikinoowauzi-naugooziwin a distinctive physical characteristic
koon(un) liver(s)
kudik(oon) forehead(s)
kun(un) bone(s)
maemae(k) eyebrow(s)
makatae-yaugummi-isheenzhigoom(n) pupil(s) of the eye(s)
meensis(un) hair(s)
meeshaebeewun(un) eyelash(es)
meeshidoonaugun(un) beard(s)
midonaeninidjigun(un) brain(s)
misqui blood
misqui-yaub(een) vein(s); an artery, arteries
misquizub(een) buttock(s)
missud(un) stomach(s); belly, bellies
naugusk(oon) palate(s)
nawae(n) cheek(s)
neezhiwaun testicles, a pair
nekaun(un) calf, calves of the leg(s)
nenishk(oon) gland(s)
ningawyh(un) armpit(s)
noogun(un) hip(s)
nugauk-ozid(un) sole(s) of the foot, feet
nugish(een) bowel(s); intestine(s)
odae(n) heart(s)
odasinaukae(n) breastbone(s)
oshkud(een) stomach(s)
oskautigun(un) thigh bone; femur
oskun(uk) skeleton(s)
ozhae body, issue, flesh, stock
ozid(un) foot, feet
peendauginah internals, innards, insides
peendumoowin(un) bosom(s)
pigaegun(un) rib(s)
pik-indibaun(un) skull(s)
pikwau-kooginaun(un) ankle(s)
pikwaush(een) kemauh pikwaunsh lung(s)
poodjaug(un) penis(es); pokers, jabbers
pun(un) lung(s)
puyoh(oon) womb(s)
quae head; hair
quaegun(un); kawaegun(un) neck(s)
shtigwaun(un) head(s)
skeeg inside the nostril
taetaek the temple
tootoobikun a cartilage
tutugaugun(un) backbone(s)
tuwug(un) ear(s)
wae-izhigid(jig) a foetus, foetuses
waubum-ishkeehnzhigoom(n) white(s) of the eye(s)
weebid(un) a tooth, teeth
weehnzoop(un) gall bladder
weenigun marrow
weenigwijih scalp
weenin fat
weenindib a brain
weeyauss flesh
weeyoow(un) a body, bodies; corpse(s); cadaver(s)
weeyoowigiziwun anatomy
wizhigun(un) skull(s)
zheegwun(un) bladder(s)
zhugyh(un) skin(s); rind(s)
zob;weehnzob; weezob bile

---

gummig(oon) *(suffix) dwellings, houses, buildings, establishments*

---

adauwae-wigummig(oon) store(s); shop(s)
anami-ae-wigummig(oon) church(es)
anookee-wigummig(oon) a factory, factories
augawaudizee-wigumming(oon) mental institution(s); asylum(s)
aukoozee-wigummig(oon) hospital(s)
awukaun-gummig(oon) barn(s); stable(s)
cheessi-akee-wigummig(oon) hut(s); cubicle(s) wherein the shake-the-earth rituals are conducted
daessigaun(un) shelter(s)
dibauk-inigae-wigummig(oon) court(s)
gabaukoodee-wigummig(oon) jail(s); prison(s)
geekitoo-wigummig(oon) council hall(s); chamber(s)

kabaeshee-wigummig(oon) inn(s); hotel(s)
kikinoomaugae-wigummig(oon) school(s); learning institution(s)
mamaundjeenoo-wigummig(oon) gymnasium(s)
mashki-akee-wigummig(oon) drug store(s)
mazin-aukizigae-wigummig(oon) printing shop(s); publisher(s)
mazin-autaess-itchigae-wigummig(oon) cinema(s)
naundiwiwae-wigummig(oon) hospital(s)
neemidee-wigummig(oon) dance hall(s); pavilion(s)
nissowau-wigummig(oon) teepee(s)
pikawae-izhigunikae-wigummig(oon) a bakery, bakeries
shungae-wigummig(oon) restaurant(s); dining room(s)
wauginoogaun(un) a dome-shaped lodge
waukau-igun(un) lodge(s); longhouse(s); cabin(s)
weegwaum(un) birch-bark lodge(s) (from *weegwauss*)
zeeginigae-wigummig(oon) beverage lounge(s)
zhaubunoogaun(un); kemauh zhauboon-dau-wigaum(un) long house(s)
zhingob-gaun(un) a lean-to constructed of green boughs
zhooni-auh-wigummig(oon) bank(s)
zhooshkawaudae-wigummig(oon) arena(s)

aen-autchikinigaudaek weegwaum *parts, divisions of a house*

anaum-sug(oon) cellar(s); basement(s)
autchikinigun(un) room(s); chamber(s); apartment(s)
auzhiwi-sug(goon) the next, other room(s)
daessaubaun(un) porch(es); vestibule(s)
iko-waundawaugun(un) stairs
ishkawaun-daem(un) door(s)
ishpi-daessi-bug(oon) the ceiling
ish-pim-sug(oon) upstairs
mitchi-sug(oon) floor(s)
neessi-eehn downstairs; below
pukwaun(un) roof(s)
waussaetchigun(un); waussaenigun(un) window(s)

meedjim; meedjiwin *food*

aumoohn-zeezibaukoot honey
baushki-meen-issigun(un) jam; preserves; jellies
bautae-weeyauss; bautaezigun dried meat
bawaetae-igun roast corn
bimidae lard; fat; grease; drippings
bwaum(un) ham(s)
cheess(un) turnip(s)
dagoonigun(un) ingredient(s)
gauskidae-weeyauss; gauskizigun smoked meat
gidjik-naewaezigun; bunugizigun corn prepared for soup, for eating
koossimaun(un) pumpkin(s) (probably from *piko*—a bulge, bump, lump, hump, clump, knot, knob)
maeziwae-auhn; mizawaewae-itchigun hardened maple sugar
naboop(een) soup(s)
- **choog-meen-aubo** tomato soup
- **maun-dau-meen-aubo** corn soup
- **minidjee-meen-aubo** pea soup
- **mino-meen-aubo** wild rice soup
- **pinee-waubo** potato soup; vichysoisse
- **zauwauk-cheessi-waubo** carrot soup
- **zhush-quaedo-waubo** mushroom soup

naessaukoohnse(uk) an ear of corn
naupaunae flour
oohnzibun juice
paubawaun an ingredient
pigaegun(un) rib(s)
pikawae-izhigun bread
pundjigun a sauce; dip; gravy
waubauk-idaeyauh a parsnip
wausgung pepper
waussigung pepper
wauwun(oon) egg(s)
ween marrow
weenin fat
weeyauss meat; the flesh of an animal or bird (from *weeyoow*—body, corpse)
- **addik-weeyauss** caribou meat
- **amik-weeyauss** beaver meat
- **bizhi-akee-weeyaus** beef
- **coocoosh-weeyauss** pork
- **zeewitauguni-coocoosh** salt pork

zauwaukoot(oon) carrot(s)

zeewaug-midae syrup
zeewitaugun salt
zeezibaukoot sugar

---

wauboo(n); auboo(n) *beverages; fluids; ades*

---

doodoosh-aubo milk
ishkotae-waubo whiskey, firewater
mashki-akik-waubo physic; laxative; tonic
mishee-meen-aubo apple juice
neebeesh-aubo tea
noonaugun-aubo milk
zeewi-aubo vinegar
zeezibaukoot-aubo sap; soda pop
zhoomeen-aubo wine

---

gawiwin(un); ayeem(un); maundidaugun(un) *clothing; apparel; costume(s)*

---

anaun(un) bracelet(s)
anik-maun(un) braces; suspenders; armbands
auhniziyaun(un) loin cloth; breach clout; (now) diapers
ayeem(un) clothing; apparel
babeeskoowaugun(un) coat(s)
beessaugunaub(een) strap(s) (e.g., a shoulder strap)
beetoo-gawaudjigun(un) lining(s)
beetooshkaudjigun(un) underwear
daebeekitchigun(un) a buckle
gabo-dayae-gawauzoon(un) trousers; pants; ass-binders
gaweengawaewoon(un) veil(s)
gawiwin(un) clothing
kishki-daussae-pizoon(un) garter(s)
kishki-doodoosh-maebizoon(un) brassiere(s)
kishki-quaendib-aebizoon(un) helmet(s)
kitipizoon(un) apron(s); a belt
matchi-goodaehn(un) dress(es) (*lit.* the bad hanger[s])
maundidaugun(un) costume(s)
medauss(un) (formerly) leggings; chaps; (now) socks (in the East); pants (in the West)
meeknoot(un) pants, trousers (from *ma culotte* [Fr.]—my breeches)
mindjikauwun(uk) mitt(s); glove(s)
moccasin(un) footwear; moccasin(s)
naub-kauwaugun(un) a tie; neckwear
piduk-indibaewoon(un) roach(es)
piquaeyaugawauzoon(un) a collar
pissi-quae-bizoon(un); weewi-quaendibae-bizoon(un) headband(s)
pupigeewaeyaun(un) shirt(s); blouse(s)
weewiqwaun(un) hat(s)
zeendipizoon(un) corset(s)
zeezing-gawauzoon(un) vest(s)
zheegun(un); zhigun(un) sock(s)

---

eegin (suffix) *fabric; textiles; material; cloth; waeyaun—material made of hide*

---

augi-goodjigun-eegin(un) drape(s); partitions
doopiwin-eegin(un) tablecloth(s)
ishkoozhigun(un) remnant(s)
kishki-gawauzoon-aeyaub(een) thread(s)
kitug-eegin(un) calico
makatae-eegin(un) black cloth
manitou-eegin(un) silk(s)
misqua-eegin(un) red cloth
nebaug-neegin(un) bedspread(s); sheet(s)
neeminauquaeyaun(un); kaudaenigun-aeyaub rope(s); hauser(s); cable(s)
ningaussimoowi-neegin(un) tarp(s); sailcloth(s)
niskitchigun-eegin(un) lace; border(s); embroidery
pishaug-inaub(een) thong(s)
pishimoon-eegin(un) sheets
pupigee-waeyaun(un) shirt(s); blouse(s)
subaup(een) string(s); rope(s)
titabeeg-waudjigun(un) fringe(s)
waubishk-eegin(un) white cloth(s), fabric(s)
wauboo-yaun blanket(s)
waussaetchigun-eegin(un) curtain(s); blind(s)
zaenibauhn ribbon(s)
zheeb-waussae-eegin(un) transparent cloth(s); gauze(s); curtain(s)

---

anookaudjigun(un) *utensil(s)*

---

aedawae-koomaun(un) a two- or double-edged knife, knives
aemqwaun(un) spoon(s)

aemqwaunaehnse(un) little spoon(s)
akik pail(s); pot(s) (from *aki*—earth, soil, meaning a clay pot; vessel; urn
bawaunauk(oon) spit(s)
bawautchigun-aubik(oon) griddle(s)
bootaugun(un) a pestle
bootaugunauk(oon) a mortar
daessi-naugun(un) platter(s)
daushkigugun(un) cleaver(s)
dubu-geezis-waun(uk) a clock; a sun dial
gabaukawigun(un) cork(s); stopper(s); lid(s); cap(s)
gaushkau-igun(un); kemauh maudau-igun(un) scraper(s)
gawaubigun(un); kemauh gawau-igun(un) dipper(s); ladle(s)
gaweetau-igun(un) corkscrew(s)
iskoobaun(un) pump(s)
iskoobaunidjigun(un) sponge(s)
kitchi-mookoomaun(un) a butcher's knife, knives
kookibi-naugun(un) woven basket(s)
meegooss(uk) awl(s)
miniquadjigun(un) cup(s); mug(s); drinking vessel(s)
moodyh(un) a bottle; a bird's crop, gullet
mookoomaun(un) a knife, knives
mooshki-moot(un) bag(s); something filled or to be filled
moozhi-waugun(un) scissor(s)
mukuk(oon) box(es); container(s)
mukuk-sug(oon) wooden container(s); barrel(s); tub(s); vat(s)
naenisso-waubidae-igun(un) fork(s); three toothed instrument(s)
naubauk-issitchigun(un) handle(s); extension(s)
naugauhnse(un) saucer(s); bowl(s)
naugun(un) dish(es); plate(s); vessel(s)
neembaugun(un) bucket(s); pail(s)
oonaudinigun(un) a kneading board
piduk-igun(un); kemauh piduk-idjeegun(un) fork(s)
waewaessaegun(un) fan(s)
waussiko-naendjigun(un) lamp(s)
zaussikoo-qwaun(un); kemauh zauzae-qwaun(un) frying pan(s); skillet(s)
zhaegwaun-aubik(oon) grindstone(s)
zhauboonigun(un) needle(s)
zheesheeb-akik(ook) kettle(s)
zhooshkawae-igun iron(s)

weegwaum anookaudjigunun *household appliances; tools; utensils*

anaukun(un) mat(s)
apiquae-ishimoon(un) pillow(s)
apishimoon(un) mattress(es)
aubaubikugun(un) key(s)
baeng-waussitchigun(un); bautae-yaussitchigun(un) dryer(s)
bim-ossae-itchigun(un) walker(s)
bunu-beewiyae-igun(un) brush(es)
cheecheebauk-naugun(un) cradle(s)
cheegitu-igun(un); waebigun(un) kemauh; cheeshi-tugun(un) broom(s)
doopwin(un) table(s)
dubu-geezisswaun(uk) clock(s); a sun dial
gaweed-biwin(un) chair(s)
gazee-ipeengawae-naugun(un) wash basin(s)
gazee-ozidae-ishimoon(un) mat(s)
gazeepeeg-issutchigun(un) washer(s)
gazee-peeg-ozhae-yaubauwitchigun(un) shower(s)
gazee-pee-yaussitchigun(un) washer(s)
gizhaupikizigun(un) stove(s)
ishpi-daessi-bug(oon) ceiling(s)
kawaundawaugun(un) stair(s)
keegitto-waubeeginigun(un) telephone(s)
kishkaupikugun(un) lock(s)
kishkudin-itchigun(un) refrigerator(s); freezer(s)
mazin-ibeegun(un) painting(s)
mazin-ininih(iwuk) statue(s) of a male figure or figures
mazin-itchigun(uk) picture(s); photo(s); an image
mazin-quae(wuk) statue(s) of a female figure or figures
meezeewi-naugun toilet bowl(s)
mitchi-sug(oon) a floor
nebaugun(un kemauh nebaegun(un) bed(s)
nebaugun-eegin(un) sheet(s); spread(s)
niki-beezigun a furnace
pubwin(un) chair(s)
pukwaun(un) roof(s)

taussoowin(un) dresser(s); cupboard(s)
tikauss-itchigun(un) fan(s)
tikinaugun(un) cradle board(s)
waewaeb-izoon(un) swing(s)
waub-oyaun(un) blanket(s)
waubumoowin(un) a mirror
waussikonaendjigun(un) lamp(s)
weessiniwaugun(un) a table
zeegi-idjiwun-aubik tap(s)
zheebau-yaudjiwun-aubik(oon) water pipe(s)

---

anookaudjigun(un); anookauzoowin(un); aubidjitchigun(un) *tools; instruments; implements*

---

anookaudjigun(un); anookauzoowin(un); aubidjitchigun(un) tool(s); instrument(s); implement(s)
aussiwaukawigun(un) prop(s); support(s)
beeminigun(un); beemissiko-igun(un) screwdriver(s)
begoonae-igun(un) chisel(s); a drill(s)
boodaudjeeshkoodae-tchigun(un) bellows
cheegi-igugun(un) broad axe(s)
dubugun(un) measuring tape(s); ruler(s)
gawaub-idauwingugun(un) spade(s)
gaweedinigun(un) lever(s)
geeshki-boodjigun(un) saw(s)
kitchi-beeminigun(un) auger(s)
mookodjigun(un) draw-knife, draw-knives
mookoomaun(un) knife, knives
nissiwi-shawae-ayauk-itchigun triangle(s); tripod(s)
nubug-aubik(oon) shovel(s)
oombau-beeginigun(un) pulley, pullies
oombaukawigun(un) hoist(s)
peendau-oodjigun(un) sheath(s); a casing
peendinik-audjigun(un) casing(s)
pikitae-igun(un) hammer(s); mallet(s)
pissikaubee-koomaun(un) a jackknife, jackknives
pugum-ishtigwaun(un) hammer(s)
shooshawaey-dubugun-aubik(oon) square(s)
siboodjigun(un) file(s)
siboodjigun-aubik(oon) grindstone(s)
tautaugidugun(un) leveller(s); flattener(s)
tikoondjigun(un) tong(s); pliers
titabae-oodjigun(uk) reel(s); coil(s)
titabauk-issaetchigun(un) roller(s)
waubigun-igun(un) trowel(s)
waugau-koomaun(un) a crooked knife, knives
waugaukoot(oon) axe(s)
wauwiyae-beeg-itchigun(un) compass(es)
zhingau-kummik-autchigun(un) level(s)
zhinoo-igun(un) pointer(s)
zhooshkoodjigun(un) plane(s)
zigu-igun(un) nail(s)

---

kitigae-anookaudjigun(un) *farm implements*

---

beegundigun(un) thresher(s), a threshing machine (from *beeg*—to break down, ruin, destroy, etc.)
bee-waubikoo-zigibidji-gun(un) chain(s); metal hauser(s)
bimidj-waugaukood(oon) hoe(s)
bimi-poodjigun plough(s); a furrow maker
binaukawae-igun(un) rake(s)
cheeshau-goonae-igun(un) small snow plough(s); snow scraper(s), shovel(s)
daess-ubiwin(un) saddle(s)
daubaun(uk) vehicle(s)
gawaubid-auwangungun(un) spade(s)
geeshk-izhigun(un) scythe(s); mower(s)
mauwindooshk-igun(un) rake(s)
mitchi-kun(un) fence(s); weir(s)
mukuksug(oon) barrel(s); wooden tub(s)
neembaugun(un) bucket(s)
nindo-baun(un) well(s); trough(s)
nisso-waubidae-igun(un) pitchfork(s)
piduk-ishkaudjigun(un) spur(s); stirrup(s)
pikwun(un) harness(es) (probably from *bikwun*—back)
pissu-kummik-poodjigun(un) harrow(s)
shkuhnzhee-kaudjigun(un) horseshoe(s)
taetibissaehn(uk) wheel(s)
taetibissaehn-daubaun(uk) wheeled vehicle(s)
tautaugidugun(un) piledriver(s); earth leveller(s), packer(s); heavy equipment
winigum-autik(ook) wheelbarrow(s) (from *winigum*—portage)
zaugi-doonae-ibidjigun(un) bridle(s)

minissino-anookaudjigun(un) *warriors' arms*

baugikawaun(un) a shield
bugu-maugun kemauh pugu-maugun a war club
bunishimah kemauh bunishimoon a shield
mamaundji-ikopidjigun(un) manacle(s)
metig-waub a bow
miss-autik(oon) cudgel(s)
peendawaeyaun(un) a quiver
peepeegiwun a flute or whistle blown to signal the launch of an attack (from *peepe-egizaehnse*—sparrow hawk, a reference to its sound, pitch, tone)
pigook(oon) arrow(s)
zhimaugun(un) spear(s)

geew-ossae-anookaudjigun(un) *hunting equipment*

adjaub(een) bow string(s)
anwih(ween) bullet(s)
augum(uk) snowshoe(s)
baushkizigun(un) gun(s); rifle(s)
beendaussinaun(un) shot pouch(es)
beendaussoowin quiver(s)
dassoo-naugun(un) trap(s)
metigwaub(een) bow(s)
ningawaugun(un) snare(s)
pigook(oon) arrow(s)
toobaugun(uk) toboggan(s)
zhawaeshk(oon) dagger(s)

geegoohnkae-anookaudjigun(un) *fishing gear*

abwih(ween) paddle(s); oar(s)
aubidjibidjigun(un) hooks(s)
audji-gawaudjigun(un) grappling hook(s)
auzhigun(un) bridge(s)
baussawae-binauk(ook) drying pole(s)
baussi-suppee-nauk(ook) net drying pole(s), frame(s)
beeminauqawaun a hauser
booni-kundjigun(un) anchor(s)
cheemaun(un) canoe(s) (*lit.* a kiss [the dip of paddle into water sounds like a kiss])
cheemaunauk(oon) paddle(s)
gaund-akeegun(un) push pole(s)
gawaub-naugun(uk) seine(s); dip-net(s)
kundeekun(uk) buoy(s)
megiskun(un) lure(s)
naubigawau-augun(uk) a net-mesh, webbing repair instrument
naupiqwaun ship(s); large vessel(s)
niminauwaetchigun(un) a wharf, wharves; dock(s); a landing, launching place; a marina(s)
nindo-pidjigun(un) grappling iron(s)
ningaussimoo-weegin(un) sail(s); tarp(s)
ningauss-mooyaub(een) ship; sailing-ship cordage
peendissaugun(un) raft(s)
piduk-ipitchigun(un) harpoon(s)
shinoodaugunaeyaub(een) a net of cord or twine
shumoodjigun bait
sidowae-ishkoodjigun(un) ballast
suppeemauhassub(eek) net(s)
waewaebunaubinautik(ook) fishing rod(s), pole(s)
wausswaugun(un) torch(es)

wukaun(uk) kemauh awukaun(uk) *domestic animals*

anim(ook) dog(s)
baezhig-oongizhee(k) horse(s) (*lit.* the one-nailed creature)
bizhi-aki(wuk) cow(s); (formerly) a buffalo
boozhaehnse(uk) cat(s)
coocoosh(uk) pig(s)
gauzhug(uk) cat(s)
maemaungishaehn(uk) donkey(s); mule(s); long-eared(s)
mauzhitaunish(uk) sheep(s)
mish-aub-ooss(ook) goat(s)

waesseehn(uk) *animals*

addik(ook) caribou(s)
adjidumooh(k) kemauh odjidumooh(k) squirrel(s)
aehnse-bun(uk) a raccoon; (formerly) a shell
amik(ook) a beaver (*lit.* one that dwells at the bottom of a pond)
baebeek-awauwigung(ook) a camel (*lit.* the crooked back)
bizheu(wuk) lynx(es)
chae-chee-pidukeehn(uk) elephant(s)

gageeb-eengawae-quae(wuk) mole(s); a blind woman
gaween-gauwigaehn(uk); gaween-waeyaugae(k); meeshigun(uk) wolverine(s); origin of the name of Michigan
gunkissaehnse(ssiwuk) chipmunk(s)
kaug(ook) porcupine(s)
kitugaukoohnse(ssuk) fawn(s)
kookidjeesh(uk) groundhog(s)
maemae-quaedoohn(uk) a mole (*lit.* one that emerges, here and there, now and then)
mauzh-aehnse(ssuk) a yearling (deer), no longer mottled
mishaewae(k) stag(s); red deer
mishauk-waukidjeesh(uk) badger(s)
moozoo(k) a moose
mukwoh(k) bear(s) (*lit.* one who goes hither and yon in search of food)
myeengun(uk) a wolf, wolves (*lit.* one who makes strange)
naepaudji-anik-aessih(ssiwuk) mole(s); gauche
nindo-maukimaesheehn(uk) a monkey, monkies (*lit.* a nit picker)
ningik(ook) otter(s)
noozhaehnse(ssuk) doe(s)
odjeek(ook) fisher(s)
pushkawau-dausheehn(uk) coyote(s)
sunigoo(k) black squirrel(s)
waub-oozoo(k) rabbit(s); hare(s) (*lit.* white-tailed)
waub-ozhaesh(iwuk) marten(s)
waugoosh(uk) fox(es)
wauwau-begoonoodjeehn(uk) a mouse, mice
wauwaushkaeshih(iwuk) a deer
wuzhushk(ook) muskrat(s)
yaubae(k) male(s)
zhaungawaeshih(wuk) mink(s)
zhigaug(ook) skunk(s)
zhigushk-aundawae(k) flying squirrel(s)
zhingoohnse(uk) weasel(s)

ae-izhi-weeyoowigiziwaut waesseehnuk *animal anatomy*

aeshkun(un) antler(s); horn(s)
beewuy(un) fur; hair(s)
bunu-beewaunaewin the shedding of fur, hair
bunuwaewin the shedding of horns
gauwi-issaungun(uk) a quarry, quarries; prey
kawaewin(un) trail(s); track(s)
kinhnsh(un) snout(s)
nitaugun(uk) the victim(s)
oozoo(wunoon) short tail(s)
oozoowaunuk(oon) long tail(s)
waunoowin tailpiece; extremity
win-ozid(un) paw(s)

benae; benaessih; benaessiwuk *bird(s)*

amik-zheeb(uk) beaver duck(s)
anaum-zigud-waesheehn(uk) wren(s)
apish-kaugaugee(uk) magpie(s)
aundaeg(ook) crow(s)
auzhidaukoon-aesheehn(uk) cross-bill(s)
baebeegiskoogaed(jik) woodpecker(s); he, she, it, or they who destroy by boring
baeshkeewae(k) nighthawk(s); one who is hoarse
baukauk-quaehn(k) hen(s)
benae(k, wuk) partridge(s)
boonissae(k) kemauh gabwun-issae(k) vulture(s)
cheecheesh-quaehn(k); cheecheeb-quaewaessih(iwuk) killdeer(s); those who leave trailing footprints; those whose heads bob back and forth
chejauk(ook) crane(s)
deendeehnse(uk) bluejay(s)
gakaushki-naedjeehn(uk) sparrow(s)
gauskauski-naudjeehn nightingale(s)
geekabeek-maesheehn(uk) meadowlark(s)
geeki-dub downy woodpecker(s); one who moves over
geeshki-munisseehn(k) kingfisher(s); one who produces a ripping sound
kaikaik(ook) hawk(s); a red-shouldered hawk
kaugaugeehn(k); kaugaukisheehn(k) raven(s); the ever present bird
kaukaubisheehn(k) screech owl(s)
kauyaushk(ook) seagull(s)
kineu(wuk) bald-headed eagle(s)
kookookoo(k) owl(s)
kookoolee; wau-oonae(k) whippoorwill(s)

maemae(k) flicker(s); a red-headed woodpecker
maeshkodae-benaessih(iwuk) prairie chicken(s); quail(s)
makatae-aunauk(ook) red-winged blackbird(s)
makatae-zheeb black duck(s)
maung(ook) loon(s)
meemee(k) dove(s); passenger pigeon(s)
migizi(wuk) brown or golden eagle(s)
mino-meeni-kaesheehn(k) snipe(s); a bird that frequents and habituates wild rice
mishi-geegoohnae(k) fish hawk(s)
mizissae(k) turkey(s)
mizuhnzih(wuk) black eagle(s)
moondawae(k) catbird(s)
mooning-wunae(k) crested plover(s)
mooshk-woossae(k) bittern(s)
naubae-ossae(k) rooster(s); a male bird; the strutter
naunookauhnssae(wuk); naunookishk-auhnse(iwuk) hummingbird(s); one who stops here and there in flight
nikah; nikak a wild goose, geese
ningibeewauhnse(uk) screech owl(s)
n'sheemaehn(k); geezhigaunaesheehn(uk) chickadee(s); my younger sister(s), brother(s)
paupaussae(k) woodpecker(s); the knocker(s), rapper(s)
peepeegizaehnse(uk) sparrow hawk(s); one whose call sounds like a bone flute
pidushk-auhnzhae(k) woodcock(s)
pishk-issih(wuk) goose, geese
pitchi(wuk) robin(s); a sudden break in vocalization
pukwaun-audjeehn(k) bat(s); one who frequents and habituates a roof, roofs
saugibuniwaun-aesheehn(k) red-winged blackbird(s)
siginauk(ook) blackbird(s)
tikwauk-zheeb(uk) autumn duck(s)
waewae(k) Canada goose, geese
waewaendjigunooh(wuk) great horned owl(s)
waub-anung-issae(k) snow-bird(s)
waubizee(k) swan(s)
waub-meemee(k) dove(s)
weenaungae(k) buzzard(s); one who is at home accustomed to dirt and uncleanliness
weendigo-benaessih(wuk) kingbird(s)
winzik(ook); oohnzik(ook) sawbill duck(s)
zaegibawaudjeehn(uk) cedar waxwing(s)
zauwae-benaessih(wuk) goldfinch(es)
zhae-aumooh(k) wood duck(s)
zhaedae(k); zhaudae(k) pelican(s)
zhaushauwi-benaessih(wuk) swallow(s)
zhauwun-aessih(wuk) bluebird(s)
zheeng-ibiss(wuk) brant(s)
zheesheeb(uk) duck(s)
zhooshigauh(k); zhooshi-gauboowih heron(s); one who stands erect
zigutaegunae-zheeb(uk) teal(s)

benaessi-weeyoowigiziwin *bird anatomy*

beewun down
koohnzh(un) beak(s); bill(s)
kuhnzh(een) claw(s); talon(s)
meegwun(uk) feather(s) removed from the bird
meegwun(un) down; feather(s)
mezaugwun down
misquawoon egg yolk(s)
moodyh(un) bird crop(s)
ningaweegun(un) wing(s)
piduk-naewoon(un); piduk-biniwae-woon(un) a bird's crest
soossiwun(un) nest(s)
wauwun(oon) egg(s)
winushkid(un) bird tail(s)

geegoohn(uk); ginaebeeg(ook); baemoodaed(jik) *fish; reptile(s); crawler(s)*

addik-maeg(ook) whitefish; caribou of the waters
aehnse(uk) a shell; small shell(s)
akiweewizaehnse(uk) a salamander
anumae(k); kemauh numae(k) sturgeon(s); one that dwells in the depths, the very bottom
ashigun(uk) a bass
baepaeshih-ginae-beeg(ook) garden snake(s); a long, striped, strand-like creature
beeg-muk-akee(k) toad(s)
beemisko-d-aehnssih(wuk) snail(s); spiralled shell(s)

beem-issae(k) eel(s)
begoonaequae(k) tree frog(s)
boodoohnse(uk) tadpole(s); pollywog(s)
dushwae(n) turtle shell(s)
geekidaunaung(ook) lizard(s)
ginae-beeg(ook) snake(s); a long, strand-like creature
gin-ozhae(k) a pike; the long-bodied one
gookaehnse(uk) small tree frog(s)
kaewiss(uk) herring(s)
kikidaungawae(k); kemauh odawuginaeg(ook) a salamander
kitchi-kikidaungawae(k) a crocodile; an alligator
kitchi-maun-maeg(ook) whale(s)
maedawaewaehn(k); zheesheegawae a rattlesnake; one that rattles
maegooss; maeg fish
maukinauk(ook); mikinauk(ook) turtle(s)
maun-maegooss(uk) catfish(es)
mauzh-maegooss(uk); zauwi-maegooss(uk) salmon(s); speckled trout
metiko-zheesheegawae(k) timber rattler(s); milksnake(s)
misheekaehn(k) turtle(s)
mishi-gin-ozhae(k) a muskellunge; the great, long-bodied one(s)
misqwaud-aehnse(uk) small reddish turtle(s)
mizundumoh(k) black water snake
mizyh(uk) catfish(es)
muk-akee(k) frog(s)
numaebin(uk) sucker(s); one that feeds off the bottom
numaegooss(uk) a trout(s); bottom, deep-water dwellers
ogauh(k) pickerel(s); walleye
sauwae(k) perch(es)
tandae(k) bullfrog(s)
ushkee(k) seal(s)
waussee(k) sun fish(es)
zaug-aesheehn(k) crab(s) or crayfish(es) that dwell at the mouth of a creek or river or that emerge from under rocks
zhauwushkoowaushkoozih(wuk) green frog(s); the green jumper
zhiginauhnse(uk) dew worm(s)
zhingwaud-aemiquam(uk) turtle(s)
zigussikawaudjimae(k) leech(es)

ae-izhi-weeyoowigizoowaut geegoohnuk *fish anatomy*

nindjigun(un) fin(s)
oskauw the flesh or meat of fish
pikwunzhi(een) bladder(s)
waukoon roe; fish eggs
winugyh(un) scale(s)
zhigwun(un) a fish tail

manitoush(uk, iwuk) *insects; worms; small creatures, so called because many change form, undergo transformation*

abidushkoon-aesheehn(uk) a dragonfly, dragonflies
aehnsaehnse(ssiwuk) clam(s); little shell
aehnsi-gauk(ook) wood louse; wood lice; tick(s)
aenig(ook) ant(s)
aenigoohn(uk) ant(s)
aeyaebig(ook) spider(s)
aumoohn(uk) a bee (from *aumoowaewin*—to beat off, repel, drive off)
auzhawaeyau-goonidjeesih(wuk) a dragonfly, dragonflies
cheecheegauwaesseehn(uk) beetle(s)
ginae-beego-kaessaehnssee(uk) cricket(s)
koodjeesh(uk) a louse, lice
kookoowaessih(iwuk) moth(s)
maemaegawaehnshish(uk) caterpillar(s)
maemaegwauhnse(wuk) a butterfly, butterflies (likely from *meegwauhnse*—little feather)
mae-minau-auwidjissaehn(uk) cricket(s)
maung-itikoom(uk) a loon louse, lice
minaugodjeessee(wuk) woodworm(s)
mish-aumoohn(uk) bumblebee(s)
mizizauk(ook) a horsefly, horseflies
niminau-goodjissaehn(uk) water spider(s)
noonimoodoowaessih(uk) a chrysalis
odjee(k) a common house fly, flies
ooquae(k) maggot(s)
pigook-issaehnse(issiwuk); pikocheessee(wuk) a blackfly, blackflies; little arrow(s)
pingwoosh(uk) a sandfly, sandflies
pubig(ook) flea(s)
pukinae(wuk) a grasshopper (from *oombaukinae*—to leap, jump, as sparks do from a fire)

skinauk(ook) nit(s)
sup(pee) kaesheehn(uk) spider(s) (*lit.* the net maker)
tibauk-waugunaenikaesseehn(uk) caterpillar(s)
tissau-waesheehn(unk) cicada(s) (from *tis-sigaewin*—to paint)
tootoowaessih(wuk) moth(s)
wauwautaessih(wuk) a firefly, fireflies
zhiginauhn(uk) earth worm(s); dew worm(s)
zigimaehn(uk) mosquito(es) (from *zigi*—to attach to, cling to)

---

paedukeedaegin; zayaug-ikeegin *plants*

---

abaupissoon false Solomon's seal—used for kidney ailments (from *inaupitaewin*—fumes)
ae-shawaeshkook; peepeegiwunushk cow parsnip—a flute-like plant; a hunter's talisman (*lit.* spread out or drooping over)
ae-zau-waukinaek(oon) north bush honeysuckle—a diuretic (*lit.* that which glows yellow)
agidae-bug(oon) marsh marigold—edible *lit.*a flosting plant)
akiwaehnzee(uk) goat's beard (*lit.* old man)
akiwaehnzee-mawi(wuk) beechdrops (*lit.* crying old man)
amik-meenushk(oon) beaver's seeds—edible
anaukoon a bullrush—used for matting
andaeg-bugoohnse(un) wild mint—a beverage; a tonic for blood (*lit.* the crow's flower)
aneeb-meen-gauwuhnsh(eek) high bush cranberries—edible
ani-geetini-gunuk wild cucumber—used as a tonic (*lit.* those/that which loosen things up)
ani-idjee-meen-ush(koon) pea(s)—edible
animakee-bug(oon) poison ivy
anim-ozid(un) sharp-lobed hepatica (*lit.* dog's foot, paw)
anim-ozidae-bugoohnse(un) Virginia waterleaf (*lit.* the dog's-paw leaf, petal)
anung-piko-ipeessae-bug(oon) fragrant water lily (*lit.* star fallen into the water)
ashkibawaun(un) Jerusalem artichoke—edible (*lit.* the raw/uncooked/green/new growth)
auboodjigun(un) a kind of reed—material used to make mats (*lit.* inverted, turned inside out)
aumoohn-gauwuhnshk(oon) oswego tea—a beverage (*lit.* the bee plant)
babau-mukoo-cheebik-issin(un); mukwo-nugishi-cheebik dogbane—a cough medicine (*lit.* the bear root found here and there; the bear's entrails root)
baebau-goondaek(oon) March cinquefoil—good for cramps (*lit.* floating here and there)
baebaumaubeeg wild sarsaparilla—used as a talisman and lure for fishing and fish (*lit.* zigzag extension)
baegawae-wunushk(oon) soft, coarse grass(es)
baemaukaweed-waubugonae(n) canada moonseed (*lit.* the climbing, snaking flower)
baessi-buguk(oon) pearly everlasting, either narrow or small leafed/petalled
baessi-buguk(oon) selfheal—female remedy (*lit.* small petalled)
baessi-bugut bladder campion (*lit.* small petalled)
baezhig-oongizhee-mashki-aki(een) vetchling—horse medicine, veterinary medicine
baupizoh(winun) false Solomon's seal—kidney purifier (*lit.* it fumigates)
beemaukoot(oon) rue anemone (*lit.* crooked span, line)
beemiss-kawaundawish(koon) hooded ladies' tresses (*lit.* to ascend in a spiral fashion)
beess-gaug-meen-gauwuhnsh(een) gooseberry bush—edible (*lit.* the small porcupine berry bush)
benae-bug(oon) slender ladies' tresses; a talisman for hunters (*lit.* partridge petals, leaves)
bigizoowin(un) mugwort; swamp milkweed—used for dysentery (*lit.* the swim)
bizhi-akee-bugaessaun(uk) a ground plum—to stem flow of blood (*lit.* a buffalo's prune)
bizhi-akeewi-guhnsh(koon) prairie sage—used for convulsions, hemorrhaging (*lit.* buffalo's food)

bizhi-akee-wuhnsh(koon) seneca snakeroot (*lit.* cattle fodder)

bugissawae-bug(oon) joe-pye weed (*lit.* the fragmented petals, leaves)

bugwudji-misquo-diss-meen(uk) a wild bean

chau-chau-boonuk-sing(oon) a skull cap—a heart remedy (*lit.* that which sways to and fro)

cheebiki-namoon(un) puccoon—a dye (*lit.* a reddish root)

cheeby-bug kemauh cheebikuh(oon) moosewood (*lit.* a ghost's root; a part of a root)

cheeby-bug(oon) leatherwood (*lit.* a ghost's plant)

cheecheego-meen(un, uk) wild lettuce—medicine for warts (*lit.* the wart plant)

coocoocoo moccasin(un); agobizoowin lady's slipper—a remedy for women (*lit.* the owl's or the whippoorwill's moccasin)

coocoosh-miniquae-meen(un, uk) long bracted orchis—an aphrodisiac, a love medicine (*lit.* the pig's beverage berry)

doodooshaubo-cheebik(oon) pawqueflower—for headaches (a milky fluid in the root of this plant)

gau-bizaun-idaeyauk(oon) hepatica—for convulsions (*lit.* that which induces or instills calm)

gaund-gawauzoon-augoot(oon); gaund-gawauzoon-nakae-izhi-naugook long-headed thimble weed—good for stomach ailments

gauwaug-bugoohnse(uk) rose(s)—edible

gauwaug-meesh(uk) kemauh; gauwaug-maewish(uk) rose-bush(es)—edible

gauzhug-aehnsewi-bug(oon) catnip, mint—a beverage (*lit.* cat's petal or leaf)

gazheeb-dayae-meeni-gauwuhnsh(eek); ginug-dayae-meeni-gauwuhnsh(eek) hawthorn—edible (*lit.* scratch your bum berry bush)

gazheeb-inushkoon kemauh; gizheeb-inushkoon scouring rushes (*lit.* the hurrying bullrushes,; the rushes that cause itching)

gee-soossawae-bugauwish green headed coneflower—for indigestion (*lit.* the old scattered flower)

geezisso-bugoohnse(un, uk); ae-ish-paendaugook ox-eye—a tonic (*lit.* the little sun flower)

geezisso-mashki-aki(een) goldenrod—medicine for fever and ulcers (*lit.* the sun's medicine)

ginae-beego-cheebik(oon) black snakeroot—for fevers

ginae-beego-meeni-gauwuhnsh(een) carrion flower—a medicine for lungs and for urinary system (*lit.* the snake plant)

gin-bugoohnse(un) rose bush—edible (*lit.* the sharp, prickly plant)

gin-ozhae-bug(oon) bead lily (*lit.* the pike flower)

gin-ozhae-guhnshk(oon) pickerel weed—childbirth medicine (*lit.* the pike's plant)

gin-ozhae-wikoon curled dock (*lit.* the pike's liver)

gozigawauk-meeni-gauwuhnsh(eek); zugauk-meen-gauwushnsh a shadebush—for dysentery and for women's ailments (*lit.* the heavy berry bush; the thorny, prickly berry bush)

gozig-meen-gauwuhnsh(een) shadbushes (Juneberries)—a prenatal remedy (*lit.* the heavy blossoming berries)

gunkissaehn-bug(oon) rose twisted-stalk—medication for eyes, kidneys (*lit.* chipmunk leaf, leaves)

gunkissaehn-meen(uk) lily of the valley—medicine for kidneys (*lit.* a chipmunk's seed)

gunkissaehn-meenushk(oon) cow wheat (*lit.* a chipmunk's plant)

gunkissaehnse-bugoohnse(un) field bindweed (*lit.* little chipmunk leaf or petal)

inini-idjeebik(oon) may-apple(s) (*lit.* man's root)

ishkotae-bugoonee(n) cardinal flower (*lit.* the fiery petalled flower)

ishkotae-idjeebik(oon) shepherd's purse(s) (*lit.* fire root)

kaudauk(oon) queen Anne's lace (*lit.* like a leg)

kaugigae-bug(oon) pipsissewa—stomach

medication (*lit.* the everlasting flower)
kaugigae-bugoohnse(un) pussytoes—afterbirth medicine (*lit.* everlasting petal[s] or leaf, leaves)
kibeehnse(un) green shrub(s)
kitchi-numae-wuhshk(oon) catnip—a beverage as well as a blood purifier (*lit.* the great sturgeon's plant or the cat plant)
kizhae-bunushk(oon) small prairie grass(es)
koossimaun(un) a pumpkin—edible (*lit.* a projection, a large lump) (from *pikoossimaun*—with food)
kundoomoon(un) the yellow water lily (*lit.* the ambusher)
mae-mashko-naukook(oon) Canada hawkweed—a hunting talisman (*lit.* firm stalked)
mae-misqwi-naugook steeplebush (hardhack) (*lit.* appears like blood)
maenowak(een) corn parsley
maesqua-koonaek orange hawkweed (*lit.* red flamed)
maesqwaub-meesh(maewish)(koon) a small red willow blended with tobacco (*lit.* a reddish plant or growth)
maesqwau-zhaubo-meenuk edible (*lit.* the red berries that purge, go directly through)
maewishkodae-ikoonaes(un) bluestem—for indigestion (*lit.* little prairie fire)
maewishkodae-meen(un) prairie bean—edible
maewishkoohnse(un); kemauh meeshkoohnse(un) grass(es)
maewishk-oohnssiwung(oon) asparagus—edible (*lit.* that which is small or slightly bladed)
maewishkoon; kemauh; meezhushk; meezhushkoon hay
makatae-anaukunushk(ook) a black reed—used to treat cramps
makatae-cheebik(oon) burr snakeroot—medicine for women's ailments (*lit.* the black root)
makatae-meen(uk) any blackberry—edible
mashki-akeewit kemauh maeshki-akeewit(chik) the common tansy—used to heal fevers; a hunting and fishing talisman (*lit.* the extremely medicinal plant)
matchi-manitou-saemauh mullein (*lit.* devil's tobacco)
matchi-mashki-aki-meen(uk) bittersweet nightshade
maundau-meen(uk) corn (*lit.* seed/berry of wonder)
maundau-meeni-cheebikaehnse(un) wood-betony (lousewort)—a love medicine; a talisman (*lit.* the wonder seed root)
mauwidaek-waegozeed-wuhnshk(oon) duckweed—duck food (*lit.* little sour plants that grow together)
mayauw-itik-waeyau-pineeg an aster (*lit.* branched in the middle tuber)
medaewi-cheebik(oon) Canada anemone (*lit.* The Medaewaewin Society medicine)
meen-bug(oon) blueberry plant(s) (*lit.* the berry plants)
meeshauwi-guhnsh(eek); gauh-baupikwo-inautik common fleabane—medication for headaches; a blend for tobacco; a hunter's talisman (*lit.* the hairy growth or plant; the stalk with little bumps here and there)
meeshi-odjee-meeni-gauwuhnsh(eek) wild currant—a food and a medicine (*lit.* the fuzzy berry bush)
meeshi-ojidumo-waunoh(wuk) tower mustard (*lit.* the hairy squirrel's tail)
megisi-bug kemauh migizibug(oon) large-leafed aster—a food and a headache medicine (*lit.* the shell plant; the eagle flower)
megissaehnse-bug kemauh; migizi-bug(oon, ook) false gromwell—a talisman (*lit.* the small shell plant; the eagle plant)
menaessi-gauwuhnsh(eek) a hawthorne bush—a food and a hunter's talisman (*lit.* the thorn bush)
mindemoyaehn(uk) dandelion (*lit.* old woman)
mini-idjee-meen-ush(koon) pea(s)—edible
minissino-wuhnshk(oon) wild pea—a food and a medicine for hemorrhages and convulsions (*lit.* the warrior's; the island's plant)
mino-meen so-called wild rice—edible (*lit.* the good seed)
mino-meen-ushk(oon) so-called wild rice—the plant (*lit.* the good seed plant)
mino-pugoo-idjeebik(oon) indian cucumber root—edible (*lit.* the good tasting root)

mino-wae-bugoohnse(un) bristly buttercup—a hunter's talisman; used as a dye (*lit.* that which pleases, satisfies)

mishi-idjee-meen(uk) the everlasting pea—a female remedy

misqui-idjeebik(oon) bloodroot—a dye and medicine

misquo-deessi-meen-gauwuhnsh(eek) red beans—edible (*lit.* red belly button seeds)

misquo-meeni-bugoohnse(un) a raspberry plant

misqwaubumeesh(un) red osier dogwood—medicine for the eyes (*lit.* the reddish plant)

misqwi-cheebik kemauh misquo-cheebik(oon) blood root—medication for sore throat; used as a dye (*lit.* the red, blood root)

mitash-akeeshinoowi-bug(oon) poison ivy

mitchig-meen(uk); matchig-meenuk wild cucumber—used as a tonic (*lit.* the bare berries, nuts)

mizaun(uk) black snakeroot—a snake bite remedy; used for heat rash (*lit.* a nettle)

mizaun-autik; mizaun(ook) a nettle tree

mizaunushk(oon) thistle(s); Canada thistle—a laxative (*lit.* a nettle growth)

moossae-djeebik(oon) sagewort(s)—for sprains (*lit.* grub-worm root)

moozoo'd'bug(oon) arrowhead—a food and a medicine (*lit.* moose leaf)

moozoo-meesh(maewish)(koon) dogwood—for the eyes (*lit.* the moose bush)

moozoo-meesh(maewish)(koon) moose plant—a blend with tobacco; a bait or lure for hunters

muk-akee-bug(oon); muk-akee-zeewaukawaun jewel weed; touch me not—for treatment of poison ivy (*lit.* frog petal; the frog's sour medication)

muk-akee-medaussun pitcher plant—childbirth medicine (*lit.* frog's leggings)

mukwo-pin(eek) large toothworth—edible (*lit.* bear's tuber)

mushkeeg-cheebik(oon) marsh cinquefoil—medication for stomach ailments (*lit.* the swamp or marsh root)

mushkeeg-meen-gauwuhnsh(eek) cranberry bush—a food as well as a curative for nausea (*lit.* the swamp growth or plant)

mushkeeg-meen-gauwuhnsh(eek) low bush cranberries—edible (*lit.* muskeg berries)

mushkeegoo-bugoohnse(un) a small tamarack—used as a beverage (Labrador tea; *lit.* a small marsh or swamp plant)

mushkoo-zoowaunoh(wun) blazing star (*lit.* elk's tail)

nae-nimbunaeyaun-quaeyauk(oon) prairie smoke (*lit.* hair on one side)

nae-nissowae-buguk(oon) red clover—fishing talisman; also blood remedy (*lit.* three leafed)

namae-wushkoohnse(un) selfheal—blood remedy (*lit.* deep-rooted or sturgeon grass[es])

Nana'b'oozoo pigook(oon) Canada lily—a snake bite remedy (*lit.* Nana'b'oozoo's arrow)

Nanabush okomissun meenississun indian paint brush (*lit.* Nana'b'oozoo's grandmother's tresses)

naunaugunushk(oon) ferns; drooping plants

nau-neebidae-widaegin Solomon's seal—a cough remedy (*lit.* clustered in a row)

neebinunauni-quae-yauk(oon) Virginia waterleaf—fodder for moose, deer, etc. (*lit.* many headed)

neeyauwi-buguk(oon) boneset—a talisman (*lit.* in the middle or center of the leaf)

neezh-kinhnzhigae-zeedi-wuhnshk(oon) silvery cinquefoil (*lit.* the two-sided plant)

nomino-ginae-guhnshk(oon) St. John's wort (*lit.* the good long seed plant[s])

nookawaezigun(un) white mugwort—a talisman (*lit.* the tenderizer)

nubug-koossimaun(un) a squash—edible (*lit.* the flat pumpkin)

nubug-ushk(oon) calamus (sweetf lag)—a medicine and fish lure (*lit.* the flat grass growth)

nubugushk(oon) coarse swamp grass(es) (*lit.* flat grasses)

nubug-ushk(oon) larger blue flag iris—a laxative (*lit.* the flat reed)

numaegoosi-bug(oon) large-leafed aster—edible (*lit.* the trout leaf, petalled plant, bush)

numae-pin(eek) wild ginger—a food and a medicine for the stomach (*lit.* the sturgeon tuber)
numae-wuhnshkoohnse(un) wild mint—a remedy for blood disorders (*lit.* the sturgeon grass)
odae-meeni-bugoohnse(un) strawberries (*lit.* heart berries)
odjidumoo-mishkish-maundau-meen(uk) Dutchman's breeches (*lit.* ornate squirrel corn)
ojibwaewae-ishiwun(un) fragrant bedstraw—for skin diseases
onaunigizidaun-bug(oon) plantain
oombuzhigowaun(un) western mugwort (white sage); Veterinary use (*lit.* that which allures, excites)
oshki-neegi-quae-neebeesh(un) a tansy—for sore throats and women's ailments (*lit.* the young woman's leaf)
pidukaudaukissin(een) umbrella plant—used for sprains (*lit.* that which stands)
pukawaeyauk-igin(een) cattail (*lit.* a plant with a growth near the crown)
pukawauzigauhnse(un); pukwaushkoohnse water hemlock (spotted cowbane)—a good luck talisman for hunting
pukwaun(un) the common plantain—a female remedy (*lit.* the chewable plant)
quae-meen(uk) a prune bush—a food and a cough medicine (*lit.* a woman's seed)
saemauhnushk(ook) tobacco—for smoking; for manitou offerings
shigaugawi-tikoon red currant—a food and a medicine (*lit.* the skunk tree, plant, bush)
soossawaeshkuk(oon) cup plant (*lit.* spread wide; broadcast)
tiki-bug-oohnse(un) arrow-arum (*lit.* a leaf or petal that cools)
tikiz-idjeebik-oohnse(un) fringed polygala (*lit.* the little root that cools)
tipo-dayae-gawaussoon(un) golden corydalis—an elixir (*lit.* a patch; to mend a hole in the rear of pants or shorts)
titaeta-meen(uk) any ripe berry(ies) (*lit.* the ripe berries; the colored, painted berries)
tootaugauhnse(un) harebell—medicine for the lungs; also bead lily or clintonia (from *tootaugun*—a bell)
tutugaug-meen(uk) flowering raspberry—edible (*lit.* backbone berry)
w'ae zauwi-cheebik-awaeyauk(oon) large-leafed bellwort (*lit.* that which is yellow- or brown- or gold-rooted)
w'ae-wauwiyae-bugug(oon) violet—a heart medicine (*lit.* the round leafed/petalled)
w'ae-zauwau-ikoonaek(oon) dandelion—a food and used to relieve heartburn (*lit.* that which glows gold/amber)
wae-zauwau-iskoonaek(oon) large-leafed avens—a remedy for female ailments (*lit.* it will glow yellow-orange)
w'ae-zauwauni-quaeyauk(oon) large-leafed bellwort—a mouthwash (*lit.* that which is brown or yellow tressed)
w'ae-zauwunushkawuk(ook) giant hyssop—a cough medicine (*lit.* that which is yellow/golden/orange)
w'ae-zhauwushkawau-ikoonaek(oon) oswego tea—a beverage (*lit.* that which glows green/azure)
w'ae-zhawuskoonaek(oon) jewel weed—remedy for headaches and for poison ivy (*lit.* that which glows orange)
waub'oozoo-bugoohnse(un) kemauh; myeengun-autik(oon) creeping snowberry bush (*lit.* a rabbit's small petals or flowers; wolves' tree)
wau-babau-bego-dayaeshing(ook) day lily (*lit.* wearing out one's rump)
waub-ishish-quae(nun) wild sarsaparilla—used for coughs (*lit.* white haired[?])
waubishki-idjeebik(oon) large-flowered bellwort—for pleurisy (*lit.* white root)
waubishkik-bug(oon) meadowsweet—a talisman for hunters (*lit.* white flowered, petalled plant)
waub-ishkik-meen(un, uk) a bedstraw—lung medication (*lit.* a white berried plant)
waubizee-pin(eek) the swan tuber—medicine
waub-oshkik-bug(oon) labrador tea—a beverage (*lit.* a white leafed or petalled plant)
waub-ozhaeshi-idjaub(een) an ivy (*lit.* fisher's bow-string)
waubugoonae(n) yarrow; a blend of tobacco

(*lit.* white petalled/leafed)

waubuno-idjeebik(oon) one-flowered cancer-root—a very good love potion (*lit.* the dawn root)

wauh-nissik-aehnssiwung(in) New England aster (*lit.* that which would kill pain)

wauwiyae-neegae-guhnshk(oon) round leafed sundew—for the heart (*lit.* round trap plant)

wau-zauwau-ikoonaek(in) butter and eggs (toadflax)—used to treat bronchitis (*lit.* that which will burst into yellow flame)

wau-zauwaus-animakee(goon) used as a dye (*lit.* the yellow thunder)

wau-zauwaus-ikoonaek(in) lance-leafed goldenrod—a medication for chest pain; a hunting talisman (*lit.* that which shines, emits a golden glow)

weebidau-bubugaunoh(wun) common chickweed (*lit.* the thin/slim, toothed flower)

weekaehn sweet flag—a medicine for colds, sore throats (*lit.* that which draws)

weekizigun(un) doll's eyes—for boils (*lit.* that which extracts)

Weengushk; Weeshkoob-maewish-koohnse(un) sweet grass (*lit.* Weeng's plant) (from Weeng—a manitou who presides over sleep)

weenizi-meen(uk) kemauh; wee-nissi-meen(uk); wee-nissi-bug wintergreen—edible (*lit.* the dirty little berry; the little killer berry)

weessauk-chechauk-meeni-bug(oon) a rose bush (*lit.* bitter soul's flower[s])

weessigi-cheebik(oon) culver's root—a laxative (*lit.* the tart, caustic root)

weessiko-cheebik(oon) red baneberry—medication at childbirth (*lit.* the bitter root)

weessugibug common burdock—a cough medicine (*lit.* that which is bitter or can inflict sharp pain[s])

wushkoohnse(un) flowering rush (*lit.* bad little grass)

zaesub(een) false nettle (*lit.* the leaf that frightens)

zau-eehnse-gauwuhnsh(eek) a bean plant(s)—edible

zaugitaug-auhnse(un) agrimony (*lit.* slightly emerging)

zauwa-cheebik(oon) gold thread—used as a dye (*lit.* the yellow-root)

zauwau-bugoon wormseed mustard (*lit.* the yellow petal or leaf)

zauwaunushk(oon) mustard (*lit.* the yellow plant)

zauwauskoonaehnse(un) wild geranium (*lit.* the little yellow flower)

zeegau-tikoom sweet cicely—for ulcers and sore throat (*lit.* the tangled bush; the spiky stem)

zeegineesh harebell (*lit.* spilling out)

zeendi-augun(un) a sunflower

zeewi-bug(oon) curled dock—used for cuts; a hunter's talisman (*lit.* the sour/tangy leafed/petalled plant)

zeewi-bug(oon) parsley (*lit.* a sour leaf, petal[s])

zeewi-bug(oon) rhubarb—edible

zeewi-odae-meeni-bug(oon) alumroot—mouthwash for cankers (*lit.* the tart, acidy berry plant)

zhaezhau-askee-bugaessing(in) common plantain—good for sprains (*lit.* the many petalled, leafed growth)

zhauboo-meen-ushk(ook) gooseberry, gooseberries—edible (*lit.* berries that permeate, go through)

zhauboozigun-bug(oon) iris—a purgative (*lit.* permeates)

zhaushae-cheebikaehnse(un); zhooshki-cheebik(oon) fireweed—used to treat carbuncles and rheumatism (*lit.* the chewable, edible root)

zhaushaug-meen(uk) bunchberry—edible (*lit.* chewable)

zhaushaugo-meen(uk) jack-in-the-pulpit—for sore eyes (*lit.* chewable seeds; barn-swallow seeds)

zheebau-kundoohnse(un) marsh skullcap (*lit.* patiently lying in ambush)

zheeg-meeshimaewish(uk); zeeg-meesh; zeeg-maewish blue cohosh—used to treat cramps (*lit.* the spill plant)

zhigaug-awuhnsh(eek) an onion—edible (*lit.* skunk plant)

zhigaug-wuhnsh(eek) an onion; a leek—edible

zhoo-meeni-gauwuhnsh(eek) a grape (vine)—edible

zigauk-meen-gauwuhnsh(eek) bearberry—a headache remedy; a food and a talisman (*lit.* the prickly brambly bush)

zigutae-bawae-bug(oon) hound's tooth (*lit.* the plant that sticks)

zigutae-b-awih(een) cleavers (*lit.* it is clinging by nature)

zigutae-koomuk kemauh zugau-koomuk clotbur (*lit.* the clingers)

---

wau-win-imoowinun *exclamations, expressions*

---

aegautch kemauh naegautch gently; easily; by degrees; carefully; slowly; etc.

aehn!; aehn-haehn! yes! agreed!

aenigook harder; louder; more force (effort); more; extended; add to; increase; enhance; supplement; entire; with all; whole; all; nothing spared; etc.

ahneen dush? why? what for? what's the point? what's the reason? etc.

ahneen nangae igoh nauh absolutely; most certainly; beyond doubt; positively; decidedly; most emphatically; etc.

ahow okay; alright; agreed; ready; yes; set; prepared; agreeable; all set; waiting; concur; in accord; etc.

anishauh for nothing; for no reason; spontaneously; without cause; etc.

apaegish would that it were; hopefully; trustfully; maybe; perhaps; if; if only; etc.

aungawaumisseedoog well, if it must be done, then it must be done; have it your way then

aussonauh be careful; take care; use caution; proceed slowly; keep your eyes and ears open

auyauh not likely; doubtful; uncertain; questionable; dubious

awuss kemauh wuss let it go; forget it; away with it; leave it alone; let it be on its way; away from me; out of my sight; get away; leave me; etc.

ayoooh!; kemauh eeeeyooooh! a cry of pain, equivalent to "ouch!" except that the expression is prolonged

baekau-ayaun be quiet; hold your speech; knock it off; that's enough; no more; shut up; be still; etc.

baub-gawaudum for nothing; out of the blue; without thought; aforethought; spontaneously; without sense; thoughtless; senseless

bizaun-ayaun be quiet; keep quiet; don't move; hold still; etc.

gaegaet suh nauh this is annoying, irritating, insufferable, aggravating, grievous, bothersome, vexatious, etc.

gaegaet right; correct; true; certainly; right on; it's a fact; there's no denying it

gagawaunissuk-kummik horrendous; appalling; unbelievable; unspeakable

gaunissidum it's a pity; regrettable; it's sad; tough; too bad; too bad it happened; it shouldn't have happened

gawaetauni-kummik extraordinary; fantastic; fabulous; prodigious; great; amazing

geessaud-kummik a pity; regrettable; sadly; rueful; mournful; awful; lamentable; etc.

how! how! hear! hear!

igoh most certainly (an emphasizer)

ikoh formerly

kauween goshah kemauh kau goshah absolutely not; certainly not; no; once and for all; etc.

kauween maemikautch not necessarily; there's no need; no longer needed; you don't have to; not required; unnecessary, etc.; no way; the answer is no

kauween ondjitah it wasn't on purpose; it isn't intentional; etc.

kauween(kau) ningot-inooh it doesn't matter a whit; I don't care; so what; it doesn't make a difference; who cares; doesn't matter one way or another; etc.

keen nitam kemauh nitum you next; you first; your turn

keeyaubih still; moreover; on and on; continual; incessant; more; add to; it hasn't stopped; doesn't end; etc.

maenoo; maunoo let it be; leave it; don't bother; forget it

maumikaud-kummik out of this world; fantastic; wonder of wonders; extraordinary

maunooh kemauh maenooh let it alone; leave it; allow it; let it pass; forget it; forebear; put up with it; etc.

mbaaaah! there!; I knew it!

mee dush and then; thereafter; as a result; consequently; subsequently; next; afterward; following; thence; at once; and that; accordingly; eventually; at last; in order; in that event; ultimately; finally; after a while

mee goshah certainly; absolutely; definitely; surely; clearly; positively; without a doubt; precisely; exactly; etc.

mee meeyow exactly; precisely; dead on; right on; etc.

mee minik that's enough, ample; no more; that's lots; that's plenty; there's more than enough

mee nah? is that so?

mee suh iwih it's done, over, finished, completed, over and done with, no more, accomplished, at last; that's all; nothing further; that's it; it's ended; no need for more; that's all there was; let it be; that's to be expected; that's the idea; precisely; exactly; etc.

meegawaetch thank you

mino-itchigae he, she has done something of benefit, done a good deed, done something commendable, worthwhile; etc. (from *izhi-itchigaewin*—a deed)

misquee'g' dae-ae-aud-kummik disheartening; discouraging; the very earth would bleed

mundji-eedoog whatever; who knows; who cares; I haven't a clue; I don't know; whatsoever; anything; it could be anything; etc.

naenipautch; naepautch gauche; clumsily; awkward; bumbling; butter-fingered; etc.

nah! look! watch! listen! look at this! watch this!

nangawoonah that is so (from *nangae igoh nauh*)

nashkae! pay attention! attend! watch out! careful! behold! regard! see!

naunidauh coincidentally; fortuitously; at an inopportune time; etc.

nawutch more; a little more; some more; over and above; something extra; besides; add to

neezaun-kummik scary; frightful; awful; horrible

ningot once; one; single; a whit

noondae too soon; not enough; short; shortfall; not up to the mark; wanting; less than; fall short; lacking; the short end; etc.

noongoom now; presently; at this time; right now; etc.

ondauss come here; come; step this way; etc.

oohn is that so? is that right? you don't say! well! that's hard to believe; I have doubts. is that true? I wouldn't have believed it. (This is an ironic expression that depends upon tone and inflection for its meaning.)

pauhnh an expression uttered for infants' amusement made by parents while they nuzzle the children's feet or stomach in affection *pauhnh* may mean stinky, smelly, etc.)

paunimauh; paumauh later; afterwards; not right now; by and by; in a little while; much later; in a bit; etc.

pootch kemauh potch still; despite; in spite of; even; even though; regardless; even if; not withstanding; leaving aside; however; if; for all that; etc.

pun gone! pffft! disappeared; vanished

sah dirty; filthy; unclean; messy; lewd; impure; salacious; raw; lecherous; lascivious; ruttish; vulgar; etc.

sheesht an all purpose expression; like *tau-hauh* and similar remarks

shimaudjee gauche; butter-fingered (an expression uttered when fumbling something)

shimaudjee-kummik! oops! drat! darn it! damn!

tau-hauh; shtauyauh; shtau-tau-hauh incredible; unbelievable; remarkable; marvellous; astounding; astonishing; amazing; extraordinary; etc.

tibee-eedoog somewhere unknown; it could be anywhere; anyplace; who knows where (the origin of the name for the Beothuks: *tibee-oodook*—somewhere unknown)

tuguh! shkaenauh! watch out!; take care!; careful!; watch what you're doing!; back off!; that's enough!; etc.
umbae let's go; let's be on our way
waendjitah as if deliberate; pre-meditated; planned; pre-conceived
waewaenih carefully; skillfully; correctly; deliberately; meticulously; prudently; etc.
waeweeb hurry up; move it; put on some speed
wauh? what? what did you say? what do you mean? what's that?
weedizih serves him right; he/she deserved it; he/she had what was coming; I don't feel sorry for what's happened to him/her; etc.
weengae carefully; skillfully; thoroughly; completely; entirely; etc.
weeshae doubtful; can't be trusted; it's a joke; unreal; fanciful; questionable; unlikely; can't be serious; etc.
weessikawautch carelessly; negligently; with little regard; for nothing; heedless; thoughtlessly; rashly; off handedly; come what may; devil may care; etc.
wuhnh serves you right! good! had it coming! that should teach him/her!
zaegaud-kummik terrifying; intimidating; the most terrorizing on earth; fearful! a world fright; panic inducing; terrible; horrible; frightening
zaum too much; more than enough; beyond limits; excessive; immoderate; etc.

---

ae-iko-dawo-dunnauk *space; as far as space extends; distance*

---

ae-apeetauk height; loftiness
ae-apeetchauk height; distance; duration; length
ae-iko-dawo-dunnauk-mishi-geezhik space; the vault of heaven
ae-iko-wauyau-kummikauk the earth's limits
ae-iqua'eeng at the terminus
ae-kawauk size; mass
aenigook-daeyauk width; breadth
aenigook-kawauk whole size, mass
aenigookwauk-kummikauk the entire world
baeshoowut close in distance
bubugaumigut; bubugauh thinness as in coats, coverings, surfaces
dawissaumigut; dawissauh; dawauh space; room; extent
dupusheesh; dupusheetch low plane; level altitude
gaussi-dawyaumigut; gaussi-daeyauh narrowness
geewitau-kummik all around the earth
ginoowaumigut; ginoowauh length; extension; span; reach
gino-weendummauh depth
ishpauh height; loftiness
kupugaumigut; kupugauh thickness
maung-daeyaumigut; maung-daeyauh width
naegaudum little; very small; small (also an expression meaning pity!)
tikoowaumigut; tikoowauh it is short; not far; deficiency of height, length
tiko-weendummauh it is shallow, lacking depth
waussuwut distance; farness

---

ae-izhi-idjeeyauk *form; shape*

---

nisso-shoo-waeyaumigut; nisso-shoo-waeyauh a triangle
nubugaumigut; nubugauh a flat surface
nubug-idjeeyauh flattish body, figure, form
piko-idjeeyaumigut; piko-idjeeyauh a bulging, bulky, body, figure, form
shoosh-waeyauh; shoosh-waeyaumigut a square, rectangular body, figure, structure
shoo-waeyauh; shoo-waeyaumigut a slanted, oblique body, figure, feature
waug-idjeewaumigut; waug-idjeeyauh a curved, bent body, figure, form, feature
wauwiyaeyauh; wauwiyauyaumigut a round, oval, circular body, figure, form
weembau-yaumigut; weembauyauh a hollow body, figure, feature; a depression
zhaugawaumigut; zhaugawauh an oblong body, feature, figure
zheebau-yaumigut; zheebauyauh a tunnel, narrow passage, narrows

---

agindaussoowinaehnsuk (gindaussoowinaehnsuk) *numbers*

---

baezhig one (1)

neezh two (2)
nissiwih three (3)
neewin four (4)
naunun five (5)
ningotwaussiwih six (6)
neezhwaussiwih seven (7)
nishwaussiwih eight (8)
zhaungissiwih nine (9)
medaussiwih ten (10)
medaussiwih ashi(d) baezhig eleven (11)
medaussiwih ashi(d) neezh twelve (12)
medaussiwih ashi(d) nissiwih thirteen (13)
medaussiwih ashi(d) neewin fourteen (14)
medaussiwih ashi(d) naunun fifteen (15)
medaussiwih ashi(d) ningotwaussiwih sixteen (16)
medaussiwih ashi(d) neezhwaussiwih seventeen (17)
medaussiwih ashi(d) nishwaussiwih eighteen (18)
medaussiwih ashi(d) zhaungissiwih nineteen (19)
neezh-tunnuh (dunnuh) twenty (20)
nissim-tunnuh (dunnuh) thirty (30)
neem-tunnuh (dunnuh) forty (40)
naunimi-tunnuh (dunnuh) fifty (50)
ningotwaussimi-tunnuh (dunnuh) sixty (60)
neezhwaussimi-tunnuh (dunnuh) seventy (70)
nishwaussimi-tunnuh (dunnuh) eighty (80)
zhaungissiwimi-tunnuh (dunnuh) ninety (90)
ningotwauk one hundred (100)
neezhwauk two hundred (200)
nissiwauk three hundred (300)
neewauk four hundred (400)
nauniwauk five hundred (500)

ningoting once
neezhing twice
nissing three times
neewing four times
nauning five times
ningotwautching six times
neezhwautching seven times
nishiwautching eight times
zhaungitching nine times
medautching ten times

nitam first
ae-iko-neezhing second
ae-iko-nissing third
ae-iko-neewing fourth
ae-iko-nauning fifth
ae-iko-ningotwautching sixth
ae-iko-neezhwautching seventh
ae-iko-nishiwautching eighth
ae-iko-zhaungitching ninth
ae-iko-medautching tenth
ishkwautch last

naen-nissiwih every third one one; triplets
naeneesh; nae-eehnsh both; two; a pair; couple

ashid-gindaussoowin addition
augaweeto-gindaussoowin; augaweeto-issitchigaewin multiplication
mauwindoo-gindaussoowin total
na'autumigauhns a fraction
na'autumigun a part
nenauwitaugae-gindaussoowin; nenauwitaugaewin division
zhaenimaugae-gindaussoowin subtraction

Adjectives, Adverbs, Conjunctions, Prepositions, and Pronouns

ADJECTIVES +

A

ae-ikoh since; for some time past
aen-dasso each; every; each and every
aen-dazhi where; at the place; at the site, location, scene
aenigook harder; more; again
aenoowaek passably; so-so; okay; alright; satisfactorily; fair; average; common; not bad
aeshkum more and more; increasingly
aetah only; solely; no other; nothing else
ahee something
ahneen apee? when?
ahneesh-ween? why? what? what for?
anauk however; in any event
anauwiz barely; hardly; scarcely
anishauh for nothing; without reason; spontaneously
anootch all sorts; potpourri; a variety; assorted; mixed bag; miscellaneous
apeetch while; during; in the course of; as; when; at the time
apeetchinauk from time to time; occasionally
ashi; ashid in addition to; include; add to or on; put another on; supplement; increase; etc.
ashitch also; as well; and; in addition to
asukummik countless; innumerable times; beyond count; infinite
atchinah for a short time; a little while; briefly; shortly; temporarily
aubidaek; aubidae-kummik most assuredly; definitely; certainly; without doubt; necessarily; it has to be
aubiding once; once upon a time; once before
auga-awo-eehn behind
aumi; auyaumee nearly; almost; on the verge; just about; at the tip, edge, ledge, lip
aundih? where? in what place? there?
aungaemauh certainly; absolutely; definitely; positively; damned right; no question
aungawaumas could be; might be; must be; may be; perhaps; that may be so
aunikaudj; aunikaudjih repetitively; recurrently; continuously; incessantly (from *aunikau; aunikoo*—tied to; related to; bound to)
aunind; naunind some; a few; others; a small number
aunungawaen nowhere; somewhere; someplace; anyplace; wherever (see also *tibee-eedoog*)
aupitchih exceedingly; very; extremely; excessively
aushiwaewih; auzhiwa-eehn on the other side; on the far side; around the corner
auwautch; missowauh; missowautch though; even though; even; despite; in

spite of; still (*auwautch* and *wauwautch* are also expressions of surprise and shock)
auwundjeesh purposely; resolutely; stubbornly
auzhigoh; zhigoh already; previously; earlier; beforehand; before
auzhook a to and fro motion
awaenaen; waenaenuk who; whoever
awuss further; away (also an expression meaning be off! get away! out of my sight! get lost!)
ayae-oshkud earlier; a long time ago; in times past; millennia ago
ayau-apee gently; easily; from time to time; occasionally; the odd time; sometimes
ayaundassin repeatedly; often; frequently; constantly; many times (from *dasso*—each; every; daily; monthly; weekly; hourly; times; frequency; per; so many times; as often as; multiplied; pressed down; crushed; trapped; *datching*—times; as often as)
ayaundji; ayaundjih over and over; cyclic; repeated; recurrent; repetitive

B

baekish while; at the same time; coincidentally; besides; in addition; along with
baenuk; babaenuk carefully; cautiously; calmly; prudently
bae-pekaun differently
bae-pungee; bae-pungeeshaehn a little at a time; little by little
baesho; baeshootch nearby; close; proximate; neighboring
baubigae at once; right away; immediately; instantly; without waiting
baubigawaudum for nothing; for no reason or purpose; pointlessly; spontaneously; on the spur of the moment; impulsively
baukidjeesh too late
bauteenut much; plenty; abundantly; amply
bayaetootch unfortunately; regrettably
beenish until; till; up to; when; as far as
beenissikauh for nothing; on a whim; impulsively; instinctively
beetoosh besides; in addition to; over and above
bidjeenaugoh yesterday
bidjeenuk just now; recently; not long ago; a little while ago; moments ago
bimi; bimidjih along; by the way; as; across; crosswise; crossed; athwart
binamauh for now; but first; momentarily
binaweego a long time ago
bizhishig whole; entire; all; entire quantity; total
bungee; pungee little in quantity

C

chibwauh before; lest; if; perchance; for fear that; in order to avoid

D

daebinauk carelessly; heedlessly; badly; awkwardly; any which way
dubusheesh low; not high
dush; mee dush and then; subsequently; consequently; therefore; following; thereafter; henceforth; as a result; next; later; after a while; while; next instant

G

gaegaet truly; factually; really; exactly; correctly
gaeg-apee finally; about time; at last; at length
gaegau-apee at last; finally; about time
gaegauh; gaegaud; gaegautch almost; nearly; closer; proximately; not quite; about; close upon
gaeg-nauh; gaegonauh if; if only; would that it were; but
gaenoowaek even though; despite; though; still
gaeshk; gaeshik; gaezik later; not now; not yet; by and by; in a while; after a while
gaetaenaum really? truly? no kidding! as a matter of fact; seriously
gaezhauwauh; gaezhauwaud; gaezhauwautch regarding; with respect to; in consideration thereof
gageedautch carefully; prudently; cautiously

ganagae at least; at the minimum; in so far as; inasmuch as; as much as
gauwauhn barely; hardly; just
gawaek; gayuk right; true; accurate; direct; on the mark; exact
gawaetch not much; not enough; short; insufficient; just so; just barely
gawaudug barely; short of; insufficiently; wanting (from *gauwauhn*—barely; hardly; just)
gayae and; also; as well; in addition to
gayaeskud; gayaeskutch suddenly; at once; abruptly
gayut; gayaut; gauyautch a long time ago; once; aboriginal; generations, millennia ago
geewautch inopportune; not quite right; not quite; odd; uneven; irregular; unbalanced
geezhau; geezhauh ready; prepared; all set; in position; available; in advance; readily
gigi whole; all; entire; complete; undivided; total
gino-waesh for a long time; extended; continuing
gomau-apee; gomau-apeetch later; afterwards; by and by; in time; in due course
gomauh moderately; tolerably
gomau-minik for some time; a period; a duration; a while; some
gonamauh perhaps; maybe

I

ishkawautch last; final; at the end; no more; finished; exhausted

K

kaetchinae personally; I, myself
kaetchishk just barely; by the skin of one's teeth
kaezhidin quickly; promptly; at once; faster
kagatin harder; with more force
kakaem suddenly; at once; unexpectedly
kakinah all; the entire; whole; every; everyone; everything
kaugigae; kaugig forever; always; everlasting; ever
kaugigae-kummik till the end of time; to the end of the world
kautchi; kautchitch just; barely
kauween baupeesh by no means
kauween weekauh kemauh kau' weekauh never; not once ever
keeshpin; keeshpinae if; perchance; should; suppose; in the event; lest; were; would that
keeyaubih; keeyaubitch still; again; more; yet
kemauh or; else; other
ketawaen despite; in spite of; still; nevertheless
kitchi greatly; abundantly; immensely; hugely; grandly

M

maegauh since; owing to; because of; considering that (poss. a contraction of *maegawauh*—while; during; as)
maegawae-eehn during; while; coincidentally; at the same time; amidst; amongst; among; mingled with
maegawauh; maegawautch while; during; as
maemaeshkoot in turn; by turn; back and forth; alternate
maemaundjeesh a little at a time
maemawaetch the most important; chief; principal; leading; pre-eminent; first; before all
maemikautch otherwise; else; or else
maemindigae especially; in particular; mainly; chiefly; principally
maem-meen here and there; sporadic; scattered; spread; hither and yon; dispersed
maeshkoot instead of; in lieu of
maewizhah a long time ago; in the distant past
mamauzh badly; indifferently; carelessly; negligently
manautch carefully; slowly; cautiously; wisely; prudently
mashi yet
maukizhauh perhaps; maybe; probably; likely; not sure (from *gonamauh goshah*—perhaps, maybe, likely, probably)

ADJECTIVES +

maumauzh; mamauzh carelessly; heedlessly; badly; awkwardly
maumoowih all together; in union
maunaed much; plenty; lots; abundantly; ample
mayaenah passably; just so; alright; averagely; so-so; adequately
mayau exact; chief; leading; in the center, middle; dead on
mee meeyauwih precisely; exactly
meedaunawae of course; certainly; absolutely; assuredly; definitely; without question
meedoog secretly; covertly; on the sly; arcanely; furtively; stealthily; clandestinely
meenawauh; meenawautch again; once more; anew; also
mikauwautch fortunately; luckily; happily; propitiously
mindjinut; mindjeenut much; plenty; lots (from *mizheenut*—aplenty, there is much)
minik an amount, quantity; so much; as much as
mininah all over; everywhere
mino-apee; mino-waugaush timely; opportunely; convenient
minootch still; yet; nonetheless; notwithstanding (poss. a variation of *pootch*—still; in spite of; despite; nevertheless; nonetheless)
mishishuh in the open; plain; manifest; clear; obvious; apparent; conspicuous; in view
missowauh; missowautch though; although; even though
mitauk; mitchih; mitu bare; unclothed; unadorned; nude
mitchi; mitu by one's own efforts; without aid or artificial devices
mitchu-eehn on the surface; on the bare ground
mizhaeg always; perpetually; constantly; on and on; over and over
mizi gaego everything; all things
mizi; miziwae everywhere; in all places; universally; all over; in every place
moozhook while; during; for a while; at length; for some time; as; often; many times

N

n'a'auh someone; he; she (an expression uttered when the name under discussion fails to come; it's like "mmm" or "ah! m.")
na-autum a little; a bit; a small amount; a fraction; a particle; few; not many; not much
naegautch; aegautch gently; easily; from time to time; occasionally; the odd time; sometimes
naepautch; naepau; naepauss gauche; backward; wrong way, side
naetaub on purpose; meant; deliberately
naeyaub return; go back
nagae-waussuh far, but not too far; a fair distance
naheehn something (an expression uttered when the name of the person, place, or thing is not readily at hand or mouth)
nakae; nakaeyauh; nakae-eehn in that direction, that way, that course
nakawae; kawae first; before all else; prior; preceding; in advance
nanaegautch gently; easily; from time to time; occasionally; the odd time; sometimes
nanaukawaesh a fence sitter; indifferent; irresolute
nanau-pigaundjih shamefully; mockingly; derisively
nanawautch for nothing; for no purpose; uselessly
nangae for certain, sure; without doubt; that is so
nanibae; naunibae; naunibaenah inopportunely; at the wrong time
naugae-eehn in some corner; a secluded place; distant; far; remote; beyond; secluded; removed
nauginah; nayauginah sooner; earlier; previously; before
naugutch later; by and by; presently; in due course; in time
naunaugae later; shortly; soon
naunaugautch exactly; precisely; right on
naunaugawaesh almost all; nearly all; majority
naunidauh; naunidautch; naunauwidauk;

na-eedauh; na-eedautch perchance; by chance; accidentally; coincidentally
naunigim often; frequently; many times
naunigotinoong sometimes; periodically; from time to time; occasionally
naunoomiyah; noomiyah recently; not long ago; lately; a short while ago; just a while ago
naupitch reluctantly; unwillingly; with reticence
naussau; naussautch; nissau between; betwixt; in the middle; in the center
naussaub same; alike; co-equal; similar
nauwautch less; least; smallest; minimum; minority
nauwi; nauwih in the middle
nauwitch far out in the middle of the lake; far off shore
nauzh; nanauzh; naunawautch later; after a while; until; at a certain time; till
nawaudut; nawaudutch too small, thus useless
nawutch more; even more; greater
nayaeg already
neebau-tibik at night; during the night
neebinuh much; plenty; lots; abundant; ample (from *neebin*—summer; the season of bounty)
neegaun in front; leading; foremost
neessa-eehn downstairs; below; lower
nindigoh as it were; it seems, appears, resembles
nindowauh; nindowautch instead; rather; therefore; preferably; instead of
ningim right away; at once; immediately; promptly; now; in a moment
ningot whatever; anything whatsoever; some; something
ningotchih somewhere; anywhere
ningoting once; one time; at one time
nishikae alone; solely; by oneself
nissituh exactly; precisely; just right
nissowa-eehn between; in the middle
nitam; nitum first; anteceding; preceding
noominug a while; for some time; during; meanwhile
noomook for some time, an extended period, a duration
noond; noondae too soon; too early; inopportune; not quite
noongoom now; at present; at this time
noopimeeng in the hinterland
nubunae(eehn) aside; to one side; on one side
numundji; mundji; mundji-eedoog unknown; uncertainty; don't know; cannot tell; who knows?

O

omauh there; in that place
ondji; ondjitch; gae-ondjih; gaed-ondih the reason; reason for; why; in order that; so that
oondaushimae this way; over here; a little closer
oondaushitah this way; over here; in this direction
oondjitah deliberately; on purpose; premeditative; meant; intended

P

pagikautch reluctantly; hesitantly; tentatively; shyly; cautiously; circumspectly
paukidjish soon; anon; not long
paumauh; paunimauh later
paupaugawaush always; continually; perpetually
peendjinah inside
pekaun different; dissimilar
pekautch differently
pekinoong; pekaenoong differently; in another way
pimae-eehn to one side; aside
pinaweego in the beginning; earlier; a long time ago; in times past; millennia ago
pootch still; in spite of; despite; nevertheless; nonetheless
pugwoonah; bugwoonah spontaneously; instinctively; impulsively; without forethought

S

saezig; saezik nearly; close; proximately
sazagoonah often; frequently; regularly

T

taedeebaun; taedibaun; tibaun separately; apart; differently; each on its own
taeyaesh next to the first or the last in age, size, height, etc.
taunauk possibly; perhaps; maybe; probably
taunausuk comparably; similarly; equally
tibi where; at or in what place
tibishkoh; tibishkootch; taubishkoh; taubishkootch like; similar; akin; equal

W

waedih that yonder; that there; there; that, he, she, it in that distance; yonder
wae-eebuh; wae-eebutch conveniently
waegawaen whoever; whomever; someone; someone unknown; anyone
waegawaenish; waegawaenish-eedoog same as above, but with a derogatory connotation
waendjitah carefully; properly; correctly; very well
waenibik for a short time; briefly; for a little while
waenigobun repeatedly; incessantly; often
waewaenih well; carefully; skillfully
waeweeb in a hurry; fast; quickly; in haste
waeweebah willingly; in quick succession
waeweengae thoroughly; fully; well; exactly
waeweesh especially; particularly
washamae; washamaetch; washamaesh more; additionally; over and over; still; besides
waugae; waukae quietly; serenely; peacefully
waussuh from afar; distantly; remotely
wauweeyaush curiously; oddly; peculiarly
wayaedautch slowly
wayaendish in spite of; despite; still; nevertheless; notwithstanding
wayaesh somewhere
weebah; waeweebah; waeweebutch soon; shortly; presently
weekauh; weekautch; waeweekaut; waeweekautch later; tardily; seldom; rarely; once in a while
weekawaed; weekawae-eehn at the far end; at the end; at the terminus
wininah very; extremely; exceedingly
wiyaeshkautch tacitly; silently; wordlessly
woodih over there; in that place; there; in the distance

Z

zaegakautch carefully; orderly; neatly
zaesikah; zaesikunnuh suddenly; unexpectedly
zaeskah; zaeskud; zaeskutch suddenly; at once; abruptly
zaugidji-eehn outside; externally; outer
zaum weekauh too late
zaum too much; over much; excessively; exceedingly; surpassingly
zhae here; in this place; over here
zhaedjau-eehn directly
zhaugootch in spite of; despite; notwithstanding
zheebau-eehn through
zibiskautch often; repeatedly; slowly; leisurely

Suffixes

aehnse; auhnse; oohnse; eehnse *small; tiny; little; puny; diminutive; few*

aehnsaehnse a little shell
aehnsebauhnse a raccoon
inineehnse a little man
mooninoohnse ironwood
quaezaehnse a girl; a small woman

aesheehn; sheehn *refers to a doer, actor, maker, performer, crafter*

nindo-maukimae-sheehn a monkey; one who seeks nits
suppeekae-sheehn a spider; a net maker
tissauwae-sheehn a cicada; a painter

aewin; eewin; oowin *a nominalizer that renders verbs into nouns*

anookeewin work; labor; employment
cheebaukawaewin cooking; food preparation
geekittoowin a word, conversation, discussion
itchigaewin (a verbalizer) do; act
meezeewin defecation; manuring; passing human waste; shitting

anoodjeewin *to loiter, habituate, strive for, haunt; importune*

abi-anoodjeehn a child, infant
pukwaun-audjeehn a bat; a habitué of roofs and eaves
wauwau-bego-anoodjeehn a mouse; the borer of holes

aub; waeyaub *refers to a rope, vine, vein, string, thread, span, line, cord, seam*

geekittoo-waubeegoonwaeyaub telephone wire or extension
inigawauzoonae-aub a thread
metig-waub a bow
misqui-yaub a vein
sup-aub a rope

aubik; waubik *refers to the character, kind, nature, quality, color of ore, metal, rock, money*

baezhig-waubik one dollar
beewi-aubik iron, iron filings
ishp-aubik a high rock
zau-waubik gold, pyrite, copper

aubo; waubo *refers to the kind, character, quality, color, density of a liquid, fluid, beverage, soup*

ishkotae-waubo whiskey; liquor; firewater
mashki-aki-waubo a tonic
maundau-meen-aubo corn soup
neebeesh-aubo tea; leaf liquid
weeshkib-aubo pop; a soft drink; a sweet drink
zeewi-aubo vinegar

aunauk; nauk; kunauk *refers to handles, extensions, or lengths of wood*

bawaun-auk a small pole used for knocking wild rice from stalks into a canoe

bawaun-auk a spit
boodawae-aunauk a poker
waewaebunaub-unauk a fishing rod, pole
waussiwau-kunauk a torch

aunimut *refers to the kind, character, quality, direction of a wind*

akeewaedin-aunimut the North Wind
mashkow-aunimut a strong wind
maud-aunimut the wind starts
mino-w-aunimut the wind is fair, favorable

autik; tik *refers to the character, kind, nature, quality of trees, wood, woods*

auzhidae-yautik the cross; a crossed stick
inin-autik a maple tree
ishk-autik a crooked rod
miss-autik a cudgel; firewood

auwuhnsh; wuhnsh *refers to flowering and fruit bearing trees, shrubs, large plants*

begaessaun-gauwuhnsh a plum tree
gozig-wauk-meen-gauwuhnsh a pear tree
mishee-meeni-gauwuhnsh an apple tree
wuhnsh the tassel of corn

bug *refers to leaves, petals*

oshki-bug a new leaf
waussi-bug a shiny leaf or petal
zauwi-bug a yellow petal
zhauwushko-bug a green leaf

bun; pun *denotes deceased, formerly, used to be, no longer is; is also a form of the imperfect sense*

aehnsebun a raccoon (*lit.* formerly a shell)
n'okomissibun my departed grandmother
n'ossebun my deceased father
ogimauweebun formerly chief
pun gone

cheebik *refers to a root*

maeshkawauwi-cheebik wild geranium
medaewi-cheebik Canada anemone
misqua-cheebik bloodroot
zhooshki-cheebik fireweed

eedoog; doog *an expression of doubt, skepticism, uncertainty, probability*

mundji-eedoog who knows
tibee-eedoog somewhere; anywhere
tibikut-eedoog it must be night, dark
waegawaen-eedoog someone unknown

eegin; waegin *refers to a fabric, cloth, textile*

doopwin-eegin tablecloth
kitug-eegin a remnant or mottled cloth
manitou-eegin silk
pishka-waegin a pelt
zheeb-waussae-eegin transparent cloth

eeng; oong; aung; ing *refers to location, site, place, scene, area, vicinity, territory; locatives*

ishpiming in the sky; above
kitchi-mookoomaun-akeeng in the United States
odaenaung in town
naeyausheeng at the point, peninsula
waubunoong in or to the east

gaum *refers to a lake, a large body of water*

awussi-gaum on the far side of the large body of water
oondaussi-gaum on this side of the large body of water
naunauwi-gaum in the middle of the lake

gawauzoon; gawaussoon *refers to a sewn article or garment*

apigunae-gawauzoon the upper part of a moccasin
beeto-gawauzoon a lining
gabo-dayae-gawauzoon pants; pantaloons
gaund-gawauzoon a thimble
kishki-gawaudussoon a sewn article

geezis *the sun, moon, month*

geezis the sun; the month
Meen-geezis July
ningo-geezis one month
tibik-geezis the moon

gummauh *refers to the character, nature, quality, of a body of water*

mautau-gummauh at the water's source
Teemi-gummauh Deep Lake
waushae-gummauh clear water

Wauwiyae-gummauh Round Lake

gummeeng; gummeek *often used in place of* gummauh; *it is the locative form*

gummeeng at the lake
Mishi-gummeeng the great lake; Lake Michigan
Teemi-gummeeng a deep lake; Lake Temagami
Waubishkigo-kitchi-gummeeng white breakers; Lake Erie

gummik *refers to a house, building*

anami-ae-w-gummik a church
anookee-gummik a factory
geewi-inaudizee-gummik a mental institution
wukaun-gummik a barn
zeezibaukootoohnse-kae-gummik a candy factory

igoon *a day*

neezh-igoon two days
nissimidunnuh-dasso-igoon thirty days
nisso-igoon three days

inaundae *refers to shade, tint, pigment, hue, tinge, color, tone, complexion*

booz-aundae it is darker
kitug-aundae it is mottled
meen-aundae it is the shade of a blueberry
nigik-waundae it is gray—the color of an otter

inummoh *refers to the nature, quality, or the direction of a road, path, trail, way*

agidau-akee-waemmoh the road goes uphill
aunikae-inummoh the road continues or joins another
gawaek-ummoh the trail is straight, direct
paupaugid-ummoh the trail, road is packed
zhooshki-d-ummoh the road is slippery

inushk; ushk *refers to a stalk, reed, grass, stem*

maewizh-ushk kemauh meezh-ushk hay
mizaun-ushk a thistle stalk
nubug-ushk sweet flag
ogimau-wuhnshk clotbur

ish; eesh; oosh; aush *a suffix that may be, depending upon tone and context, either derogatory or salutary*

animishish an old, useless dog; a cur, bitch, mutt
mashkimootaush an old bag
matchi-auwish the evil one
matchi-gawaehnish a scoundrel, rogue
mukwoosh a nuisance bear
pineesh a rotten potato
weegwaumish a dilapidated house

ishkih *habitually; customarily; frequently; constantly*

gautchi-mawishkih in the habit of crying
geenawishkih a habitual liar
meegaushkih ready to fight at a moment's notice; in the habit of fighting; disposed to fight
miniquaeshkih an alcoholic; ever drinking

itchigun; igun *refers to an instrument, tool, device, implement; a manufacture; a product; an ornament*

baeng-waussi-itchigun a clothes dryer
geeshki-boodji-igun a saw
neem-ishkugun a headdress; dancing apparel
nishki-itchigun lace; a frill

kaun *the character of a place, location, site, grounds, area, patch, sector, field, district*

geegoohn kaun fishing area
geewi-ossae-kaun a hunting territory
maewishkoohnse-kaun a meadow
ningo-kaun burial grounds; a cemetery

kummik *refers to place on, or to the nature, character, quality, form of the earth*

aedawae-kummik on both, or on either side of the earth
agid-kummik on the surface of the earth
anaum-kummik in the bowels of the earth
zoong-kummik strong, firm ground

kunnuh; kun *a roadway, path, trail (from* meekunnuh—*a way, route, course, passage)*

aedawae-kunnuh on either side of the road
agaum-kunnuh on the other side of the road

cheegi-kunnuh near the road
naunauwi-kunnuh in the middle of the road

maewish; meesh; mish *refers to a certain kind of tree*

gibaumaewish a hazelnut tree
metig-meesh a red oak
mishi-meesh an oak
quae-meesh a cherry tree
zhigaug-mish blue beech (a variation of *zhigaug-maewish*—skunk beech)

meen *refers to a berry, seed, fruit (often pronounced* min*)*

maundau-meen corn, maize; the seed of wonder
mino-meen wild rice; the good seed
mishee-meen an apple; the great seed, berry
odae-meen strawberry; the heart berry

onaugun; naugun *a vessel, dish, instrument*

cheecheeb-naugun a rocker, crib
dasso-naugun a trap
gawaub-naugun a dip-net; a seine
piskitae-naugun a woven basket

oonuk; oonukut *refers to the shape, form, structure, part, place of or in a vessel; the hull*

anaum-oonuk the keel; under the boat
gauss-oonuk narrow hulled
ishkawae-oonuk the stern
peend-oonuk in the hold

ooshkin *refers to capacity, fullness, measure, extent of goods, liquids*

aupit-ooshkin half full
nauwi-ooshkin contents are depleting, decreasing
neezh-ooshkin two bags
ningot-ooshkin a bag full

pin *a tuber*

aundaeg-pin bugleweed; crow's tuber
numae-pin broad leafed arrowhead; sturgeon's tuber
pin a potato

pizoon *an article of clothing; an ornament*

gabi-dae-pizoon a vest
gitchi-pizoon an apron
naub-ozhae-pizoon an earring
tipi-inindjee-pizoon a ring

quae *refers to a woman or to the length, color, texture of hair*

misqawaun-quae red-haired
Mizzu-kummik-quae Mother Earth
oshki-neegi-quae a young woman; a girl (*quae*—woman, hair, head)
quae a woman; head (of the family); long haired

sug *refers to boards, floors*

ishpim-sug upstairs
mitchi-sug the bare floor
mukuk-sug a wooden barrel; a keg
nubug-sug a plank; a board

waewaun *a pair*

neezho-waewaun two pair
ningot-waewaun one pair

waeyaun; ooyaun *hide or skin of an animal; a covering for humans (such as clothing or a blanket)*

amik-waeyaun a beaver skin
auhnz-ooyaun a loincloth; a diaper
mukwo-waeyaun a bearskin
waub-ooyaun a blanket

wauk *a hundred*

medauss-wauk one thousand
medautching medauss-wauk one hundred thousand
neezho-wauk two hundred
ningot-wauk one hundred

waunoh; oozoowaunoh *refers to the length, color, character, nature of an animal's tail*

bizhi-akee-waunoh a cow's tail; a buffalo's tail
makatae-oozoowaunoh black-tailed
moozoo-waunoh a moose tail

myeenguni-waunoh a wolf's tail
ojidumo-waunoh yarrow

---

waush; waudj; wish *a den, cave, hole, lodge, burrow*

---

aenigoohn-wish an anthill
amik-waush a beaver's lodge
migiz-waudj an eagle's nest
nigik-waush an otter's den
ojidumo-waush a squirrel's burrow
wizhushk-waush a muskrat's lodge or den

Verbs

A

abee-tchigaewin *bring; fetch*

abeed-aussoowin to bring
abeed-auwissoowin to bring
abeed-oonigaewin bring; deliver (from *abi-atoon*—to bring and set down)
abee-tchigaewin to bring
gawau-oodauwissoowin to unload
gawau-oodoo-auwissoowin to unload and bring to land
maudjeed-auwissoowin to bring; to take to
neesi-auwid-auwissoowin to bring down
peendigaed-auwissoowin to bring indoors
pissikaub-auwid-auwissoowin to bring back

abeetumoowin *wait; await; bide*

abeetumoowin to wait; to bide one's time
baubeewoowin to await
beetumoowin to wait; to bide time
beewoowin to wait

abee-wiwaewin *expect; wait; anticipate (see also* abeetumoowin—*wait; await; bide)*

abee-wiwaewin to wait in expectation; to anticipate
kawae-tumoowin to wait for someone for a period

abi-ayauwin *come*

abi-ayauwin to come; to be on the way
abi-izhau'd'iwin to come; to be on one's way
oohnz-ikauwin to come for some purpose

abi-boon *winter*

abi-boon to come to a stop; winter, the season when growth is suspended
abi-boonigiziwin to age; to calculate age by winters
abi-boonishiwin to winter (somewhere)

abiz-igaewin *warm*

abiz-igaewin to warm up; to defrost
aubiwiz-igaewin to thaw; to defrost
geezhoo-shinoowin to hunker in under blankets; to get cozy, warm
gizhiz-igaewin to heat, warm up, warm
wuhzoowin to warm up

adjauwaewin *trade; exchange; barter; swap*

adauwaewin to grant right of passage to nonresidents upon payment of a fee or toll (toll collectors were known as Attawau or Ottauwau warriors)
aushi-toonigaewin to exchange; to switch; to swap
maeshi-toonigaewin to barter; to switch; to swap
odjauwootumoowin to peddle

ae-iquayauk-issitchigaewin *limit; enough*

ae-ayauqawaek-issitchigaewin to go to the very end
daebissae-tchigaewin to have enough

agawau-igaewin *ladle; scoop*

agawau-igaewin to ladle
gawaub-igaewin to ladle; to scoop

agawauk-issinoowin *rust; mold*

agawaubik-issinoowin rust
agawauk-issinoowin mold

agindaussoowin *add; total; count; sum up; estimate; read*

aenigo-queenoowin the entire number, all
agindaussoowin to add; to total; to count; to sum up
ashid-gindaussoowin to add; to add to
dabi-gindaussoowin to estimate; to guess (total number)
maumoo-weenoowin all; the entire number; everyone
maumoow-issitchigaewin to compile
mauwindoo-gindaussoowin to total
mizi-waeshinoowin all; everything; altogether; whole; everything in place, integrated, assembled, complete

agookaewin *stick; glue; cement; solder, paste*

agook-issigaewin to stick on; to paste; to cement; to wallpaper
bautau-shinoowin stuck; caught
bizook-issaewin fuse; solder; glue; stick to
chika-wigaewin to stick into
dagoo-waubik-idaewin to solder; to melt to
piduk-akee-igaewin to quilt
piduk-awigaewin to stick; to stab; to sting as does a bee

agudji-inaewiziwin *shy; bashful; coy; embarrass; demure*

agudji-ayauwin coy; demure
agudj-inaewiziwin to be bashful
zhaugo-waenimoowin shrinking; timid

akeegaewin *plant; work the earth*

aund-akee-igaewin to transplant
maudjee-igi-itchigaewin to plant; to assist growth
ningowudji-akeegaewin to cover seeds
ningowudji-igaewin to plant; to cover over
ningowudji-meenikaun-igaewin to plant seeds; to bury seeds
peend-akee-issitchigaewin to plant; to set in
piduk-ishingaewin to plant; to set upright as a tomato plant

akeewaewin *home; go home*

akeewaewin to go home
azhae-keewaewin to return home

ako-daudiwin *succeed; follow; replace*

ako-daudiwin to follow after
aunikae-ishkaugaewin to follow, succeed another
gukaudjigaewin to prosper, flourish; to work for gain
kishki-tchigaewin to succeed; to attain; to gain
kishki-tumauzoowin to accomplish; to profit for oneself
naub-ishkaugaewin to substitute for; to succeed
sukaudjigaewin to prosper; to flourish; to work for gain

amauzoowin *premonition; presentiment; alarm; sense*

amauzoowin to have a presentiment
kabaewaewin to augur, prophesy, market forecast
moomiziwin to alarm; to put on alert
munissoowin to alarm; to alert
nawautchigaewin to prefigure, foretoken

anaukinikaewin *weave*

anaukunikaewin to weave mats
pukwaekaewin to weave mats, partitions

anaum-ingaewin *blame; accuse*

anaum-ingaewin to blame
baut-aungaewin to tell on, report on
mizh-ingaewin to let slip an inculpatory remark

anibae-itauwin *stoop; slouch; droop; bend*

anibae-tauwin to lean
initauwin (root) to shape, flex, contort, twist oneself
nau-witauwin to stoop down
nawae-tauwin to slouch, droop

zhigushk-itauwin to bend, stoop low

ani-baek-auwin *incline; slant; lean; slope*

ani-baek-aukissitchigaewin put something aslant
ani-baek-kummikauh slope; incline
shawae-aukimoowin to angle, tilt, curve
shawae-quaeniwin to incline one's head to one side

anim-akeekauwin *thunder*

anim-akeekauwin thunder
baug-inigaewin the strike of lightning
baushk-umoowin to explode; to create an explosion
bimi-waewidumoowin to go by clamoring; to clamor during passage

animi-kaugaewin *greet; salute; hail*

anim-kaugaewin to greet; to hail

animikooss-itchigaewin *invert*

animikooss-itchigaewin to turn upside down
aubood-inigaewin to turn inside out/outside in

anim-oodjigaewin *track; trace; trail; tail*

anamaetumaewin to leave tracks, a trail
anim-oodjigaewin to track
bimi-kanawaewin to leave tracks
bimi-kawaewin to leave tracks
cheecheesh-kawaewin to leave a trail distinguished by furrows on the surface produced by the drag of feet, paws, or claws as does a killdeer
inaegaewin (root) direction of one's search, course, bearings, route, beat, ambit
inikawaewin (root) the character, aspect of trail left behind
inishkum (root) state, quality of tracks left behind
kawae-tchigaewin to follow tracks
kawaewin (root) to track, trail, tail
mamaung-ishkawaewin to leave large tracks, prints
mamaung-ishkummeewin to leave large tracks, prints
mamaung-ishkummoowin to leave large tracks, prints
nawa-zoowaunauwin to trail someone
nawuz-inaegaewin to shadow; to dog
noozoowaun-aegaewin to trail someone

animukowiwin *faint; lose consciousness*

animukowiwin to faint, lose consciousness
nik-aubindumaewin to lose sight of; to fade from sight

anoodjee-kaewin *frequent; habituate*

anoodjeekaewin to frequent, habituate
dazheekaewin to trifle, dawdle, idle away, putter, fiddle, dally, play, fool around

anookeetumaewin *order; command*

anookeetumaewin to order some work to be done
mindjidawaewin to send for

anookeewin *work; do; perform*

anookeewin to work; to hunt and fish; to harvest; to derive, obtain, acquire sustenance from the earth
anoon-akeewin to perform a specific form of work; to labor
meekimoowin to toil, drudge, labor

apaenimoowin *trust; rely on; count on; hope; aspire; depend upon*

apaenimoondaugaewin to rely on
apaenimoowin to rely on
sugin-aendjigaewin; sigin-aendjigaewin to cling to in mind

apeet-aendaugooziwin *value; worth*

apeet-aendaugooziwin to have worth
inugindaussoowin to charge; to price; to set a value on

apeet-issaewin *pace; rate; speed*

apeess-ikauwin a given pace or rate of movement
apeetch-itauwin to work at a certain pace or rate
inikauwin (root) motion
itauwin (root) action, inclination, disposition, preference

VERBS

asaekaewin *tan; make brown, beige, yellow*

asaekaewin to tan hides
zauwae-gizigaewin to tan a hide
zauwau-issiwidizoowin to seek a tan

ashid-inigaewin *increase, add*

aenigo-iqueenoowin all; the whole, entire body
ashid-gindaussoowin to add up
dabi-gindaussoowin to estimate, guess quantity, numbers
maumoo-weenoowin all, everyone, the entire number, all gathered
maumoow-issitchigaewin to compile
mauwindoo-gindaussoowin to total
mizi-waeshinoowin all, everything, all together, whole, everything in place, integral, integrated, assembled, complete aggregate

ashi-waubindumoowin *watch; observe*

ashi-waub indumoowin to mark; to keep under surveillance
iko-waubindumaewin to watch; to keep an eye on

atchigaewin *set*

aedawaug-inikaewin to set apart, aside
atawaug-inikaewin to set apart
atchigaewin to put
geezhi-issitchigaewin to set in readiness
izhi-issitchigaewin to set in order

aubawae-waendumoowin *forgive, pardon; overlook; relent*

aubawae-waendumoowin to forgive; to warm up
auniss-aendumoowin to overlook, forgive, conciliate, reconcile
booni'gid-aetumoowin to pardon
winissida-waendjigaewin to relent

aub-awaewin *bake; roast*

aub-aewin to roast; to broil

aub-cheebauwin *revive; resurrect; recover*

aubi-cheebauwin to return to life; to resurrect
aubizee-audiziwin to survive, recover, recuperate
boomaewin to recover from fright

aubeendjiwaewin *torture; torment; victimize; persecute; harm; hurt; injure; maltreat in the extreme*

aubeendji-waewin violate; batter; trounce; defile; torment
bawaenishinoowin to inflict internal injuries
inaup-inozhiwaewin to inflict wounds
inaup-inunigaewin to inflict certain kinds of injuries
inikaugaewin to inflict wounds, injuries in a certain manner
inishinoowin to be injured in a certain manner
kotug-iwaewin to abuse, torment
matchi-doodaugaewin to maltreat, ill-treat
mazhi-auwaewin to injure; to bruise; to cut; to wound
week-audjiwaewin to victimize
weessigaup-inunigaewin to inflict extreme pain

aubeez-oongaewin *slander*

aubeez-oongaewin to shame, disgrace, insult
augaw-ingaewin to belittle, detract
beenish-ingaewin to defame, revile, dishonor

aub-igaewin *untie*

aub-igaewin to loosen, untie
aubiss-ikoobidjigaewin to untie, loosen
aub-iwaewin to untie
binisk-oobidjigaewin to untangle, unravel
bunung-aussinoowin blown loose by the wind
gaeshikauwin to unfasten
gaesh-iwishkauwin to become unbound, untied; to come loose
geetchig-ooshkauwin to come loose
gidis-akeewin to break free
gidis-kauwin to come loose and off
gidjish-keeweewin to break free
gidjish-kikauwin to break free
pekwae-ishkauwin to break off
piko-ishkauwin to break off

auboonoowin *drift; float; carry by current*

auboonoowin to drift along with the current

babaum-waeboogoowin to be driven about by wind and current; to drift
bimau-bugoowin to float along
bimi-boogoowin to drift by
bugoowin (root) the direction and pace of drift
neessau-boogoowin to drift downstream on ice, an ice floe
neessau-boonoowin to drift downstream
waebi-boogoowin to drift away
wae-bugoowin to float or drift away

auboot-issaewin *tumble; somersault*

adjid-akeessaewin to fall upside down
auboot-issaewin to fall heels over head, inside out

audauk-ishinoowin *strand; stick; maroon; isolate*

audau-igoon-aeshinoowin to be snow-bound
audauk-ishinoowin restrained; to be bound; to be locked, barred
audi-gaumig-ishinoowin stranded on the far side
audugau-gummee-shinoowin to be marooned by flood waters

augawaud-iziwin *wild*

augawaud-iziwin to be unrestrained

augi-goodjigaewin *veil*

augi-goodjigaewin to veil

aug-oonaetumoowin *deny; refute; object to*

augoon-aetumoowin to deny
aunoo-waetumoowin to refute

auhnz-pizoowin *wrap; bundle; gird; bind; bandage*

auhnzi-pizoowin to gird
kishki-pitchigaewin to bind up, swaddle, envelope
mikindauwissoowin to wrap up furs
titabee-waeginigaewin to wrap, swaddle
weewiquae-iginigaewin to wrap, bundle
weewiquae-pitchigaewin to wrap, bundle
zeehnzoob-inigaewin to bandage

auhnz-waendumoowin *forget; omit*

auhnz-waendumoowin to forget, omit
winaendumoowin to forget, to lose in one's mind
wineekaewin to forget, to leave behind in mind

aukooziwin *sick; ill; unwell*

anaum-inaeziwin to have boils and skin inflammations
aubeendji-inaewin to experience agonizing, excruciating, unremitting pain
auki-mundjiwoowin to feel sick
auk-ishkudaewin to have cramps, stomach pains, indigestion
aukoo-waundumaewin to experience injury, pain, hurt
aukooziwin to be sick
aundji-inaewin to have a relapse, fall sick again
aunimiziwin to experience agony, excruciating pain
auzhookood-inigae-waupinaewin to have a contagious disease
baug-eengawaewin to have a swollen face
baushk-eegawaegaewin to let blood
beenissisiwin to have numbness
beetawae-doonaewin to froth at the mouth
beeto-ipeeg-ozhaewin to have a blistered body, covered with blisters
bigum-aukooziwin to arrive sick
bigum-aupinaewin to arrive sick
biziniwin to have a mote in the eye
bunug-doonaeshkauwin to have the skin around the mouth peel off
bunug-zhuguyaewin the skin, epidermis, peels off
chauchaumoowin to sneeze
chaushinoowin to limp
cheeby-inaewiziwin to have numbness, stiffness
cheeby-itukoowin paralysis, rigor mortis
cheecheeb-ibinigoowin to have convulsions
cheecheeb-ishkauwin to have involuntary movement, twitching
cheecheegoomiwin to have warts
cheeshigoowin to be scarred, marked
cheesidae-binigoowin to suffer cramps in some part of the body

VERBS

daewi to have pain, ache, throbbing
daewi-quaewin to have a headache
daubishkauwin to have cramps, a fit, a seizure
gaboo-inaumoowin to have a blockage of nasal passages
gageeb (gabi)-suggizhaewin to have constipation
gageeb-eengawaewin to be blind
gageeb-ishaewin to be deaf
gageeb-naquaewin to have dumbness; to be mute, speechless
gageetae-igaewin to extract a thorn, a foreign substance from the body
gaup-doonaewin to have chapped lips
gaupiziwin to have a stiffness; delicateness
gawauk-idoozoowin to have thinness, leanness; to be spare (from *pauguk-idoozoowin*—to be skeleton thin)
gawinaewin to be felled by sickness
gazheeb-ozhae-waupinaewin to have scabies or any other condition that causes itching such as a rash
gazhizoowin to have a fever
gazhiz-waupinaewin to have a fever, a temperature
geediziwin, gaugeediziwin to have sore muscles, joints, tenderness of bruised area
geewi-inaewin to be crazy with pain, delirious, delirium
gidisk-anik-aeshinoowin to dislocate an arm
gidisk-maungun-aeshinoowin a shoulder separation
gikikauwin to have the flu, influenza, a cold
inaumoowin (root) breath, breathing, inhalation, exhalation (*pagid-, ishkwau-, gazheeb-, kishki-, gabo-* and any number of other prefixes may be affixed to the root to denote some condition of breathing)
inaupinaewin to experience the nature and intensity of illness
kautoonaewin to suffer a relapse
kikudjiwin to be cold; to catch a cold
kininoo-wauzi-inaugooziwin to have distinctive characteristics, features, marks
kotugitoowin to experience suffering
mamaedauw-idjeewin to have constipation
mamaundji-igooziwin to be lame; to halt
maukiwaewin to wound, hurt, injure and to leave a bruise or scar
maukizee-waupinaewin to have smallpox
mauk-iziwin to have a wound; to have a scar, red wound
maunaud-aupinaewin to have a pestilence
maun-ikaugoowin to have nausea, queasiness
maun-mundji-oowin to have nausea
mauz-aubiwin to have impaired vision
mauzh-ayauwin to have nausea, queasiness
mauzh-odae-aewin to have nausea, indigestion
migeewin to be scabby
mineewiwin to have an abscess
misquwee-waupinaewin to have tuberculosis, consumption, TB
misquweewiwin to experience bleeding; to hemorrhage
misquwo-ozhae-waupinaewin to have measles
moossae-weengawaewin to have pimples; to be pimply
naunoozi-minaessiwin to get worse
nekaubundumaewin to faint; to experience unconsciousness
pungishkoon-aeziwin to have a sudden illness
seemiziwin to feel unwell
shugawaewin, shushiguwaewin to vomit, puke, bring up
soossidumoowin to experience coughing; to cough
tiki-inindjeewin to have cold hands
tiko-wauk-ozid-aewidjiwin to have cold feet
weeg-wing-odae-aewin to have a fast heartbeat
weessigitoowin to suffer; to be in agony
zaessaeg-eengawaewin to have snow blindness
zaugiskau-geewaewin to experience bleeding
zaugis-kawaewigoowin to bleed from a wound
zauwa-inaeziwin to have jaundice
zhaubookaugoziwin to have diarrhea, dysentery
zhaushaug-waubaewiziwin to be emaciated
zhee-waubiwin to have cataracts

aumoowaewin *ward off; repel*

agawaun-igoon-auwaewin to beat off, back
aumoohnwaewin to force retreat, as do bees
iko-inauzh-iwaewin to evict, drive away

aunau-zoongaewin *restrain; hold back; check; curb; stop; halt*

aunau-zoongaewin to talk out of, dissuade
ningau-bidjigaewin to halt, stop
ningau-kummee-tchigaewin to hold back, check
ningaushk-augaewin to curb

aundauwaewin *shed; molt*

aundauwaewin to shed fur by a dog
aundji-gwunaewin to molt
bawi-beewunaewin to shed down
bawi-oonaewin to shed, lose fur
binauwaewin to shed fur
bini-winaewin to lose, shed antlers
bunauk-awaeyauwin to lose leaves
bunug-ozhae-shkauwin to lose skin; skin peels off
piki-waneewin to shed, lose bark

aund-issitchigaewin *transfer; shift; hand over*

aund-aki-nigaewin to transplant
aund-issitchigaewin to transpose, shift, relocate
aunikaen-imaugaewin to pass on, delegate, cede, bequeath a heritage

aundjeewin *change; reform; revise; reconstruct; rearrange; move*

auhnss-akeewin to change place, move
aundjeewin to change; to move
aundj-issitchigaewin to rearrange
aundj-itchigaewin to revise, alter, reconstruct
gawaek-eewin to change affiliation

aundji-igiwoowin; needjauniss-ikaewin *to conceive, get pregnant; to beget a child*

abi-anoodjeehnss-ikaewin to sire an infant; to conceive
aundji-igiwoowin to conceive; to change; to become part of another
gigishk-augaewin to be with child
needjaunissikaewin to beget a child; to make a child

aungawiziwin *tame; domesticate*

aungawiziwin to be tame, docile
aungi-witchigaewin to tame, domesticate
waengawiziwin to be tame, docile

aunikae-inootumoowin *translate; interpret*

aunikae-inootumoowin to translate
gawaek-gawaek-itumoowin to put in other words
naub-inootumoowin to translate
nee'inawaetimoowin to interpret

aunikae-ishkaugaewin *follow; succeed; replace; go after; chase*

aunikae-ishkaugaewin to succeed another
ishkawae-ikaugaewin to follow behind
naugu-izhiwaewin to follow
naugutoo-waewin to follow a trail
noopinukeewin to run after
noop-inuzhiwaewin to chase after

aunikae-issitchaegaewin *join; extend; couple; bind*

aunikae-issitchigaewin to join ends, extend
dagoon-igaewin to blend, mesh
tikoo-bidjigaewin to bind or secure to
zigi-bidjigaewin to tie to, to fasten to

aunikaeni-maukaewin *hand; pass; transfer; give; transmit*

abeed-inigaewin to pass in this direction
aunikaeni-maukaewin to pass on, transmit, bequeath
ininigaewin (root) to hand over to, to pass on to
ininimaukaewin to hand to, pass to

aunikoo-bitchigaewin *connect; join; hitch; bond between generations*

aunikoo-bitchigaewin to hitch, connect, tie to

aunimut *storm*

gootaumikoot stormy

VERBS

neessikaudut unsettled, inclement
nitcheewut a punishing, angry storm

---

aun-ishee-tumoowin *discourage; submit; give in; lose heart; despair*

aunishee-tumoowin to be discouraged
waussuda-waendumoowin despair; lose hope

---

auniss-aendumoowin *reconcile; make up; remedy; assuage*

auniss-aendumoowin to mend, remedy, make up

---

auniwi-toowin *fail; flag; fall short*

auniwi-itchigaewin to cause failure
auniwi-tumoowin to flag, enfeeble
bawauniwi-tumoowin to fail despite attempts
noondae-ishinoowin to fall short

---

aunoo-waendumoowin *reject*

aunoo-waendumoowin to reject in one's mind
aunoo-waubumaewin to be displeasing to the sight

---

aunoo-witumoowin *deny; disbelieve; refuse*

augoon-aetumoowin to deny
aunoo-waetumoowin to refute

---

auskaugaewin *support; help; abet*

auskaugaewin to support, favor, foster, back
auskoowaewin to support, favor, foster, back
weess-ookaugaewin to support, favor, foster, back in the commission of an offence

---

aussi-wauk-awigaewin *brace; lean on/to/ against*

aussi-wauk-awigaewin to nail something against
aussi-wauk-issitchigaewin to lean something against

---

aussiwauk-issitchigaewin *lean; abut; press against*

aussiwauk-issitchigaewin to lean against, support
shood-aukawigaewin to nail against

---

aussoodjeep-itchigaewin *tighten; bind; lace; tie*

aussoodjeep-itchigaewin to bandage, bind tightly
inaukiwigaewin (root) to affix, attach
inupizoowin (root) manner, style and type of dress or binding
kishkee-waukiwigaewin to seal
maundjigo-ibidjigaewin to bind securely
naubidjaush-ibidjigaewin to tie temporarily
naubidoo-igaewin to lace
tikoo-bidjigaewin to tie, bind
zeend-aukiwigaewin to wedge
zigi-bidigaewin to tie to

---

autae-itchigaewin *extinguish*

auttae-itchigaewin to put out a fire, blaze
auttawae-itchigaewin to put out a fire

---

auwaetchigaewin *tell a parable*

auwaetchigaewin to tell a parable

---

auwiwin *become; be*

abeetumoowin to abide, infuse, instill, inspirit
abiwin to be present; to be there, insensate
anaum-aend-augooziwin to have guilt; to be culpable; to take responsibility, accountability; to blame; to be liable, at fault, etc.
ani-auwiwin to become different or other in the course of time
apeetchi-nawaeziwin to have impatience, restlessness; to be anxious to get going; to be in the course, presence of passion, anger, a fit of temper
ataewin to be there, insensate
aubauk-awiziwin to recover one's senses; to recover consciousness
augad-aendaugooziwin to feel shame, humiliation, dishonor, mortification, discredit, embarrassment, discomfiture, etc.
auga-waudiziwin to express instability; to be unbalanced, psychotic, crazy, nuts; to express lunacy; to be demented, insane, deranged, paranoid, etc.
aukooziwin to have illness, unwellness, sickness
auk-waudiziwin to express testiness, grouchiness, grumpiness, a sour disposition; to

be touchy, prickly, irritable; to be peevish, huffy, crabby, ill-natured, sensitive, etc.

aundji-ayaewin to change

aungawaum-iziwin to be circumspect, cautious, prudent, careful, watchful, wary, discreet, mindful, etc.

aunga-wiziwin to be tame, subdued, trained, broken, meek, mild, peaceful, quiet, docile, etc.

auskauwi-naeziwin to be ambitious, self-seeking

auwiwin to be; to become; to exist; to be such condition

ayau'd'iwin to be present

baek-audiziwin to be meek, gentle, quiet, docile, pliant, tractable, submissive, agreeable, well-behaved, etc.

been-audiziwin to be clean, tidy, neat, organized, trim, spruce, prim, dainty, well kempt, etc.

beeniss-iziwin to be paralyzed, numb, insensitive, stunned, without feeling

bizu-waudiziwin to be clumsy, awkward, muscle bound, ungainly

bugwoon-iwiziwin to be backward, untutored, ignorant, without manners, dumb, stupid, rude, rough, crude, untamed, etc.

chaep-iziwin to be agile, quick, fast, nimble, high spirited, rapid, etc.

cheen-iziwin to be bashful, timorous, shy, diffident, timid, reserved, coy, etc.

cheeshitau-inaewiziwin to be reserved, introspective, reticent, grave, serious, reflective, sober, solemn, etc.

daeb-iziwin; daebinaewiziwin to be deserving; to merit; to be entitled to; to have a right to; to claim; to have an interest in; to deserve and to be entitled to certain rights and goods and services according to one's needs, aspirations, efforts

dagoowin to be; to inhabit, domicile, lodge, stay; are

daneewin to remain; to increase possessions, wealth, assets

daniziwin to reside

dazheewin to habituate, frequent; to be in one place

gageebaud-iziwin to exhibit foolishness, mischief, silliness; to be irresponsible; to indulge in folly; to have bad or poor judgement

gaugaetau-wiziwin to be careful, prudent, watchful, vigilant, cautious, weary, etc.

gaupo-iziwin to be unyielding, unbending, intractable, stubborn, bull-headed, obstinate, fixed, dogmatic, headstrong, brittle, etc.

gawaek-awaudiziwin to have rectitude; to be upright, moral, ethical, honest, principled, law-abiding, etc.

gawaushk-awaeziwin to be nimble, agile, quick, bouncy, dexterous, etc.

gazhee-ozhae-wiziwin to have vigor, energy, vitality, vim, animation, verve; to be robust active, lively, etc.

geedji-naewiziwin; gudji-naewiziwin to be shy, timid, inclined to be reserved, bashful

geewi-audiziwin to be vagrant, nomadic, transitory, migratory; to have wanderlust, etc.

geewi-inaudiziwin to be demented, crazy, a lunatic, mad, psychotic, irrational, etc.

geewi-iziwin to be abandoned, orphaned, forsaken

geewish-quae-iziwin to be giddy

gizhaud-iziwin to express generosity, kindness; to be liberal, charitable, unselfish, unsparing, tender, considerate, helpful, understanding, sensitive, etc.

goop-idiziwin to be inept, incapable, incompetent, awkward, clumsy, bumbling, etc.

goozikee-wiziwin to be cautious, wary, careful, conservative, afraid, etc.

gotaumig-awaendaug-ooziwin to be mighty, overwhelming, overpowering, potent, dreadful, horrible, daunting, intimidating

gotaumig-ooziwin to be ambitious, inspired, energetic, avid, ardent, earnest, industrious, zealous, fervent, spirit; to undertake something with all energy and ability

inaendaug-iziwin to seem; to appear to be; to give an impression; to show, resemble, etc.

inaudiziwin the character, nature, state of being; to exist, live; to have a certain manner, mood, character, style, nature, etc.

ina-wauzoowin to make a presumption, assumption, guess; to take things for granted, to indulge in pretension, pretext; to accept, surmise, etc.

ini-gauziwin to experience poverty, wretchedness, need, want, destitution; to be impoverished, beggared; to deserve pity, sympathy, help, etc.

ishi-waebiziwin to suffer; to endure an event, accident, occurrence, happening, incident; to have an experience of some kind, etc.

izhi-ayauwin the state of being, character, personality

izhi-ayauwin to be; to be in such a state, condition

izhi-naugooziwin to appear, seem, look like, resemble someone; to give an impression of, etc.

kikaed-iziwin to be grave, stern, serious, sober, reflective, meditative, etc.

kikaund-aendaugooziwin to be grave, stern, serious, sober, reflective, meditative, etc.

kitim-audiziwin to have a disposition, tendency toward sloth, laziness, indolence, idleness, etc.

kitim-augiziwin to experience poverty, destitution, want, need brought about by sloth, indolence, laziness

maenishi-iziwin to experience embarrassment, mortification, humiliation, discomfiture, etc.

mauk-iziwin to be scarred, bruised, marked, blemished; to have a wound, a laceration, abrasions, etc.

mauminaud-iziwin to have vanity, conceit, pride, haughtiness, etc.

maun-aendaug-iziwin to seem evil, bad, mean, base, vile, vulgar, cross, dangerous, etc.

maunaud-iziwin to have plainness, ugliness, homeliness; to be frightful, etc.

mayug-iziwin to seem, appear to be strange, different, alien, foreign, etc.

migooshk-audiziwin to experience trouble, affliction, anguish, turmoil, upset, etc.

min-audiziwin to be fastidious, selective, picky, choosy, biased, etc.

mindau-waewiziwin to be moody, temperamental, low spirited, irritable, irascible, peevish, glum, high strung, etc.

mino-neewig-iziwin to have a, a sunny disposition; to be good natured, happy, even-tempered, cheerful, pleasant, sunny, etc.

mino-waendaug-iziwin to experience happiness, joy, elation, gladness, exaltation, bless, rapture, ecstasy, revelry

mussug-awaudiziwin to be unlucky, unfortunate, not blessed, cursed, damned, ill starred

nana-waudiziwin to be useless, worthless, aimless, purposeless, idle, unfit, ineffectual, incompetent, inept, unable, etc.

neegaun-iziwin to lead; to have leadership traits and aspirations

nimb-audiziwin to indulge in gluttony, excess, overeating, greed; to be voracious, indulgent, piggish, etc.

ningud-iziwin to be familiar, acquainted, practiced, used to, accustomed to, experienced, skilled, wise, trained, qualified, etc.

nishin-audiziwin to be corrupt, ruined, bankrupt, rotten, wasted, immoral, ravaged, dissipated, broken, disorganized, confused, muddled, etc.

nishk-audiziwin to be displeased, vexed, testy; to experience anger, annoyance, irritation, rage, temper, etc.

niss-audiziwin to be sober, grave, serious, reflective, in control, composed, calm, etc.

ni-waeziwin to pout, sulk; to be sullen, in a snit, petulant; to feel slighted over some comment or behavior and then to refuse an offering or service or apology

nook-audiziwin to express docility, meekness, gentility, mildness, tenderness, tractability

pussug-awaudiziwin to be caught in the web of bad luck (possibly from *bizug*—sticky, to be glued to)

sumi-iziwin to be spry, agile, supple, etc.

wanushk-awaeziwin to be easily distracted, diverted, misled, ready to drop one's duty, work, etc.; to pursue another interest, lack concentration and commitment, etc.

wayaeyaud-aend-augooziwin to express drollness; to be droll

weed-aend-augooziwin to be amusing, droll, funny, comical, ludicrous, humorous, laughable, witty, jolly, etc.
weediziwin to suffer deserved punishment; to receive just desserts, poetic justice; to get what one deserves
weegiziwin to be abject, wretched, woeful, poor
ween-audiziwin to be dirty, filthy, unclean, impure, messy, soiled, blemished, tarnished, etc.
zaeg-iziwin to be fearful, apprehensive; to be full of dread, fear, timidity, misgiving, foreboding, anxiety, etc.
zaug-iziwin to have selfishness; to be stingy, mean, tight fisted, niggardly; to have love of self, etc.
zhawaend-augooziwin to be lucky, fortunate, blessed, favored, successful, prosperous, rewarded, deserving of benefits
zhazheeb-inaewiziwin to be persistent, resolute, unwilling to give in, to take no for an answer, tenacious, determined, etc.
zheeng-aend-augooziwin to be annoying, vexatious, a nuisance, irritating, pesky, etc.
zoong-iziwin to have resolution, firmness; to be strong, durable, robust, vigorous, sturdy, brawny, etc.

---

auwish-ingaewin *threaten; warn; caution; intimidate; menace*

auwish-ingaewin to menace with words, daunt
naneem-awauwaewin to caution, intimidate, cow
naunib-oongaewin to curse, damn

---

auyauzhee-keewaewin *scream; yell; whoop; screech*

ayauzhee-keewaewin scream; yell
zausauk-keewaewin to war cry, war whoop

---

auzhid-aendjigaewin *challenge; dare*

auzhid-aendjigaewin dare risk
maun-aeningaewin to dare
nindo-gagawaedibaendjigaewin to test, tempt

---

auzhidaewauwae-itaugaewin *revenge*

auzhidaewauwae-itaugaewin to avenge, pay back
mazhimauwaewin to betray

---

auzhi-waewin *ford; cross over; portage*

auzhi-waewin to cross from one side to the other
tikum-akeekumoowin to cross some tract of land
wini-gumoowin to portage with a canoe

---

auzhookood-inigaewin *infect; contaminate*

auzhookood-inigaewin to communicate, transmit a disease
mazhin-igaewin to be, become infected; to catch a disease

---

awiwaewin *lend*

awiwaewin lend

---

awun *fog; haze; mist*

agikina'um mist
awun fog
bigikna'um haze
madookoot dew; haze

---

ayaek-aweetchigaewin *flag; tire; exhaust; weary*

ayaek-aweetchigaewin to grow tired
baedjee-itumoowin to slow down
chaugin-inigaewin to exhaust; to spend
chaugin-itchigaewin to exhaust; to spend

---

ayaekooziwin *tire; weary; exhaust; spend; deplete; expend*

ayaekooziwin to be tired; to tire
chaug-eeweewin to exhaust energy, strength
chaug-inigaewin to expend all, everything
noondae-weewaewin to become exhausted

---

ayau'd'iwin *present*

abee-tumoowin to dwell, habituate
ayau'd'iwin to be present; to be
dazhee-woowin to habituate; source of livelihood

---

ayaudjigaewin *acquire; have; purchase*

VERBS

ayaudjigaewin to acquire; to have (note the relationship to *ayauwin*—to be [whatever one acquires adds to his or her being])

ayaumi-tawauwauwin *bless*

anami-ae-itchigaewin to bless, sanctify
ayaumi-tawauwauwin to bless

ayau-waewin *stutter; stammer*

ayau-waewin to stammer so as to be incomprehensible
bae-bizhi-goowaewin to miss syllables
bununee-widumoowin mutter; mumble; to be inarticulate, incomprehensible
bunu-waemoowin; bunu-weendaussoowin to mispronounce
chippawaemoowin to stutter
maun-inawaewin to be ungrammatical
naepaud-oomoowin to use language ungrammatically
oomoowin (root) an utterance

ayoowiwin *use; employ; hire*

anookauzoowin to use; to use an implement
anookeewin to hire
aubidji-tchigaewin to use a tool
ayoowiwin to use
inaubidiziwin the use, purpose of someone
weeyoowiwin to make use of another's body, fornicate

B

babeesh-augaewin *travel; wander*

abeed-auzhi-gummaewin to come in this direction by water
babaum-audiziwin to travel abroad; to live here and there
babaum-ishkauwin to travel about by canoe
babeesh-augaewin to wander, travel, roam, meander
bigum-ishkauwin to arrive by canoe
bimi-daubaunikoowin to travel on board a vehicle
bimi-daudigaukoowin to travel, walk on ice
bimi-ishkauwin to travel by canoe
bim-oomigoowin to travel on a horse or other animal
binaushkauwin to travel from place to place; to be nomadic
gawaek-ishkauwin to go directly by canoe
geewitau-igaewin to walk around the perimeter of a point or bay
geewitau-ishkauwin to walk around the perimeter of a point or bay
geewitau-yauzh-gummaewin to walk around the perimeter of a point or bay
goopeewin to go inland
inauzhi-gummaewin to go by water on foot, wade
inikauwin the direction, purpose and pace of one's course, destination
ishkauwin the direction, purpose and pace of one's passage by canoe
ishk-oomoowin to travel upstream
ishkumoowin; umoowin to travel by water
maudjee-ishkauwin to begin setting out by canoe
mindau-ipeewin to go down to the shore
nanau-ishkumoowin to travel upstream
nanau-oomoowin to travel upstream
nanau-umoowin to travel in the middle of a stream going against the current
neebau-ishkauwin to travel at night
neebin-ishkauwin to travel in summer
niminauwae-ishkauwin to launch or to push one's canoe from shore to open waters
oomb-oomigoowin to mount a horse
tibaewae-ishkummaewin to go along the shore; to follow the shore
tikum-ishkauwin to cross a body of water

baegidaewin *burp; belch*

baegidaewin to burp

baekautch-ayauwin *calm; peaceful; serene; tranquil; quiet; pacific (see also* baekaudji-ummoowin*—peace)*

baekautch-ayauwin to be pacific
baekautchigummoowin to be peaceful, serene
bing-ataewin it is still and quiet
bingun to be quiet
bizaun-ataewin it is still
bizaun-ayauwin to be still; to hold still

bizaun-odae-aewin to be peaceful, calm, unruffled
nawautinoowin a calm on a lake
nissutaewin to be calm, without life
wibauh a calm in the forest

baekautchi-igummoowin *silence*
baekaudj-ingumoowin to be tranquil
bingun to be quiet, still

baekaudji-ummoowin *peace; tranquil; serene*
naezhinaunig-aendumoowin to have peace of mind
waunakeewin to lay things to rest

baesho-witumoowin *draw near; approach; advance; get close to; shorten*
baesho-witchigaewin to seek intimacy, familiarity
baesho-witumoowin to draw near
naussik-augaewin to advance upon,; to go to
noondoong-awaugaewin to draw nearer

baesk-ikauwin *slow; tardy*
baedj-itauwin to slow in work
baess-ikauwin to be slow; to be tardy
inikauwin (root) the direction, pace and stage of motion

banaud-aundaewin *stain*
banaud-aundaewin to discolor
nitibut to be marked, black and blue

banaudjiwaewin *violate; despoil; debauch*
banaudjiwaewin to violate, despoil

baug-ishkauwin *swell*
baug-ishkauwin to swell

baup-eengawaeniwin *smile*
baup-eengawaeniwin to smile broadly
eengawaeniwin (root) to change the expression of one's face
gagaundji-eengawaetumoowin to smirk
zhoom-eengawaeniwin to smile wryly; to make a face like a dried grape

baup-iniwaewin *joke; banter; clown*
baup-iniwaewin to clown; to cause laughter
baupishi-itaugooziwin to cause laughter
wauwiyauss-itaugooziwin to banter; to joke
weeshkawi-itaugooziwin to parody; to ridicule

baupiwin *laugh*
baupiwin to laugh

baushk-auwaewin *hatch*
baushk-auwaewin to hatch; to burst out

baushk-idaewin *burst; explode; thunder*
baushk-idaewin to burst; to explode
baushk-inuniwin a sore opens as a blister may break

bautaewin *dry*
baenga-wigaewin to wipe dry
baussae'igaewin to dry by heat or flame
baussauwin to dry by heat or flame
baussimaewin to dry meat
baussitae'igaewin to dry pelts
bautae'igaewin to wring or beat dry
bautaewin to dry
bigikeewaewin to dry and desiccate meat
pissataewin to dry wet clothes
sakazoowin to dehydrate
zheebautae'igaewin to dry pelts

bautauwaewin *tattle; inform; tell on*
bautauwaewin to tell on; to talk another into trouble

bauzh-itchikaugaewin *exceed; surpass*
bauzh-itchikaugaewin to surpass
zaum-itchigaewin to exceed

bauzigob-ozhae'b'inigaewin *scratch; score; scrape*
bauzigob-ozhae'b'inigaewin to scratch
gaushki-gushki-waundjigaewin to clamp in claws and to tear and rip
gaushki-igaewin to scrape

bawaezoowin *sweat; perspire*
baushki-bawaezoowin to break into a sweat

bawaezoowin to sweat
bawautaezoowin to sweat from hard labor, effort
cheesi-geewaewin to perspire, sweat profusely

---

bawaudjigaewin *dream*

bawaudjigaewin to dream
bawaun-aegaewin to seek or conjure a dream
inaubindumoowin (root) to imagine

---

bawaun-iwitumoowin *fail; weaken*

aun-iwitumoowin to fail; to weaken
auno-iwitoowin to fail
bawaun-iwitumoowin to be unable; to fail

---

bawaushaukidiwin *naked; nude; undressed; bare*

bawaushaukidiwin to be nude, unclothed
mitauk-ozhaewin to be naked, bare
mitchi-issinoowin to be bare, unadorned, as is
nebaudj-issinoowin to set in lewd position

---

bawautaewin *fade; lose color; disappear; vanish; dissolve*

aungoshkauwin to fade away
bawautaewin to fade slowly; to lose color
mitug-awaeshkauwin to slip from sight
nauwau-buminaugooziwin to fade from sight
neewautaewin to dissolve, dry up
nikaewaewin to disappear, vanish
ningosh-ikauwin to disappear
wautae-bugauwin to fade as plants and flowers do

---

bawi-aegaewin dust; brush

bawi-aegaewin to brush, sweep down
bunu-igaewin to brush

---

beeg-awigaewin break; destroy; smash; pulverize; crumble; wear down

bauss-ikauwin to crack
beeg-awigaewin to puncture, splinter, smash
beegishkauwin to come apart, fall apart, disintegrate
beegissaewin to collapse
beeg-issikawigaewin to bore, drill
beessi-gugaewin to pulverize
begosh-kaugaewin to break down, make holes
bigishk-augaewin to bust, crash
bigishk-issaewin to bust, smash
book-issaewin to snap, break, fracture
bootaugaewin to pulverize with mortar and pestle
bugundigaewin to thresh, winnow
bunaudji-itchigaewin to wreck, destroy
bunaudji-waewin to cause ruin
bunug-kummik-ishkauwin to crumble
naubeeg-unaeshinoowin to splinter
neessauk-ibidjigaewin to pull down, dismantle
neessauk-ishkaugaewin to cause collapse
weemb-bunug-ishkauwin to cave in

---

beeg-ozhae-binigaewin *maul; rend; gore; shred; gash*

beeg-ozhae-binigaewin to gore, gash
beeg-ozhae-izhigaewin to rip to ribbons

---

beem-igaewin *twist; screw; wind; warp; augur*

beemauk-igaewin twist
beem-inigaewin to coil up; to reel in
ikowau-beegigaewin to wind up
titabaubee-ikoodjigaewin to coil

---

beem-inigaewin *screw; twist; reel*

beem-inigaewin to twist
beemissi-kawauk-iwigaewin to reel
beem-issikawoogaewin to screw
gawaek-awaek-iwigaewin roll up

---

beenissiziwin *numb; insensate; paralysis*

beenissauwin to be paralyzed
beenissiziwin to be numb; to be frozen
cheeby-inaewiziwin to be without sensation
cheeby-itauk-anikaewin to be without feeling in the arm

---

been-itchigaewin *clean; tidy; arrange*

been-itchigaewin to clean
gaezib-issitchigaewin to set in order; to tidy up
gaussee-aukizigaewin to purge, cleanse by fire
na'eekaudjigaewin to clean up

oonatoochigaewin to arrange

beetoo-abeetumoowin *infuse; inspire*

beeto-abeetumoowin to infuse, inspirit, enter into, dwell, imbue, instill

beetoo-ipeeg-ozhaewin *blister*

beetoo-peeg-ozhaewin to have blisters on the body
oombatae-peeg-ozhaewin to break into blisters throughout one's body
oombatae-peewin to break into blisters

beetoo-issitchigaewin *layer; tier*

augaweetoo-issitchigaewin to set in layers
beetoo-issitchigaewin to line; to coat; to overlay; to wrap

begonaegaewin *bore; drill; make a hole; perforate; puncture; corrode; erode*

begonae-boodjigaewin to bore; to drill a hole
begonae-gaewin to drill; to make a hole
begonae-idjeegaewin to puncture
begonae-ishkaugaewin to cause corrosion
begonae-izigaewin to blast a hole
begonae-yaukizigaewin to burn a hole
begoshkauwin to come apart at the seams; to tear; to tatter

begoogaewin *mend; patch; repair*

begoogaewin to patch

begoshiwaewin *beg; ask for; demand; implore; beseech*

aushundaegaewin to ask for alms
begoshiwaewin to ask for charity, alms
begoss-aendjigaewin to beg
begoss-aendumoowin to plead for
nindo't'umaugaewin to ask for, demand

begushk-inutoowin *rot; decay*

banaudiziwin to deteriorate
banaudjiwaewin to corrupt
banaudut it is ruined, wrecked
beeg (root) to break
beegushkinuniwin; bigushk-inuniwin to rot, putrefy
bunaud-itchigaewin to spoil, ruin
neeng-inutiwin to spoil, taint
suttae-ssinoowin it is rancid
wanaudut to spoil, waste
zhae-gummissinoowin; zeewau-gummissin to go sour
zheeg-waussinoowin to wither away

bigumeewin *arrive; reach*

bigum to arrive on foot
bigum-audigaewin to arrive by swimming
bigum-audigauwin to arrive by water or to come ashore by wading from another point
bigum-aushiwin to arrive by flight or by sailing vessel
bigumeewin to arrive
bigum-ishkauwin to arrive by vessel
daeb-akeegaewin to touch the bottom
daeb-inigaewin to catch, reach
dagooshinoowin to arrive; to join up with, become one with
dittumoowin to reach one's goal; to fulfill aspirations
mauwi-dittumoowin to reach, attain, jointly
mizhauwaewin to reach; to get there

bimee-auwissoowin *raise; nurture; breed; rear*

bimee-auwissoowin to rear
koogin-auwissoowin to raise
ondum-ozhaewin to be tied down with children

bimeekaugaewin *tend; care for; manage; supervise; look after*

bimeekaugaewin to look after; to administer; to supervise; to manage; to conduct
gauta-waendjigaewin to care for another in illness to health

bimee-taugaewin *serve; employ; hire*

anoodaugaewin to hire; to employ
anookee-taugaewin to work for
bimee-taugaewin to serve; to attend to

bimidae-winigaewin *lubricate; oil*

bimidae-waubik-inigaewin to lubricate
bimidae-winigaewin to grease
noom-aubik-inigaewin to oil

VERBS

bimi-daubaudjigaewin *drag; pull; haul (see also* week-iweewin*—pull)*

auwidji-daubeewin to haul; to transport
bimi-daubaudjigaewin to draw; to drag

bimi-ishkauwin *travel by canoe, rowboat*

babaum-ishkauwin to travel about by canoe
bigum-ishkauwin to arrive by canoe
bimi-ishkauwin to travel by canoe
gawaek-ishkauwin to go directly by canoe
maudjee-ishkauwin to begin setting out by canoe
niminauwae-ishkauwin to launch or to push one's canoe from shore to open waters
tikum-ishkauwin to cross a body of water

bimoodjigaewin *shoot; fire; launch*

baushkizigaewin to fire a gun
beemoodaukawaewin to do archery
bimoodjigaewin to shoot with bow and arrow
dautigau-igaewin to fire upwards
gagawaed-aukawaewin to practice marksmanship; to fire at a target

binaukawae-igaewin *rake; comb*

binaukawae-igaewin to rake; to comb

bingutaewin *lull; peace*

baekaudji-ingumoowin to have peace, everything at rest, tranquility, serenity
bingun to be quiet
bingutaewin to be quiet, still, silent
naezhinaunig-aendumoowin to have peace of mind
nissutaewin to have dead silence
waunakeewin to lay things to rest

binu-inaugaewin *miss; pine for*

bini-itumoowin to miss hearing
bini-kaugaewin to miss meeting someone
binu-auwaewin to be off the mark
binu-ginaundjigaewin to knock off a perch, footing
binu-inaugaewin to miss the target
maess-inigaewin to miss; to long for; to pine for
pishko-inaugaewin to graze

binu-maungaewin *nip*

bini-kawaetchigaewin to graze someone
binu-maungaewin to intend biting but succeeding in grazing the skin or to bite lightly in play as does a dog

bizhi-ibigaewin *stab; skewer*

bizhi-ibigaewin to stab
piduk-igaewin to skewer

bizhi-naewin *endanger; risk; jeopardize*

bizhi-naewin to experience a close call
neezaun-aewin to represent a danger

bizig-aweewin *rise; raise; elevate; lift*

bizig-aweewin to get up
ishp-auk-issitchigaewin to raise to a height
ishp-ishkauwin to heighten
ishp-ooshkauwin to grow tall (said of grasses)
kooga-umoowin fish rising to surface
onishkauwin to get up, rise from a reclining position
oomb-aukawaewin to brace upwards; to elevate
oomb-ishkauwin to ascend

bizi-waudiziwin *inept; clumsy; awkward; gauche; ungainly; incompetent*

bizi-waudiziwin to be clumsy, awkward
mauzh-eeweewin to be unskilled; to be slovenly
naepautch-itchigaewin to be gauche
pissoog-iziwin to be inept and unlucky
weessik-wiziwin to be incompetent

bizo'g'aeshinoowin *stumble; trip; fall*

adjid-akeessaewin to tumble heels over head
bizo'g'aeshinoowin to tumble
biz-ossaewin to stumble
biz-ozid-aeshinoowin to trip
chacheenga-waessaewin to fall face down
peend-issaewin to fall in
pikit-aeshinoowin to trip, dash one's foot against an obstruction
pitauk-ozid-aeshinoowin to dash one's foot
zhaub-issaewin to fall through

bizung-waub-issaewin *blink*

bizung-waub-issaewin to blink

boodaudjigaewin *blow*

boodaudjigaewin to blow; to blow a horn, flute

boodauk-awaessaewin *plunge, fall in*

boodauk-awaessaewin to fall in water
piko-ipeewin to enter water

boodaukawaewin *dip; dunk; immerse*

boodaukawaewin to dunk, immerse
dawaushiwin to fall through ice
gindau-ipeeg-inigaewin to immerse
ispo-quae-issaewin head completely submerged
nanitigaub-uminaugaewin to launch
nindo-ipeeg-inigaewin to dip into
piko-ipee-issaewin to fall into water

boodawaewin *enkindle; set fire to*

boodoowaewin to start a cooking or warming fire
cheecheek-kizhaegaewin to stoke
niki-zhaegaewin to stoke
pissikauk-inaendjigaewin to set a fire

boodji-awaewin *poke; jab; prod; jog*

boodji-awaewin to poke, jab with a finger or stick
took-inaugaewin to poke
took-inidjeesh-awigaewin to poke, jab, prod, jog

boogidiwin *fart*

boogidiwin to fart
oombauzimaug-itchigaewin to create a stink
zaebawaen-igaewin to deflate, pass gas

book-issaewin *break; fracture*

bauss-ikauwin to crack
beeg-awigaewin to puncture; to splinter; to smash
beegishkauwin to come apart; to fall apart; to disintegrate
beegissaewin to collapse
beeg-issikawigaewin to bore, drill
beessi-gugaewin to pulverize
begosh-kaugaewin to break down, make holes
bigishk-augaewin to bust; to crash
bigishk-issaewin to bust; to smash
book-issaewin to snap; to break; to fracture
bootaugaewin to pulverize with mortar and pestle
bugundigaewin to thresh, winnow
bunaudji-itchigaewin to wreck, destroy
bunaudji-waewin to cause ruin
bunug-kummik-ishkauwin to crumble
naubeeg-unaeshinoowin to splinter
neessauk-ibidjigaewin to pull down; to dismantle
neessauk-ishkaugaewin to cause collapse
weemb-bunug-ishkauwin to cave in

boon-aendjigaewin *pardon; absolve; excuse; forgive*

boon-aendjigaewin to absolve
boonigidaetumoowin to excuse; to forgive

booneewin *land; alight; go ashore; beach; dock*

agawautau-igaewin to come out of the water
agawau-umoowin to go ashore
boon-akeessaewin to plunge and come to rest on the earth
booneewin to land as a bird
gawau-issitchigaewin to unload a vessel
gawau-oodoon-igaewin to draw a vessel ashore
gawautauwin to come out of the water
naudigaumaewin to paddle, row, go ashore

boonimoowin *lay an egg*

abi-naundumoowin to lay an egg
boon-imoowin to lay an egg; to quit cackling once an egg has been deposited

boon-kundjigaewin *anchor; hold down; ballast*

boon-kundjigaewin to anchor; to affix to one place
sidawae-ishkoodjigaewin to ballast

boo-poodaudjeesh-kawigaewin *inflate*

boo-poodaudjeesh-kawigaewin to inflate, fill with air

VERBS

moozh-inaebawaewin to fill; to pack; to stuff; to swell; to breathe life into; to infuse

booz-aundaewin *darken; dark*

boozaundaewin to be of dark shade, hue
makatae-waussoowin to be darkly tanned
nikeewigut dark
tibikut night
weeshkotae-ozhaewin to have dark skin
weessaukotae-waussoowin to be half-burned

booz-itaussoowin *load; store; stock*

booz-itaussoowin to put on board
taussoowin to heap; to amass; to store; to stock

booziwin *board; get on*

booziwin to get on board

bugwoon-wiziwin *backward; unlearned; slow; undeveloped*

bugwoon-wiziwin to be unlearned, backward

bunug-koodjigaewin *peel; pare; skin*

bizhugauk-koobidjigaewin to debark trees
bizhug-eegimaewin to skin an animal
bizhug-ibinigaewin to skin
bunug-koodjigaewin to pare; to peel; to skin

C

chaek-inaewin *run aground; ground*

agawauy-aussinoowin to be blown ashore or aground
chaek-ipidaewin to run aground onto a shoal
chaek-issaewin to run aground involuntarily

chauchaumoowin *sneeze*

chauchaumoowin to sneeze
zeenis-keegoomaewin to have a snotty nose
zeezikawi-idjaunaewin to have a running nose

chaug-boodaewin *wear out; erode*

chaug-boodaewin to erode

cheebaukawaewin *cook*

abawautigaewin to warm up
aboomin-aetigaewin to roast corn
anook-oohnzaekawaewin to tenderize; to cook to tenderness
apaubawaewin to admix; to flavor; to season
aubawaewin to roast
baushki-meen-issigaewin to make jams, preserves, jellies
bautae-zigaewin to dry meat, flesh
beegi-waezigaewin to make maple toffee
boodaukawaewin to put in water
bootaugaewin to pulverize corn to a powder
bunug-zigaewin to cook corn; to prepare corn
cheebaukawaewin to cook; Feast of the Ghosts
dagoonigaewin to blend; to add ingredients
gabaushingaewin to boil
gaboozoowin to broil; to cook in a closed vessel
gausk-izigaewin to smoke meat, flesh
gazhi-zaekawaewin to warm up food
geezh-oohnzaekawaewin to finish cooking
gidjik-nawaewaezigaewin to cook corn till kernels come off
inoohnzaekawaewin the manner of cooking
inuk-idoodaewin to cook to a stage or state
mino-daewin to cook well to doneness
mino-oohnzaekawaewin to cook well to doneness
naboop-eekaewin to make soup
namaetchigaewin to smoke meat
ningo-aubawaewin to bake in closed container or in sand
ningo-waubauwae-tchigaewin to boil down; to dissolve
oohnzaekawaewin (root) to steam, scald, scour
oombidjeezigaewin to make and bake bread
oonau-zigaewin to smoke meat
pikwae-izhigun-ikaewin to bake bread
sautae-tchigaewin to fry
zaug-buwaun-aezigaewin to barbecue
zaussikookawaewin to fry

cheeby-itautchi-iziwin *cramp*

cheeby-itautchi-iziwin to suffer a cramp, stiffness

nibo-winaetch-iziwin to be paralyzed

cheecheebeewin *shiver; twitch*

cheecheek-ozhae-ishkauwin to twitch
giniskaw-ozhae-ishkauwin to twitch
naning-aukitchiwin to shiver from the cold

cheechee-gumikawaewin *chew; gnaw*

cheechee-gumikawaewin to gnaw
zhaushau-gumikawaewin to chew

cheegi-nugaek-iwigaewin *strip; peel*

baug-aukawigaewin to pound repeatedly until the fibers or layers are loosened
bunugaek-ibidjigaewin to peel off bark
cheegi-nugaek-iwigaewin to strip off bark

cheemaewin *paddle; row*

cheemaewin to paddle
geewitau-oomoowin to go, paddle around a point, island
inuk-izhoowaewin (root) to row, propel a boat
naneema-umoowin to paddle upstream

cheengaewin *kiss*

cheengaewin kiss
daungi-doon-aeshinoowin touch lips
zigi-doon-aeshinoowin to engage in a long passionate kiss
zoob-daeniniw-taudiwin French kiss

cheeng-initauwin *kneel*

cheeng-initauwin to kneel
cheeng-inubiwin to sit on one's knees

cheeshiziwin *bruise; contusion; scar*

cheeshiziwin to have, suffer bruises, abrasions
maukiziwin to have a scar
nitibiziwin to have a contusion

cheess-akeewin *shake; tremble; spasm; quake; twitch; jiggle*

cheebab-inigoowin to convulse, spasm
cheecheeb-ibinigaewin to shake, wiggle, jiggle
cheecheebi-kaud-aeniwin to swing a leg back and forth
cheess-akeewin vibrate; to cause the earth to tremble
kooshkawaek-itumoowin to pound, rumble, pitch
mamig-issaewin to shake, tremble
mamig-issutchigaewin to shake; to blend, churn
naning-ishkauwin to shake
odaup-ibab-inigoowin to have spasms
odaupin-issaewin to have spasms; to twitch
paupauwae-igaewin to shake out dust
waewaeb-quaeniwin to nod the head

cheessimoob-inigaewin *pinch*

cheessimoob-inigaewin to pinch

cheess-ingaewin *sting*

cheess-ingaewin to sting as a bee
weessi-ginaeziwin smart, burn from a sting

D

daeb-inaewiziwin *right; entitle; deserve; merit; aspire to*

daeb-inaewiziwin to be entitled to necessities of life—food, clothing, shelter, etc.
gawaek-itchigaewin to do things right
meeyoow-issitchigaewin to put things in order and in place
oondiziwin to aspire to; to covet

daeb-indoowaewin *promise; vow; give one's word; undertake; vouch*

daeb-indoowaewin vouch
wau-weendumaugaewin to promise; to give one's word

dae'b'ingaewin *true; right; correct*

dae'b'awaewin to tell what one knows according to his/her perception and according to one's fluency; to have the highest degree of accuracy; to be right, correct; to have truth
dae'b'ingaewin to tell the truth about someone
gawaek it is true, right, correct, accurate
gayuk it is true, right, correct, accurate

daeb-ibinigaewin *capture; catch; seize; hold; lay hands on*

daeb-ibinigaewin to catch; to hold

daeb-waetumoowin *believe*

baukau-tumaewin to have faith in revelation
baukau-tumoowin to trust in what one hears
dae'b'waetumoowin to believe

daess-inigaewin *welcome*

daess-inigaewin to welcome

daewiziwin *ache; pain; throb*

daewi-quaewin to have a headache

dago-waukawigaewin *nail; fasten; stick; attach; clamp; affix; brace*

agawaub-ikigaewin to stick, attach
ashi-shood-aukawigaewin to fasten to; to press
aussi-waukawigaewin to nail something to
dago-waukawigaewin to nail something onto; to nail an extra board or other fixture
gindjig-aukawigaewin to clamp down
mindjim-aukawigaewin clamp, nail down
zig-aukawigaewin to nail, fasten

dago-weendjigaewin *vouch; mention*

daebawae-audjimoowin to verify; to substantiate
daebindoowaewin to swear to
dago-weendjigaewin to vouch
dago-weendjigaewin to include the name or names of others in conversation, discussion; to implicate
dago-weendumaewin to include the name or names of others in conversation, discussion

daub-inaenimoowin *please; soothe; placate; satisfy; gratify*

daeb-aenimoowin contentment, satisfaction, gratification
daebig-aenimoowin contentment, satisfaction, gratification
gizhautchitoowin to placate, satisfy
mino-inaendumitaugaewin to satisfy, gratify, cheer
mino-nawaetchigaewin to appease, please, soothe, mollify

daudjigookaewin *troll*

daudjigookaewin to troll

daung-inigaewin *touch; feel; explore*

daung-inigaewin to touch, feel
dautaung-akee-issitchigaewin to sound the depth, bottom
gagawaed-idjeenigaewin to explore, feel the body of another
gagawaed-inigaewin to test the weight, texture
nindo-idjeenigaewin to grope for, feel around
took-inigaewin to nudge

daupinigaewin *take; adopt; usurp; welcome; accept*

daupinigaewin to take; to take up
kidisk-inumaugaewin to snatch; to seize; to take by force
kiti-nimaudizoowin to take for oneself; to usurp
kitin-imaugaewin to take from
maudjee-atchigaewin to take with
odaes-inigaewin to welcome; to take into one's heart
pitchi-nimaugaewin to take by mistake
waungoomaewin to adopt a child

dauwingaewin *borrow*

dauwingaewin to borrow

dibaendaussoowin *own; have; possess*

dae'b'issaewin to have enough; to have no need for more
danee-igaewin to own; to add to one's possessions, worth, wealth; to improve, increase one's possessions
dibaendaussoowin to own, possess, have, have claim
dibaendjigaewin to own, possess, have, have claim
minaeziwin to need; to be short of; to need and want more
waundiziwin to have more than enough; to

have a surplus; to have an abundance; to be rich, wealthy, fortunate

diminaegaewin *overtake*

diminae-igaewin to catch up to
kab-ikaugaewin to overtake and pass
oditau-oonaugaewin to catch up to someone by canoe

dittumoowin *achieve; accomplish; fulfill; carry or bring about; realize*

dittumoowin to reach or fulfill a goal, a dream
kishkitum-auzoowin to gain, achieve, earn, reap for oneself

doodumoowin *do (*see also anookeewin; izhitchigaewin—*act, performance)*

anookeewn to hunt, fish, harvest; to draw sustenance from the earth
dazhee-kaewin to dabble, putter
doodumoowin to do, perform; to do with purpose
indiwin to perform a culpable act, deed
izheewin the capacity and style of performance
izhi-tawauwin to act out of belief, conviction
izhi-tchigaewin to do something in a particular manner
matchi-izhi-itchigaewin to do evil, harm, wrong
mino-itchigaewin to perform well; to do a good deed

dootoossinoowin *thicken; pile on; add to; curdle; congeal*

dootoossinoowin to thicken, curdle
dootoo-waugumm-issitchigaewin to congeal
kupug-issitchigaewin to pile on, heap
kupug-itchigaewin to make thick

dubaubee-ishkoodjigaewin *weigh*

dubaubee-ishkoodjigaewin to weigh
good-inigaewin to weigh freehand, guess the weight of

dubauk-inigaewin *judge; assess; evaluate*

dibauk-inigaewin; dubauk-inigaewin to judge, evaluate, assess

dubugaewin *pay; compensate; reward; remunerate; originally measure*

dubugaewin to pay; to measure
geezheekauzoowin to retire a debt

duminoowin *play; amuse; frolic; gambol; carouse; cavort*

ataugaewin to play for stakes, contest
atawaugaewin to play for stakes, contest
dazhee-kaewin to play or to preoccupy oneself at something in one place
duminoowin to play; to pretend; to amuse oneself
geewaupeewin to cavort
geewiniziwin to cavort; to frolic; to gambol; to caper
oombu-kummikiziwin to play uproariously; to carouse

E

eengawaewin *face; facial expressions*

abeedj-eengawaeshinoowin to face in this direction
baup-eengawaeniwin to grin; to smirk
inauss-eengawaetumoowin face to face
inaussim-eengawaetaudiwin face to face
mauzh-eengawaeniwin to glower; to frown
neessik-eengawaeniwin to grimace
nishkaudjee-eengawaeniwin to scowl

eenoowin *many; plentiful; numerous*

bauteenoowuk they are numerous
bauteenut there is much
eenowin refers to numbers
mizheenoowuk they are plentiful, rife
mizheenut there is more than enough
neebinut plenty; abundance
zaumeenoowuk there are too many
zaumeenut there is an overabundance

G

gabauk-iwigaewin *close; shut; blanket; enclose; cover; seal; secure*

agawoon-aubishkoodaewin to weigh down

VERBS

shut, to place a weight on a cover or lid to keep it in place
aud-aukawigaewin to shut
bidub-aubiwin to close eyes
bidubau-bugooneewin the act of flowers closing
gab-aukawigaewin to shut
gabo-igaewin to cover with a sheet, shroud
gawo-ozhaewin to cover with blanket
kishkaub-ikigaewin to close tightly
kishkee-waukawigaewin to seal
mitchi-kun aukikaewin to erect a fence
pidug-inugaewin to cover with blanket; to cover something; to cover over for concealment

---

gabauwin *get off; disembark; debark*

gabauwin to get off a boat, vehicle

---

gabi-naewaeb-inigaewin *choke; strangle*

gabi-naewaeb-inigaewin to choke; to strangle
nae-goondjigaewin to gag
pikawae-nishkaugoowin to hack

---

gabis-gazheewin *constipation*

gabiss-gazheewin to be constipated

---

gabishk-kaugaewin *hinder; impede; block; foil; obstruct; interrupt; meddle*

awo-ayaek-itautchigaewin to weary someone
gabish-kaugaewin to impede
gageeb-ishkaugaewin to be in someone's way
kishkidauk-augaewin to block someone's passage
neessi-ikaugaewin to be in the way
ningau-ishkaugaewin to stand in someone's way
wayaegitautchigaewin to meddle

---

gabo-inaumoowin *smother; suffocate*

gabo-inaumizoowin to be overcome by smoke
gabo-inaumoowin to suffocate

---

gaeshi-waubeeg-inigaewin *relax; slacken*

gaeshi-waubeeg-inigaewin to loosen a line, rope
kagee-ozhae-wizeewaewin limber

---

gaessik-waubungaewin *notice*

gaessik-waubingaewin catch sight of; glimpse
mukwo-waubingaewin to behold

---

gaezi-beeg-inigaewin *fold; pleat; crease; plait; bend*

auhnz-umawaeg-eenigaewin to fold as a loincloth
bidubau-bugooneewin petals folding or closing
gaezi-baubeeg-inigaewin to wind up and coil a rope, string
gaezi-beeg-inigaewin to fold neatly for storage
naun-abawaeg-eenigaewin to fold in half
nubug-waeg-inigaewin to flatten textiles, fabrics (see also *kaukau-kummikaewin, nubug-ishkoodjigaewin,* and *zhingu-kummik-igaewin*—flatten)
nubug-waungaewin to fold wings
pissikeeg-inigaewin to fold; to pleat
pissiki-taenigaewin to fold as a birch bark container

---

gagaundji-iwaewin *tease; excite; arouse; bedevil; provoke; taunt*

aubee-zoongaewin to ridicule; to scorn; to slander
aushi-waewin to tantalize; to arouse; to excite
bae-waendjigaewin to have little confidence in
baup-inoodjigaewin to ridicule; to make fun of
cheesi-waewin to tease, tantalize a child
gagaundji-waewin to pester; to annoy
gaund-aupiwin to laugh at
goopiz-oongaewin to smear; to revile
maunaudj-aungaewin to be contemptuous
meekindjiwaewin to taunt; to provoke; to incite; to bedevil
migooshkauz-oongaewin to upset with disturbing accounts
nanae-beegizhi-oongaewin to disparage; to belittle; to calumniate
nanaundiko-itaugooziwin sarcasm, provocation, sneering

nimiskaugaewin to insult with gestures, motions; to give the finger to; to thumb one's nose at
nishi-baupin-oodjigaewin to deride, making a laughing stock of
oombauz-oongaewin to incite; to rouse
pishigawau-zoongaewin to slight; to belittle
pissi-taugooziwin to provoke by tone and/or tenor of language and voice
pugindjiwaewin to impute something to; to imply
pugi-zoongaewin insinuate; intimate
zaessaemi-aungaewin to reduce to tears by taunts
zhaugooz-oongaewin to out-talk, out-argue; to best in argument

---

gagauz-oongaewin *advise; counsel; advocate; recommend; exhort; guide; urge; exemplify*

aush-ingaewin to counsel to do evil; to entice; to seduce; to beguile
ausk-aungaewin to second; to abet; to back; to support
gagauz-oongaewin to advise; to advocate; to exhort; to urge
gaugeetaudjimootaudiwin consult, advise
geek-ingaewin to advise; to counsel
kikinoowaezh-ingaewin to guide; to show the way; to exemplify

---

gagawae-dabaendjigaewin *tempt; test*

cheesh-ingaewin to tease a child
gagawae-dabaendjigaewin to tempt; to test; to try
oombush-ingaewin to arouse; to incite

---

gagawaed-akeegaewin *measure or gauge depth; sound*

gagawaed-akeegaewin to sound depth; to measure depth

---

gagawaediwaewin *ask; query; question; inquire*

gagawaediwaewin to ask a question; to test someone's knowledge

---

gagawaedji-kuzhiwaewin *race*

gagawaedji-kundawaewin to race; to contest
gagawaedji-kuzhiwaewin to race; to contest

---

gageeb-eengawaewin *blind; impaired vision*

biziniwin to have a mote in the eye that impairs sight
biz-waubiwin to have blurred vision
gageeb-eengawaewin to be blind, sightless
mauz-aub-indumoowin to have fuzzy vision
shee-waussoowin to be dazzled
zaussi-geengawae-waussoowin to be snow blind

---

gageeb-inuquaewin *mute; speechless; dumb; muzzle*

gageeb-ishaewin to be mute

---

gageeb-ishkaugaewin *check; block; hinder*

gageeb-ishkaugaewin to block; to distract
inushkawae-itchigaewin to hinder; to harry; to interfere

---

gageeb-itaewin *deaf; impaired hearing*

gageeb-ishaewin to be deaf
gageeb-itaewin to be inattentive

---

gageed-waewidumoowin *lament; keen; wail*

gageed-waedaemoowin to wail
gageed-waewidumoowin to keen

---

gageetau-igaewin *pull out; extract*

gageet-igigaewin to extract
geetchi-koobitchigaewin to undo; to take off, out
maumi-koobitchigaewin to pull off
weekoozau-peewin to suck out

---

gagunugidjee-binigaewin *tickle*

gagunugidjee-binigaewin to tickle
gagunug-ozhae-binigaewin to tickle

---

gauboowin *stand*

aussiwauk-gauboowiwin to lean on something while standing
cheessi-gauboowiwin to stand on tiptoe
naunauw-itauwin to stoop, bend over while standing
neebidae-gauboowiwin to stand in a row, line

VERBS

neeboowin manner of standing
piduk-ishinoowin to stand as planted, fixed
piduk-izoowin to stand as planted, fixed, erected

gaud-auwissoowin *hide; conceal; secrete*
gaud-auwissoowin to hide, conceal something
gaudjigaewin to hide; to conceal; to secrete
gauzoowin to hide, conceal one's self

gaukikishkauwin *tear; rip; unstitch*
aub-izhigaewin to unseam
cheega-aumiquaegaugaewin to gouge
daushk-ibidjigaewin to tear along the grain or in half
daut-issaewin to rip asunder
gaukikishkauwin to come apart at the seams; to rip
gaukikishk-izhigaewin to rip; to unstitch
geeshk-ibidjigaewin to tear
geeshk-issaewin to tear or rip spontaneously
ibidjigaewin (root) the manner and form of pulling something apart, asunder
kaukikishk-ibidjigaewin to unstitch

gaund-inigaewin *push; shove; propel*
gaund-akeegaewin to pole along
gaund-inigaewin to push
gaund-issutchigaewin to push, shove suddenly, violently
gaundji-waebinigaewin to push; to shove
zhaub-inigaewin to push through

gaundissi-kummeewin *bolt; dash; make a sudden break*
gaundissi-kummeewin to bolt
waebeewin to run from; to flee

gaushkau-igaewin *scour; scrape; scrub*
cheeshaukawae-igaewin scrape and scrub; to clear away
cheeshau-ozhae-gaewin to scrape skin off
gaushkau-igaewin to scrape
gaushkaush-imaegaewin to scale fish
gaushkaushki-igaewin to scrape
mauda-igaewin to scrub

gaushki-bauzoowin *shave*
gaushki-bauzoowin to shave

gausk-eewaewin *croak; rasp*
gauska-waewidumoowin to rasp
gausk-eewaewin to speak with a hoarse voice

gausk-inoozoowin *hush; quiet; whisper*
baekaudumoowin to speak in hushed tones
gausk-inoozoowin whisper

gaussee-igaewin *erase; wipe out; expunge; wipe; delete*
bawish-kumoowin to cover up tracks
beegozi-nabeegaewin to destroy writing
gaussee-ibeegaewin to erase; to wipe out
gaussee-igaewin to dust; to wipe

gauta-waetchigaewin *nurse; care for; give medical care*
gautawaetchigaewin to tend to; to administer care and medication

gauwaewin *envy; jealousy*
gauwaewin to be jealous of a rival, real or imagined
gizhau-waendjigaewin envious, covetous of another's love or possessions
zhee-waubumaewin jealous and envious; to look on with envy, jealousy

gawauk-idoodaewin *stale*
gawauk-aukidoodaewin stale and crisp
gawauk-idoodaewin stale and crisp

gawaushkawae-ssitchigaewin *bounce; bob; spring*
gawaushkawae-ssitchigaewin to bounce
nanik-issaewin to bob up and down in water

gawaushkin-itaugaewin *attack; assault; onslaught*
gawaushkin-itaugaewin to leap on
kawaun-ootawaugaewin to bring to bay; to corner
mawi-inaegaewin to charge; to cause a victim to cry

mookee-taugaewin to attack from an ambush

gawaushkiniwin *jump; leap; bounce; rebound*

gawaushk-awaessinoowin to bounce; to rebound
gawaushkiniwin to jump; to leap
geep-agawaushkiniwin to cavort; to jump down
kooga-umoowin fish jumping for flies

gawautaewin *shade; shadow*

bawautae-ishimoowin to cast a shadow
bawautae-tchigaewin to shadow
gawautaewin to shadow; to shade

gawau-widaussoowin *unload*

gawau-widaussoowin to unload
gawauwin-aussoowin to unload

gaweeniwi-inaendumoowin *perplex; befuddle; bewilder; puzzle*

gaweeniwi-doodumoowin to fail to know what to do
gaweeniwi-inaendumoowin to be undecided; to be of several minds

gaween-oomaugaewin *desire; long for; want; aspire to*

gaween-oomaugaewin to pine for; to miss
misso-waendjigaewin to covet; to aspire
nindo-waendumoowin to want

gaweeshkizhiwin *whistle*

gaweeshkizhiwin to whistle
seeseenga-waewaewin to whine; to whir

gawishimoowin *lay; lie down*

gawishimoowin to go to bed; to settle down; to fast and to seek dream or vision
inishimoowin (root) position and angle of lying down

gawo-aushiwin *blow down*

gawo-aushiwin blown down by the wind

gawo-igaewin *chop; hew; cut down; fell*

dawau-igaewin to clear; to make an opening
gawogaewin to fell
geeshkau-gawogaewin to hew; to chop; to cut down
geeshkau-kawaewin to hew, fell trees
minissaewin to cut wood
pissa'igaewin to cut cedar splints

gawo-inaundumoowin *starve*

gawo-inaundumoowin to collapse from hunger

gazee-ipeeg inigaewin *wash*

gazee-ipeeg-inigaewin to wash; to cleanse
gazee-suguk-aewin to wash, mop, clean the floor

gazee-ipeeg-ozhaewin *bathe*

gazee-ipeeg-ozhaewin to wash; to bathe

gazheebaub-issaewin *whirl; spin; twirl; turn*

aubumoo-waunimut a whirlwind, cyclone, twister
aubumoo-widjiwun a whirlpool
aubumoo-witumoowin to spin around
gazheebaub-issaewin to whirl
gazheebaub-waebinigaewin to crank
gazheebau-pidaewin to spin

gazheebeewin *itch*

gazheebeewin to itch
gazheeb-ozhaewin to itch somewhere on the body; to have scabies

gazheek-umoowin *roar*

gazheek-umoowin roar

geegoohn-kaewin *fish; angle; seine; trawl; spear*

agawauwaewin to spear fish
cheecheeb-inaubeewin to jig fish through ice
gawaub-inauwin to seine
geegoohn-kaewin to fish (a general term)
goondum-oodjigaewin to angle
naud-aubee-iginigaewin to draw in lines; to go lift lines
naud-suppeewin to lift nets
pagid-aubee-iginigaewin to release a line; to let down a line

VERBS

pagid-iwauwin to set nets
peendunaugaewin to net fish
pishi-ibin-augaewin to fail to land a fish
pitchi-ibin-augaewin to hook a fish accidentally
shum-oodjigaewin to bait a hook; to set a bait
waewaeb-inaubeewin to angle
waussi-waugaewin to fish by torchlight

---

gee-iwaewin *avoid; evade; shun; elude; avert; flee*

---

gee-'iwaewin to evade; to elude; to escape
medakawaewin to evade
meedaugawae-ishtaugaewin to avoid meeting; to shun
waem-autaugaewin to avoid

---

geekaundiwin *quarrel; squabble*

---

auzhidaendiwin to talk back; to squabble
geekaundiwin to quarrel
geekau-widumoowin to dress down; to castigate; to call down; to denounce

---

geekee-pungooshiwin *doze*

---

geekee-pungooshiwin to drowse; to doze

---

geekittoowin *talk; chat; converse; discuss*

---

dago-weendjigaewin to include, implicate, name another person in one's discussion; to testify, swear, avow, vouch for
dazh-ingaewin to gossip
inaudjimoowin (root) the character, tone, nature, purpose, flavor of talk
inaunigidoonoowin to talk
inaun-kittoonoowin to talk
kittoowin (root) to utter

---

geemeewin *escape; flee; make off; slip away; break free*

---

gee'iwigaewin slip away (from)
geemeewin sneak away; make off unnoticed
geetauk-aweewin to break free from someone's grasp
gidisk-eewaewin break free as from bondage
waebeewin run off; bolt away

---

geemootaugaewin *scout; spy; sneak; observe; survey*

---

geem-ootaugaewin to spy on; to sneak
nindo-waetchigaewin to scout; to seek signs

---

geeshk-ikauwin *rip; tear; come loose*

---

gau-kik-ishkauwin to come loose; to rip
geeshk-ikauwin to tear

---

geeshk-izhigaewin *cut*

---

babeeto-ozhae-igaewin to fillet; to skin
binizh-imaegaewin to cut off a slice; to shear
gaussi-koodjigaewin to cut into small pieces, slice thinly, etc.
geen-koodjigaewin to cut to the point
geeshkauni-quae-izhigaewin to cut hair
geeshk-izhigaewin to cut
geetchi-kunae-izhigaewin to cut meat from a bone
gidizh-igaewin to cut or trim
gizhoowid-izoowin to cut one's self accidentally
ini-zhigaewin (root) the style and manner of cutting
in-ozhae-igaewin to cut body, flesh
ishko-izhigaewin to leave remnants
kidau-weeyoowi-igunaewin; kidau-weegunaegaewin to fillet
mandjidaewin to cut brush, boughs
mazin-beeg-kookidjigaewin to carve designs
mino-ishko-zawaewin to cut reeds
mitchi-kunae-izhigaewin to cut to the bone
moozhaegaewin; mizheegaewin to cut clear, as of trees, hay, like a moose
moozhiwaewin to cut hair
naunau-izhigaewin to cut, divide, separate
piti-izhigaewin to cut, slice accidentally
pukwae-ozhigaewin to slice
waugae-kawaegaewin to tap maple trees
weenan-itchigaewin to quarter an animal at site of kill
zaugee-kawaegaewin to tap maple trees

---

geeshp-inudjigaewin *buy; purchase; acquire*

---

geeshp-inudjigaewin to buy, purchase
mazinigaewin to buy on credit; to charge
nipu-zinugaewin to pawn

---

geessaud-aendumoowin *regret; rue; repent; mourn*

---

geessau'd'aendumoowin to regret
matchi-nawaeziwin to experience discontent, displeasure; to go into a snit
mindaunauwaewin final farewell, a sadness

---

geetau-kiwitchigaewin *save; remove from danger; leave; set aside (see also* sundjigoowin—*store)*

geeta-kiwitchigaewin to remove from danger to safety
geeta-witchigaewin to remove from danger to safety; to save
ishko-issaewin left over, residue
ishkoon-imaugaewin put away for others
naegautch-itchigaewin thrift
naekautchi-itchigaewin to practice thrift
shingo-biniwaewin to save from fire or death
ziguk-inigaewin to save; to set aside; to store away

---

geetchi-kooniyaewin *disrobe; unclothe; shed clothing; divest*

geessi-kooniyaewin to disrobe; to take off garments
geetcheewin to take off shoes and socks
geetchi-kooniyaewin to disrobe; to take off garments
inukooniyaewaewin (root) manner and quality of clothing

---

geewaut-issutchigaewin *trick; outwit*

geewaut-issutchigaewin to trick; to fool
wiyaezh-ingaewin to deceive

---

geewi-naudiziwin *crazy; demented; nuts; lunacy*

geewi-naudiziwin to be crazy, without sense

---

geewin-imoowin *lie; fib; deceive; mislead; cheat; cozen*

awiyaezh-ingaewin to deceive
awo-yaezh-oongaewin to deceive
geen-iwishkeewin to lie; to deceive; to mislead
geewin-imoowin to lie; to talk in circles
neezhi-yaendjigaewin to deceive; to betray; to mislead; to speak with two meanings

---

geewi-ossaewin *hunt*

geewi-ossaewin to hunt deer who circle back to point where they were perceived
iwaewin (root) to seek, track down, and flush
mukwo-iwaewin to hunt bear
nindo-kanawaeyautchigaewin to look for evidence of the presence of animals
nindo-kawaetchigaewin to seek and follow tracks
nindo-waendjigaewin to hunt following one's intuition
nindo-waetchigaewin to hunt following one's intuition
nindo-wautoowin to scare up game as with dogs
nookitumoowin to hunt beaver
wauwaushkaesh-eewaewin to hunt deer

---

geewish-quaewin *dizzy*

geewish-quaewin to be dizzy

---

geewitau-ishkaugaewin *surround*

geewitau-ishkaugaewin to surround

---

geewitau-ishkauwin *circle; coil; twist; spiral*

geewitau-ishkauwin to go around; to circumnavigate
pizhibaub-eeshkauwin to twist; to wrap; to spiral
titibaub-eeshkauwin to coil; to roll; to twist
wauwiyau-ishkumoowin to walk around

---

geezhee-tauwin *end; finish; terminate; conclude; stop*

boon-itauwin to quit
geezhee-tauwin to finish what one started
geezhi-itchigaewin to finish a specific project
ishkawae-ssinoowin something comes to an end
ishkawau-tauwin to finish, end permanently
nawau-tauwin to suspend work or some other endeavor, take a break
ningau-gaewin to brake
noog-ishkauwin to stop one's travel

---

geezh-igiwin *mature*

bizis-kaudiziwin to mature; to be free
geezh-igiwin to attain full growth

meeniwun to mature; to ripen
netau-wigiwin to attain full growth, strength, etc.

gimiwunoowin *rain*

abeedji-ipeessauwin the rain is coming
autae-ipeessauwin the rain is over
bigum-ipeessauwin to bring rain
boon-ipeessauwin the rain is over
gimiwun to rain
ipeessauwin (root) character, quality, density of rainfall

gimoodiwin *steal; rob; pilfer*

gimoodiwin to steal; to take by stealth
zhee-boodjigaewin to draw away; to entice; to steal away (from)

ginae-waubindumoowin *guess; estimate; reckon*

dubub-aubindumaewin to estimate
ginae-waubindumoowin to size up, from sight

gindaussoowin *read*

anami-aetchigaewin to read
gindaussoowin to read

ginoo-aundizoowin *health; well-being; fit; sound*

gino-aundiziwin good health, well, fit
mino-mindjiwowin to feel fit, sprightly, good, in fine form

ginoo-wauk-issitchigaewin *extend; lengthen; stretch; continue*

aunikae-issitchigaewin extend; add to
ginoo-wauk-issitchigaewin lengthen; extend
inaukumootchigaewin the angle, bearing, direction and setting, alignment of foundation, walls, beams, joists, etc.
naubauk-issitchigaewin attach
zhaugawaugoowin elongate
zheesheeb-inigaewin stretch

ginoo-weendum-autchigaewin *deepen*

gino-weendum-autchigaewin to deepen
teemi-itchigaewin to go deeper

gizhaud-igaewin *guard; safeguard; defend; shield*

gizhaud-igaewin to guard; to babysit
iko-waubindumoowin to watch; watch out; scout
kinokaewin stand watch; guard as a dog
kipeewau-oossoowin to side with; to take up children's side; to cause

gizhaudiziwin *kind; generous*

gizhaudiziwin to be kind, generous, warm
mino-odae-aewin to have goodness of heart

gizhizigaewin *heat*

abizigaewin to warm, heat
aubawauwin to become mild
gazhidaewin warmth, heat
gazhi-naumidaewin sultry, humid, close
gizhautaewin a hot day

gizikaewin *take flight; take off*

gizikaewin to take flight
oombi-pizoowin to fly up

goob-izoowin *bind; bandage*

goob-idjigaewin to bandage
goob-izoowin to bandage; to be bandaged
zeen-zoopizoowin to be swathed; to be bandaged

googeewin *dive*

googeewin to dive

goondaewin *float; drift*

goomoowin to float
goondaewin to float
goondjinoowin to float
taetaeb-goondaewin to rock gently while afloat

goondjigaewin *swallow*

goon-aendjigaewin to keep in the mouth
goondjigaewin to swallow
ishkumoowin (root) to put in the mouth

goonub-issaewin *upset; overturn; capsize; tip over; upend*

aubood-issaewin to pitch over

goonub-issaewin to tip over
kootig-issaewin to keel over

goonugauwin *snow*

aungo-wadauneewin to cover a tree, trees with snow
goon (root) the quality, character, nature, texture of snow
goonugauwin (root) the quality, character, nature, texture of snow
ipoowin (root) the quality, character, nature, texture of snowfall
ningo-wadaunee to cover a tree, trees with snow
onaubunu-goonugauwin to harden snow (crust)
oombaushk-inaewin to swirl, whirl, raise snow by the wind
pizhi-baubeewoon to fly in circles
shakau-goonugauwin wet snowfall
wadaeyauh-goonugauwin to harden snow (crust)
zoog-ipoowin to snow
zoong-ipoowin to snow

goozau-ipeewin *sink*

goondau-igoowin to be drawn under
goondau-ishkaugaewin to cause sinking
goondau-kummik-issaewin to sink into the earth
goondau-shkauwin to be sucked down
goozau-ipeewin to sink; to go under
niki-ipee-ishinoowin to vanish into waters

I

ibigaewin *spear; stab; thrust*

bizhi-ibigaewin to stab
ibigaewin (root) to thrust; to spear
zhimaugaewin to spear

idumoowin *mean; imply; connote*

idumoowin (root) to mean; to intend

igaewin *make; construct; build; fabricate; manufacture*

igaewin; ikaewin; itchigaewin; itchikaewin (roots; also verbalizers) to make
pukoodjigun-ikaewin to manufacture roofing materials
pukwaun-ikaewin to roof; roofing
waubigun-igaewin to plaster
waubigun-ikaewin to plaster; to make plaster
waugunogaun-ikaewin to construct a dome shaped dwelling, lodge
waukau-igun-ikaewin to construct a log house
weegwaum-ikaewin to erect a birch bark dwelling
wizhigaewin to construct a house; to prepare trees for maple syrup making; to tap maple trees; prepare
wizhi-tchigaewin to make or do something
wizhi-tumaugaewin to make, construct something for another

igugaewin *chop; hew; chip; indent; notch; cleave; slash*

dawau-igaewin to clear, make an opening
gawogaewin to fell
geeshkau-gawogaewin to hew; to chop; to cut down
geeshkau-kawaewin to hew, fell trees
minissaewin to cut wood
pissa'igaewin to cut cedar splints

ikowau-beegigaewin *wind; coil; reel*

beem-inigaewin to coil up; to reel in
ikowau-beegigaewin to wind up
titabaubee-ikoodjigaewin to coil

imaugootiwin *smell; odor; aroma; fragrance*

imaugootiwin (root) the kind of odor given off by an insensate object
imaugooziwin (root) the kind of odor given off by a sensate being
imaundjigaewin (root) the quality, character of smell
imautaewin (root) the aroma of smoke; the kind of odor given off by an insensate object
izhi-maundjigaewin to detect a certain odor
maun-imaugootiwin to emit a foul odor
mauzh-maundjigaewin to detect a foul odor

VERBS

mino-imaugootiwin to be fragrant
mino-maundjigaewin to emit a pleasant odor, fragrant
nindo-maundjigaewin to attempt to detect an odor
oombauz-maugooziwin to stink to high heaven
weeshaugi-imaugoot to be fragrant

---

inaendjigaewin *opinion, perception, attitude, emotion and sentiment generated by external causes and directed at someone or something*

---

apeet-aendjigaewin to hold a certain person, persons, object or objects in contempt or respect to an unseemly degree
auniss-aendjigaewin to forgive, pardon, excuse, while admitting or owning up to one's fault or part in alienation
auno-waendjigaewin to scorn, despise, disdain, reject a person or persons, an object or objects as unworthy, of little value, etc.
daessido-waendjigaewin to feel sorry for, pity for, sympathy for another person or persons or living creature(s)
dupuss-aendjigaewin to scorn, look down on, despise, disdain others; to have a superiority attitude
gagawae-dibaendjigaewin to tempt, test, try, etc.
gizhau-waendjigaewin to be covetous, jealous, avaricious, envious, greedy; to resent the good fortune of another person; to ascribe the gains of another to dishonesty, or even to theft
goopit-aendjigaewin to regard others as awkward, bumbling, fumbling, clumsy, ne'er do wells, inept, incompetent, not equal to, etc.
kitimaug-aendjigaewin to regard with pity others as poor, unfortunate, destitute, unlucky, needy, ill-starred, etc.
misso-waendjigaewin to hanker, long for, care, want, like; to be fond of; to have affection for; to be biased in favor of, prefer someone, something
ningud-aendjigaewin to be accustomed to, familiar with, friendly toward, practiced, used to the ways of others and to the environment
pishig-aendjigaewin to like, favor, prefer, to be fond of, have an affection for, an attachment to a person or persons or to an object or objects
sida-waendjigaewin to have a general prejudice, bias, discrimination directed at people by virtue of race, creed, politics, or for any other reason
zheeng-aendjigaewin to harbor hate, enmity, hostility, antipathy, dislike, aversion, revulsion

---

inaendumoowin *think; will; an operation of the mind*

---

abeed-aendumoowin to expect, await, anticipate, look forward to, assume, etc. (*lit.* a waiting mind, thought)
anaum-aendumoowin to blame, suspect, impute fault, mistrust, distrust, implicate, indict, connect with, etc. (*lit.* thinking under, beneath)
anish-aendumoowin to be scornful, disdainful, haughty, skeptical; to dislike; to have no use for, etc. (*lit.* a baseless thought, feeling)
ani-waendumoowin to prefer, select, choose, like better, favor, fancy, opt for, etc. (*lit.* the inclination of the mind, feeling)
apaendumoowin kemauh apaenumoowin to hope, trust, rely on, depend on, look on/to, count on, lean on, etc. (*lit.* a depending mind, feeling)
apeet-aendumoowin to value, cherish, esteem, treasure, honor, love, like, admire; the pace or rate of thought, feeling; in the course, duration of thought, feeling, etc. (*lit.* the rate, pace, value of feeling, thought)
ashid-aendumoowin to include another in one's resentment, suspicion, distrust, anger, etc. (*lit.* something added to the mind)
aubawae-waendumoowin to forgive, absolve, reconcile, pardon, excuse, exculpate, bury the hatchet, etc. (*lit.* to warm up or to loosen up one's mind, feelings)
aubizee-waendumoowin to be encouraged, uplifted, revival of spirit, refreshed; to

have recovery of hope, renewal of courage, revival of spirit, to regain composure, etc. (*lit.* a revived mind, feeling)

augoonaet-waendumoowin to be skeptical, in denial, suspicious, dubious; to disbelieve, mistrust, doubt, disallow, renounce, repudiate, etc. (*lit.* a rejecting mind, feeling, sense)

aukoowaud-aendumoowin vexation, annoyance, irritation, pique, provocation, touchiness, grumpiness, etc. (*lit.* an angry mind, feelings)

aundji-aendumoowin to change one's mind, view, opinion (*lit.* reconsider)

aungawaum-aendumoowin to proceed with caution, prudence, wariness, circumspection; to be watchful, careful, scrupulous, mindful, discreet, etc. (*lit.* a careful mind)

aunim-aendumoowin to be unable to bear, endure; to have dismay, distress; to be daunted, demoralized, dispirited, dejected, etc. (*lit.* an unsettled, stormy, windy mind, thoughts, feelings)

aunisheetumoowin to be discouraged, disheartened, dejected, unnerved, intimidated, daunted (*lit.* discourage)

auniss-aendumoowin to reconcile, conciliate, come to terms with, accept things as they are, make peace, assuage, compose, make up, propitiate, accord, patch up, etc. (*lit.* to compose minds, settle feelings)

aunood-aendumoowin to have avarice, greed; to indulge in voracity, excess, acquisitiveness, intemperance; to be overwhelmed, daunted, cowed, intimated by fears, etc. (*lit.* overcome, overwhelmed by thoughts)

auno-waendumoowin to turn down as unsuitable, not good enough; to discard, rebuff (*lit.* a rejecting mind, feeling)

auzhidae-waendumoowin to have opposing thoughts, beliefs, feelings; to counter, disbelieve; to intend revenge, retaliation, settling scores, getting back at, reprisal, square accounts, etc. (*lit.* to cross in mind, feeling)

auzhidaewau-waendumoowin vengeance, revenge, retaliation, getting even, reprisal, etc. (*lit.* a retaliatory mind, feeling)

awi-inaendumoowin to forget, neglect, leave behind, overlook, ignore, omit, think of no more, etc. (*lit.* lost in mind, thought; distant from recall)

awo-ani-inaendumoowin to err, mistake, misjudge, miscalculate, misunderstand, incorrect, etc. (*lit.* to lose one's way in one's mind)

ayaek-waendumoowin to be weary of mind; to tire of; to lose patience, tolerance, etc. (*lit.* a weariness of mind, spirit)

babaum-aendumoowin to heed, pay attention to, tend to, keep in mind, notice, be aware of, care for, keep a mind on, etc. (*lit.* a minding mind, spirit)

baebeezh-waendumoowin to be distracted, inattentive (*lit.* a mind that meanders, wanders)

baed-aendumoowin to think slowly, indecisive; to be tardy in making decisions, etc. (*lit.* slow of thought, mind)

baekaud-aendumoowin to be peaceful, serene, tranquil, composed, collected, calm, unmoved, unconcerned, placid, self-possessed, etc. (*lit.* a meek, mild mind, feeling, disposition)

baesho-waendumoowin to desire, covet, want, lust for; to know carnally (*lit.* close in one's thoughts)

bae-waendumoowin to have little faith, trust, confidence, hope in something, someone; to regard something, someone as unreliable, untrustworthy, incompetent, unable, etc. (*lit.* a weak, frail, feeble mind, feeling; a weakness of thought, mind, feeling)

baezhigo-aendumoowin to have solidarity, one mind, one purpose, agreement, concurrence, consensus, unanimity, etc. (*lit.* one mind or oneness of minds)

banaud-aendumoowin to have confusion; to give up, lose hope; to be discouraged, disheartened; to have despair, dejection, dismay, daunt; to be pessimistic (*lit.* broken, battered thoughts)

baup-inaendumoowin to be amused, delighted, humored, cheered, in good

VERBS

humor (*lit.* an amused mind)

bauskausk-inaendumoowin to crave food, long for certain foods, etc. (*lit.* a mind, feelings, raspy, brittle from craving)

been-aendumoowin to nurture clean, pure, modest, chaste, innocent, moral, decent ideas, thoughts, etc. (*lit.* a clean mind, thoughts)

beewi-inaendumoowin to scorn, hold in contempt, disdain, dislike, abhor, despise, etc. (*lit.* to regard as small, as of little worth)

begoss-aendumoowin to wish, long for, pine for, crave, yearn, aspire for, desire, hope, etc. (*lit.* a begging mind, thought)

bizaun-aendumoowin to be satisfied, content, peaceful, reconciled, accept things as they are, resigned, serene (*lit.* a quiet mind, feelings)

bizisk-aendumoowin to have good judgement; to make a mature decision; to have thoughtful, sage reasoning; to be wise, prudent; to have common sense; to use sound logic, etc. (*lit.* a mature, grown-up mind);

book-waendumoowin to be dispirited, disheartened, dejected, broken hearted, discouraged, despairing, etc. (*lit.* a broken mind, spirit, feelings)

boon-aendumoowin to stop thinking about, overlook, forbear, forgive, absolve (*lit.* to stop thinking)

buguk-aendumoowin to understand clearly, lucidly; to see through and through; to comprehend completely; to grasp, know, conceive, master, distinguish, discern, etc. (*lit.* a clear mind)

buni-inaendumoowin to forget; to have on the tip of one's mind, tongue; to have in mind one moment and then gone the next, etc. (*lit.* to drop from one's mind)

chaunim-aendumoowin to be anxious, troubled, perturbed, worried, bothered, vexed, distressed, upset, etc. (*lit.* an anxious mind, thought)

cheesig-aendumoowin to covet a neighbour's goods, etc. (*lit.* a mind moved by want)

dae'b'awae-waendumoowin to have belief, confidence, faith, intuition, understanding, supposition, thesis, hypothesis, presumption, impression, certainty, conception, etc. (*lit.* to believe as far as the mind can grasp ideas, notions, events, etc.)

daebig-waendumoowin to ponder, reflect, cogitate, deliberate, contemplate, meditate (*lit.* to reach to the ends of one's mind and feelings)

daessido-waendumoowin to feel sorry for, have compassion for, pity on, sympathy, empathy, etc. (*lit.* an open heart)

dago-aendumoowin to include, incorporate, inject, combine in one's thoughts and feelings, other matters, parties (*lit.* to blend into thought, feelings)

dan-aendumoowin to guess, assume, presume, reckon, figure, surmise where a person or object might be, etc. (*lit.* the mind focused upon a certain place)

dazhin-aendumoowin to guess, assume, presume, reckon, figure, surmise where a person or object might be, etc.(*lit.* the mind focused upon a certain place)

dubug-aendumoowin to guess, estimate, figure, rate, surmise, reckon, speculate, hypothesize, conjecture, etc. (*lit.* a weighing mind)

dupuss-aendumoowin to despise, slight, look down on, disdain, scorn, dislike, hold in contempt, deride, ridicule, look on as inferior, worthless, etc. (*lit.* low, base thoughts, ideas)

gabo-waendumoowin to have claustrophobia, cabin fever, a persecution complex, etc. (*lit.* a locked in mind, feeling)

gae-izhauwaud-aendumoowin to aspire to, have a fixed goal, ambition, object, purpose; keep in mind, remember, set a date, etc. (*lit.* the mind's destination)

gagaund-aendumoowin taunting, teasing, daring, challenging, provocative, inciting, goading, etc. (*lit.* a pushing, prodding mind, feeling)

gagawaunnisug-aendumoowin to feel deep sorrow, remorse, detestation, hate, dislike, horror, revulsion, etc. (*lit.* feelings, mind, in the extreme)

gageebaud-aendumoowin to entertain foolish, frivolous, stupid, ridiculous, flippant, absurd, simple ideas, notions, etc. (*lit.* a foolish mind, thought)

gageetau-waendumoowin kemauh gaugaetau-waendumoowin to be wise, prudent, sage, intelligent; to display common-sense, etc. (*lit.* a well-rounded mind, sense)

gaung-waendumoowin to be jealous, envious, etc. (*lit.* longing, yearning mind)

gauta-waendumoowin to tend and care for as a nurse does a patient, etc. (*lit.* caring mind)

gau-waendumoowin to be jealous of; to covet another's sweetheart, good fortune; to believe a spouse or sweetheart is in love or interested in another, is cheating, etc. (*lit.* to want for oneself, to suspect the fidelity of another without cause)

gawaeki-waendumoowin truth, certitude, correctness, accuracy, certain, assurance, right, etc. (*lit.* the right mind, feeling)

gawaek-waek-waendumoowin to have a change of mind; to review (*lit.* to turn one's mind over and over)

gaweeniwi-inaendumoowin to be undecided, puzzled, confused, perplexed, befuddled, confounded, etc. (*lit.* an unsettled mind, thought)

gawo-aendumoowin to collapse and die from fear, anxiety, loneliness, sadness; to languish, etc. (*lit.* to be felled in mind)

gazhee-aendumoowin to be impatient, anxious; to have a quick mind; to be quick of thought and decision, etc. (*lit.* a fast mind, feeling)

gazheeb-inaendumoowin to consider, contemplate, ponder, meditate, etc. (*lit.* present in the mind for some time)

geemood-aendumoowin to suspect, surmise, presume, speculate, assume, suppose, guess, etc. (*lit.* sly thoughts, ideas)

geessaud-aendumoowin to have regret, remorse, sorrow, repentance, penitence, compunction, contrition; to lament; to be rueful, sorrowful (*lit.* a rueful mind, thought)

geewid-aendumoowin to think in circles; to be irrational, confused, unreasonable, illogical, senseless, muddled, mixed-up, befuddled, etc. (*lit.* circular thinking, feeling)

geewinaud-aendumoowin to have crazy thoughts, insensible ideas, wild, irrational, half-crocked, illogical schemes, etc. (*lit.* a mind that revolves)

geezhauta-waendumoowin to be reluctant to leave, unwilling to go; to want to remain, etc. (*lit.* a mind, heart warmed to one place)

geezhi-aendumoowin to make up one's mind; to be decided, resolved, fixed, settled, firm of purpose, determined, etc. (*lit.* mind made up beforehand)

geezhin-aendumoowin to invent, dream into being, imagine, create, compose, conceive, envisage (*lit.* already or pre-formed in the mind)

gina-waendumoowin to safeguard, keep, hold in trust, guard, keep an eye on, babysit, etc. (*lit.* to keep in mind for some time)

ginib-aendumoowin to be resolute; to endure, fixed, determined; to have tenacity, will, etc. (*lit.* a clinging mind, thoughts, feelings)

gizhau-waendumoowin to be jealous of, envious, greedy, desirous; to covet, begrudge, crave, feel ill-will toward someone else's good fortune, etc. (*lit.* a hot, heated, inflamed mind, feelings)

goopit-aendumoowin to regard as worthless, useless, good for nothing, of little worth, value; to scorn, despise, disdain, etc. (*lit.* useless, inept thought, feeling)

goossikee-waendumoowin to be afraid, scared, wary, expectant, apprehensive; to have qualms, dread, misgiving, foreboding, etc. (*lit.* an apprehensive mind, spirit)

gotaumig-waendumoowin to have resolution, ambition, determination; to be sure, certain, definite, positive, convinced, without doubt, determined and sure—all extreme, awesome, excessive, inordinate (*lit.* an extreme mind, feeling)

gotug-aendumoowin to have a feeling or belief or conviction in one's wretched state, poverty, suffering, a persecution complex, etc. (*lit.* a suffering mind, feeling)

inaendumoowin (root) to think, imagine,

VERBS

will; surmise, have in mind, conceive, guess

ishp-aendumoowin to prize, honor, respect, revere, treasure, regard, exalt, uplift, cherish, elevate, admire, celebrate, etc. (*lit.* high thoughts, mind)

ishp-aenimoowin to have pride, conceit, vanity, airs, a high opinion of oneself; to be haughty, supercilious, etc. (*lit.* a high mind, an uplifted mind, feeling)

kik-aendumoowin to know; to have knowledge, understanding, familiarity, wisdom, learning, insight, education, etc. (*lit.* the images in the mind correspond to the images, sounds, that exist in the outside world)

kikinae-yaub-aendumoowin to review, reconsider, re-examine, re-analyze, look over again, re-study, etc. (*lit.* a reviewing mind; to go over again in mind)

kishk-aendumoowin to feel grief, sorrow, sadness, melancholy, lonesome, miserable, mournful, despondency, heartache, gloom, desolation, etc. (*lit.* tight thought)

kitchi-inaendumoowin to be glad, happy, grateful, joyful, encouraged, inspired, satisfied, blissful, ecstatic, bubbling over, etc. (*lit.* big thoughts)

kitchitawau-waendumoowin to meditate, exalt, glorify, laud, sanctify in mind, etc. (*lit.* an exalted mind, sense, spirit)

kitim-aendumoowin to express unwillingness, reluctance; to be disinclined, hesitant, apathetic, procrastinating, etc. (*lit.* a lazy mind)

kitimaug-aendumoowin to have a low opinion of others, other things; to believe others to be poor, needy, wretched, abject, requiring or deserving pity, sympathy, help, etc. (*lit.* poor, wretched, miserable mind, thought)

kooshka-waendumoowin to be startled; to shock, surprise, astonish, etc. (*lit.* a startled mind)

kooshk-awauwaud-aendumoowin to be melancholy, dispirited, morose, dejected, gloomy, depressed (*lit.* a cramped, squeezed mind)

maeniss-aendumoowin to feel shame, embarrassment, mortification, humility, chagrin, discomfiture, abashment, etc.(*lit.* inadequacy of mind, thought)

maesso-waendumoowin to pine for, long for, miss, yearn for, etc. (*lit.* a pining mind)

maetissi-waendumoowin to miss, yearn, long for, etc. (*lit.* something missing in mind)

mamaundau-waendumoowin to be puzzled, bewildered, befuddled, perplexed, etc. (*lit.* a strangeness, wonder in the mind)

mamidon-aendumoowin to ponder, consider, analyze, scheme, plot, etc. (*lit.* everything in mind)

mashkowi-aendumoowin to be resolved, resolute, firm, strong in mind, fixed, determined, persistent, tenacious, persevering, stout hearted, etc. (*lit.* a strong, hard mind)

matchi-inaendumoowin to intend evil; to be evil minded; to have evil plans, criminal intent, ill-will, etc. (*lit.* a bad mind, thought)

maud-aendumoowin to start thinking, feeling, etc. (*lit.* thoughts, feelings begin)

maumayau-waendumoowin to express thankfulness, gratitude, a collective feeling and expression, etc. (*lit.* all thoughts are conjoined)

maumayau-waendumoowin to understand fully, comprehend, recognize; to be aware, cognizant, enlightened, etc. (*lit.* the blending of all thoughts, feelings)

maumeek-waendumoowin to express enthusiasm, excitement, admiration, deference, praise, regard, fondness, adoration, etc. (*lit.* an admiring mind, sense, feeling)

maumikaud-aendumoowin to feel awe, wonder, astonishment, amazement, bewilderment, disbelief; to marvel, etc. (*lit.* an awe-struck mind, perplexed)

mauminaud-aendumoowin to be choosy, picky, selective, biased, careful, particular, etc. (*lit.* a particular, selective mind, spirit)

mau-mino'd'aendumoowin; mau-mino-in-aendumoowin to remember; to recall fully, exactly, in every detail; to recall fondly (*lit.* to hold fondly in mind)

maun-aendumoowin to feel bad, remorse, regret, sorrow, penitence, blue, dejected, disheartened, despondent, depressed, melancholy, sad, etc. (*lit.* baneful thoughts, ideas, feelings); to think ill, evil of; to regard something, someone as too ambitious, too vain, haughty, evil, as deserving of chastisement (*lit.* evil in mind, feeling)

maunaud-aendumoowin to be unsettled, disturbed, agitated, troubled, vexed, apprehensive, grieved, anxious, bothered, uptight, etc. (*lit.* bad thoughts)

mauzh-aendumoowin to be depressed, penitent, remorseful, sorry, sorrowful, etc. (*lit.* a bad mind, feelings)

mauzh-waendumoowin dismal, downcast, dejected, inconsolable, despondent, etc. (*lit.* bad feelings)

meedaug-waendumoowin to wish, want that something were not so; to wish to avoid; to wish that an event would not come to pass, etc. (*lit.* a wish, longing to avoid or evade)

meedau-waendumoowin to agonize, anguish, grieve, feel distress, etc. (*lit.* a remorseful mind; a helpless mind, spirit)

meegawaetchi-waendumoowin to express thankfulness, gratitude, appreciation, sense of obligation, etc. (*lit.* a thankful mind)

meekoonooy-aendumoowin to be enthusiastic, thrilled, excited, eager, exhilarated, ardent, zealous, fervent, ecstatic, etc. (*lit.* a mind, feelings equal to any)

meendaud-aendumoowin to feel disappointment, disillusionment, frustration, dissatisfaction, etc. (*lit.* to have less than satisfaction of mind)

midon-aendumoowin to think, have an idea, imagine, scheme, etc. (*lit.* to examine every aspect of an idea, plan, etc.)

migooshkaud-aendumoowin to be troubled, disturbed, distressed, disquieted, afflicted, apprehensive, perturbed, worried, anxious, agitated, upset, etc. (*lit.* an unsettled mind, thought, spirit)

mindjim-aendumoowin to remember, keep in mind, recall, retain in memory, etc. (*lit.* to hold in mind, feeling)

mino-inaendumoowin to feel good will, contentment, pleased, happiness, delight, joy, etc. (*lit.* good thoughts)

mino-waunig-waendumoowin to feel joy, bliss, happiness, rapture, ecstasy, celebration, good humor, revelry, etc. (*lit.* merry in mind)

misqui-eeg-odae-aendumoowin to feel exasperation, extreme irritation, annoyance, chagrin, discouragement, dismay, disheartenment (*lit.* heart bleeding thoughts, feelings)

misso-waendumoowin to like, desire, covet, want, fancy, take an interest in, etc. (*lit.* a wanting mind)

mooni-aendumoowin to suspect; to harbor an idea, an inference; to deduce; to believe something without proof, etc. (*lit.* dredged up thoughts)

moozh-aendumoowin to have intuition, sensation, feeling, a sixth sense, telepathy, instinct, etc. (*lit.* a feeling mind)

moozhi'g'aendumoowin to feel joy, inspiration, uplifted, exhilaration, cheer, elation (*lit.* mind picked up or collected thoughts)

mukwo-aendumoowin to remember, recall, recollect, refresh a memory, bring to mind, look back on, etc. (*lit.* to find one's mind)

nagata-waendumoowin to care for, tend, look after, mind, oversee, guard, watch over, safeguard (*lit.* keep something, someone in mind)

nagauwaug-aendumoowin to examine one's self (introspection; *lit.* to dig deep and to scrape the mind)

nanaezhinaunig-aendumoowin to be calm, peaceful, serene, untroubled, unaffected, composed, etc. (*lit.* a loosening mind)

nanawaud-aendumoowin to have vain hope; to be annoyed for nothing; to desire, want, wish for, crave, long for; to waste time in thinking about something, someone, etc. (*lit.* a wasted mind, feeling)

naneezaun-aendumoowin to apprehend, suspect, foresee, expect, anticipate danger (*lit.* a mind preoccupied with danger)

naunaugata-waendumoowin to reflect, think, ponder, consider, contemplate, speculate, meditate, etc. (*lit.* a mind that goes over again and again)

naung-aendumoowin to be relieved, carefree, calm, happy, cheerful, composed, serene, relaxed, etc. (*lit.* a light head, mind,

VERBS

thought)

naussaub-aendumoowin to agree, concur, assent; to have like or similar reasons, concord, accord; to go along with, have the same goals; to think alike (*lit.* to share like views)

nay-aen-inaendumoowin relief, composure, alleviation, release, a load off the mind, relaxation, ease, mitigation, etc. (*lit.* a lightening of the mind)

needa-waendumoowin kemauh naneeda-waendumoowin to be sad, sorrowful, morose, unhappy, desolate, abject, miserable, etc. (*lit.* a sorrowful, burdened mind)

neena-waendumoowin to be on the verge of breakdown; to give in to tears; to have weakening resolve; to be about to give in to emotion, dispirited, overcome by grief, sorrow; to give in to feelings, etc. (*lit.* the weakening of the mind, feelings)

niboo'd'aendumoowin to be melancholy, lonely, sorrowful; to pine, long for; to be homesick, desolate, solitary, forsaken, etc. (*lit.* dead thought)

nigau-aendumoowin to commiserate, feel sorry for, sympathize, pity, grieve with; to feel sorry for another's abject condition, etc. (*lit.* a grieving, pitying mind, feeling; a low mind, thought, feeling)

nindo-kik-aendumoowin to investigate, research, dig around, study, examine, inspect, inquire into, probe, explore, check out, put to the test, etc. (*lit.* to seek to know)

nindo-waendumoowin to want, desire, long for, crave, aspire, yen for, etc. (*lit.* to seek in one's mind, soul, spirit)

nindum-aendumoowin to be preoccupied, absorbed, deep in thought; to be rapt (*lit.* to have a busy mind)

ningud-aendumoowin to feel familiarity; to be accustomed; to have acquaintance; to know well; to habituate; to be well acquainted, etc. (*lit.* to feel free and easy with another)

nishinaud-aendumoowin to be confused, perplexed, puzzled, discomfited, unable to think straight, befuddled, confounded, bewildered, muddled, etc. (*lit.* a disordered mind, thoughts)

nishki-aendumoowin anger, resentment, vexed, annoyed, agitate, indignation, provoked, inflame, etc. (*lit.* an angry mind)

nissaud-aendumoowin to be sober, grave, collected, composed, unruffled, calm, dispassionate, cool, etc. (*lit.* a sober, objective mind, feelings)

nissitot-waendumoowin to recognize, to know, make out, distinguish, recall, etc. (*lit.* to recall in one's mind through the senses)

nissu-aendumoowin to believe, feel oneself to be alone, abandoned, deserted, forsaken, forlorn, destitute, desolate, etc. (*lit.* a killed mind, feeling)

noogi-aendumoowin to cease thinking; to suspend ideas, wishes; to be conciliatory, soften attitude, etc. (*lit.* to stop the mind, feelings)

onaunig-waendumoowin to be happy, joyful, cheerful, content; to have gladness, bliss, serenity, peace of mind and being, elation (*lit.* a well pleased mind, thought, feeling)

ondug-aenimoowin to have conceit, vanity, a superiority complex; to have a self-serving attitude, self-love, pretension, vainglory, arrogance, etc. (*lit.* a grasping mind)

pagid-aendumoowin to give up, let go, forget; to resign oneself to a loved one's death; to surrender, abdicate, etc. (*lit.* to let go one's mind, feeling, attachment)

pekaun-aendumoowin to believe otherwise; to hold another opinion; to be contrary; to hold another view, etc. (*lit.* a different mind, feeling)

pishigawaud-aendumoowin to have immoral thoughts, desires, lust, sex in mind; to long for sex, etc. (*lit.* immoral thoughts, feelings)

pishig-waendumoowin to be fond of, sweet on, enamored with; to feel affection for; to like, care for, etc. (*lit.* a liking mind, spirit)

pit-aendumoowin to think of the wrong event, object, time, person; to misunderstand, misconstrue, misconceive, etc. (*lit.* to bear in on some object other than the right one in mind, feeling)

pitchi-inaendumoowin to think of something accidentally, by chance; to have an idea pop into one's mind, etc. (*lit.* to think of something inadvertently)

shoo-waendumoowin kemauh ashoo-waendumoowin to be wary, circumspect, watchful, suspicious, vigilant, etc. (*lit.* a leaning mind, feeling)

sida-waendumoowin to have bias, bigotry; to look down, scorn, despise, disdain, etc. (*lit.* weighted, burdened feelings, thoughts)

takon-aendumoowin to keep in mind, remember; to hold in memory, memorize, etc. (*lit.* to capture, imprison in the mind)

tautagaud-inaendumoowin to have a lazy, lethargic, slow, sluggish, dull mind, etc. (*lit.* a flat mind, even disposition)

teemin-aendumoowin to think deeply, concentrate, meditate, study, cogitate, etc. (*lit.* a deep thinking, feeling)

waenipun-aendumoowin to regard work, challenges as easy; to have confidence, etc. (*lit.* ease in the mind, feeling)

waeweeb-aendumoowin to be anxious, in a hurry, impatient, eager, earnest, restless, etc. (*lit.* a mind in a hurry)

waun-akee-aendumoowin to be carefree, blithe, unconcerned, happy-go-lucky, nonchalant, casual, blasé, devil may care, etc. (*lit.* a mind in the hollow of the ground)

waussido-waendumoowin to be discouraged, disheartened, daunted, intimidated, dejected, etc. (*lit.* an embittered, soured mind)

wauwin-aendumoowin to be amused' to think of something funny, droll, whimsical, facetious, etc. (*lit.* a round mind, thoughts)

weed-aendumoowin to be amused, droll, bemused' to entertain humoros thoughts (*lit.* an accompanying mind, thought, feeling)

weedooki-waendumoowin to abet, aid, support, encourage, bolster, comfort, approve, stand behind, sponsor, assure, second, etc. (*lit.* to help in mind, thought)

weekood-aendumoowin to wish, desire, yearn, long for something to occur, happen, by act of mind, will; to invite by act of mind, telepathy; to invoke by wish, will, etc. (*lit.* to draw into the mind)

ween-aendumoowin to harbour impure, dirty, carnal, perverted, lascivious, lustful thoughts, desires, etc. (*lit.* a dirty mind, thought, desire)

weenga-waendumoowin to have a fondness for something, an attachment, etc. (*lit.* a complete mind, feeling)

weeshitau-waendumoowin to dislike, averse to, disfavor, detest, loathe, etc. (*lit.* a tart mind)

weessig-aendumoowin to have, to feel, to experience excruciating sorrow, regret, sadness, contrition, remorse, etc. (*lit.* tart, sour mind, feelings)

weessiki-waendumoowin to be bitter, sour, skeptical, critical; to have cynical thoughts, feelings, etc. (*lit.* sour thoughts, feelings)

weessooki-waendumoowin to aid and abet, conspire, connive, incite, sanction, approve, encourage in the commission of a wrong, go along with, etc. (*lit.* to go along with in mind, concur)

weezh-aendumoowin amusement, mirthfulness, gleefulness, drollness, merriment (*lit.* mirth in the mind)

zaeg-aendumoowin to be apprehensive, anxious, worried, daunted; to feel misgiving, alarm, foreboding, etc. (*lit.* a fearful mind)

zaessaess-aendumoowin to be terror stricken, frantic; to panic; to have horror, dread, etc. (*lit.* an agonized, excruciating mind, thought)

zaub-aendumoowin to care for, cherish, prize, treasure, ador; to feel spirited, ecstacy, etc. (*lit.* a fervent mind)

zaug-aendumoowin to trust, hope, depend upon, rely, look to or on another, have faith in, etc. (*lit.* a loving, trusting mind)

zaum-aendumoowin to be overwhelmed by thoughts; to entertain high expectations; to be confused; to think too much; to be daunted by one's own thoughts; to disapprove of someone; to be disillusioned (*lit.* excessive thought, mind)

zhaug'd'aendumoowin to overcome doubts; to exercise will power; to overcome in mind (will); to cow, daunt another by force of will, etc. (*lit.* an over-powering mind, will, thought)

zhaugo-waendumoowin to have reservation, reticence, timidity; to be reserved, withdrawn, hesitant, fearful, shy, etc. (*lit.* a regressive mind, feeling)

zha-waendumoowin to sympathize; to feel solicitude, pity, compassion; to express consolation, etc. (*lit.* a sympathetic mind, feeling)

zheeb-aendumoowin fortitude, long suffering, enduring, resolution, persistence, tenacity, stamina, to hang in there; to persist, etc. (*lit.* to cling to thought, resolve)

zheeng-aendumoowin to hate, dislike, abhor, detest, disdain, loathe, scorn, despise, resent, feel disgust, etc. (*lit.* a hateful mind, thought)

zhigud-aendumoowin to weary, tire of someone, something; to be too familiar, too accustomed, etc. (*lit.* to know thoroughly, too thoroughly)

zoong-aendumoowin to be firm of conviction, resolute, assured, confident, determined, firm, etc. (*lit.* a strong mind, will, feeling)

zunug-aendumoowin to be discouraged, to be disheartened, to find things difficult to deal with in one's mind, anticipation of difficulties, etc. (*lit.* a difficult mind, thought)

---

inaewin *pain; agony; hurt; smart; wound*

iginaewin (root) to have pain

weesig-itumoowin to suffer agony

weessi-ginaewin to suffer agony

---

inaubae-wiziwin *shape; form; construct*

boodawiziwin to have soundness; to be stout, sturdy; to have density

inaubae-wiziwin (root) figure, human figure

inauwaewin (root) form, shape of the human body

inaweewin (root) malleability of form

inigaumoowin (root) bulk, fatness

inoodjuzoowin (root) girth, frame

izhi-eengawaewin (root) form, shape of the face

izhi-ishkeehnzhig-awaewin (root) tone, shade and lustre of the eye

namaeshinoowin to profile, shadow, outline

nitchig-aushinoowin to silhouette

piko-inaubae-wiziwin to shape, structure

---

inaubaugawaewin *thirst*

gaushki-aubaugawaewin to thirst

gauski-naubaugawaewin to thirst

inaubaugawaewin to have degree of thirst

noondae-aubauwaewin to thirst; to be dehydrated (*lit.* too soon dry)

---

inaubauwaewin *wet; soak; drench; drown; saturate; souse; immerse*

aubau-widjigaewin to moisten

booz-aubauwaewin a soaking, drenching

gabo-naubauwaewin to drown; to be engulfed

gindjidau-peeg-inigaewin to put, stick in water

goondjigaewin to soak, steep

madookoot dew

niki-ipeeyauh it is flooded

ning-aubau-widjigaewin to dilute, dissolve

nipeekauh it is wet

nipee-witchigaewin to soak

niss-aubauwaewin to get wet; to drown

tik-aubauwaewin to get, receive a cool, cold dunking or drenching

tipau-bauwae-itchigaewin to drench

tip-aubauwidjigaewin to moisten

---

inaubeewin *string; row; line; band; stripe*

inaubeeg-inigaewin to mount; to deploy; to arrange; to extend to; to line up a cord, band, line

inaubee-issitchigaewin to line up or arrange in some order

inaubeewin (root) direction, angle, contour of a line, stripe, strip, string, margin, etc.

---

inaubiwin *look*

aub-inaubiwin to look back

aubiz-aubiwin to stare

aungawaum-aubiwin to look carefully

begooss-aubiwin to look on beseechingly

cheeb-eengawaeniwin to wink
cheech-aubiwin to squint
cheecheeb-eengawaeniwin to wink repeatedly
cheezigeez-peengawaewin to see through bleary eyes
gagaweeniwi-inaubiwin to look, search in vain
geemooz-aubiwin to spy on, peek, sneak on, observe
geezhig-aubingaewin to stare
gino-waub-indjigaewin to spectate, look on
gino-waubiwin to stare, look at for some time, examine, observe
iko-waubiwin to watch, keep on eye on, observe
inaubiwin (root) to look
kikinoo-waubiwin to imitate; to copy; to do as one sees
mau-mino-aubiwin to see everything
mauz-aubiwin to have impaired eyesight
naeg-waubiwin to look askance
naunaukizo-waubiwin to observe, scrutinize
nindo-waubiwin to look for
nishk-aubiwin to frown, scowl, glare, glower
oohnz-aubiwin to look from
tip-aubiwin to look through, in, out of; to peek, peer
waweemb-aubiwin to look out from sunken eyes
zhee-aubiwin to see through, clearly, thoroughly
zhigudji-aubiwin to tire of watching

---

inaudigaewin *swim*

---

bigizoowin to swim to cleanse oneself
bim-audigaewin to swim
gabaushimoowin to bathe
inaudigaewin (root) the form, style of swimming

---

inaudigaukoowin *walk on ice*

---

abeed-augum-ossaewin to come in this direction by snowshoe
abeed-audigaukoowin to come in this direction on ice
anim-audigaukoowin to leave by way of ice
gawau-waudigaukoowin to get off the ice; to come ashore off ice

---

inaudiziwin *exist; live; to be*

---

bim-audiziwin
life; to live, exist
inaudiziwin (root) the quality, state, nature of life, being, living

---

inaudjimoowin *tell; report; narrate; account; explain; describe*

---

abeed-audjimoowin to bring news
aud-waudjimoowin to speak allegorically
aunikae-audjimoowin the continuation of a story, report, etc.
auttissookaewin to create, invent, make up a story
auwaetchigaewin to tell a story, a parable
baup-inaudjimoowin to tell a humorous story; to narrate in a humorous fashion
bautauwaewin to tell on, inform, squeal, snitch
daebingaewin to testify
geenawishk-audjimoowin to lie, misrepresent, deceive
imaugaewin (root) to transmit an idea, news, feelings, etc
inaudjimoowin the manner, purpose, style, character, nature and quality of a report, narration, news, description, explanation
mazhinawaendauwaewin to send messages, report
meeshit-audjimoowin to give an indistinct, fuzzy, misleading account
pishi-ingaewin to accuse, blame, implicate falsely
pissi-taugooziwin to provoke by tone and/or tenor of language and voice
pitchi-ingaewin to accuse, blame, implicate falsely
pugidji-issidumaugaewin to imply, impute, allege
w'd'inaun he/she tells, says to him/her
weendumaugaewin to tell, report, narrate
zaum-audjimoowin exaggeration
zaum-doonoowin to talk too much; to be a blabber mouth

VERBS

inaugooziwin *appear; seem; resemble; look; aspect; emerge; come into sight*

gagawaunissug-inaugooziwin to be or appear to be horrible, grotesque
inaubim-inaugooziwin to appear, seem
inaugooziwin (root) to appear, resemble, seem
inoowauwaewin to resemble, look like
izhi-inaugooziwin to seem like; to appear in a certain way
mino-inaugooziwin to be comely, handsome
mookeewin to appear, make an appearance
mook-ipeewin to emerge from the water's depths
mook-issaewin to emerge suddenly; to bob to the surface
mooshkawoon-indjissaewin to burst to the surface
nitcheewi-inaugooziwin to be ugly, repulsive
zaugi-ipeewin to emerge; to stick out of the water
zaug-itauwaewin to emerge; to make an appearance

inaugummi-issitchigaewin *brew*

inaubookaewin to make soup
inau-gummissitchigaewin to brew
naboopeekaewin to make soup
neebeesh-aubookaewin to make tea

inaugummiwin *water; liquid; fluid*

auboo (root and suffix) kind, character of soup or beverage
been-aubau-widjigaewin to cleanse by spraying; to wash down
bimi-idjiwun it flows
gazheeshkau-idjiwun to flow swiftly (the origin of Saskatchewan)
geezho-gummi-tchigaewin to warm water
inaubauwaewin (root) the manner, degree, and form of getting wet
inaubau-witchigaewin (root) the manner of watering someone, something
inaubau-wizoowin to have purpose and manner of washing oneself
inaugummi-issitchigaewin to brew spirits
inaugummiwin (root) state, quality, taste, character of water
inidjiwun (root) the pace, direction, force and sound of flowing water such as a river, falls, etc
ipeewin to draw or fetch water; to approach or enter water (from *nipi*—water, drinking water, wet, moist)
mashki-akik-wauboo-kaewin to brew a tonic, lotion, prescription
mino-wau-gummiwin to have the pleasant flavour of a liquid
nauzh-ipeewin the drop in the level of water
nauz-ipeewin to draw water, sap
neebeesh-auboo-kaewin to make a beverage from leaves
niss-aubauwaewin to get wet; to drown
piko-ipeewin to enter water
soossawae-yaubau-widjigaewin to spray, shower
tikau-bauwizoowin to swim to cool off
waukau-gummiwin to have the clarity of water
zhauboo-waubauwaewin to get soaked, drenched

inaukawauwin *woods; forest; bush*

inaukawaeyauh (root) the nature, character, density of a forest, woods
inaukawauh the composition, color, structure, character, nature of a forest

inauk-inigaewin *settle; decide; resolve; judge; set; plant; plan; intend; mean; will; propose*

boon-akeegaewin to settle; to put in place; to plant; to sink
inaukinigaewin to decide, judge, resolve

inaukiziwin *form; shape; posture; frame; structure; outline; figure*

inaukiziwin (root) contour of a body
inautaeshinoowin (root) form or shape of shadow, outline
inigaumoowin (root) state or condition of plumpness
namaeshinoowin to outline
oskun-iwaessinoowin articulation of bones
pigaeg-aunkaewin to make a frame, form
saeningiwish-inootauwin to spread wings out
zhaeyaungaetauwin to spread wings in flight

inaumoowin *respiring; breathing; panting*

gabo-inaumoowin to suffocate
gazhee-waewae-inaumoowin to wheeze
inaumoowin (root) to respire
medawae-ingawaumoowin to snore
naessaewin to breathe
nana-inaumoowin to clear the throat, breathing passages
nissu-naumoowin to sigh
pagid-inaumoowin to exhale
piku-inaumoowin to gasp
zhazheeb-inaumoowin to have long, drawn out breathing

inaundaewin *color; tint; shade; hue; tone*

inaundaewin (root) the hue, tone, quality of color
tissigaewin to color
titaewin to ripen

inaundumoowin *hunger*

bining-unaeziwin to feel hunger pangs
inaundumoowin (root) degree and character of hunger
noondae-iskudaewin to be too soon empty, depleted
pakadaewin to be hungry
shakawayaewin to be famished

inaunimut *wind; breeze; blow*

aubumoo-yaunimut a whirlwind, tornado
beess-ipeessido-ossaewin a water-spout
inaunimut a wind; the direction of wind
inaushiwin (root) direction, pace, manner of being driven by the wind
inaussinoowin (root) direction, pace, manner of being driven by the wind
inaussitchigaewin (root) to cause or influence the course and direction of flight, navigation
noodiniwin (root) to blow wind
noodinoowin (root) to blow wind
waeb-aussinoowin to blow away
waessae-aunimutiwin to blow a gale
zeegimi-noodiniwin a wind causing ripples
zhauwuni-noodiniwin the south wind

inauniquot *cloud*

inauniquot (root) the state of clouds; cloudiness
mizhu-quot to be cloudless
ning-awaunquot to be overcast

inaupinaewin *disease*

aukooziwin to be sick, unwell
inaupinaewin (root) cause and nature of an illness
mazhin-igaewin to become infected; to contract
meezhiziwin to become infected; to contract

inaupitaewin *fume; smoke*

geek-inaumindaewin suffocating with smoke
geek-inaumizigaewin to create smoke to repel mosquitoes
imaussoowin (root) to smell of smoke
imautaewin (root) the aroma of smoke; the smell of something burning
inaumindaewin (root) the density and quality and temperature of smoke
inaupitaewin (root) the pattern, texture, tone of smoke
kiki-noodaewin to smoke
oomb-aupitaewin the rise of smoke
pukawaenaewin to fume
titabee-aupitaewin the swirl, curl of smoke
zugussawauwin to smoke a pipe or cigarette

inaushiwin *sail*

abeed-aushiwin to sail in this direction
anim-aushiwin to sail away
augawau-yaushiwin to steer for or to be driven to shelter by storm and wind
ayau-zhaewaeb-ayaushiwin to tack
babaum-aushiwin to sail about
bigum-aushiwin to arrive by sail
bim-aushiwin to sail
gawo-waushiwin to beach one's vessel; to go ashore
geewitau-yaushiwin to sail around some point, island
inaushiwin (root) to sail, fly; the rate, direction, tone, pitch, quality of motion produced or generated by the wind
iqawaushiwin to be driven off-shore by winds, currents

kawau-ishiwin to drift away from shore to the open sea
zaugi-aushiwin to hove into sight

inaushkaugaewin *chase; pursue*

akeewae-inaushkaugaewin to chase home
bimi-inaushkaugaewin to pursue, chase
inaushkaugaewin (root) manner of pursuit
noopinukeewin to run after
noop-inuzhawaewin to run after

inaushkauwin *wave; billow; swell*

boon-aushkauwin the settling down of waves
inaushkauwin (root) the character, form, nature, sound, pace, appearance of waves
maud-aushkauwin the commencement of waves
medawae-aushkauwin sound, echo; resonance of breakers
oogoowin (root) the direction, pace, character of waves

inauss-igaewin (root) *light; sunlight; sunshine; sunrise; sunset*

geezh-aussigaewin already shining, finished shining
geezhig-autaewin moonlight; moonlight as bright as day
geezhoo-aussigaewin a warming light
inaukinaewin (root) nature, quality, character of fire and light produced by fire or blaze
inaussigaewin (root) quality, character of sunlight
inautaewin (root) quality, character of sun and moonlight
inauzhaewin (root) quality and character of light
mishish-waussigaewin to brighten and to make plain
nanig-awaussaeyauwin mirage
pissikaukin-aessaewin flickering light
waussae-ayaumigut it is bright, clear
waussae-tchigaewin to make a light; to illuminate
waussi-waugaewin to illuminate with a torch
zaug-aussigaewin to shine through
zheeb-waussigaewin to shine through; to make transparent

inauzhigaewin *drive; direct; conduct; steer*

abeedji-daubeewin to drag, haul something in this direction
anim-daubeewin to drag, haul something in the opposite direction
bimi-daubeewin to drag, haul something
bimi-inauzhigaewin to drive, steer
cheeshi-daubeewin to drag, haul and to scrape
ginub-daubeewin to drag, haul something; to overturn
idaubeewin to drive, direct, guide, control a vehicle
inauzhigaewin (root) to drive, to direct, conduct
zaugidji-daubeewin to drag, haul something out

inawaewaewin (root) *sound*

abeed-waewaewin emit sound, coming sound
anim-waewae-ishinoowin the resonance of retreating footsteps
anim-waewaetoowin to create a din as one leaves and goes further into the distance
anim-waewaewin the sound, music recedes, fades, etc.
gausk-bugauwin rustling leaves
gausk-eewaewaewin a rasping, rustling sound, noise
gazhee-waewaewin loud sound, a loud person, loud speech
inawaewae-ssinoowin (root) sound, chime, peal
inawaewaetoowin to create sound or commotion
inawaewaewin (root) sound
inawaung-awaewin to create melody
mamaud-awaewin to begin to utter sounds, calls
maud-waewaewin the sound, music begins
medawae-aubid-aeshinoowin the squeak of grinding, gnashing teeth
medawae-aukinaewin the roar of fire
medawaewae-aushkauwin the roar, crash, pound of waves, surf
medawaewae-augummidae the sound of boiling liquid
medawaewae-gummizoowin the sound of

the bronchial passages; intestinal passages; the purr of a cat
medawaewaeshkauwin to crackle
meda-waewae-waung-awaewin to drum
medawaewae-yaubik-issaewin the jingle of metal, coins
medawaewae-yaungissaewin the flutter, beat of wings
medawae-yaukinaeshkauwin to crackle as in a fire
nawautoowin to create a din
oombeegiziwin to create clamor, tumult
oombeeg-waewaewin the sound is too loud, raucous

inawaewin *language*

auyauwae-itaugooziwin to be incomprehensible, inarticulate
baewi-itaugooziwin to have no conviction in speech from either tone or reason; to be inaudible, barely audible
dazhingaewin to gossip; to talk about, discuss
dinaunikittooniwin to say; to talk
gaganootumaugaewin to speak for; to act as an advocate; to represent; to intercede
geekittoowin to have a word, conversation, discussion
geeshk-iwaewin to suspend speech
geezhawaewin diction, syntax
ginoongaewin to discuss
idumoowin (root) to mean
idumoowin connotation and definition
imoowin (root) language, call, utterance, locution
inawaewidumoowin (root) pitch of voice
inawaewin (root) language
initaugooziwin (root) tone, inflection of voice
keewaewin (root) to articulate, enunciate, pronounce; vocalize
kittoowin (root) to say, utter,
mauzh-geezhiwaewin to have arrogant, impudent speech
mazhinawaewin to communicate a message
migooshkauz-itaugooziwin disturbing, annoying, troublesome words
muzz-itaugooziwin to produce a wakening sound; to call
naepaud-oomoowin to be ungrammatical
ningudawaemoowin fluency
oongaewin to communicate; to impart
wauwin-itaugooziwin to sound confusing, incomprehensible; to confound, perplex, mystify
waweezhi-geezhi-waewin to have rambling speech
weendumaewin to articulate; to pronounce
wini-taugooziwin to speak in riddles
zaeg-itaugooziwin to fear monger

indaendiwin *absence; to be elsewhere, abroad, away, not at home*

aub-oohnzikauwin to be gone for some time
indaendiwin to be absent

indauwin *dwell; live; abide*

daneewin (root) the source, origin of one's fortune, means; the source of one's livelihood, income
daniziwin to abide; to work
dazheewin to haunt; to abide; to while away one's time by the place that provides one's livelihood (from dazhi)
indauwin to dwell; to reside

iniboodjigaewin *saw; cut; etch; flute; score; harrow; furrow*

beessi-boodjigaewin to cut into small pieces, lengths; to make sawdust
daushki-boodjigaewin to saw logs and timbers lengthwise
geeshk-iboodjigaewin to saw
iniboodigaewin (root) to flute, cut, etch, harrow

inidjeen-igaewin *handle a body; to skin*

inidjeenigaewin (root) the manner of handling a body
pika-ozhauwaewin to gut a fish
piki-ishkoonigaewin to defur
piki-oonigaewin to skin
piko-idjeenigaewin to skin; to flay

inidjiwun *spurt; flow*

abi-idjiwun or abeedji-idjiwun to flow in this direction

VERBS

ayaubimoo-idjiwun to eddy, whirl
gazheeskau-idjiwun swift current (the Cree name for the Saskatchewan River)
gidau-idjiwun the watershed, divide, upland
inidjiwun (root) the manner, direction, rate, force, nature, quality, character of a flow of water, i.e. a river
izhae-taubee-idjiwun to flow in reverse
nanau-idjiwun to flow in reverse
neesau-idjiwun below, lowland

inigauziwin *impoverish; deprive*

inigauziwin to be in a sorry state
kitimaug-iwaewin to impoverish
kitimaug-iziwin laziness, poverty (from *kitimiwin*—lazy; indolent)
weeg-iziwin to be deprived, disadvantaged

inigawaudjigaewin *sew; knit; weave; stitch*

azheeg-inigaewin to knit socks
babeem-daubee-ginikaewin to weave
beem-ikeeg-iwaewin to weave
beeto-gauwauzoowin to line
googawaudjigaewin to sew something, as an addition, to a garment
inigawaudjigaewin (root) form, design of sewing, stitching
inigawaussoowin (root) form, quality, design of sewing, stitching
kishki-gawaussoowin to sew, stitch
kooko-medauss-ikaewin to make leggings; to knit socks
mazin-gawauzoowin to embroider
mazin-ibeeg-wauzoowin to embroider, sew lace
mazin-manitou-meenaehnse-gawauzoowin to sew on beads
naubidoo-gawauzoowin to thread; to sew things
niski-gawaudjigaewin to sew on ruffles
onutiga-igaewin to knit
pidukeegishta-igaewin to quilt
pidukee-igaewin to make blankets, quilts
titabee-gawaudjigaewin to sew on a border
wawae-gawauzoowin to repair garments
zigi-gawaudjigaewin to sew two fabrics together end to end

iniginoowin (root) *size; bulk; mass*

gausheehn-iwin to be small
mindidoowin to be large, big

inikaudjigaewin *fit*

daeb'ishkigaewin to fit to a "t"; to be just right
inikaugaewin (root) form and quality of fit
inikingaewin (root) form and quality of fit
mino-kaugaewin to fit comfortably

inikauwin *move*

bimoodae-gooziwin to move family to another place
cheebeewin to twitch
geek-inigaewin to move something over slightly
gooziwin to move, to change residence
inikauwin (root) direction and angle of motion
issaewin (root) involuntary motion
koogauwin to withdraw
koonigaewin to evict
mamaun-idjeenoowin to limber up; to exercise; to stretch the limbs; to do gymnastics
maudjeewin to move; to stir; to begin to come to
maunaud-issaewin to malfunction; to be incompatible
mauz-ikauwin to incite; to rouse
mino-issaewin to operate; to function; to move; to work well, harmoniously

ininigaewin *drop; fumble; fall; mishandle; bumble*

bimi-inigaewin to fumble
buni-inigaewin to fumble and drop; to mishandle
buni-oondumoowin to drop a load
ininigaewin (root) to handle; to manage
nishinaud-inigaewin to mishandle
oondu-goodaewin to fall
pishig-ibidjigaewin to drop a thrown object
pishig-inigaewin to fumble; to drop
pungi-issitchigaewin to drop

inishaewin *hear*

beebaug-ishaewin to hear a ringing, tingling

in the ears
daeb'itumoowin to perceive a faint and distant sound
gaweeniwi-ishaewin to hear indistinctly
geewauss-itumoowin to misunderstand; to mishear; to fail to understand owing to a speaker's pronunciation or dialect; to misconstrue
inishaewin (root) to perceive by hearing a sound
initumoowin (root) to perceive by hearing a voice
noondaugaewin to hear something, someone
noondumaewin to hear
wini-itumoowin to misunderstand

---

inishinoowin *recline; to be inert, prostrate, prone*

---

animik-ooshinoowin to lie face down
ap-ishimoowin to lie on a mattress, etc.
aund-ishinoowin to change position, place
aussiwauk-idjeeshinoowin to recline on something at an angle
auzhi-agid-ishinoowin to lie face up
ayubiwin to lie prostrate
bimauk-ishinoowin to lie prone
bim-aungizoowin to lie stretched out
bizaun-ishinoowin to lie quietly, without moving
gawaek-ishinoowin to turn
geek-ishinoowin to move over slightly
geezhoo-ishinoowin to lie snug as a bug
inaungizoowin angle and posture of collapsed body
iniquae-ishinoowin (root) angle and direction of reclining head
inishinoowin (root) angle and direction of reclining body
izhishinoowin (root) angle and direction of reclining body
maun-ishinoowin to lie uncomfortably
mino-ishinoowin to lie comfortably
nubug-ishinoowin to lay flattened
shawae-idjee-ishinoowin to lie at an angle
zhing-ishinoowin to lie prostrate

---

initumoowin *listen; hear*

---

babaum-itumoowin to heed
bizindumoowin to listen; to obey
geemooss-itaugaewin to eavesdrop
inishaewin (root) perception obtained by hearing a sound
initumoowin (root) perception obtained by hearing a call, voice
nanau-nindo-ishae-itaugaewin to listen for gossip
nindo-ishaewin to listen
nindo-itumoowin to listen for a particular sound, message, story

---

inizhauzoowin *urinate; piss*

---

inizhauzoowin (root) to piss
peend-izhauzoowin to urinate into
zaukumoowin to urinate (woman)
zheesheegiwin to urinate (man)

---

inoodaewin *creep; crawl*

---

bimoodaewin to crawl
inoodaewin (root) pace, direction of crawl

---

inoogaewin *aim; point; make for; course*

---

inoogaewin (root) to point to, direct
inukawae-igaewin to steer, bear in the direction of
izhi-inoogaewin to point; to aim

---

inoomaugaewin *teach; instruct; point the way*

---

inoomaugaewin (root) to point the way
kiki-noomaugaewin to teach

---

inootaugaewin *imitate*

---

inootaugaewin (root) to do as one perceives; to mimic
kikinoo-wautchi-beegaewin to trace
kikinoo-wautchi-itchigaewin to imitate; to practice; to drill; to exemplify
naub-inootumoowin to imitate the voice or words of another; to interpret

---

inoowaunigaewin *resemble; look like*

---

inoowaunigaewin to resemble

---

inossaewin *walk*

---

augum-ossaewin to walk by snowshoe

VERBS

auzhi-gummaewin to go across a lake
baubeenau-ossaewin to stagger
bim-auwinidiwin to walk in a body; to march; to parade
bim-ossaewin to walk
doong-dayae-ossaewin to walk bowlegged
gau-geemood-ossaewin to walk stealthily
ikishinoowin (root) pace, direction, manner of strides
inaudigaukoowin (root) to proceed on foot on ice
inaudigauwin (root) to proceed on foot in water
inaudigauzeewin (root) to proceed on foot on water covered ice
inauwinidiwin (root) to walk in a group, en masse
inauwizoowin to walk in a body; to march; to parade
inossaewin (root) pace, direction, manner of walking
inudoowin (root) to follow and to leave a trail, road
izhi-gummaewin (root) to progress by foot along waterway
kooshki-wae-ossaewin to stagger; to lean; to cant; to pitch
maun-ossaewin to waddle
mayau-ossaewin to walk erect, to lead an upright life
na'eek-ossaewin to walk upstream
nanau-ishkumoowin to walk by snowshoe upstream
nauwi-kummeewin to walk in balance; to walk in the middle
neebidae-ossaewin to walk in a column, single file
neegaun-ossaewin to walk in front; to lead the way
nitau-uhmeewin to walk upriver
shaushoodaukawo-oomaewin to walk against something
tikum-audigaukoowin to cross on ice
tikum-ossaewin to walk across
uhmeewin (root) pace, direction, manner of steps
uhmoowin (root) to walk on an established trail, road, path
zhae-ossaewin to step back; to walk backwards
zhaeyauwae-doowin to walk back

---

inubiwin *sit*

daess-ubiwin to straddle
inubiwin (root) the manner, style of sitting
numiss-ubiwin to sit on haunches
numu-dubiwin to sit
waukaubee-dubiwin to sit in a circle

---

inudaemoowin *cry; weep*

gautchi-mawishkiwin to cry readily
inudaemoowin (root) reason for and tone of crying
mawiwin to cry; to weep
mookinae-mawiwin to cry for food
mook-wauk-idaemoowin to cry, weep for someone who is leaving; to cry to accompany
needawae-widumoowin to keen
nishi-geedawae-imoowin to sob; to sniffle

---

inudauwaewin *sell*

dauwaewin to sell
inudauwaewin to reason for selling; the rate at which an article is sold; the manner of sale

---

inugauwin *dance*

babau-tangissaewin to leap about like a ballet dancer
inugauwin (root) the style and meaning of a dance
mino-waez-inugauwin war dance, an act, pantomime
neemiwin to dance
nishinaudji-pugizoowin to cast one's self about in a lewd manner, to go-go dance

---

inug-inaundjigaewin *hit; strike; belt; slam; knock; smite; club; batter*

gawo-ishkawaeg-inaundjigaewin to knock someone down
geewish-quaeg-inaundjigaewin to stun someone
inuginaundjigaewin (root) character of a blow
mauk-awigaewin to leave a bruise or mark

on object struck
meek-awigaewin to strike an object, target, mark
naunee-noowaewin to batter; to bludgeon
paupaug-aukawigaewin to rap; to tap
piki-taegaewin to smite
piss-eengawaegaewin to slap a face
pugumaugaewin to club
pugund-igaewin to pulverize
puss-eengawae-igunaundjigaewin to slap a face
taetae-waukawigaewin to rap
tautaug-idugaewin to pound
waep-itumoowin to knock back and away

---

inugindaewin *price; value*

---

apeet-aendaugootiwin to cost, value, estimate
inugindaewin to price; to set a value
weendauwaewin to put a value on

---

inugindaussoowin *price; charge; valuate*

---

inu-gindaussoowin to price; to put value on

---

inugoodjigaewin *hang; suspend*

---

goodaewin to hang; to suspend
goodjigaewin to hang; to suspend
goodjinoowin to hang; to suspend
inugoodjigaewin (root) manner of hanging, suspension

---

inuk-issitchigaewin *erect; construct; build; put up*

---

inuk-issitchigaewin to put up; to erect
neem-aukawigaewin to nail in place
neemauk-issitchigaewin to set in place
oombauk-issitchigaewin to prop up
oombauk-oonigaewin to raise up
oonauk-issitchigaewin to set up
pidukauk-issitchigaewin to set upright
piduk-issitchigaewin to erect; to set up
wizhigaewin to prepare; to make a place ready

---

inuk-koodjigaewin *carve; sculpt*

---

inuk-koodjigaewin (root) to carve in a certain manner, style
mazin-koodjigaewin to sculpt

---

inukooniyaewaewin; inupizoowin *dress; clothe*

---

auhnssi-kooniyaewin to change clothing
beecheewin to put on footwear (shoes and socks)
beessi-kooniyaewin to dress up; to put clothing on
inukooniyaewaewin (root) manner, style of dress

---

inumauzoowin *chant; sing*

---

beebaug-itumaewin to chant a death song
inumauzoowin (root) to chant with words to the accompaniment of a drum; to sing a psalm (the word may be from *anami-au-win*—prayer; petition)
ningumoowin to sing

---

inumindji-woowin *feel*

---

inaukidjiwin (root) the nature, character and quality and intensity of a chill or freeze
inikaugoowin kind, nature, character of mark, injury inflicted
inudjiwin (root) to feel or sense the cold
mooshitumoowin to feel, sense someone, something
munsoowin to sense; to feel something is going to happen, or already occurred
nissitoziwin to perceive; to sense

---

inupidjigaewin *fasten; bind; tie*

---

inupidjigaewin (root) the manner and character of fastening
mindjim-aukawigaewin to fasten securely against
mindjimauk-ibidjigaewin to tie securely against
tikoo-bidjigaewin to tie; to bind

---

inushk-awaetumoowin *intrude*

---

awo-ayaekit-autchigaewin to cause weariness
inushk-awaetumoowin to distract; to disrupt
naunibae-tumoowin to enter at the inopportune time

---

ipidjigaewin *savor; taste; sample*

---

ae'poogook (root) quality of flavor

VERBS

goodji-pidjigaewin to taste; to sample
ipidjigaewin (root) quality, nature of taste, flavor

ishkauwin *move; advance; make progress; press ahead*

maudjee-ishkauwin to move ahead; to stir; to prosper
maudjee-ishkumaewin to move forward

ishkawae-igaen *swerve; turn; change course*

beemisko-itauwin to twist; to turn
gawaek-ishinoowin to turn; to change position
gawaek-issitchigaewin to set right; to correct
itauwin (root) to be in motion; to move

ishkawautauwin *quit*

boon-itauwin to quit
geezhee-tauwin to finish what one started
geezhi-itchigaewin to finish a specific project
ishkawae-ssinoowin something comes to an end
ishkawau-tauwin to finish; to end permanently
nawau-tauwin to suspend work or some other endeavor
ningau-gaewin to brake
noog-ishkauwin to stop one's travel

ishkaweewin *stay; remain; sojourn*

dazhee-kinigizhaewin to dally; to remain; to sojourn
ishkaweewin to stay; to remain behind; to go no further
kabaeshiwin to stay over; to camp
katugooneewin to spend a night away from home
niganaubiwin to stay over one night
ningo-inaubiwin to stay over one night
ningo-nebauwin to stay over one night

ishko-naewin *last; endure; survive*

ishka-waugaewin to last to the finish; to survive
ishkawau-inaewin to survive; to be spared
ishko-awautumoowin to last to the end; to survive
ishko-inaewin to survive; to be spared
kabae-eetumoowin to last long
kabae-tumoowin to last long
wae-abi-boon-ishaewin to survive the winter
waebauzoowin to survive the night (said of the sick)

ishp-aenimoowin *pride; conceit; haughty; vain; arrogant*

ishp-aenimoowin to be proud; to be conceited; to be haughty
oondug-aendizoowin to be vain; to be arrogant

ishpi-ishkauwin *ascend; rise; rise up; scale; mount*

agid-aukeewaewin to climb a hill
agidau-widjiwaewin to climb a mountain
aumidjiwaewin to rise as of water
aundawaewin (root) to change place; to move
bizig-aweewin to rise from bed or chair
gizikaewin to take off; to rise in flight
ishp-aundawaewin to climb higher
ishpi-ishkauwin to rise up
ishpi-waungaewin to ascend, as birds do
ka-waundawaewin to climb
oomb-aukishkauwin to rise spontaneously
oomb-ishkauwin to ascend

ishp-inigaewin *heighten; raise*

ishipauk-issitchigaewin to raise higher (as a building or tower)
ishp-inigaewin to raise upward with one's arms

iskidaewin *burn; blaze; singe*

autae-aukodaewin to smoulder
autae-ishkodaewin to smoulder
baushk-aukinaewin to burst into flame
chaugauk-izumaewin to burn all of one's wood
chaug-idaewin to burn completely
cheecheesawauk-izigaewin to singe off pinfeathers, etc
dani-aukodaewin to be in the course of burning

inaukidaewin (root) the cause, character, and nature of a blaze
ishkawau-aukoodaewin to cease burning
ishp-aukinaewin to burn with high flames
iskidaewin to burn
iskugaewin to set fire to
maetizoowin to burn oneself
maudjee-aukodaewin the fire starts
mizheewauk-idaewin to raze
weessauk-idaewin to burn to a crisp, black

iskugaewin *kindle; enkindle*

bizum-augaewin to make smudge fire
inaukidaewin (root) form and manner of fire
iskizigaewin to set ablaze
iskugaewin to set afire; to light a fire
isku-puwaugun-aewin to light a pipe
nawudidaewin catches on fire
pugwaussi-waugaewin to set fire to

isku-ipeetchigaewin *pump; drain*

boo-poodaudjeesh-kawigaewin to pump up
isku-ipeetchigaewin to pump out

isku-ipeewin *strain; screen; sift; drain; pump*

beem-ipeeg-inigaewin to twist dry
eeweewin (root) to put forth energy, strength; make an effort; to try to the utmost
iskoo-baudjigaewin to soak up
iskoo-ipeeg-inigaewin to strain; to wring
isku-ipeewin to drain; to pump
iskutaewin the riverbed, lake bed is dry
koodjeeweewin to strain; to try
nanawaudjeewin to strain for nothing
noozh-ikaudjigaewin to strain; to drain

iskutaewin *empty; void; arid; dry; drained; depleted*

bizhishig to be alone; to be unadulterated
chaug-issaewin to deplete; to exhaust
inishkiniwaewin (root) form, manner, degree of fullness, fit
iskutaewin dry, arid, drained
mizhee-ginigaewin to spill contents out
naun-iwishkinaewin to empty; to exhaust
nauwidudaewin receding, depleting, getting less
nauwo-ishkinaewin less than half full
noozh-kinaewin to be too small; to contain all there is to be contained
zaugidji-nawaessinoowin to void

issutchigaewin (root) *jerk; shove*

gaund-issutchigaewin to shove; to push violently
week-issutchigaewin to jerk toward oneself

izhau'd'iwin *go; travel*

izhau'd'iwin to do
waequawaey-aushkumoowin to go to the very end

izheewin *act; do; perform*

anookeewin to perform any form of labor, be it hunting, fishing, trapping, harvesting, tanning, cooking, making clothes, shoes, snowshoes, etc.; to draw sustenance from the earth; to fulfill one's duties to his family and community
dazhee-kaewin to persist; to persevere; to continue in one task in one place until one is rewarded; to play as children do in one place
doodumoowin to do; to perform; to act; to bring about some result
izheewin (root) the character and style of an act, performance
izhi-tawauwin to be disposed or inclined to a certain political or religious belief
izhi-tchigaewin to perform an act or task in a particular manner
matchi-izhi-tchigaewin to commit an evil, harmful, wrongful deed
mino-tchigaewin to do or perform a good deed

izhi-inumoowin *imagine; conceive; fancy; envision*

izhi-inumoowin to imagine; to have an impression

izhin-izhoowaewin *deliver; take to; dispatch; send*

abeed-umaugaewin to bring to someone
izhin-izhoowaewin to send; to dispatch
maudjeetawaewin to deliver to another
maudjee-tumaugaewin to take to someone

VERBS

izhiwaebut *occur; happen; take place*

adjiteh-issaemigut to happen; to come to pass
inukummikut to occur (an event)
izhiwaebut to happen
kabik-isaemigut to transpire

izhi-winiwaewin *guide; conduct; lead; exemplify; represent; escort; take*

izhiwiniwaewin to conduct; to lead; to guide
kikinoo-waezhiwaewin to show the way
maudjee-izhawaewin to take someone along; to guide; to escort
wini-nawaezhiwaewin to lead astray; to get lost
zaugidji-nauzhiwaewin to lead out

K

kabaeshiwin *lodge; stay over*

kabaeshiwin to stay over

kabik-audjigaewin *pass*

kabik-audjigaewin to pass someone, something
kabik-issaewin passage of time

kabik-issaewin *time*

adjitch-issaewin to occur; to take place
kabik-issaewin the passage of time, events

kaetchinae-wiziwin *freedom; free; independence*

animaewauweewin to do as one needs, wants, and pleases
dibaunoodaewiziwin to be free to come and go
kaetchinae-auwissoowin to exercise freedom; to get one's own way; to do what one wants without regard for others
kaetchinae-wiziwin freedom
tibinawae-auwissoowin to exercise one's will, choice, mind, for one's own benefit, freedom
tibinawae-iwiziwin to have freedom, independence
tibinawae-tumoowin to exercise one's freedom, right of freedom

kagauk-igaewin *harvest; reap; gather in*

kagaukigaewin to gather ripened fruits, vegetables
mauwindooshk-igaewin to gather up

kaugeed-umeewin *limp; hitch; lurch; hobble*

chauchaung-kummeewin to hobble
chau-ossaewin to limp
chaushinoowin to limp
kaugeed-umeewin to shuffle; to step gingerly
taudji-ossaewin to hitch

kaukau-kummikaewin *level; flatten*

kaukau-kummikaewin to level the land
ona-kummika-igaewin to prepare land for seeding
zhingukau-kummikaewin to bulldoze; to flatten; to level
zhingukauwin to flatten

keewae *utter; tone, pitch of voice*

baesh-keewaewin to rasp
gabis-keewaewin to rasp
gee-keewaewin to preach
kittoowin to utter a word; to say
w'd'inaun to say something to someone

kenae-kenaegaewin *mingle; blend; mix; admix*

dago-issitchigaewin to blend
kenae-kenaegaewin to mix
kinigau-wauwi-gummoowin to mix in fluid
oondau-au-gummigaewin to stir

kik-aendumoowin *know*

kageetau-inaendumoowin to see the entire picture
kik-aendumoowin to know
maumoowi-d-aendumoowin to see the entire picture

kikau-igaewin *mark; sign*

kidjigae-beegaewin to draw lines
kidjigaewin to mark in small lines
kikau-igaewin to set up post markers
kikinoo-wautchitchigaewin to set an example; to show the way
waussi-waukawigaewin to blaze a trail

kikauwin *age; grow old*

apeeti-ziwin to attain or to be of a certain age
kaetae-audiziwin old age, senility
kikauwin to grow old
kitiziwin to be old, of advanced age
zazeek-iziwin to be older than . . . [a comparative term]; to be wrinkled

kiki-noonoonwauwaewin *predict; forecast; foretell; foreshadow*

dub-aubindukawaewin to forecast the weather from a reading of signs
iko-zaubindukawaewin to foretell, or to see as far as one can see into the distance, future, as far as one is enabled to do so by the manitous
kiki-noonoonauwaewin to forecast weather from a reading of the stars
kiki-noonoo-waubindakawaewin to read skies to predict weather
kiki-noonoo-waudjimoowin to prophesy

kiki-nootaugaewin *mock*

inootaugaewin (root) to imitate, interpret
inoota-waetchigaewin to mock
kiki-nootaugaewin to imitate a voice
nanau-bidoo-waetchigaewin to mimic
nanau-gizootawaetch-igaewin to mimic

kikinoo-waudidumoowin *see describe*

kikinoo-waudaudjimoowin to describe; to amplify
kikinoo-waudidumoowin to describe
kikinoo-waudjimoowin to describe; to explain

kishk-aendumoowin *mourn; grieve; depress; deject*

kishki-aendumoowin to be sad
naetawae-aendumoowin to mourn
naeto-aetchigaewin to cause grief, sadness
needawae-aendumoowin to mourn
waussitauwaewin to be dejected

kishki-aewiziwin *ability; aptitude; proficiency; skill*

kishki-aewiziwin to be able
kissing-awaudjeewin to do passably
kook-waudjeewin to be willing to do
na-waudjeewin to be willing; to be ready
netau-witchigaewin to do with ease and skill
weengaeziwin to work, to do with care

kishki-ingaewin *persuade*

kishk-ingaewin to convince; to persuade

kishki-meewaewin *urge; press; encourage; convince; cajole; exhort*

gagauhn-zoongaewin to urge, encourage, press, cajole
gageebauz-oongaewin to counsel to evil, mischief, foolish deeds
kishki-ingaewin to persuade; to convince; to prevail upon
kishki-meewaewin to persuade; to convince; to prevail upon
naubauwid-aungaewin to recite
oombauz-oongaewin to incite

kishk-itchigaewin *earn; succeed*

kishk-itchigaewin to earn; to succeed
kishki-tumauzoowin to earn for oneself

kishkoona-waewiziwin *surprise; astonish*

chees-ibiniwaewin to startle; to unsettle
chees-ikaugaewin to stun; to shock
gaessikaugaewin to come upon another during the commission of an act; to overtake someone at the point of departure; to be on time
kishkoona-waewiziwin to be surprised
kishkoo-tautchigaewin to startle; to astonish

kishkoziwin *wake; awaken*

aubizeengawaumoowin to awaken from sleep slowly
aubizeeng-awishiwin to awaken fully
kishkoziwin to waken
madjiwaewin to awaken
maudji-issaewin to waken abruptly
mudji-issaewin to waken abruptly
muzz-imiwaewin to awaken with the voice
muzzi-zoongaewin to rouse with calls
pautauwin to rouse; to interrupt someone's sleep by creating excessive noise
pauwaewin to rouse from sleep

waukau-oongaewin to awaken with a call

kishk-udinoowin *freeze*

agawauskudjiwin to freeze to thin coating of ice
gab-udinoowin to freeze over
inudinoowin (root) tone, degree of freezing, ice, snow
kishk-udinoowin to freeze hard, solid
mashkoow-udinoowin to freeze solid
nanoob-unudinoowin to freeze unevenly, here and there
niguk-udinoowin frost
paupaushk-udinoowin the crack of trees and ice in intense cold

kitigaewin *farm; till the soil; plant*

babeess-kummikugae-boodjigaewin to harrow
bimi-boodjigaewin to plow
kitigaewin to farm; to till the soil
maewishkookaewin to cut and gather hay
mauwund-ooshkigaewin to rake
meeshk-ookaewin to cut and gather hay
pugundigaewin to thresh

kitimiwin *lazy; indolent*

kitimaugooziwin poverty, sloth, the cause of poverty
kitimiwin sloth, laziness, indolence, idleness

kitin-maugaewin *seize; grab; snatch; take; grasp*

kautch-igushk-aundawaewin to latch onto
kitin-maugaewin to seize; to take from
mukundawaewin to seize; to plunder; to appropriate
nawud-inigaewin to seize
pitin-maugaewin to take by mistake
zigauni-quae'n'-igaewin to seize by the hair

kittoowin *say*

kittoowin to say a word

kogaediwin *convene; assemble; gather; collect; amass*

kogaediwin a camp, an assembly, convocation, a summer village consisting of a collection of families
maumoo-wissitchigaewin to put altogether
mauwihnzoowin to gather berries
mauwindj-idiwin to come together
mauwindj-itchigaewin to collect; to amass
mauwind-oonigaewin to amass
meen-kaewin to pick berries

koob-idjigaewin *pull up; hoist*

koobi-idjigaewin to pull up; to raise

koodjeewoowin *try; attempt; essay*

gagawaedjitumoowin to try
koodjeewoowin to try (probably from a contraction of *week-idjiwoowin*—to try by force)
koodji-itchigaewin to essay
week-aweewin to physically try
week-idjiwoowin to try by force
weeki-idjitoowin to attempt

koodji-pidjigaewin *taste; flavor*

beeniss-ipitchigaewin to have a bland taste; to be flavorless
inaugummi-pidjigaewin the flavor of a beverage
inipidjigaewin (root) to derive a certain flavor from taste
koodji-pidjigaewin to taste
kood-oondaunawaewin to taste
mauzh-ipitchigaewin to taste something foul, unpleasant
mino-ipitchigaewin to taste something pleasant, agreeable
weeng-ipitchigaewin to have a sweet tooth for something

koogauwin *vacate; leave*

koogauwin to leave; to vacate; to withdraw

koog-inauwissoowin *bring up; rear; raise*

bimee-auwissoowin to rear
koogin-auwissoowin to raise
ondum-ozhaewin to be tied down with children

kookoobi-naugunikaewin *basket making*

gauweekaewin to gather quills
gauweek-audjigaewin to do quill work

kookoobi-naugunikaewin to make baskets
weegwauss-kaewin to gather birch bark
zhizhookee-wigaewin to apply to pitch to seal containers

kooss-itchigaewin *pile*

agaweed-issitchigaewin to raise a pile still higher
apeet-issitchigaewin to pile so high
kooss-itchigaewin to pile

kotug-iwaewin *misuse; abuse; mistreat; torture; torment*

aubeendj-iwaewin to torment
kotug-iwaewin to torture
matchi-doodumoowin to perpetrate an evil
nigau-iwaewin to abuse

kundoowin *ambush*

kumaugaewin to lie in wait; to waylay someone/for someone
kundoowin to lie in wait; to waylay

M

madootizoowin *purify*

madootizoowin to purify oneself in a "sweat lodge"

maeniss-aendumoowin *shame*

agudji-ayauwin to be shy; to be self-conscious
augid-aendumoowin mortify; humble
maenishiziwin to be discomfited
maeniss-aendumoowin to be ashamed; to be abashed; to be embarrassed

mamaundji-igooziwin *lame; cripple*

mamaundj-igooziwin to be lame; to be bound; to be crippled

mamaup-inaewin *groan; murmur*

mamaup-inaewin to groan

manitou-kaewin *commune with the manitous*

manitou-kaewin to commune with the spirits
manitouwun supernatural, mystery

mashkoowauwin *harden; stiffen; temper*

agawauk-idoodaewin to harden with age, time, or from overcooking
ishkauk-ooziwin to have an erection
mashko-udinoowin to freeze stiff; to freeze solid
mashko-waubik-itchigaewin to temper steel
mashko-waukidjiwin to freeze to near hardness

mashkowut *solid; firm; strong; sound; stable; stout; durable*

mashkow-issitchigaewin to plant solidly
zoong-itchigaewin to strengthen

matchi-doodumoowin *bad; wicked; evil; base; mean; vile*

matchi-doodumoowin to do an evil deed
maunaud-issaewin circumstances go badly
pitchi-doodumoowin to do something accidentally, inadvertently

matchi-geezhi-waewin *swear; curse*

geezhiwaewin (root) the nature and character of remarks
matchi-geezhiwaewin to use bad language

matindaudiwin *share; give; distribute*

matindaudiwin to share
matoondiwin to share
nanauwidau'oonimaukaewin to distribute
naudau-oonimaukaewin to distribute
nenauwidau'oonimaukaewin to distribute

maud-idjiwaewoowin *surge*

maud-idjiwaewoowin to begin to surge

maudjauwin *leave; depart; desert; abandon; vacate*

koogaudiwin to vacate
koogauwin to vacate
maudjauwin to leave; to go away
ninguzh-iwaewin to desert: to forsake
oondjik-inigaewin to leave; to abandon
pungissau-gummissinoowin to leave a sediment

VERBS

maudjee-igiwin *wax; grow; swell; rise; expand; enlarge*

maudjee-igiwin to grow
oombi-idjeeshkauwin to rise (as bread)

maudjee-ishkauwin *proceed; go forward; prosper*

maudjee-ishkauwin to begin to go forward; to prosper

maug-inigaewin *depress*

maug-inigaewin to depress, to pull a trigger

maumeek-awaungaewin *praise; exult; laud*

maumeek-awaungaewin to praise; to laud

maumoow'd'aendumoowin *agree; treat; bargain; negotiate; concur*

daebindoowaewidiwin to enter into mutual obligations (a treaty)
maumoowi'd'aendumoowin to concur; to be of one mind; to reach accord
nauk-oongaewin to bargain; to negotiate
ningot-aendumoowin to be in accord, concord

mauwi-dittumoowin *visit*

mauwi-ditumoowin to visit
nebawautch-iwaewin to visit and to sleep over

mauwid-ookeewin *unite; join; combine*

aussikoo-idaudiwin to support mutually
maumoowi-weekoodaudiwin to combine efforts
mauwid-ookeewin to collaborate
mauwi-indjidiwin an assembly, gathering
mauwizoo-kaugaediwin to unite forces
mauwizoo-kaugaewin to gang up on

mauwundji-itchigaewin *collect; reap; amass; save*

mauwundji-itchigaewin to collect; to save; to put away
mauwund-oonigaewin to collect; to gather; to amass
mauwund-ooshkigaewin to reap
nindoo-ishkigaewin to dun; to ask for money owed

mazhi-auwaewin *harm; injure; abuse; maltreat*

inaup-inunigaewin (root) form and nature of harm inflicted
inigau-auwaewin to devastate, ravage; to put to a sorry, pitiable condition
kotug-iwaewin to abuse; to torment
matchi-doodumoowin to do an evil deed
mazhi-auwaewin to injure

medaewaewin *sound; music; drum; rattle*

abeed-waewaewin the sound arrives, comes
anim-waewae-ishinoowin the resonance of retreating footsteps
anim-waewaetoowin to create a din as one leaves and goes further into the distance
anim-waewaewin the sound, music recedes, fades, etc.
gausk-bugauwin rustling leaves
gausk-eewaewaewin a rasping, rustling sound, noise
gazhee-waewaewin loud sound, a loud person, loud speech
inawaewae-ssinoowin (root) sound, chime, peal
inawaewaetoowin to create sound or commotion
inawaewaewin (root) sound
inawaung-awaewin to create melody
mamaud-awaewin to begin to utter sounds, calls
maud-waewaewin the sound, music begins
medawae-aubid-aeshinoowin the squeak of grinding, gnashing teeth
medawae-aukinaewin the roar of fire
medawaewae-aushkauwin the roar, crash, pound of waves, surf
medawaewae-gummidaewin the sound of boiling liquid
medawaewae-gummizoowin the sound of the bronchial passages; intestinal passages; the purr of a cat
medawaewaeshkauwin to crackle
meda-waewae-waung-awaewin to drum
medawaewae-yaubik-issaewin the jingle of metal, coins

medawaewae-yaungissaewin the flutter, beat of wings
medawae-yaukinaeshkauwin to crackle as in a fire
nawautoowin to create a din
oombeegiziwin to create clamor, tumult
oombeeg-waewaewin the sound is too loud, raucous
peepeeg-waewaewin a shrill sound, call, like the screech of a hawk, flute
pidik-waung-awaewin to make a drumming sound by the beat of wings
titawaetoowin to cause a disturbance
weemb-waewaewin to create a hollow sound; to sound hollow
zeepi-waewaewin to squeak; to squeal
zheen-waewaewin to rattle
zheesheeg-waewaewin to jingle

---

meda-waewae-issitchigaewin *ring*

meda-waewae-issitchigaewin to ring something (a bell)

---

meegaudiwin *fight; battle; war; combat*

dapininidiwin to inflict wounds and death
gagawaedjee-wauzoowin to wrestle
inaupinun-igaewin (root) form of injury inflicted
meegaudiwin to fight; to battle; to war
meegauzoowin to fight another
oondjininidiwin (root) cause of a battle, fight, war
zhauboodaug-inigaewin to Indian wrestle

---

meegawaetch-iwiwaewin *thank*

maumooyauwaewin to give thanks in a body, as a group
meegawaetch-iwiwaewin to give thanks
meegawaewin (root) to give

---

meegawaewin *give; hand over; donate; share*

a'eedaegaewin to give or share what little one has
meegawaewin to give; to hand over

---

meekinaewiziwin *equalize; equality*

meekinawaewin to be alike; to be related
meekinidiwin to rival; to compare; to match; to equal
naenauwaendaugooziwin to deem equal; to accept as equal

---

meek-issaewin *compare; match; correspond*

meek-issaewin to match
naussaub-issaewin to synchronize; to coincide
neezho-inaugaewin to compare
neezho-waetchigaewin to match; to pair
tibishiko-issitchigaewin to set side by side
tibishko-issaewin to coincide; to take place; to be concurrent

---

meek-waundizoowin *boast; brag; crow*

meek-waundizoowin to boast; to exalt oneself
oondug-aenimoo-taugooziwin to crow; to bluster
waeweezhi-waundizoowin to brag

---

mee-wautaewin *reflect; glare*

mee-wautaewin to glare
wauss-aukissinoowin to reflect
wauss-inoodaewin to reflect; to glare; Northern Lights

---

meezeewin *defecate; shit*

meezeewin to defecate
moowitchigaewin to make waste
zhaubookaug-ooziwin to have diarrhea

---

megooshaewin *feast; festival; celebration*

megooshaewin
to have a festival with feasting

---

migooshk-audjiwaewin *trouble; disturb; bother; pester; harry; annoy*

migooshk-audjiwaewin to disturb; to trouble; to annoy

---

minae-ayauwin *scarce; rare*

minae-ayau'd'iwin to be scarce; to be scanty; to be short; to be deficient
minae-ayauwin to be scarce; to be lacking; to be wanting

---

minaeziwin *need*

VERBS

maendaut-issaewin to be short of; to have less than is necessary
minaeziwin to be short of; to need
nindo-waendaussoowin to need; to want
noond-aessaewin to run short of

minau-waunaewin *court; romance; woo*

babau-nindo-waukishkaugaewin to go seeking sex (female)
minau-waunaewin to court; to romance
neezho-babaunikumigaugaewin to seek a mate, partner; to go seeking romance
noodi-inineewaewin to seek out; to court a man
noodi-quaewaewin to seek out; to court a woman

mindau-waewidumoowin *murmur*

mindau-waewidumoowin to murmur

mindji-aungaewin *owe*

mindji-aungaewin to owe; to be obliged to

mindjig-inigaewin *hold; bear*

mindjig-inigaewin to hold
tikoon-auwissoowin to hold a baby
tikoon-igaewin to hold; to have in arms
zig-inik-aenigaewin to hold hands

mindjimauk-ibidjigaewin *bind; tie; secure*

mindjimauk-ibidjigaewin to bind securely to something
tiko-bidjigaewin to tie; to bind

mindjim-inigaewin *keep; retain; hold*

gino-waendumoowin to keep
mindjim-inigaewin to keep and to hold

mindjiwaewin *let*

inaendjigaewin let, permit
mindji-iwaewin to lend or to give something on condition that a like or comparable article be given in return in the future

minduzoowin *net; enmesh*

minduzoowin to become enmeshed, entangled
peend-uzoowin to be, to become inside entangled
pida-inauwaewin to entangle; to catch in a net
pidau-inaugaewin to entangle; to catch in a net

mingiwin *bark*

mingiwin to bark

miniquaewin *drink*

dani-ipeewin the time of drinking
dazhi-ipeewin the place of drinking
geewish-quae-ipeewin to get drunk, dizzy in the head
iski-undjigaewin to drink the entire contents
miniquaewin to drink
mino-ipeewin to be pleasantly drunk, giddy
mozhig-ipeewin to be happy, boisterous from drink
nauz-ipeeg-awaewin to go down to the shore for a drink
week-goondjigaewin to draw into the throat
week-indjigaewin to draw drink as through a straw
wini-ipeewin inebriation, dead drunk, hammered

mino-audjiwaewin *honor; respect; revere; esteem*

kizhae-aendjigaewin to esteem
mino-audjiwaewin to honor; to respect

mino-ayauwin *prosper; good health*

mino-ayauwin to be well to do;to be in comfortable circumstances
mino-waubumaewiziwin to be lucky; to be favored; to be blessed

mino-waen-idjee-nigaewin *embrace; hug*

aukawau-gidaginaewin to embrace by placing arm around back with hand on shoulder
auko-quae-nigaewin to encircle arm about neck
aupito-idjee-nigaewin to encircle arm about waist
mino-waen-idjee-nigaewin to embrace pleasingly

mino-waen-igaewin *like; cherish; to be fond of; caress; stroke*

mino-waen-igaewin to like
misso-waendumoowin to covet; to like; to want
pizhig-aendumoowin to cherish
weeng-meenaewin to be fond of fruit

mino-wauwae-ishkauwin *thrive; improve; prosper*

mino-maudjee-ishkauwin to prosper
mino-wauwae-ishkauwin to enhance one's fortune

mishishu-wissitchigaewin *expose; divulge; open; reveal; bring to light*

baukauk-inigaewin to open
mishishu-wissitchigaewin to make plain and open
mook-inigaewin to bring into open

misqui-eengawaewin *blush; flush; redden*

misqui-eengawaewin to blush; to flush; to redden

misqui-eewin *blood*

baushk-awaewin to let blood
gabi-taugaewin to bleed from the nose
misqui-weewin to bleed
zaugeeskawae-giziwin to let blood

misso-waendumoowin *covet*

misso-waendumoowin to covet; to long for

missug-iziwin *unlucky*

missug-awaudiziwin to be unlucky; to be unfortunate
missug-iziwin to be unlucky; to be unfortunate

mookeewin *emerge; come out; appear; stick out; protrude*

mook-eewin to emerge; to open; to reveal
zaug-aewaewin to appear
zaug-akeewin to break through the earth as a plant does
zaug-aukoowumaewin to emerge from the woods
zaug-aussigaewin the act of the sun, moon breaking through clouds
zaug-umoowin to go out; to exit

moon-aendjigaewin *suspect*

anaum-aendjigaewin to blame
geemood-aendjigaewin to mistrust; to suspect
mooni-aendjigaewin to suspect
moozhi-inaendjigaewin to have an intuition

mooshkin-udjigaewin *fill; put in; heap; fit in*

daeb'ishkinaewin to fill; to fit in
daeb-ipeewin it is full to the brim (liquid)
gawaushk-inudjigaewin to fill; to stuff; to cram
gawaushkwashk-inudjigaewin to fill to the brim
inishkinaewin (root) the manner, mode of filling a container
inudjigaewin (root) to put something in a container
mooshk-aubawaudjigaewin to fill up (liquid)
mooshkinae-ipeedjigaewin to fill with a liquid
mooshk-inudjigaewin to fill; to heap
peendau-ishkoodjigaewin to put in; to ram in; to stuff
winushk-inudjigaewin to load
zaum-ishkinaewin to overfill

moozhig-aendum-itchigaewin *cheer; gladden; hearten; delight*

moozhig-aendum-itchigaewin to make; to create; to generate gladness

moozhig-aendumoowin *uplift; hearten*

baupin-aenimoowin to be amused
mino-waunigooziwin to be amused; to be joyful
moozhig-aendumoowin to be uplifted

moozhig-inigaewin *pick up*

moozhig-inigaewin to pick up

mukaundjeewin *find; discover; uncover; come upon*

mukaundjeewin to find; to locate; to discover
mukoo-idjeenigaewin to grope for and find

VERBS

by touch
mukooshkautchigaewin to find by accident; to do something that leads to the discovery of someone, some object

mukawoowin *aware; conscious; self discovery*
aubizee-ishinoowin to come to; to recover consciousness
mukawoowin to be aware, conscious
zhauzheebau-mukawoowin to be clear headed

muko-wautch-itchigaewin *create; invent*
auttissookaewin to create stories
baubigawaudum-itchigaewin to do things ex tempore
baubigawaudumoowin to be spontaneous
beenissik-autchigaewin to do things ex tempore
bugwooniw-itchigaewin to improvise
manitou-witchigaewin to create
muko-wautchitchigaewin to create; to improvise; to devise

mukundawaewin *plunder; dispossess; appropriate; seize*
gitini-maugaewin to dispossess
mukundawaewin to take from; to plunder; to dispossess

mukwo-waendumoowin *remember; recollect; recall*
gino-weekaewin to memorize
mindjim-aendumoowin to remember; to hold in mind
mukwo-waendumoowin to recall; to find in one's mind
takwo-inaendumoowin to always remember some small act or token

munissoowin *sense; presentiment*
inum-indumaewin to know, sense; to have an intuition
munissoowin to have a premonition, presentiment

N

na-auwiziwin *thin; narrow; slender*
bubugau-itchigaewin to make thin
na'auwiziwin to be slender
weebawau-taewin to make an aisle, corridor, alley
weebawau-waetchigaewin to make narrow
zheeb-aukawaeyauwin sparsely treed

naesh-wishkauwin *slacken*
gaesh-wishkauwin to come loose; to come unseamed
naesh-wishkauwin to come undone

nakawae-ishkaugaewin *meet; date; rendezvous*
kiki-maugaewin to meet by arrangement
nakawae-ishkaugaewin to meet by chance
nakawae-waugaewin to meet another, others at sea

nakawae-pitchigaewin *catch*
nakawae-pitchigaewin to catch
nawud-inigaewin to seize

nakawaetumoowin *answer; reply; respond*
nakawaetumoowin to answer; to reply

nanaukaweewin *rebel; revolt; resist*
aubumeetumoowin to strike back; to resist
nanaukaweewin to resist
nanaupugautumoowin to oppose; to retaliate

nanawautch-itchigaewin *useless; ineffective*
auk-awitchigaewin to waste time
auk-awitumoowin to work for nothing
bawaukidaewin to deplete
nanawaudut it is of no use, useless
nanawautch-itchigaewin to do work for nothing; to expend effort for naught
naunaum-itchigaewin to waste time and effort
naunau-witumoowin to trifle; to waste time

naneed-awaewin *wail*
naneed-awaewin to keen

naneewi-itaugooziwin to lament; to lack strength of voice
wau-oonoowin to wail

naneena-waewidumoowin *grieve; sorrow; lament; mourn; wail*
naneena-waendumoowin to grieve; to lament; to mourn
naneena-waewidumoowin to wail; to keen

naning-kummik-ikauwin *quake; tremor*
naning-kummik-ikauwin to earthquake
naning-kummik-ishkauwin to earthquake

naub-oongaewin *curse; hex; jinx; denounce; execrate*
beem-ishkawaungaewin to execrate
bimi-waushkawaungaewin to execrate
cheessik-aungaewin to denounce
medaekud-aungaewin to invoke evil upon
naunib-oongaewin to curse
noodji-gayaungaewin to hex; to jinx
zaessikood-aetchigaewin to practice witchcraft

naudawaewin *get; fetch; acquire*
gaween-oondu-ipeewin uncertainty in locating water
naudi-inigaewin to go and get
naudin-issaewin to fetch wood
naud-ipeewin to fetch water
naudjid-aubeewin to fetch; to go get; to haul something by a vehicle
naudji-meedjimaewin to go get food
nauz-ipeewin to fetch water
nindo-ipeewin to search for water
ondinimaugaewin to receive from another; to receive for another
oond-inigaewin source of acquisition
oondu-ipeewin (root) the source of water

naud-imaugaewin *help; aid; abet; assist*
aussikaugaewin to give support and encouragement
naud-imaugaewin to fetch something for another
neebawi-itaugaewin to stand by someone in support, sponsorship
weed-ookaugaewin to assist directly
weess-ookaugaewin to aid and abet in the commission of an evil deed

naugutch-auwissoowin *put off; delay; defer*
apeetchitauwin to take one's time
baedau-shkumoowin to saunter; to dawdle
baessikau-tumoowin to go slow
naunookishkau-tumoowin to hesitate; to stop and go
ningau-kummeetumoowin to brake
weekaud-aetchigaewin to be tardy

naunaup-gauzoongaewin *complain*
gageem-doongaewin to complain
nanaup-gauzoongaewin to murmur

naunau-witaukaewin *reduce; lessen; diminish; subtract*
nauwaudj-itchigaewin to lessen; to make smaller
naunau-witaukaewin to reduce gradually
zhae-nimaukaewin to subtract; to take back

naundawiwaewin *heal; cure; doctor*
gagawaedjee-isqawaubeeginigaewin to feel the pulse
kee'igaewin to dress a wound
keegaewin to dress, heal a wound
kikinoo-wautchitchigaewin to vaccinate, inoculate
naunaundiwiwaewin to doctor; to medicate; to treat
neebikeewaewin to administer to during sickness; to doctor
nindo-weeyoowi'iwaewin to treat
noodjimoowin to heal; to improve
pugawaussaewin to express the effectiveness of a medicine person's medicine
sussigoo-tchigaewin to operate
zhaubooz-igaewin to administer a laxative, emetic, purgative

nauzhaewin *dim*
dauhnzhaewin to bedim, to turn down a light
inauhnzhaewin (root) the quality, character of light

VERBS

nauzhaewin to dim

nauzh-eewaewin *descend; go down*

nauzh-eewaewin *to descend*

nauzh-waungaewin the descent of a bird
neesi-aundawaewin to go down

nauzh-inigaewin *lower; set down; take down; slacken*

binauk-koonigaewin to let a sail down
bunu'igaewin to take down
dubuss-inigaewin to set down; to lower
nauzh-aubeeg-inigaewin to let down a line
nauzh-aungaewin to descend by flight; to glide down as a bird
nauzh-inigaewin to lower; to pull down
neess-aubeeg-inigaewin to lower a line
neessi-inigaewin to unhoist
neess-inigaewin to let down
pagid-aubeeg-inigaewin to lower a line
pagid-inigaewin to let go; to set free; to give up; to conduct a funeral
pagidji-waeb-inigaewin to drop

nauzh-waungaewoowin *swoop*

nauzhi-waungaewoowin to swoop down; to dive down

nawaendaugaewin *kinship; relationship*

aungishaehni-maugaewin to be related to another woman
nawae-maugaewin to be related to
nawaend-augaewin to be related to
weetauwissi-maugaewin to be related to another man

nawaudjeewin *eager; ready; keen; willing*

mino-waeziwin to be industrious; to be eager
nawaudjeewin to be willing
saubaudji-ayauwin to be ready
saub-ayauwin to be ready
waenib-auneewin to be available

nawautauwin *rest*

nawaebiwin to rest
nawautauwin to pause for a rest

nawazh-oonaegaewin *choose; select; pick out; elect*

kik-aubindumaewin to pick out
nawazh-oonaegaewin to choose; to select
wae-naubindumoowin to choose; to select

nawuz-inaegaewin *tail; trail*

anamaetumaewin to leave tracks, a trail
anim-oodjigaewin to track
bimi-kanawaewin to leave tracks
bimi-kawaewin to leave tracks
cheecheesh-kawaewin to leave a trail distinguished by furrows on the surface produced by the drag of feet, paws, or claws (as does a killdeer)
inaegaewin (root) direction of one's search, course, bearings, route, beat, ambit
inikawaewin (root) the character, aspect of trail left behind
inishkum (root) state, quality of tracks left behind
kawae-tchigaewin to follow tracks
kawaewin (root) to track; to trail; to tail
mamaung-ishkawaewin to leave large tracks, prints
mamaung-ishkummeewin to leave large tracks, prints
mamaung-ishkummoowin to leave large tracks, prints
nawa-zoowaunauwin to trail someone
nawuz-inaegaewin to shadow; to dog
noozoowaun-aegaewin to trail someone

nebauwin *sleep*

awi-iningawaumiwin to be lost in sleep; to sleepwalk
awi-iningooshiwin to sleepwalk
bim-ossae-ingawaumiwin to sleepwalk
gawoong-ishiwin to fall asleep
gazheeng-gawishinoowin to be drowsy
geekeep-ingooshiwin to drowse
iningawaumiwin (root) the character, quality, kind, duration and density of sleep
kizhingawo-ishinoowin to be sleepy
nebaun-kawaewin to sleepwalk
nebauwin to sleep
neess-ingawaumoowin deep slumber
nikin-gawishimoowin to fall into a deep

sleep, slumber
pauwaeng-awishimoowin to have insomnia
pishi-ingooshiwin to fall asleep
weepaewin to sleep with another
zaum-ingawaumiwin to sleep too long
zheeb-ingawooshiwin to sleep lightly; to nap

nebau-yauwaewin *yawn*
nebau-yauwaewin to yawn

nebawaukauwin *wise; clever; smart; learned*
nebawaukauwin to be smart, wise

neebaubiwin *hold a wake; keep vigil*
neebaubiwin to watch at night, to hold a wake

neebawiwin *marry; wed; stand*
neebawiwin to marry
neezhoo-naubae-igaewin to marry two men (bigamy); to court two men
neezhoo-quae-igaewin to marry two women (bigamy); to court two women
oonaussiwin to have a wedding
oshindiwin to marry
weedigaendiwin to marry, wed

neebidae-issitchigaewin *line; align; file; row*
neebidae-ishinoowin to be in order; to set in order
neebidae-issitchigaewin to set in rows
neebidae-ossaewin to walk in a file, a line, formation
neebinae-ossaewin to walk in a file, a line, formation

neegaewin *trap; snare*
dassoo-izoowin to be pinned down
dassoo-naugaewin to deadfall
neegaewin to trap
ningawaugaewin to snare

neegi-auwissoowin *birth*
neegi-auwissoowin to bear and rear
netau-ozhaewin to be fertile, fruitful

neegiwin *grow; flower; flourish; increase*
baedj-igiwin slow growth
geezh-igiwin fully grown, mature
ginib-igiwin fast, quick, accelerated growth
maudjee-igiwin to grow, thrive; to begin to grow
meeniwun it bears fruit
neegiwin (root) to grow
netau-wigiwin to mature; to flourish
oshki-neegiwin new growth, shoots, saplings
skundjeewun unripe, immature

nee-hinoo-wiziwin *alike; related; similar; identical*
inoowaetchigaewin to resemble
nawae-ingaewin to be related, alike in some respect
nawaend-augaewin to be related, alike in some respect
nee'hinoo-wiziwin to be identical; to be a facsimile; to be parallel
taubishkoo-tchigaewin to clone; to correlate

neekimoowin *growl*
neekimoowin to growl

neendauwaewin *send; dispatch*
auzhi-inauzhiwaewin to send back
iko-nauzhi-waewin to send off; to send away
izhi-nauzhigaewin to dispatch; to send; to commission
izhinizhoowaewin to send; to dispatch
maudjeen-auzhigaewin to send; to drive off, away; to dispatch
mazhin-awaewin to send word, news
mindjidawaewin to send for
neend-auwaewin to send with

neessauk-issaewin *collapse; fold; crumble; cave in*
ispo-kummik-issaewin to cave in
nauzh-issaewin to collapse; to fold
neessauk-issaewin to collapse
neess-inushkauwin to sink in; to give way
ningowau-kummik-issaewin to crumble; to cave in

neessi-kaung-itchigaewin *litter*
neessikaung-itchigaewin to litter
ween-itchigaewin to create dirt

VERBS

neezaun-iziwin *danger; peril; risk; hazard; jeopardy*

bizhi-naewin a close call, close shave, near death
neezaun-iziwin to be dangerous
waun-akeetumaewin to be close to digging one's own grave

nenauwitaugaewin *distribute; allocate; divide*

mauwid-oonimaugaewin to divide evenly
naudau'oonimaukaewin to divide
nenau-witaugaewin to distribute

niboowin *death*

babanaud-iziwin to destroy; to be destroyed
dapinaewin the manner, place, scene of death and killing
ishkawau-inaumoowin to breathe no more
ishkwau-bim-audiziwin to die; to be at the end of life
maudjau'd'iwin to leave
nibowin to die
noondae-yaubauzoowin to fail to survive the night
ondji-naewin the cause of death
weebinaenautumoowin to die quickly
weeg-inaewin to die wretchedly, miserably, dismally

niboo-wiziwin *paralyze*

niboo-wiziwin to paralyze

niki-ipeewin *submerge; dive*

googeewin to dive; to submerge
niki-ipee-issinoowin to submerge; to sink
niki-ipeewin to submerge; to engulf
spo-quae-issaewin to be dunked

niminauwaewin *launch*

nimin-auwaewin to launch a canoe, boat
pissi-kawae-boodjigaewin to launch a rock with a sling

nimisk-aundjigaewin *insult; revile; ridicule*

aubeez-ingaewin to call down; to revile; to malign
nimisk-aundjigaewin to slight; to ridicule; to mock; to give the finger to

nindo-binikaewin *kidnap; take prisoner; raid*

nindo-binikaewin to raid, conduct a foray into the territory of another to pillage, plunder, or take prisoner; a retaliatory armed mission

nindo-inaegaewin *search; look for*

nindo-waubiwin to look for
sooka-waetchigaewin to look for and to sound beaver

nindo-kik-aendjigaewin *learn; study*

kik-aendjigaewin to learn; to know
nindo-kik-aendjigaewin to research; to study

nindo-meegawaewin *offer; proffer; tender*

nindo-meegawaewin to proffer
pagid-inigaewin to set down

nind-oongaewin *call; summon; convoke; beckon*

beebaug-oongaewin to yell a summons
beebaug-waewidumoowin to shout a summons
nindo-omaewin call for help
nind-oongaewin to summon; to call forth; to call hither
nindo-waewaewidumoowin to call; to summon
weeki-zoongaewin to invite; to entice

nindot-umaugaewin *demand*

nindot-umaugaewin to demand; to ask for

nindo-waendaussoowin *want; crave; desire; long; covet*

gauwaudumoowin to crave
maudagaez-aendumoowin to long for
misso-waendumoowin to desire; to covet
nindo-waendumoowin to want

nindo-waubiwin *look for; search*

nindo-inaegaewin to look for; to search
nindo-waubundjigaewin to seek

nindum-eewin *hesitate*

nindumeewaewin to dally; to dawdle

ningau-ishkummaewin *delay*

apeetchitauwin to take one's time
baedau-shkumoowin to saunter; to dawdle
baessikau-tumoowin to go slow
naunookishkau-tumoowin to hesitate; to stop and go
ningau-kummeetumoowin to brake
weekaud-aetchigaewin to be tardy

ningawaugaewin *snare*

ningawaugaewin to snare, enmesh

ningidaewin *melt; thaw; dissolve*

ningidaewin to melt
ningiz-ikoodaewin to dissolve in heat
ningizoowin to melt

ningo-akeewin *bury; inter*

naengaweek-audjigaewin to cover up with soil
ningo-akeewin to bury; to inter
ningo-idjigaewin to cover, bury seedlings, plants with soil
ningo-igaewin to cover with earth, soil
ningo-waungigaewin to cover with sand
zeegaun-iwunginugaewin to scatter sand upon

ningo-waupitaewin *evaporate*

ningo-waupitaewin to evaporate; to vaporize

ningud-iziwin *familiar; intimate; accustom*

nauzhi'ayauwin to feel at home; to accustom
ningud-aendjigaewin to be intimate with
ningud-iziwin familiar, habitual, intimate
weessookaewin to aid; to abet; to boost in friendship

nipee-waupitaewin *vapor; steam*

nipee-waupitaewin to emit steam

nipeewut *wet; dampen; moisten; soak; drench*

aubau-widjigaewin to moisten
booz-aubauwaewin a soaking, drenching
gindjidau-peeg-inigaewin to put in water; to stick in
goondjigaewin to soak; to steep
madookoot dew
niki-ipeeyauh it is flooded
ning-aubau-widjigaewin to dilute; to dissolve
nipeekauh it is wet
nipee-witchigaewin to soak
niss-aubauwaewin to get wet; to drown (see also *inaubauwaewin*—drown)
tik-aubauwaewin to get, receive a cool, cold dunking or drenching
tipau-bauwae-itchigaewin to drench
tip-aubauwidjigaewin to moisten

nishikae-wiziwin *solitary; alone*

nishikae-wiziwin to be alone
nissutae-wiziwin to be alone; to be solitary

nishiwaewin *kill; slay; murder*

dapininidiwin to battle for life; to war; to contest
geem-inunaegaewin to plan and execute a murder
nishiwaewin to kill; to murder
nitaugaewin to kill an animal, bird, etc. for food
nitauwissoowin infanticide
oondjinimoowin to kill for a reason
oondjininidiwin to attempt to kill or maim one another

nishkaud-iziwin *anger; annoyance; ill-temper; rage; fury*

aukawaud-iziwin to be cross; to be grouchy; to be sullen; to be testy; to be touchy
geezhi-gidauzoowin to be already angry or getting over a bout of bad temper
inigidauzoowin (root) cause, character, nature, intensity of anger
nishkaud-iziwin to be angry
nishki-naewin to resent pain, illness, suffering

niss-audiziwin *sober; grave*

niss-audiziwin to be sober

nissauk-inigaewin *unlock (see also nissauk-issitchigaewin—open)*

aub-igaewin to untie; to loosen; to unlock
nissauk-inigaewin to unlock and open

nissauk-issitchigaewin *open; unlock; bare*

baukauk-issitchigaewin to open; to reveal; to uncover
biniskau-bugoneewin the act of flowers opening
daessi-anik-aeniwin to spread arms out
daessi-inindjee-inigaewin to open one's hand, extend fingers
dawau-igaewin to clear, widen, make space
nissauk-issitchigaewin to uncover
taudauw-issitchigaewin to make room, space
zhae-aukissitchigaewin to open

nissaut-umaegaewin *fast; abstain*

ginoowau-poonaewin to fast; to abstain from food
nissaut-umaegaewin to abstain
pakadaekaewin to hunger; to make hunger

nissib-ibinawae-wiziwin *restless; jumpy; agitated*

nissib-ibinawae-wiziwin concerned, worried, disquieted, flustered, bothered
wunushk-awaeziwin restless, hyper, jumpy, agitated

nissi-quaewoowin *comb*

naunauzhaun-quaewoowin dress hair
nissi-quaewoowin to comb

nissitoowin-igaewin *recognize; identify*

nissitoowaenigaewin to recollect; to identify
nissitoowinigaewin to recognize

nissit-otumoowin *understand; comprehend*

nissis-tumoowin to understand
nissit-otumoowin to understand

nissitoziwin *feel; intuit; sense; perceive*

inaukidjiwin (root) the nature, character and quality and intensity of a chill or freeze
inikaugoowin (root) kind, nature, character of mark, injury inflicted
inudjiwin (root) to feel or sense the cold
mooshitumoowin to feel, sense someone, something
munsoowin to sense, to feel something is going to happen or has already occurred
nissitoziwin perceive, sense

nitam-eekaewin *lead; antecede; precede*

chaeni-mikaewin to beat another to the punch; to steal another's thunder
neegauneewin to lead the way
nitam-eekaewin to assume the lead, first position; to take risks first

nitam-itauwin *begin; start; commence; initiate*

maudj-itauwin to start
nitam-itauwin to begin before others do

nitchee-witchigaewin *scold*

geek-aungaewin to call out, dress down
naneeb-ikau-widumoowin to belittle; to disparage
nitchee-witchigaewin to scold; to berate

nitibut *blot; blemish*

nitibut (from nitibiziwin) to have dark mark

noogi-ishkauwin *stall; stop*

noog-ishkauwin to stop

nook-iziwaewin *soften; tenderize*

ninga-kummutaewin soften the soil
nook-audjigaewin to soften
nook-itchigaewin to temper
nook-iziwaewin to tenderize

noom-inigaewin *rub; knead; massage*

mamig-oonigaewin to knead
mayau-weewin to rub oneself against something to relieve an itch
naunauzh-idjeeb-inigaewin massage
noom-inigaewin to rub, knead with oil, liniment
zashoo-nigaewin to rub down
zheeshoob-inigaewin to rub
zinig-idjeeb-inigaewin to rub with oil, liniment

noondae-issaewin *lack; need*

minaeziwin to lack; to need
noond-aessaewin to be short of

noossik-awaudjigaewin *lick*

noossik-awaudjigaewin to lick; to lap; to tongue

nubug-ishkoodjigaewin *crush; flatten; mash; squash*

nubug-ishkoodjigaewin to flatten
paupaug-ishkoodjigaewin to crush
tautaug-ishkoodjigaewin to mash; to crumble
zeendauk-iwigaewin to squeeze
zhimug-ishkaugaewin to flatten; to squash

O

odissigoowin *receive; get*

odissigoowin to receive, get something
odit-inumoowin to receive; to gain; to reach; to achieve

odji-kun-aetumoowin *slouch*

odji-gauwi-kunnaetauwin to slouch one's shoulders forward
odji-kun-aetumoowin to slouch; to be slumped down

odjitauwin *shrink*

chib-waukidaewin to shrink in the heat
odjitauwin to shrink from
ojib-waubauwaewin to shrink because of wetness
zheeshee-beeg-ibidjigaewin to shrink something
zheeshee-beeg-ishkauwin to shrink

odjitumoowin *withdraw; retire*

ayaum-pissaewin to fly back (birds)
naeyaub-eeshkumaewin return to same place
odji-quae-waeniwin to withdraw or draw in one's head as does a turtle
odjitumoowin to withdraw
pissik-aubeewin to return (same day)
zhae-akeewaewin to return home
zhaemoowin to fall back; to retrace steps; to go back

ogimauk-indaugaewin *govern; lead; administer; operate; manage; conduct*

bimeek-augaewin to operate; to administer; to manage
dibaugimauwin to oversee; to supervise; to superintend
neegaun-iziwin to lead
ogimauk-indaugaewin to govern

onaunigawaess-itaugooziwin *cheer*

onaunigawaess-itaugooziwin to cheer

onawaeziwin (root) *luck*

mino-waubum-aewiziwin to be fortunate, lucky
onawaewiziwin to be lucky

ondji (root) *purpose; cause; origin*

ohnzikauwin to go for a purpose
ondiziwin to purpose; to aspire to
ondji (root) origin; reason for

onushk-inudjigaewin *pack*

onushk-inudauwissoowin to pack; to cram; to fill; to stuff
onushk-inudjigaewin to pack; to cram; to fill; to stuff

oohnziwin *ooze; seep; pus*

mineewin to pus
oohnziwin to ooze; to seep

oombauh-iwaewin *excite; arouse; interest; stimulate*

aumino-oozoowaewin arouse sexually
aushiwaewin to arouse; to excite; to incite
oombauh-iwaewin to arouse; to interest
oombi-yauwaewin to pique; to stimulate
oombuzhi-oongaewin to tease; to tantalize

oomb-inigaewin *lift; boost; pry; lever; hoist; raise; elevate*

dautig-issitchigaewin to tilt, slant slightly upwards
gaweed-inigaewin to pry; to boost; to elevate
koowaeg-inigaewin raise slightly
nikae-eek-issitchigaewin to hoist
oomb-anikaeniwin to uplift, raise an arm, arms

VERBS

oomb-aukawigaewin to hoist
oomb-aukinigaewin to hoist; to elevate
oomb-aukoodjigaewin to hoist a sail
oombi-inimaunginaeniwin to shrug one's shoulders
oomb-inigaewin to raise; to lift
oombi-quaeniwin to raise one's head

oomb-oomoowaewin *mount*

oomb-oomigoowin to mount a horse
oomb-oomoowaewin to hoist something, someone to one's back

oombuzh-eekaugaewin *molest*

megooshkaudj-iwaewin to annoy; to vex; to trouble
megooshkautch-itchigaewin to annoy; to vex; to trouble
oomb-uzheekaugaewin to pester; to hector

oonaewin *carry; bear; transport; shoulder; tote*

ani-numdjigaewin to carry in one's mouth as do animals and birds
ani-numigaewin to carry in the beak
auwidji-inaewin to carry, transport on one's back
awid-aussoowin to transport
bauwaun-oowinaewin to be unable to carry a load, burden
bimi-oonaewin to carry on one's back, as does a horse
bim-oongaewin to carry on one's back, as does a horse
gozig-oonaewin to bear a heavy load
mamaudjee-izhiwaewin to take elsewhere
mamigaewin to remove
maudjeed-auwissoowin to carry off
maudjee-itum-augaewin to deliver
naung-oonaewin to bear a light load
neessikig-oonaewin to carry ill wrapped, cumbersome articles that impede movement
oombi-oonaewin to hoist to one's back
oonaewin to carry
weewizhi-oonaewin to bear troubles
winigumaewin to portage

oonaewiziwin *menstruate*

aundj-igaesseewaewin to change blood
oonae-wiziwin to menstruate

oonaubaewauwin *smoothen; gloss; sparkle; polish*

oonaubaek-itchigaewin to polish and gloss
zhooni'auh silver, sparkling
zhooshaun-igaewin burnish; glaze
zhooshk-idjigaewin to polish and slick
zhooshk-oodjigaewin to plane

oonauwaewin *hiccup*

oonauwaewin to hiccup

oondaewin *boil*

aubau-gummizigaewin to heat up
inau-gummidaewin (root) the manner of boiling
iskee-gummizigaewin to boil down
oomb-igummidaewin to boil up; to bubble
oondaewin to boil

oondau-igaewin *stir; blend; mix; mingle*

mamaudau-gumm-issitchigaewin to stir a liquid; to begin brewing
oonau-igaewin to stir
oondau-au-gummig-aewin to stir a liquid
oondau-igaewin to stir
oondau-itchigaewin to cause the stirring of fluid
tamoonga-igaewin to slap and to stir water as does a beaver with its tail

oondjeewin (root) *origin; source; cause; begin; issue; start*

oondjeewin to originate
oondjibauwin to come from

oondjigaewin *suck*

indjigaewin (root) to take into the mouth
weeki-indjigaewin to draw into the mouth
zoob-indjigaewin to suck

oondjigauwin *leak; seep; ooze; dribble*

oondjigauwin leak; seep; ooze; dribble

oondji-maugaewin *forbid; dissuade; warn; prohibit; disallow*

aungawaumi-maugaewin to warn

aunisheet-maugaewin to dissuade
gina-maugaewin to forbid
oondji-maugaewin to prohibit; to disallow

oondumeewin (root) *busy; diligence; occupy; industrious*

meekawaud-iziwin to be industrious
meekwaud-anookeewin to be diligently at work
oondum-eewin to be preoccupied
oondum-iziwin to be preoccupied
oondum-tauwin (nindumtauwin?) to be busy

oondumiwaewin *distract*

nushkawae-itchigaewin to distract
nushk-waetumoowin to distract
oondum-iwaewin to divert attention

oonoowin *howl*

oonoowin (root) to howl
wau-oonoowin to howl as a dog, wolf, whip-poorwill

oshki-bugauwin *bud; blossom*

meenikauni-bugauwin to sprout buds
oshki-bugauwin to bloom
waub-bugonaewin to blossom
waussi-bugauwin to bud, bloom, break into bud, petals
zaug-aunawaewin to sprout; to tail out
zaug-bugauwin to sprout
zaug-buniwin to bud

P

pabushk-iziwin *immature; young; fresh; unripe; raw; green*

pabushk-iziwin to be immature

pagid-inigaewin *yield; give up; give in*

aunisheetumaewin to give up
niwaeziwin to go into a snit when one doesn't have one's way
wawaunitoowin to give in out of misery and helplessness

pagiz-oongaewin *taunt; slight; ridicule; censure; slander*

baupi-zoongaewin to slight; to ridicule
bugwo-inoongaewin to slander
meekindjiwaewin censure; call down
pagi-zoongaewin to accuse; to cast aspersions

papag-ininigaewin *invent; create*

papag-iningaewin invent; create

paubawaewin *season; blend*

paubawaewin to season; to blend

paugaukid-ooziwin *lean; thin; skinny; scrawny*

paugaukid-ooziwin to be as thin as a skeleton

peendigae-ishkaugaewin *invade*

peendigaeshkaugaewin to walk, march into someone's home or territory

peendigaewin *enter; go in*

chaek-aukoowumaewin to enter the woods
peendig-aenissaewin to bring wood indoors
peendig-aessaewin to fall indoors; to fall into the house
peendigaewin to enter
zhaeg-aukoowimaewin to enter the woods
zhae-weetumoowin to enter backwards; to go back in
zhashood-aukoowumaegaewin to skirt woods; to go along the edge

pekaediwin *separate; part; break; split; cleave*

pekaediwin to separate; to diverge

pekaunaeyauwin *different*

maunae-yaugidinoowin to differentiate; to contrast
pekaunae-yaugidinoowin to distinguish

pidug-inigoowin *nightmare*

pidug-inigoowin to have a bad dream

pishko-ibinigaewin *pluck; defeather*

pishko-ibinigaewin to pluck; to defeather

pissaun-ikaewin *trench; canal; ditch*

VERBS

pussaun-ikaewin to make a ditch, canal
zeepee-kautchigaewin to make a ditch

---

pissikaugaewin *bump; collide; run into*

pissi-kaugaewin to crash into
pitauk-ishinoowin to bang into
pitauk-ishkaugaewin to collide with; to bump
pitauk-ishkoodaudiwin to collide into one another

---

pitchi-boonaegaewin *poison*

matchi-mashki-akeetaugaewin to administer poison
pitchi-boonaegaewin to give poison to (from *pitchi-niboonaegaewin*—to administer a poison that brings about death that looks accidental)

---

pizhuhnzhae-igaewin *punish; whip*

pishuhnzhaeg-igaewin to punish; to whip

---

pizoowin *fly*

anim-aushiwin to fly a certain course
auhnz-pizoowin to fly together as a flock
aunississauwaewin fly as a flock
aushoowin; aussoowin (root) manner, form, rate, character, etc. of wind-generated flight
bimaushiwin to sail
bimi-issaewin passage of time
bimi-pizoowin to fly by
gaweeshk-waewaewin whiz in flight
geewitau-ayaushiwin fly in circles
gizikaewin to take flight; to lift off
inaungaewin; inawaungaewin (root) flight of a bird
ishpi-waungaewin to ascend, gain altitude
issaewin (root) manner, form, rate, character, etc. of involuntary motion
izoowin (root) manner, form, rate, character, etc. of conducted, voluntary motion—spontaneous
nauzhi-waungaewin to descend; to fly lower
ond-aushiwin to fly from
oomb-aussitchigaewin to cause objects to fly up or take flight
oomb-ipizoowin to take flight
oomb-issaewin to take flight
pazigawawin to rise in flight
pizub-aussoowin to fly in circles
sokipizoowin to fly together as of a flock
zhooshk-waewaewin-aushiwin whiz in flight

---

pukwauk-iweewin *double up; clench; clinch; scrunch up*

pukwauk-inindjeetauwin to clench a fist

---

pungishinoowin *fall; drop; plunge; collapse; pitch down*

binaungaewin to fall in, during flight
bin-aussinoowin blow down
binu-goodaewin to fall, drop involuntarily
cheeng-idjissaewin teeter and totter and then collapse
gawo-issaewin to collapse; to fall
geep-goodaewin fall from a perch, moorings
geep-issaewin to fall from a ledge
inigoodaewin (root) form, state, nature of suspension
oondu-goodjinoowin to fall from a perch
pung-ishinoowin to fall; to drop; to plunge

---

pungu-oowin *pulse*

pungu'oowin to pulse; to fall drop-by-drop

---

puss-waewae-kunaundjigaewin *slap*

pussa-waebitumoowin to slap
puss-eengae-kunaundjigaewin to slap a face, in the face
puss-eengaewauwin to slap in the face

---

putoowin *run*

putoowin (root) run

---

puwaewin *run away; flee*

puwaewin (root) run away; flee
zhae-puwaewin to run back; to run backward

S

---

shau-wautchigaewin *flush out; scare up*

aumau-bizigaewin to smoke out
shauk-awitchigaewin to alarm one's quarry
shau-wautchigaewin to flush up quarry

shawae-issitchigaewin *tilt*
shawae-issitchigaewin to set at an angle

shoowaudjeewin *improve; get better*
aub-izeeshinoowin to improve; to get better; to revive
shoowaudjeewin to improve slowly; to recover

shugawaewin *vomit; puke*
augidaewin to be nauseous
shugawaewin to vomit, puke
shushigawaewin to vomit, puke

shum-oodjigaewin *bait; lure*
kookae-yautchigaewin to bait; to attract
shum-oodjigaewin to bait

shungaewin *feed; nourish; serve food*
doodooshkaewin to suckle, nurse at a breast for nourishment
noon-auwissoowin to nourish from a breast; to breastfeed a child
shum-auwissoowin to feed infants, little children
shungaewin to feed; to serve food

siboodji-igaewin *sharpen; hone; taper; put an edge to*
geen-iboodj-igaewin to hone; to taper
geen-ikootchigaewin to put an edge to
siboodj-igaewin to file

skwaudjigaewin *spit*
skwaudjigaewin to spit

soossawaewae-ishkaugaewin *scatter; broadcast; disseminate*
soossawae-waeb-inigaewin to broadcast; to scatter
soossawaewae-ishkaugaewin to disperse
soossawaeyau-itaegaewin to disseminate

sooss-idumoowin *cough*
sooss-idumoowin to cough

sukaudjigaewin *gain; prosper; achieve; profit*
abeetumoowin to achieve; to arrive; to gain
daneewin to prosper; to add to one's lot
kishkitchigaewin to achieve with difficulty
sukaudjigaewin to prosper

sumiziwin *quick; supple; fit; agile; nimble*
chaepiziwin to be nimble, supple
gawaushki-waeziwin to have agility
gazhee-ozhae-wiziwin to be hale, hearty, fit, supple
sumiziwin spry

sundjigoowin *deposit; store; put away; stash; put; place; set*
atchigaewin to put; to set
pagid-inigaewin to set down; to release, let go
wizh-issitchigaewin to set; to prepare

T

taetib-ishkauwin *roll*
taetib-ishkauwin to roll and pitch

taugaewin *gamble; play; complete*
taugaewin to play; to gamble
week-itchitoowin to try; to attempt

tautaug-ishkumoowin *trample; stamp on; batter*
paupaug-idjeesh-kawigaewin to pack, tramp down
paupaug-ishkumoowin to pack down
tautaug-idugigaewin to pulverize
tiko-kaud-itchigaewin to step on; to trample upon

tibissitawaugaewin *duty; responsibility; obligation*
tibissitawaugaewin to owe a duty
tibissitawautumoowin to discharge a duty

tikauyauwin *cold; cool; chilly*
beengaedjiwin to be cool, chilly; to have chills
gawudjiwin to be cold
inaukidjiwin (root) the manner, character of a cold, chill
kikudjiwin to catch a cold or flu
kissinaumigut it is cold
tikauyauh it is cool

VERBS

tikudjiwin to catch a cold

tikoongaewin *bite; nip*

nawud-ingaewin to nip
pika-waendjigaen to bite off a morsel, chunk
tikoongaewin to bite

tikumeewin *cross*

auzhidae-ikaugaewin to cross paths, trails, courses without meeting; to miss meeting another
auzhi-waewigaewin to cross over to the other side
auzh-oogaewin to cross over and back; to go back and forth
tikumeewin to cross over

tissigaewin *paint; color*

shooss-igugaewin to paint with a brush
tissigaewin to paint; to color

tungishkigaewin *kick; boot*

tungishkigaewin to kick; to boot

U

ummeewin *step; stride; pace*

binu-kummeewin to miss a step; to misstep
daumeewin to step
inukummeewin (root) manner, character of pace, step
ishkummeewin (root) manner, character of pace, step
kummeewin (root) a step, footing
mino-kummeewin good footing
mituh-oomaewin to walk on snow without snowshoes
muzaekawae-kummeewin to walk with snow sticking to snowshoes
nawau-ummeewin to stumble
tiko-akeewin to step
ummeewin (root) manner, character of pace, step

W

waebeewin *flee; escape; elude; run away*

gee'iwigaewin slip away from
geemeewin sneak away; make off unnoticed
geetauk-aweewin to break free from someone's grasp
gidisk-eewaewin break free as from bondage
waebeewin run off; bolt away

waeb-igaewin *sweep; dust; clean*

bawae-iginigaewin to shake off dust
bawi-ae'igaewin to shake off dust
bawin-waeb-inigaewin to shake dust from
cheeg-itugaewin to sweep off
cheeshau-goonaegaewin to clear snow
cheesh-itugaewin to sweep off
waeb-igaewin to sweep away

waeb-inigaewin *throw; cast; pitch; hurl*

assineegaewin (root) the force and direction of pitching stones
beem-assineegaewin to pitch stones at
beem-autikawae-gaewin to throw sticks at
inaussitchigaewin (root) the rate, direction and force of flight
neessi-waeb-inigaewin to throw; to cast down
oombi-waeb-inigaewin to throw up, aloft
pikitae-yauk-issitchigaewin to throw, smash, dash, an object against something
pugitchigaewin to throw; to cast; to pitch
pugizoowin to throw oneself
waeb-aussitchigaewin to let fly
waeb-inigaewin to cast aside; to abandon; to forsake

waendautchigaewin *skill; do with ease; leisure*

kishki-aewiziwin to be able
kissing-awaudjeewin to do passably
kook-waudjeewin to be willing to do
na-waudjeewin to be willing, ready
netau-witchigaewin to do with ease and skill
weengaeziwin to work; to do with care

waewaeb-aussinoowin *flag; wave; flutter*

pikitae-aussinoowin to flap with resonance

waewae'b'aussinoowin to wave and flutter

waewaeb-issaewin *wag*

waewaeb-aunoowaewin to wag a tail
waewaeb-aussinoowin to flutter and flap in the wind
waewaeb-ishkauwin to wag
waewaeb-issaewin to wag

waewae-ipizoowin *sway; swing; wave*

auyauzhook-ipizoowin to sway, back and forth
chaucheebauk-issaewin to rock back and forth
waewae-ipizoowin to swing
zhaushoobauk-ipizoowin to bend to and fro

wae-waetikoogaewin *wave; flutter; flag; flap*

kidjigaun-inaussinoowin to flutter in a breeze; to flap
wae-waetikoogaewin to wave
wau-wautikoogaewin to wave

waeweeb-itauwin *hurry*

gazheekauwin to be swift, fleet
ginibitumoowin to be rapid
tautibeewin to be quick, fast, brisk
waeweebitauwin to make haste

waezhi-itchigaewin *fix; repair; patch; mend; restore; refit; remodel; rebuild*

bego-igaewin to mend; to repair a hole, tear, rip
nanautch-itchigaewin to repair, patch, mend, restore
nau-tchitchigaewin to repair
waeshi-itchigaewin to fix; to rebuild

wanaudut *rot; deteriorate; go bad; taint; spoil; corrupt; debauch*

banaudiziwin deteriorate
banaudjiwaewin to corrupt
banaudut it is ruined, wrecked
beegushkinuniwin; bigushk-inuniwin rot, putrefy
bunaud-itchigaewin to spoil; to ruin
neeng-inutiwin to spoil; to taint
suttae-ssinoowin it is rancid
wanaudut to spoil; to waste
zhae-gummissinoowin; zeewau-gummissin to go sour
zheeg-waussinoowin to wither away

waubidaewin *ripe; aged; mature; ready*

geezhi-meenigauwin it is ripe, ready, fit
titaemingut it is ripe, fully colored
waubidaewin it is ripe, aged

waubundawaewin *prove; verify; substantiate; show; reveal; open; bring out; bare; disclose*

waubundawaewin to show

waubundumaewin *see; imagine; perceive; observe*

auko-waubundumaewin to look on in anger
baushk-aubiwin to see through swollen, bleary eyes
bizung-waub-issaewin to blink
bizung-waubiwin to close the eyes
buguk-aubiwin to see clearly, plainly; to open eyes widely
daeb-aubiwin to be able to see an object in the distance
dautig-aubiwin to look upward, aloft
doosk-aubiwin to see through half-opened eyes
geewauz-aubiwin to have blurred vision
inaubindumoowin (root) to perceive
izhinumoowin (root) to perceive
maumikauz-aubiwin to behold something unusual, wonderful, inspiring, new, awesome, etc.
mau-mino-waubiwin to have 20:20 vision; to see clearly
mauz-aubindumaewin to have impaired vision
mino-waubiwin to see well, clearly; to have an unobstructed view
mishi-geeshk-ibikutae-bindumaewin to be dazzled to temporary blindness
ninkaubindumaewin to lose sight of; to faint
oombaunaet-aubindumaewin a mirage
tibikinae-waubiwin to lose sight; to have failing sight
waubindumaewin sight
waubiwin to see
waussae-aubindumaewin to have a vision, revelation

waussi-aubizoowin to be dazzled
zaeg-aubindumaewin to behold a frightening, traumatic spectacle
zauss-aubizoowin to be dazzled

waubishkauwin *whiten; lighten; illuminate*

waub (root) to lighten, clear, whiten
waubidaewin to ripen
waub-ishkugaewin to paint white
waubun-aewiziwin to pale; to ashen; to blanch
waut-aetchigaewin to illuminate

waubunoowin *dawn; daybreak*

abeed-aubun to dawn
waubunoowin to dawn

waug-inigaewin *warp; bend*

waug-inigaewin to bend, warp something

waukae-yauwin *clear*

mishee-igaewin to clear a forest; cut down to clear
mishee-tikwoon-aegaewin to lop off limbs
mishishiwauk-aeyauwin to be lucid
pagukau-waeyauwin to be clear; to be lucid
waukae-yauwin to be clear
waushae-gummauwin clear water
waussae-yauwin to become clear; to brighten; to clear up

waun-ikaewin *dig; dig up; pull up; hoe; till*

dubuss-aunikaewin to hollow out
moon-igaewin to dig up
moon-ishkawaewin to hoe
piko-wauk-cheeb-idjigaewin to dig for and pull up roots
puss-aunikaewin to dig a ditch, moat, trench; to make a canal
waun-ikaewin to dig

wauni-waungaewin *warn*

ashawa-munissoowin to be forewarned
ashweegaewin to be vigilant
aungawaumeewin to be cautious
aungwaum-aungaewin to caution
kaugeed-auweewin to take precaution
wauni-waungaewin to warn

waussae'n'igaewin *illuminate; brighten; shine; glitter*

waussae'n'igaewin to illuminate
waussae-tchigaewin to illuminate
wautae-tchigaewin to brighten

waussi-waugaewin *light; shine; illuminate; brighten*

geezh-aussigaewin already shining; finished shining
geezhig-autaewin moonlight; moonlight as bright as day
geezhoo-aussigaewin a warming light
inaukinaewin (root) nature, quality, character of fire and light produced by fire or blaze
inaussigaewin (root) quality, character of sunlight
inautaewin (root) quality, character of sun and moonlight
inauzhaewin (root) quality and character of light
mishish-waussigaewin to brighten and to make plain
nanig-awaussaeyauwin mirage
pissikaukin-aessaewin flickering light
waussae-ayaumigut it is bright, clear
waussae-tchigaewin to make a light; to illuminate
waussi-waugaewin to illuminate with a torch
zaug-aussigaewin to shine through
zheeb-waussigaewin to shine through; to make transparent

wau-weendaussoowin *pronounce; articulate; enunciate*

wau-weendaussoowin to pronounce; to articulate

wau-weendumaugaewin *vow*

wau-weendumaugaewin to promise; to undertake

wauwiyaeziwin *round; circle; gird; rotate; cycle*

geewitau-ishkumaewin to go around
titabaussaewin to spin; to gyrate
titabauyauk-itchigaewin to encircle; to gird
titabeessaewin to whirl; to twirl; to rotate
waun-inishkauwin to go around

wauwi-yautumaewin to make a circle

weedjeewaewin *accompany; go with; escort; keep company*

weedjeendiwin to accompany; to associate with
weedjeewaewin to go along with; to follow

weedji-akiwaendiwin *befriend*

abinzibeewin to warm up to; to befriend
weedigik-inaendiwin sorority
weekau-inaendiwin brotherhood
weekji-akiwaendiwin to befriend

week-ingaewin; weekiz-oongaewin *induce; invite; lure; entrance; tantalize*

aushi-augaewin enchant; entrance; tantalize; tease
aushi-waewin enchant; entrance; tantalize; tease
waebee-ingaewin to coax
weekiz-oongaewin invite; lure
week-waudjigaewin draw; attract; enchant

week-iweewin *pry; lift; lever (lift); exert strength*

adaubau-peeg-ibidjigaewin to pull a canoe up rapids
bimi-daubaudumoowin to draw or drag an object
weeki-bau-beeg-inigaewin to pull, draw in a rope, string
weeki-daubaudumoowin to draw an object to oneself
weeki-ibidjigaewin to draw an object to oneself
week-iweewin to exert oneself in pulling an object

weendaussoowin *name; nominate; appoint; designate; delegate*

anoodaugaewin to nominate; to delegate
inikauzoowin (root) a name
izhi-inikauzoowin a given name
weehnzoowin to give a name to
weendaussoowin to name; give a name to; call
zeegundaugaewin to baptize

weendumaugaewin *proclaim; make known; spread news; tell*

kikaendumoonigaewin make known
mazhin-awaetchigaewin to deliver word
weendumaugaewin to tell

weeninoowin *fat; corpulence*

inigaumoowin (root) the degree and aspect of corpulence
weeninoowin fatness, corpulence

ween-itchigaewin *dirty; soil; tarnish; pollute; clutter*

pingiwi-yaussitchigaewin to cause sand or dust to fly
ween-augummugaewin to muddy the waters; to pollute a liquid of fluid
weenaung-itchigaewin to litter; to clutter
ween-itchigaewin to mess; to soil; to mar
weeniziwin impurity, lust, lechery
ween-ozhaewin dirty of body

weeshki-bugaewin *sweeten*

weeshkibugaewin to sweeten
zeezibaukootookaewin to sugar something; to process maple sugar; to sweeten

weessaup-oongaewin *charm; lure; allure; entice; draw*

weekibi-ozhiwaewin to entice; to lure
weessaup-oongaewin to lure; to enchant

weessigitoowin *suffer*

aunimitoowin to be in torment
inigauziwin to be wretched
kotugitoowin to suffer
nanaedjitumoowin to cause great suffering, agony
weessigitoowin to be in agony

weessikiwautch-itchigaewin *careless; slovenly; slipshod*

daebinauk-itchigaewin to be careless; to be casual; to be indifferent
mamauzh-eeweewin to be slovenly; to be slipshod
weessikiwautch-itchigaewin to be negligent; to be haphazard

VERBS

weesiniwin *eat; dine*

adoopoowin to eat on something (such as a table)
amoowauwaewin to feed on
aneemikookaewin eat and forage along the way
baedj-issineewin to eat slowly
biniskawau-gizumaewin to digest
cheechee-gindjigaewin to gnaw on
daeb-issineewin eat to fullness
dazhi-weessiniwin during the course of a meal; at the site of a the meal
gaukaup-indjigaewin to crunch and crackle
goodaunawaewin to eat everything; eat all
inundjigaewin (root) manner of form of eating
kishk-undjigaewin to bite through something hard
meedjiwin to eat
moozhig-undjigaewin to eat remains, crumbs; to eat off the floor or ground
nawupoowin a lunch
neessiniwin, weessiniwin to eat
nindo-wissineewin to seek a meal
ningau-poonaewin eat and forage along the way
nipaudiziwin to eat to excess
oshkimoowin to eat raw, uncooked
pundjigaewin to eat with condiments, sauces, gravies, etc.
tootoo-gindjigaewin to nibble on
weedoopingaewin to eat, dine with company
zeewaukawaewin eat corn
zhaushau-gindjigaewin to chew on

weeyoowiwin *copulate*

boodji-cheedinaegaewin to poke
boodji-kidinaegaewin to poke
naeg-inigaewin to insert
peend-inigaewin to put in
weeyoowiwin to copulate (*lit.* to flesh)

wineekaewin *lose; leave behind*

wineekaewin to lose; to leave behind
winishinoowin to lose one's way, one's bearings
winitaussoowin to suffer a loss
winitchigaewin to lose; to misplace
winu-audjigaewin to lose one's way

winikauwin *stray; wander; digress; branch off*

inikauwin (root) direction of one's course
pekaediwin to separate
pekae-ishkaugaewin to force someone to step aside
pekaewin to leave the course, route, road
winikauwin to lose one's bearings

winissaewin *mistake; error*

bautau-idiwin to sin; to get oneself in a mess, trouble
binu-kummeewin to be errant; to go astray
pissi-itumoowin to misunderstand
pita-indauwaewin to bite accidentally
pitchi-aetchigaewin to do a misdeed
pitchi-doodumoowin to act unintentionally
winissaewin to make an error

wiyaezh-ingaewin *cheat; chisel; hoodwink; fleece*

wiyaezh-ingaewin to cheat

wizheewoowin *ready; prepare*

ae-shooweetumoowin to be all set
awae-nubiwin to be ready, seated
geezh-eetauwin to be ready, completely finished with other matters
wizhee-itauwin to make ready; to prepare
wizhi-issitchigaewin to set the table

wizhigaewin *prepare; build; construct*

wizhigaewin to prepare a stand of maples for sugaring

wukaun-aetchigaewin *enslave*

wukaun-kaewin enslave

Z

zaebawaewin *deflate*

zaebawaewin to deflate

zaeg-iwaewin *scare; startle; frighten; worry; intimidate; threaten*

chaunimae-wiziwin to be worried; to be anxious
gooss-ikeewin to be wary

gootaudjiwin to be timid
kishkoowaewin to startle someone by some sudden act, word
neezaun-itchigaewin to create danger and rouse fear
noodjaunimae-wizeekaewin to cause anxiety, apprehension
paupizh-akee-waewin to startle and drive away quarry
shauk-iwitchigaewin to scare an animal, bird
shau-waetchigaewin to scare an animal, bird
zaeg-itchigaewin to cause fear
zaeg-iwaewin frighten; scare
zaegiwaewin to frighten someone; to threaten
zhaemoo-tautchigaewin to make another cower
zhaug-odae-aewin to shrink in fear; to cower, etc.

---

zaegiziwin *dread; fear; daunted; timid*

---

gootaudjiwin to fear; to be afraid, timid
zaegiziwin to be daunted; to be intimidated

---

zaessae-gautchigaewin *adorn; beautify; primp; enhance*

---

binaukawae-oowin to comb, brush the hair
gino-waudj-itchigaewin to beautify, make beautiful; to enhance something, someone to the extent that it/he/she deserves a second look
kaudaenigaewin to braid hair
maundaug-tchigaewin to render remarkable, extraordinary
mino-inaugooz-tchigaewin to impress beauty, charm on someone, something
zaessae-gautchigaewin to doll up, dress up

---

zaugi-akeewin *sprout; shoot up; spring up; burgeon*

---

mook-akee-issitchigaewin to emerge from the earth
zaug-akeewin to sprout; to shoot up; to burgeon
zaug-auk-akeewin to come out of the earth

---

zaugidji-waeb-inigaewin *put out; throw out; cast out*

---

zaugidji-waeb-inigaewin to throw out

---

zaugiwaewin *love*

---

zaugidiwin love, mutual love, affection
zaugiwaewin love; to love someone

---

zaugiziwin *mince; scrimp*

---

minae-gaud-inigaewin to scrimp; to save; to economize
nae-gautch-itchigaewin to scrimp; to save; to ration
zaugitumaewin; zaugitumaugaewin to withhold from another
zaugiziwin to hold back

---

aum-aundumaeshkiwin *sensual; sexual; carnal*

---

zaum-aundumaeshkiwin to be carnal, sensual

---

zaussau-keewaewin *yell; bellow; whoop; shriek; holler*

---

ayauzhee-keewaewin to bellow
beebaug-keewaewin to holler at someone
beebaug-oongaewin to hail someone
noondaugooziwin to call out; to shout; to holler
zaussau-keewaewin to yell; to howl; to shriek; to whoop

---

zauzeenikoo-ipee-goondji-gaewin *sponge; soak up*

---

zauzeenikoo-ipee-goondji-gaewin to sponge up

---

zeeba-waewae-ishkauwin *grate; squeak; scrape; rasp; grind; screech*

---

neeyaubid-aeshinoowin to grind one's teeth
zeebawaewae-ishkauwin to squeak; to grate

---

zeeg-eengawaewin *wither; wrinkle; crease; line*

---

zeeg-eengawaewin to have a wrinkled face
zeeg-iwaegin-igaewin to crease cloth, fabric

---

zeegissaewin *spill; pour*

---

zeeg-issaewin to spill
zeeg-waeb-inigaewin pour out
zeeg-waeb-itchigaewin to spill out

---

zeegwun *to flow (as sap)*

VERBS

mino-kummik the good earth, soil; the latter part of spring
zeegwun the flow; the early part of spring

zee-ipeengawaewin *tears*

mooshkinae-zeepeengawaewin to have tearful eyes, so full that one is unable to see clearly
zee-ipeengawaewin tears

zeendau-kawi-igaewin *clamp; squeeze; compress*

dagoo-waukawigaewin to nail; to clamp to something
zeendau-kawi-igaewin to squeeze; to clamp

zeen-inigaewin *milk*

zeen-inigaewin to milk

zeewit-augunigaewin *salt*

zeewit-augunigaewin to salt

zeewut *sour*

zeewi-issitchigaewin to cause to go sour
zeew-issinoowin to go sour
zheewi-issitchigaewin to cause to go sour

zeezibi-doonaewin *slobber*

minis-keegoomaewin to have a runny nose
zeenis-keegoomaewin to drip mucous
zeezibi-doonaewin to slobber

zhae-abwi-yaewin *row; scull*

zhae-abwiyaewin to row; to scull

zhaeg-eeweewin *weaken; enfeeble*

baedji-eeweewin to be weak
chaug-eeweewin to lose strength
neenim-itchigaewin to enfeeble
neenim-iziwin to be weak
zhaeg-eeweewin to lose strength
zhaeg-iziwin to lack strength

zha-waendjigaewin *sympathy*

zha-waendjigaewin to feel sorry for; to favor, do a favor for, show kindness to, take care of, patronize

zhaewauwin *dull; blunt*

zhaegawauwin to dull; to blunt
zhaewauwin to dull; to blunt

zhaugood-inaugaewin *beat; overcome; defeat; master*

piki-inaugaewin to defeat
zhaugood-inaugaewin to best
zhaugood-inigaewin to best

zhaugood-inigaewin; zhaugooss-kummoowin *master; overcome; better; subdue; overpower; beat*

mauzhiwaewin to overcome; to overpower; to beat; to subdue
mawi-inauzhiwaewin to drive off an opponent in tears
zhaugood-inigaewin to overcome; to overwhelm; to vanquish
zhaugoodji-ayauwin to master; to overcome; to subdue
zhaugooss-ikaugaewin to overpower, outdo someone

zhaugoonaessi-kaugaewin *daunt; intimidate; scare*

zaegiwaewin to frighten; to scare
zhaug-odaetumoowin to daunt
zhaug-onaewiziwin to intimidate

zhauwushk-waundaewin *blue; purple; green; indigo*

zhauwushk-waundaewin to be blue, purple, green, indigo

zhawae-iginigaewin *spread; stretch out; extend; distend*

babeegi-waeb-inugiziwin spread out
beega-waeb-inugiziwin the tree is branched, limbed
daessi-ineegauwin to be distended
daess-inigaewin to outstretch
doongi-dubiwin to sit with legs open and outspread
sae-ningaweegun-aetumoowin to spread wings out
zhawae-iginigaewin to spread
zhinga-daess-itchigaewin to extend; to stretch

zhazheeb-inaewiziwin *endure*

zhazheeb-audiziwin to endure; to last
zhazheeb-inaewiziwin to be long suffering; to be steadfast

zheebau-umoowin *go through; inject; insert; put in*

bood-aunik-inigaewin to put an arm through
gindjid-aunigaewin to stick in
naeg-inigaewin to squeeze in
peend-aubau-widjigaewin to pour into
peend-inigaewin to put in
peend-issitchigaewin to put in; to insert
tipauk-issitchigaewin to stick or poke through
zheeb-aushkauwin to go through
zheebau-umoowin to go through a tunnel or passage

zheebeeg-inigaewin *stretch; extend; spread*

daess-inigaewin to spread or stretch out
daess-itchigaewin to spread or stretch out
neessikauk-inindjeeniwin to stretch, flex one's fingers
zhae-ozhae-witumaewin to flex and stretch
zhaezh-awitumaewin to stretch muscles
zhawaeg-inigaewin to spread out as a sheet
zhazheeb-itae'igaewin to stretch a pelt
zheeb-anik-aeniwin to stretch one's arms
zheebeeg-iginigaewin to stretch
zheeb-itae-igaewin to stretch a pelt
zheeb-itauwin to stretch as does a cat

zheegau-wiziwin *bereave; widow*

mindaunauwaewin the last farewell
zheegau-wiziwin to be left alone, solitary, bereft

zheeng-aendjigaewin *hate; loathe; abhor; detest; dislike*

anishinaenigaewin to scorn
daessido-waendumoowin to feel repugnance; to look down on; to have prejudice
weeshtu-waendumoowin dislike
zheeng-aendjigaewin to hate; to abhor

zhingu-kummik-igaewin *flatten; level; even; plane*

kaukau-kummikaewin to level the land
ona-kummika-igaewin to prepare land for seeding
zhingukauwin to flatten
zhingukau-kummikaewin to bulldoze; to flatten; to level

zhoobaug-inigaewin *bend; flex; warp; fold; stoop; crook; curve; bow*

nawug-itauwin to crouch; to bend down
nawug-quaeniwin to bend, bow the head
nawukeewin to bend down
pidubaub-ikinigaewin to fold
pisk-anikaeniwin to fold one's arms
piski-kaudaeniwin to cross one's legs
shawae-keewin to curve
shoozoo'igaewin to make flexible, malleable
waugauwin to crook
waug-inigaewin to curve
wauwiyaeyau-ginigewin to bend around
wishk-augauwin to warp
zhae-itauwin to bend; to lean backwards
zhigushk-itauwin stoop
zhoobaug-inigaewin to bend; to flex
zhoodae'gaewin to make plastic
zhooshaud-inigaewin to flex
zibiskau-beegaewin make malleable

zoong-dae'aewin *brave; courageous; bold; pluck; fearless*

mashkowi-odae'aewin to be brave
maung-idaussaewin to be bold; to be plucky
waed-aussaewin to be bold
zoong-dae'aewin to have courage

zhooshk-ishinoowin *slide; slip ski; toboggan*

cheeshi-boozoowin to scrape one's skin; to burn and scrape one's skin from sliding, slipping
zhooshk-ishinoowin to slip
zhooshki-widjiwaewin to sleigh ride; to ski

zhooshkiwae-igaewin *press; iron*

zhooshkiwae-igaewin to press; to make smooth; to iron

zugau-beessinoowin *tangle; snarl*

biza-waubeessinoowin to tangle a rope, line, string, wire

biza-waubeessitchigaewin to tangle a rope, line, string, wire

zugau-beessinoowin to tangle; to snarl

Prefixes

Introduction

Our language, Anishinaubae or, as it is commonly known, Ojibway (Chippewa in the United States), is a beautiful language, soft and musical, full of meaning. Perhaps the Kiowa author M. Scott Momaday best expressed his tribe's regard for language when he said, "Words were medicine; they were magic and invisible. They came from nothing into sound and meaning. They were beyond price; they could neither be bought or sold." To the Anishinaubae and other tribes, words and language were analogous to medicine, and sacred; they could heal or injure, comfort or offend, enlighten or mislead.

Instead of venerating our language as our ancestors did, those of us who still cling to it have taken our language for granted, speaking it carelessly, loosely, negligently, without regard for its beauty, rhythm and cadence, and by so doing, have taken the grace and elegance from it. The chief abuse of language comes from the human predilection to try to talk as fast as ideas race across one's mind. Of this tendency, Fred Wheatley, of Parry Island, an old friend, noted that "One's tongue can never keep pace with the velocity of ideas. To try to do so will only result in cacophony." Perhaps it is because of our tribe's tendency to speak too quickly and to abbreviate our words that we have come to earn the name of Chip-wae—the people who slur.

But taking language for granted is a fairly common affliction among other speakers; and this is because speech comes naturally and easily for most people, so its exercise needs no more thought or effort than breathing or blinking. English is not without its careless speakers who abuse their language with mispronunciations such as *gonnah* (whatcha gonnah do?), *tomaters*, and other such absurdities. Equally as bad is the slovenly expression of terms without regard for their meaning or sense: "It's raining outside"; "She's a personal friend"; "Is Alex there by any chance?"; "There will be a fumigation process"; "Comprehensible Input Hypothesis." Daily speech and even learned articles are replete with such nonsensical expressions. Many speakers of the tribal tongue are just as lax in their usage.

To be sure, they are as familiar with their language as are the speakers of any other tongue, capable of easily understanding and expressing the most common meanings and applications of words. Where many fall short is in the knowledge of the more fundamental, essential meanings of words and their derivations. They readily understand *mashki-aki* and *w'daebawae* as meaning "medicine" and "he/she is telling the truth," but few know that *mashki-aki* also means the strength of the earth operating as a healing agent, or that *w'daebawae* also means that a speaker casts his knowledge and his voice only as far as his perception and his fluency with language will enable him. Few know that *w'daebawae* is also a philosophic proposition that denies that truth can ever be absolute.

It is to assist teachers, students, scholars, grammarians, writers, linguists, and orthographers that this list of prefixes, along with their meanings and examples of usage, was compiled. Although much effort and diligence was put forth to glean as many prefixes as possible from existing sources, there are a number of prefixes still at large. So long as these prefixes remain loose, the list is incomplete, and I make no claim that it is the be-all and end-all.

As difficult as was the task of compiling this list, much more difficult was the task of settling upon the spelling, owing to the similarity in the sound of many of the prefixes and roots and other parts of speech, and owing to the difference of sound in the pronunciation of the same terms, depending upon its position in a word. As evidence of the difficulty of assigning a spelling to similar sounding terms with the roman alphabet, I submit the following which constitutes but a small portion of a great many:

goon snow
igoon day

nook soft
noog stop

ikoh formerly
igoh most certainly (an emphasizer)

kummik of the earth
gummik of or pertaining to a dwelling
gummeeng of or pertaining to a large body of water

matchi evil; bad
mindji hold; press down
maudji begin; start
mitchi naked; without clothing; bare
matchau large
mashi yet
mishi a piece of firewood
mishi huge; large; immense

gazhee fast
gizhee hot
geezhi ready

apaegish would that it were
baekish while

While these affixes and roots, whether they be identical twins, triplets, quadruplets, or even octuplets, may easily be distinguished in speech, they are not so in print. Hence it is to render them more readily discernible to the eye that each was written to bear its own individual spelling, along with its variations, as well as its many meanings. By doing so, some measure of stability may be brought to the tribe's orthographic system. Furthermore, by spelling the affixes and roots in the fullness of their sound, the articulation and enunciation may be fostered so that the grace and elegance and style in speech that once was there may be restored. Instead of contractions *chi, naebik, dauss, daewaegun, ssiwih, paumauh, kau,* there are here set down the full terms from which these contractions were derived: *kitchi, ginaebig, medauss, medawaewae-igun, nissiwih, paunimauh,* and *kauween.*

The affixes and roots and other terms are as full and as distinct as the roman alphabet is capable of making them. As necessary and as important as is the task of documenting and affixing individual spellings to each part, the affixes do not readily lend themselves to one fixed spelling, owing to their mutability in sound when conjoined with other prefixes and other words. Hence their variations were included as well in the list.

PRESENT TENSE

n'waub	I see
k'waub	you (*sing.*) see
w'waubih	he/she sees
w'waubiwuk	they see
n'waubmim(n)	we (not including you) see
k'waubmim(n)	we (all, including you) see
k'waubim	you (*pl.*) see

PAST TENSE

n'gee waub	I saw
k'gee waub	you (*sing.*) saw
w'gee waubih	he/she saw
n'gee waubumim(n)	we (not including you) saw
k'gee waubumim(n)	we (all, including you) saw
k'gee waubim	you (*pl.*) saw
w'gee waubiwuk	they saw

IMPERFECT

n'waubunaubun	I was seeing
k'waubunaubun	you (*sing.*) were seeing
w'waubunaubun	he/she was seeing
n'waubumiminaubun	we (not including you) were seeing
k'waubumiminaubun	we (all, including you) were seeing
w'waubunaubuneek	you (*pl.*) were seeing

The following is offered as but one example to illustrate not only the application of prefixes but also the number that may be affixed to one verb, in this instance *puto*—run. The list, though extensive, is not exhaustive. It is set down in the present tense, third person singular.

w'abeedji-putoo	he/she comes running
w'abeed-waewae-putoo	his/her advancing running footfalls reverberate
w'agidau-akeewae-putoo	he/she runs uphill
w'akeewae-putoo	he/she runs home
w'ani-putoo	he/she runs by way of
w'anim-putoo	he/she runs in the opposite direction
w'anim-waewae-putoo	his/her retreating running footfalls fade away

Prefixes

w'apeetchi-putoo	he/she runs at a certain pace
w'aubidji-putoo	he/she runs constantly
w'augawau-putoo	he/she runs to shelter
w'auzhoog-putoo	he/she runs back and forth
w'awini-putooi	he/she loses way while running
w'babaum-putoo	he/she runs hither and yon
w'baedji-putoo	he/she runs slowly
w'bawaunawi-putoo	he/she is unable to run
w'bigum-putoo	he/she arrives on the run
w'bimi-putoo	he/she runs
w'booni-putoo	he/she stops running (for some time)
w'boozi-putoo	he/she runs aboard
w'buzawaewae-putoo	he/she runs creating echoes
w'chaekauk-putoo	he/she runs into the woods
w'chaunimi-putoo	he/she runs in a frenzy
w'cheegi-putoo	he/she runs nearby
w'daebi-putoo	he/she wearies of running
w'dago-putoo	he/she runs in company with others
w'gaundji-putoo	he/she sprints away
w'gawaeki-putoo	he/she runs in a direct line
w'gawaekawaek-putoo	he/she runs round and round
w'gawaetauni-putoo	he/she runs beyond belief
w'gawau-putoo	he/she runs ashore
w'gaweeniwi-putoo	he/she runs uncertain as to where
w'gazheekau-putoo	he/she runs swiftly
w'geemootchi-putoo	he/she runs stealthily
w'geewini-putoo	he/she runs aimlessly
w'goopee-putoo	he/she runs inland
w'gooskee-putoo	he/she runs warily
w'gotaumigo-putoo	he/she runs with extreme speed, pace
w'gozig-putoo	he/she runs heavily, pounds, etc.
w'ishki-putoo	he/she changes course running
w'kawaundawae-putoo	he/she runs upstairs
w'kikinoowautchi-putoo	he/she runs in imitation, practice
w'kishki-putoo	he/she breaks loose running; able to
w'kooshkawae-putoo	he/she so runs as to rouse others by the uproar created
w'maudjee-putoo	he/she commences to run
w'maundaudji-putoo	he/she runs badly
w'mayauwi-putoo	he/she runs upright
w'mindau-ipee-putoo	he/she runs down to the shore, lake
w'mino-putoo	he/she runs well
w'mitauk-ozhae-putoo	he/she runs naked
w'mitauk-ozidae-putoo	he/she runs bare footed
w'miziwae-putoo	he/she runs in all directions
w'mooki-putoo	he/she runs out of nowhere into sight
w'naegautchi-putoo	he/she runs easily, without effort
w'naepautchi-putoo	he/she runs in the wrong direction, awkwardly
w'nanawautchi-putoo	he/she runs for nothing

w'naung-putoo	he/she runs lightly
w'naunoogi-putoo	he/she stops now and then while running
w'naussaub-putoo	he/she runs in like manner
w'nauwi-putoo	he/she runs in the middle
w'neegaun-putoo	he/she runs ahead
w'neessau-keewae-putoo	he/she runs downhill
w'neessaundawae-putoo	he/she runs downstairs
w'neezaun-putoo	he/she runs carelessly, recklessly
w'netau-bimi-putoo	he/she runs well and frequently
w'nikawae-putoo	he/she runs out of sight
w'ningodji-putoo	he/she runs somewhere
w'nishkaudji-putoo	he/she runs in a fit of temper
w'nishinaudji-putoo	he/she runs without purpose
w'nitam-putoo	he/she runs first
w'noogi-putoo	he/she stops running
w'ondji-putoo	he/she runs with some object, purpose
w'onishkau-putoo	he/she leaps from sleep and runs
w'peendigae-putoo	he/she runs inside
w'pekae-putoo	he/she runs off course
w'piko-ipee-putoo	he/she runs into the water
w'pimae-putoo	he/she runs to or on one side
w'pissikaubee-putoo	he/she runs back
w'shawae-putoo	he/she runs aslant
w'tibaewi-putoo	he/she runs along the shore
w'tikum-putoo	he/she runs across
w'waun-ani-putoo	he/she runs around by some other way
w'zaesaegi-putoo	he/she runs in terror
w'zaugaewae-putoo	he/she runs into sight
w'zaugidji-putoo	he/she runs outside
w'zaum-putoo	he/she overruns
w'zhae-putoo	he/she runs backwards
w'zhazheengi-putoo	he/she runs with endurance
w'zheebau-putoo	he/she runs through
w'zoongi-putoo	he/she runs with vigor

PREFIXES

A

abau; abaub; aut *a key; to open with something; unlock; release; loosen*

abaubi-ikugun a key; an opener
n'wee aub-aun I will unlock it
aubawaewae-inimishin forgive me

abau; aub; aubau *to warm; to heat; to dry*

w'abaugummizaun naboop he/she warms up some soup
abawau-nauk a roasting spit
abaushkoo-peetae the water is lukewarm
w'abauk-aukunaezih he/she warms his/her chest
aubawae-itchigun a drying, smoking apparatus

abee; abi; aubee *here; in this place; thither; to be here; to be in one place; set; it is; it is there*

a'abi-izhauh he/she comes, arrives (*lit.* to this place he/she goes)
abi-boon winter; the season during which growth is suspended
w'abeetum he/she resides here

abeeshk; abeeshkawae *blister (from* nipeesh—*water)*

n'abeeshkawae-beeg-inindjee I have a blistered hand

adji; adjitch; odji; odjitch • *move; move slightly; stir; shift; yield; draw back; draw away* • *invert; turn upside down*

w'adjitch-gaubowih he/she moves over
w'adji-quaewaenih he/she draws her head in
adjidumoo or **odjidumoo** a squirrel
adjitchissaemigut it occurred, took place; an incident, event, time passes; it came to pass

ae; aen; aeni *each; every; every other, respectively; each and every; as; according to; direction; manner; mode; style; angle; during; along; bearing*

ae-dasso-geezhiguk every day
mee w'aen-doodung that is what he/she is doing
mee w'ae-inaudjimoot according to his report
ae-inumook the direction or bearing of a road, avenue, etc.

aedawae *on either side, both sides, each side; at both ends, extremes; at*

ae-aedawaeyeehn on both sides
aedawae-geezhig at either end of the day
aedawae-anik both arms
aedawae-meekun on either side of the road

ae-inauss; inauss *in the direction of; in the face of; face to face*

woodih w'inauss-imishin he/she faces in that direction while he/she is lying down
w'abee'd'aussim-ossae he/she is coming this way
inauss-eengawaetaudiwin face to face

aesh; aeshi *to guard, defend, safeguard; keep vigil; sentinel*

aeshkeewee a guard, sentinel

agau *nothing; void; vain; empty; for nought*

w'agauwizih he/she gains nothing; to go round and round and round

agaut; agauti; agautch; agautchi; agutch; agutchi *withdrawn; withdraw; backward; ashamed; bashful; retire; shy; timid; shrink; embarrass; reserved; wanting self-esteem; confidence and/or pride; make, feel small, humble, abased, chagrined (from* gauss—*small)*

w'agutchih he/she is shy
w'agutchi-inaewizih he/she is shy by nature
agautaendaugoot it is shameful

agawau • *to cause hurt, damage, injury, pain to another or oneself, so as to occasion resentment* • *shelter; haven; sanctuary; harbor; shade; safety*

n'd'agawau-beekiss I am burned
w'd'agawaudji-aun he/she hurts someone
agawautae-oon a parasol, umbrella
augawa-eehn in the corner, a nook
w'agawautauh he/she comes ashore to shelter

w'agawau-puwae he/she flees to shelter

agawauk; agawauki *moldy; rancid; fungus; blight; mildewed; decayed; bad; spoiled; musty; stale*

agawaukissin it is moldy
agawauki-poogoot it tastes moldy

agid; agidau; agidji; agweed; agwid • *on top; astride; mount; ascend; scale a mountain; make one's way up; climb; apex; crown; summit; clamber* • *lever; a lift; hoist*

agidau-aki on top of the hill
agweed-inigun a lever
w'agidau-widjiwun on top of the mountain; watershed; river source
w'agidau-aki-wae-putoo he/she runs up the hill
w'agiweediwi-issitoon he/she piles it on

agidjaub; agidjaubi *poke; jab; drive; prod; poke into; project; poke in the eye (see also* cheek—*poke; stoke; jab; butt; dig; nudge; thrust; prod; jolt—and* boodji—*prod, thrust)*

w'gee agidjaub-ishin he/she fell and hurt his/her eye
w'gee agidjaub-iwaun he/she poked him/her in the eye

agik; agika; agikin; pagik; pagika *hazy; unclear; misty; cloudy; foggy; vaporous*

agikina-um(un) it is misty
pagikina-um(un): it is hazy

agind; agindau *read; count; sum up; number; letter(s); tell; list; enumerate; calculate; compute; tally; score; figure; total; quantify*

w'agindaussoowuk they count or read
w'mauwindo-agindaussoh he/she totals everything
gindausso-beegin a number or a letter
ogimauh (agimauh) a leader; one who counts many followers, and conversely, many count him/her

agindji *to press down*

w'agindji-idaunaun nipeeng he/she forced it down into the water
w'agindji-idau-peeginaun he/she forced it into the water
w'agindji-idaunaun he/she forces it down

agoob; agook, agookae, agooki *to bind; to stick to; bandage; dress; viscous; adhesive; attach; fuse*

agoobizoowin a bandage
agookae it sticks
agookaehnse a little tree frog (*lit.* the little one who sticks)
w'agookissigaewuk they are putting up wallpaper
w'gee agoobinaun he/she bound him/her with bandages

agoosk; agooskee; agooss; agootau *cautious; afraid; fearful; wary; guarded; careful; uneasy; apprehensive; worried; perturbed; anxious; disquiet*

w'agooskee-waudizih he/she is cautious by nature
w'agooskee he/she is uneasy, leery, nervous
w'agoostaugoonaezih he/she inspires fear

agoowau *stick to; weld; adhere; attach; cement; glue (from* agook—*to bind)*

w'agoo-waubikigae he/she welds, affixes something to another surface or object
agoo-waubikissin it is soldered, welded
w'agoo-waubik-izigae he/she solders

akauk; akauki; akuk *carbonized; brittle; fragile; delicate; breakable; friable*

n'd'akaukinikizaun I burn it to charcoal
akukizhae- charcoal or ashes

aki *earth; land; soil; world; ground*

w'aki-eewae he/she goes home
n'weedji-aki-waehn my friend; the person with whom another would like at his/her side in the course of his/her passage along the path of life
mashki-aki- medicine (*lit.* strength of the earth)
agidau-aki- on top of the hill
akik pail; pot; clay vessel
aki-waehnzee an old man

PREFIXES

aki-weewizaense a boy

---

anagabae; anigabaeg *divided; divergent; split; spread; open; separate; fork; part; sunder; bisect; sever; cleave*

anigabaeg-idjiwun the river divides
w'anigabae-aushiwuk the flock separates in flight
anigabaeg-kummikauh the land opens up
w'anigabaeg-izhaun he/she bisects it

---

anagusk; anaguski *wide; broad*

anagusk-oonigut it is broad of beam
anaguski-daeyauh it is wide
anagusk-aukoozih it is thick

---

anaum; anaumi; naum; numae • *under; below; beneath; neath; lower; bottom; downstairs* • *blame; put suspicion on; charge*

numae sturgeon
numaebin sucker
numaepin a tuber
w'd'anaumimaun he/she blames him/her
anaumi-kummik under the earth (Hell)

---

ani; anim *on his/her way; along the way; his/her path, course; underway; route; lane; avenue; run; trail; process; sequence; direction; approach; means; mode; drift; bearing; launch; commence* • *start; initiate; begin*

mee woodih w'wauh ani-izhaut he/she is going in that direction
w'animi-waewidum he/she is heard to talk or shout as he/she makes his/her way
w'ani-maudjauh he/she is on his/her way

---

anibae; anibaek; anibaeki *sloping; aslant; slant; angle; oblique; grade; bank; gradual; lean; tilt; cant; inclined; a slope; higher and higher; ascend gradually*

anibaek-kummikauh the land slopes; a slope
w'anibaek-itauh he/she leans
w'anibaek-quaenih he/she tilts his/her head
anibaek-issae it tilts of its own accord

---

anim; animi • *greet; hail; hello; salute; shake hands; make welcome; dog; canine* • *to fall or turn upside down*

k'd'animikooninim greetings, welcome; I welcome you
w'anim-ikooshin he/she lies upside down
w'anim-ikoossae he/she flips upside down
anim a dog
w'anim-mukowih he/she faints
w'anim-ossae he/she walks away (back turned)

---

anishauh *for nothing; for no reason; without cause (see also* nenawautch*—useless, good for nothing)*

w'anishi-inautchitoon he/she wastes it

---

apau *to season; to flavor; to add an ingredient*

coocooshun w'gee apau-bawae he/she flavored it with pork
apau-bawaudae it is seasoned

---

apeesi; apeet; apeetau; apeetch; apeetchi • *of a certain height, dimension, length, size, weight, age; measure; extent; range; compass; gauge; volume; capacity; span; growth; pace; speed; value; estimate; appreciate; appraise; cost* • *while; during; in the meantime*

w'apeetizih he/she is of such age or height
mee igoh w'ae-apeessi-ikaut that is as quickly or slowly as he/she goes
ahneesh ae-apeetchauk what time is it? (*lit.* how high or long is it?)
ae-apeetchi-anookeeyaun while I am working

---

api *in, by, for the head; head rest; pillow; at; on; around*

api-quae-ishimoon a pillow
api-quan a packing strap, tump line
api-ganaegawauzoon top part of moccasin

---

ashi; ashid *and; in addition to; plus; increased by; and also; together with; joined with; coupled with*

neezh-tunnuh-ashi-baezhig twenty-one
ashid-agindaussowin addition

---

ashki *green; raw; immature; callow; unripe; uncooked; rare (see also* oshki*—new)*

n'd'ashkundaun I eat it raw
ashkin it is raw

ashki-poogoot it tastes raw

atawau *set aside; put aside; store; stock; store away; stash away; reserve; stow; keep; husband*

atawau-gunikaewin to set aside for future use

atawau-poonauwissaewin to set aside for one's child

atchi *squint*

w'atchitchi-aubih he/she squints

aub; aubee *to an exceeding degree; too much; excessive; extravagant; beyond bounds; unreasonable; undue; inordinate; unwarranted; extreme; abuse; maltreat; mistreat*

w'aubeez-oongae he/she calls down, reviles another

w'aupitchih igoh nauh w'd'aubeendjaun he/she abuses him/her to an excessive degree

w'd'aubeendji-aun he/she maltreats him/her

aub; aubidae; aubidji; aubidjih *always; all the time; constantly; habitually; routine; daily; never stopping; without fail; practice; chronic; hardened; usual; regular; frequent; repetitive; persistent; continual; perpetual; ongoing; nonstop; permanent; use*

mee igoh w'gee aubidae-aendit he/she is gone for good

w'aubidji-aukozih he/she is always sick

w'dah aubidji-atoon he/she will use it

k'wee aubidji-auh nah? are you going to use him/her?

aub; aubiss; aubiz; aubizee • *recover senses; revive; renew; resuscitate; reanimate; revitalize; regenerate; start over; refresh; rekindle; come alive; regain consciousness; draw out* • *untie; release; unbind; forgive; loose; set free; clear; vindicate; relieve; extricate* • *absolve; pardon; amnesty*

aubawau-migut it is mild, warm; it loosens up

w'aubawae-waenimaun he/she forgives him/her

w'aubau-oodjigae he/she reels it out

w'gee aubizee-ishin he/she recovered

auboo; auboodji *upside down; inside out*

w'gee auboss-ikaun pupigiwiyaun he/she put his/her blouse on inside out

w'gee auboodji-nissae he/she fell head over heels

aud; auda • *to accompany; go with by boat —on water* • *take with; share; accompany; consort; go with; attend; escort; support; guide; conduct; usher*

w'auda-omaun he/she goes with him/her by boat

w'aud-oomaun he/she guides another person in the same "vessel"; he/she shares the same vessel with another party in an expedition

w'aud-issookae he/she creates, tells a story; to conduct others through an imaginary adventure; to call upon the manitous for their assistance in the creation and narration of a story

aud; audau; audaub; audauk • *obstacle; impediment; check; constraint; barrier; stop; block; lock; bar; confine; seal off; enclose; bolt up; strand; to buckle; clasp; hinge; hook; catch; snap; fasten; hasp; brooch; pin; tie; join; hitch* • *to hinder; to prevent; to bar; to stop*

audaukawigun a bolt, deadbolt, lock

audau-pikissin it is buckled up

audau-pikissitoon buckle it up

n'd'audaukumikishin zeepi, zaugigun the river or lake bars my way

w'audauk-ishin he/she is locked out

w'audaukawigae he/she bolts up

audj; audji • *repeat; encore; over; once more; anew; afresh* • *to hook; grapple* • *a hitch*

n'd'audji-ossae because of a lameness I have a hitch in my walk

audji-ozidaebizoon a stirrup

n'd'audji-gawaudaun I hook or grapple it

audji-gawaudjigun a grappling iron

augaw; augawau • *to ferry; to carry; to bear; to convey; to transport; to transmit from one shore to another by boat* • *crazy; demented;*

PREFIXES

insane; mad; lunacy; deranged; unbalanced; advanced; getting on; ancient; getting old

augawau-geezhigut it is getting on to midday
augawau-neebin summer is nigh
augawau-abi-boon in the dead of winter
w'd'augawauwidoon he/she carries it from ship to shore
w'augawaudizih he/she is crazy
w'augawaud-aendaugozih he/she seems deranged

augaw; augawi; augawitch; autchi • *behind; behind something; in the shade; in the shadows; as to be unseen; blindfold; cover; mask; blinder; blinker; shutter* • *to cover; protect; shelter; shield as with blankets, mantles, comforters* • *to cushion; to lift; a rest; a stand; a kneeler; support; brace; bracket; prop; shore; stay; buttress; strut; truss (from* gawau*—to go, get ashore)*

gawautae-oon a parasol (a contraction of *augawautae-oon*)
w'augawitchi-ozidaeshin; w'augaweed-ozidaeshin he/she stands or has one or both feet on a footstool
w'augawaukeeda-igae he/she pries something
w'augawau-puwae he/she flees, runs to shelter
w'augawau-gaweeng-awaebizoh he/she is blindfolded

augo; augoon; augoonae • *contradict; deny; refute; dispute; rebut; repugn; discredit; belie; confute; controvert; show up; retort* • *to stop up; a lid; a cover* • *blind; curtain* • *disobedient*

gaegauh igoh n'd'augoonaetoowauh I'm almost inclined to disbelieve him
w'netau-augoonaetum he/she is fond of taking issue
w'augoonaetaudiwuk they contradict one another

augum *walk on top of, on the surface*

augumuk snowshoes
w'augum-ossae he/she snowshoes
augumikaewin snowshoe making

auhnz; auhnzi *bind; wrap; swaddle; enfold; tuck in; enwrap; bundle up; bandage; drape; shroud*

auhnziyaun loincloth (archaic); diaper
auhnzi-pizoowin a bandage
w'auhnz-pizoowuk they fly as a flock; they are bound together

auhnz; auhnzi *omit; forget; leave out; neglect; except; exclude; miss; overlook; pass over; skip*

w'auhnz-waubumaun he/she overlooks him/her
auhnz-waendumoowin forgetting
w'gee-auhnzi-waegimaun he/she forgot to include it in wrapping

auk; auko • *sick; unwell; ill; constricted; tighten; ailing; nauseated; aching; squeeze; contract; cramp; pinch; bind; press; astringe; impede; obstruct* • *dangerous; fierce; temper; ill humored; petulant; peevish; surly; volatile; sullen; mean; irascible; explosive; vicious; truculent; violent; furious; raging; despicable; useless; wasted; for nought; fruitless squander; fritter away; no avail*

auk-oziwin sickness
w'aukozee-winaugozih he/she has a sickly pallor
w'auko-shkudae he/she has stomach cramps/pain
w'auko-waudizih he/she is ill-tempered
w'auko-wauni-kidoon he/she has a tart tongue
w'auko-wauzi-inaugozih he/she looks or appears ill-humored
w'auk-ozih he/she is sick
w'auko-wiziwih he/she is good for nothing
w'auko-wishkauwuk they go for nothing

aumidae *to overflow by boiling (poss. from* zaum; azaumi*—excessive)*

aumidae-gumizoh zheesheeb-akik the kettle is boiling over
aumidae-gumidae it overflows

aun; aund; aundi; aundj; aundji; auhnse *again; repeat; over again; encore; duplicate;*

once more; anew; afresh; in addition; another time; further; change; alter

w'auhnsi-kooniyae he/she changes his/her clothing
aundi-audiziwin change in character, style
w'aundji-gaubowih he/she stands elsewhere
aundau-bikissitchigun a gear, shifter

aun; auni; aunim; aunimi *exceedingly; suffer; unendurable; to have a difficult time; unbearable; pain; suffering; violent; arduous; troublesome; bothersome; plight; trial; tribulation; ordeal; hardship; distress; urgency*

w'aunim-aendjigae he/she can hardly bear it in his/her mind
w'auni-imizih he/she has a difficult time
aunimut it is hard to endure

aun; aunishee; auno *give up; abandon; turn from; forsake; discard; despise; reject; turn down; disdain; scorn; contempt; spurn; look down on; slight; snub; dislike; hate; abhor; detest; loathe; discourage; dishearten; discomfit*

n'd'auno-wishkoowauh I make him/her give up
auno-waewiziwin inability
w'd'auno-waendaun he/she despises it
w'aunishee-itumook they are discouraged

aung; aungawau(waung) • *caution; care; beware; circumspect; watchful; wary; prudence; discretion; vigilance; heed attention; guardedness; regard; mindfulness* • *tame; circumspect; domesticated; broken; trained; docile; submissive; meek; tractable; subdued*

aungawaumizin take care
w'aungawaum-ayauh he/she is wary
w;aungawaumimaun he/she warns him/her
w'd'aunga-wimaun he/she tries to conciliate with words
w'gee aungi-wiyaun he/she tamed, subdued him/her

aung; aungo *abolish; vanish; disappear; evaporate; annul; quash; repeal; put out of sight; annihilate; cancel; do away with; put an end to; terminate; dispense with; expunge; obliterate; raze; demolish*

n'd'aungo-waubundaun I lose sight of it
w'ningo-waubumaun he/she loses sight of him/her
w'gee aungoshkauh he/she disappeared, vanished
aungo-issuk driftwood; demolished wood
aungo-waubauwidoon dissolve it

auni; aunikae *add; adjoin; affix; append; unite; connect; superimpose; join; continue; succeed; transfer*

auni-koobidjigun great grandchild
w'd'aunikae-inimoowaun he/she passes it on to the next person
w'aunikae-ishkaugae he/she succeeds, replaces
n'gah aunikae-audjim I will continue my story
w'aunikae-anootchigae he/she translates; to transmit what one has heard
aunikae-kummaukaewin heritage; legacy (*lit.* leaving a trail)

aunissi; aunissis *evaporate; vaporize; mist; steam; melt; warm*

aunississin it evaporates; it changes into something else
w'aunississ-atoon he/she evaporates or steams it

aupid; aupidae *for good; for always; ever; always; permanently; absence (see also* aubid; aubidae*—all the time; habitually)*

mee igoh w'gee aupidae-indit he/she left and never came back
w'gee aupidji-maudjaubun he/she had gone, never to return
w'aupidi-ingawaum he/she is in permanent sleep

aupissee *blue black; violet*

aupissee-bug the violet
aupissee-inaundae it is violet in color

aupit; aupitah; aupito *half; 50 percent*

aupita-wipee it is half full
aupita-wizih half-breed
aupitau-tibikuk midnight

PREFIXES

aupitchi; aupitchih *exceedingly; to a great degree; exceedingly but not excessive; extremely; especially surpassingly; incomparably; highly; greatly; supremely; over and above*

w'aupitchi-ishin he/she suffered permanent injury

w'aupitchi-zoongizih he/she is exceedingly durable

aush; aushi; ausho; ausso; autch • *to tease; to discourage; to tempt; lure and deny* • *deject; dishearten; dismay; despair; check; close in* • *base; foundation; bottom; basement; cellar; stand; support; underpinning; footing* • *hard; settled*

n'd'aushi-auh; n'cheeshi-auh I tease or tempt him/her

w'd'aushoossikoowaun he/she falls on him/her

n'd'autchiniss I am afraid

aushootchissitchigun foundation

n'd'aushiwauh I scare him/her away

w'aussoowaukishin he/she leans away

aussaunae-goonugauh the snow is settled (hard)

aussae-autae *moss; lichen*

aussae-kummik swamp moss

autae-kummik water moss

aussee; ausseek *tan; brown; change pigment (from* nauss*—pigmentation)*

quaewuk w'ausseekaewuk women are tanning

w'ausseek-ozhae his/her body, skin is brown

ausseek-inaundae it is beige in color

aussik; aussiko; ausso *aid; abet; approve; follow; second; replace; succeed; next; supplant; accede*

k'wee aussikoowauh nah? are you going to support him/her?

w'ausso-waukishin he/she is leaning on something

w'd'ausso-waukawaun he/she props it up

autae *put out; extinguish; snuff out; quench; douse; blow out; smother; snub out*

w'autae-itchigae he/she puts out the fire

autae-itchigae-ininih a fireman

autch; autchi • *to partition; to set off; to isolate; to enclose; to shut* • *to be shy, introverted; to set off one's self*

autchi-kinigun a room; a corral; a park

autchi-ozid-aebizon a footboard in a cradle

w'autchinizih he/she is shy

autiss; autisso *to confer; pass on; bestow; tell stories (legends, myths, tales); to pass on the knowledge and understandings of one generation to another*

autissokaunuk the muses (*manitouwuk*)

w'autissookae he/she tells a story

autissokaun a story, fable

auwaetch; auwaetchi *compare; make or give an example; moralize; side by side; liken; equate; analogize; teach by example; simile; enlighten or instruct through stories; parable; chronicle*

auwaetchigun a parable; simile; a comparison; an example

w'auwaetchigae he/she tells a story

auwudj; auwudji; auwo *to carry; transport; convey; tote; haul; cart; lug; move; deliver; transfer; freight; truck*

w'auwudji-adaubee he/she carries or transports

w'auwud-aussowuk they freight or truck

w'auwudoon he/she carries it

auwo-daubaun a transport

auyaen *roll about; pitch (a boat)*

auyaen-ibissae the canoe rolls

auyaen-goondae the canoe rocks, pitches

auyau *to circle; to return; come back; retrace; retract; turn about*

auyaub-bimoodjiwun a whirlpool, eddy

auyaub-bimissaewin migration of birds

w'auyaub-imossae he/she walks back

auyauss; auyaussi *to gird; to bind; against (from* ausso*—to bind against, gird)*

w'd'auyaussipitoon he/she binds it
auhnssiyaun loincloth (archaic); diaper

auzh; auzhi; auzho; auyauzhi • *across; the other side; ford; far side; cross-wise; cross transversely; back and forth; ferry; to and fro; to return to source; tit for tat; rebut; refute; retort; return; give back; answer back; retaliate; reply in kind; measure for measure* • *a bridge for going back and forth* • *to force someone to do something; blackmail, coerce*

auzhidau-koonaeshee crossbill (a bird)
Auzhiwae Oshawa (Ontario), a fording place
w'auzho-wigae he/she goes back and forth
w'gee auzhidae-kawaun quaewun he/she missed meeting the women on or along the way

auzhag *face up(ward); on one's back (from* auzhi*—to lie on one's back +* agid*—on top of something)*

w'auzhagid-ishin he/she lies on his/her back
auzhagid-aukoossin it lies right side up

awo *to that place; there; destination; purpose; intent; thither; goal; aim; ambition; aspiration; target; mark*

w'awo-minissae he/she goes to cut wood
w'awo-weessiniwuk they are gone to eat

awun; awuss *moist; foggy; damp; drizzle; dew; dank; steamy; humid; muggy; vaporous; misty*

awun-beessauh it is drizzling
kaugigae-awung permanently misty
kitchi-awun it is very foggy
awun-quot foggy cloud

awuss; awussi *yonder; beyond; next; day after*

awussi-woodih over yonder
awussi-waedih that which is beyond
awussi-inaugoh day before yesterday
awussi-omauh away from here (to a dog)

ayaek; ayaeki *tire; weary; exhaust; fatigue; wear out; do in; enervate; run down; bushed; pooped*

aki-waehnzee w'ayaekozih the old man is tired
w'd'ayaeki-waenimaun he/she is wearied of him/her
quae w'ayaeki-gaubowih the woman is tired of standing

ayeem-ayeemi *clothing; articles; personal possessions; chattels (from* ayaun*—to possess)*

n'd'ayeemun my clothing, possessions
w'd'ayeemun his/her possessions

azhae *backwards; back; to the rear; reverse; to the stern; astern; return; backtrack; retract; retreat (see also* zhae*—backward)*

w'azhae-ossae he/she steps backwards
w'azhae-gawaushkinih he/she leaps backwards
w'azhae-aushiw he/she is blown backwards by the wind
azhaemook! retreat! go back!

azhaug; azhaugi *to spoil; corrupt; sour; rancid; deteriorate; acid; fermented; curdled; acerbate*

azhaugi-imissin the liquid is spoiled
azhaug-imidae the liquid is spoiled

B

babau; bau; baum *here and there; hither and yon; around; about; action repeated; done again*

w'babaum-ossae he/she walks around
babaum-tigiwaeyauh the stream meanders
w'babaum-aushih he/she sails around

babee; pabee; paubee; baebee; baubee *to stagger; weave; meander; uneven; zig-zag; crisscross; sway; wind; curve; bend; turn; change direction*

w'baubee-inossae he/she staggers
baebeek-idauwingauh serpentine mounds; a ridge
babeek-waukummikauh the ground is rough, rugged

babeeg; babeegi; beeg; beegi; beego; beegooshk; beegwauk • *to break; demol-*

ish; destroy; ruin; fall apart; smash; shatter; bust; burst; crash; tear; crack; disjoint; crush; wreck; mutilate • pimply; broken

beegwau-kummikauh the land is rough, broken

w'bego-ozidaeshin he/she wears a hole in his/her shoe

gee-beegi-ishkauh it broke (is ruined)

bae-beegi-iskoogaet a woodpecker

babeeshk; beeshki; pissikau; pissik *lose periodically; intermittent; from time to time*

w'baubeeshki-waendum he/she loses his/her mind periodically

w'babeeshki-waupih he/she laughs intermittently

babeeski; beeski *wrinkled; creased*

w'beesk-eengawae he/she has a wrinkled face

w'beesk-inindjee his/her hands are gnarled

beeski-wae-igut it is creased

babeewi; beew; beewi *small; tiny; wee; diminutive; runty; chip; puny; dwarfed; shrunken; fragment; crumb; scrap; shaving; chunk; piece*

w'beewi-ozidae he/she has small feet

beewi-koodjigun shaving

beewauh it is tiny

w'beewi-beegae he/she writes small characters

babeez; babeezi; beez; beezi *curly; frizzled; coil; ringlet; wavy; kinky (from* babee; pabee; paubee, *etc.—curve)*

w'babeezig-indibae he/she has curly hair

w'babeezig-aukizigae he/she curls his/her hair

babeez-wauki-dae it curls as it burns

bae; baess; baessi; baewae *• slow; plod; no hurry; dawdle; lag; linger; pausing; hang back; not on time; leisurely; unhurried; measured; gradual • soft; low; relaxed; tranquil; serene; subdued; muted; faint; inaudible; • hardly; scarcely*

owih quae w'bae-d-awae that woman speaks very softly

baekauh igoh take your time

n'baewitoowauh I think little of his promises

w'baewaenimaun he/she doesn't think too much of him/her

w'baessi-ikauh he/she is slow

baessi-ikaumigut it is slow

w'bae-d-awae he/she speaks slowly or in low tones

baeng; baengi *to dry; to spin dry; wipe; swab; towel*

w'baengi-onaugunae he/she dries dishes

baengi-waussitchigun a dish dryer

baengi-waussin it is wind dried

baepaesh; baepeshi; baesh; baeshi *striped; streak; band; lined*

baepaeshi-ginaebig a garden snake

w'baepaeshi-aubee he/she is banded or goes streaking by

w'gee baepaeshi-beegae he/she draws lines

baesho *near; close; not far*

w'baesho-witoon odaenah he/she makes the town seem close with his/her pace

w'baesho-waubundaun he/she examines or sees it near

w'baesho-witoowaun he/she courts, woos him/her; attracted to

baezhig *one; single*

w'abi-baezhigoh he/she comes alone

baezhi-gaubowih he is a widower

w'baezhigo-inaendumook they are all of one mind, thought; they are agreed

baezhig-waubik one dollar

banau; banaud; banaudji; banauss; banaussi; baunaud *ruin; break; destroy; mess up; demolish; ravage; desolate; fracture; mangle; maim; spoil; vandalize; mutilate; spoilate; raze; tear down; tumble; topple*

banaudut it is ruined

w'banaudji-aun he/she corrupts him/her

w'banaudi-aendum he/she is utterly discouraged, disheartened

w'gee banauzi-imaun he/she completely disheartened him/her

bashi; bizhi • *near; close; almost; close call; just about; all but; not quite; well nigh* • *to spear; knife; stab; score*

w'gee bizhi-boowaun he/she stabbed him/her
w'gee bizhi-inae he/she had a close call
bizhi-bigun a spear
bizhi-aki the buffalo (from its habit of scoring the earth with its hooves)
bizheu the lynx (from its habit of scoring the flesh of its victims)

baubauk; bauk; baukauk; baupauk *knock; rap; tap; bang; pound; hammer* • *to open; unshut*

w'baukaukinaun moodyh he/she opens the bottle
w'baupaugaukiwigae he/she knocks on the door
baupaussae the woodpecker
baukiwaessikauh it becomes unglued
baubauk-inutae there are patches of ground opening up in the snow
bauk-aukiwigun; baug-aukiwigun black ash splint, lath

baubeeg; baubeegi *peevish; surly; short (poss. from* beegi—*to break; to disrupt)*

w'baubeegi-odae-ae he/she is surly

baudaug; baudaugi *to burn, scald*

w'baudaug-ozidaezoh he/she burns his/her foot
w'baudaug-eengawaezoh he/she burns his/her face

baug; baugi *swollen; bump; expand; extend; distend; inflate; dome; intumesce; well up; protrude; project; stick out (up); bulge; bilge; lump; knob; knurl; node; shoal*

w'baugi-nawae he/she has a swollen cheek
baugi-waushkauh there is a surf
baugawauh there is a shoal
baugawau-tigawaeyauh the river is shallow or is characterized by many shoals (origin of Bauwiting—Sault Ste. Marie)
w'gee baug-ishin he/she ran aground

baumae; bimau; bimee; bum *to look after; operate; manage; direct; administer; run; conduct; supervise; superintend; care for; busy; business; absorbed; engrossed; occupation; preoccupied; care; tend*

bimee-taugun an employee
w'bimee-kaun he/she manages it
w'bim-aenimaun he/she cares, tends him/her

baup; baupi *laugh; laughable; funny; comical; chortle; chuckle; ridicule; deride; mock; jeer; satirize; parody; amusing; risible; humorous; jolly; mirthful; merry; jovial; playful; sportive*

w'baupi-inaendum he/she is amused
w'baupi-izhi-inaugozih he/she looks funny
w'baupishkih he/she is ever ready to laugh
baupinooz-waugun a clown; a comedian

baupaushk; baushk; baushki; bausk *burst; explode; asunder; blow apart; to overswell; break (burst) open; rupture; detonate; fulminate; blow up; bust; to bleed*

baushkizigun a gun
baupaushkidaehnse a firecracker
baushki-meen-sigun jam; preserves
w'baushki-idaemoh he/she burst into tears
w'baushki-aupih he/she bursts out laughing

baupauss; bausk; bauski *split; divide; crack; rive; halve; bisect; sever; rend; sunder; chop; cut; hew; cleave; slit; gash*

mukwoom bauskauh the ice cracks
baupaussi-bigiw balsam
waussaetchigun gee bauss-issae the window cracked
bauss-ikauh wauwun the egg is cracked
bauss-ikauh assin the stone is cracked

bauss; baussae; beeshau; bees; beessau; beessi *small; shred; minuscule; grain; morsel; flake; shard; seed; kernel; particle; grist; bit; speck; mite; mote; dot*

beessi-boodjigun ground up (grounds)
beeshau gonaub a thong
beesauh it is minuscule

bauss; baussi; baut; bautae *dry; wring out; dehydrate; arid; thirsty; without water;*

PREFIXES

rain; parched; rainless; drought; unwatered; withered; dry up

bautae it is dry
w'baussoh he/she is dry
bautae-kummikauh the ground is dry
bautae-aussitchigun a dryer

baut; bautau; bautauk • *stuck; mired; embedded; bogged down; defiled; sullied; tarnished; sunk down; entangled; enmeshed; sinfulness; iniquity; incorrigible* • *close; seal*

w'gee bautau-kaukoowaun he/she sealed it with nails
w'bautaushin he/she is stuck, mired
w'gee bautau-maun he/she informed on him/her
bautau-idiwin a sin; a felony

bautee *much; lots; quantity; a great deal; loads*

bauteenut there is much
bauteenoowuk there are many (same as *w'mizheenoowuk; w'zaumeenoowuk*—they are many)
w'bautee-inaun he/she has many

bauz; bauzi *to scratch*

w'gee bauzigoobinaun he/she scratched him/her

bauzh; bauzhi *overfill; overflow; too full; leap over; hurdle; jump over; brim over*

w'bauzhi-idji-gawaushkinih he/she leaps over
bauzhidae-ipee it overflows
w'gee bauzhi-idinaun he/she lifted him/her over

bawau; bawaun; bawauni(auno)(aunowi) *deplete; exhaust; use up; consume; spend; run out; empty; drain; bleed*

w'bawaun-awitoo; w'abwaun-awiwoh he/she is unable because he/she is exhausted
w'bawaun-aukizigae he/she burns it all
bawaupikizigun a stove; that which uses up wood

bawau; bwau • *before* • *in advance of* • *unable; cannot; incapable; powerless; impotent; incompetent; unfit; too weak; unqualified; inept; unsuited; unskilled (from* chibawauh; chibwauh—*before)*

w'bawau-dagooshinoowaut before they arrive
bawau-tibikuk before night
w'bawaun-witooh he/she is unable (falters)

bawi; bawih *to knock down; sweep away/down; brush; whisk; groom; curry; fell; level; raze; devastate*

bawi-ozidaeshinoon chibwauh peendigaeyin wipe your feet before you come in
bawi-igun a brush
w'gee bawi-waeginaun he/she shook it free of dust
w'bawi-beewiyae animoosh the dog shakes himself/herself

beed; beedau; beedi *coming this way; to here; to this place; hither; arriving; approach; draw near; near; to close in; bear down upon; draw nigh; confront (poss. from* abi—*here)*

Beeda-waewae Petawawa, Ontario (*lit.* the coming sound; the sound drifts/wafts this way)
beed-auniquot coming clouds
Beed-aussigae Petoskey, Michigan (*lit.* the sun comes shining)
beedaubun dawn
beewodae a guest; the awaited one; The Messiah

beedauss; beedaussi *face this way (poss. from* abi—*here)*

w'beedaussl'm'ossae he/she is walking in this direction
w'beedaussi-mubih he/she sits facing this way
w'beedaussoh he/she is bringing something with him/her

beeg; beego; bigo *to break, rupture, fracture, demolish, destroy, tear apart, ruin*

w'beeg-ishkauh it is broken down
w'beeg-iskwogae he/she drills, bores a hole

beem; beemi; beemiss; beemissik *twist; screw; turn; twirl; pirouette; whorl; spiral; rotate; crank; wind; plait; braid; wrench; distort; contort; coil; spin; revolve*

beeminigun an auger
w'beemissi-iquashih he/she twirls
w'beemissiko-igae he/she drills
beemi-inauquan a cable, hauser
w'beemi-doonae he/she twists his/her mouth

been *clean; tidy; chaste; virtuous; spick and span; clear; unsullied; untarnished; spotted; pure; cleansed; washed; immaculate; refined; purged; unpolluted; scour; sweep; orderly; neat; trim*

w'been-itchigae he/she cleans
beenut it is clean
w'beenizih he/she is clean
been-itchigun-aubo liquid cleanser

beenae; babeenae *dry*

babeenae-kummitae the ground is dry

beengae *thoroughly; completely; too much; excessive; overmuch*

w'beengae-ingawaum he/she sleeps too much
w'beengae-itchigae he/she does it thoroughly
w'beengae-wizih he/she is thorough
w'beengae-idjih he/she is cold through and through

beenissis *without feeling; numb; deadened; anaesthetized; bland; without flavor*

beenissi-poogwood it is bland
w'beenissi-ozidae he/she has a numb foot
w'beenissi-izih he/she is without feeling
w'beenissi-idoon he/she has a numb mouth

beensh; beenssi *for nothing; falsely; without proof; unverified; unsupported; unsubstantiated; without cause*

beenissi-ikauh for no reason at all
w'gee beenishi-imaun he/she accuses him/her falsely

beepee; beepeeg; beepeegi *shrill; high pitched*

beepeegizaehnse; peegwiss; peguis sparrow hawk
beepeegwun flute
beepeeg-awaewae it is shrill

beesk; beeski *put on; dress; clothe; vest; garb; don; slip on; adorn*

w'babees-ikooniyae; w'bees-ikoonigae he/she dresses
babees-ikoowaugun; bees-ikoowaugun a coat
w'wee babeetchee; beetchee he/she will put on socks and shoes

beet; beetau; beeto *between; sandwiched; betwixt; in the middle; midst; halfway; midway; intermediate*

beeto-ishkaudjigun undergarment
beeto-kummik between levels of earth
beeto-nebaug-ineegin sheet(s)

beetae; beetau; beeto *to froth; foam; bubble; spume; suds; head; fizz; effervescence*

beetae-waushkauh the waves created a foam
w'beetae-widoon he/she froths at the mouth
beetae-gimidae it fizzes

beew; beewi; beewih • *small; slight; slender; slim; thin; narrow; spare; lean; wispy; chip; fragment; crumb* • *hew; nick; notch; whittle* • *shard; chunk; shaving* • *fur; small; tiny fur or hairs; fuzz*

w'beewi-ikoodjigae he/she makes small shavings or small carvings
beewiyun fur of an animal
beewi-auniquot small clouds
w'beewi-shkeehnzhigowae he/she has small eyes

beezug; bizo; bizug; bizugi • *sticky; adhesive; syrupy; thick* • *entangled; snarled; twisted; matted; ensnare; enmesh; entrap; snag*

w'gee bizo-zidaeshin he/she tripped (one foot stuck somewhere)
n'gee bizo-gaewauh I tripped him

PREFIXES

bizugawauki-meenuk bill berries
bizugawau-gummih the fluid is syrupy

---

begaun *nut*

begaun-ushk a nut-bearing tree
begaessaun a plum

---

bego • *a hole; repair; aperture; opening; vent; orifice; cut; perforation; incision; rift; gap; breach; leak; puncture; spike; pierce; stick* • *repair a hole; mend; patch; service; fix (from* beeg*—to break)*

begooshkauh it has a hole in it
w'bego-inaegae he/she makes a hole (drills)
w'bego-igae he/she mends a hole
Begonae-geezhig a notable chief's name (*lit.* either Hole in the Day or Hole in the Sky)

---

begoosh; begooshi; begooss; begoossih *beg; ask; implore; beseech; seek; request; entreat; plead; crave; petition; solicit; supplicate; seek alms; bum; mooch; panhandle*

w'begooshiwae he/she begs
w'begooss-aendum w'wee izhaut he/she wishes also to go
w'begoossi-aubungae he/she pleads with his/her eyes

---

bidik; bidiki *rumble; roar; echo; reverberate; roll; resound; din*

bidik-awaewae it resonates
bidik-kummikauh the earth rumbles and trembles
w'bidik-ishae he/she perceives, hears a thundering sound

---

bidub; bidubau *to close; fold; infold; tuck in; crimp; gather; plait; enclose; envelope; enwrap*

bidubau-bugoonee a flower folds up
w'bidabau-beeginigae he/she folds, rolls in sheets, etc.
bidabau-ibeeshkauh it closes, crimps of its own accord

---

bigiz; bigizi *dim; blurred; blurry; unclear; indistinct; becloud*

w'bigizi-waubih he/she does not see well
w'bigizi-waubundaun he/she sees it but dimly
bigiz-waubuminaugoot it is indistinct

---

biguk; biguki *clear; plain; sober (poss. from* baukauk; paukauk*—open; to see, make clear)*

w'dah biguk-aendaun he/she will know it clearly
w'biguk-waubih he/she sees clearly
biguk-aendaugoot it is clear

---

bigum; bigumi *to arrive; to get here; arrive (from* abi*—here—and* gum*—on foot)*

bigum-beessauh the rain arrives
bigum-aunimut the wind comes
w'bigum-ishkauh he/she arrives by sail
w'bigum-audigaukoh he/she arrives by means of crossing on the ice

---

bigun; biguni; bigund *to break down; thresh; flail; flog; pummel; beat; batter; thump (from* beeg*—to break, pulverize)*

w'bigundigaewuk they are threshing
bigumaugun a war club

---

bigushk; bigushki • *break down; thresh; flail; batter; pummel; crush; grind; pulverize; mash; granulate; hash; crumble* • *spoil; rot (from* beeg*—to break, pulverize)*

bigushkinut it is rotten
w'gee bigushki-aun he/she crushed or pulverized it
bigushki-boodaek weeyauss ground meat

---

bigusk; biguski *resound; echo; slam; slap; clap; resonate; ring; peal; clang; sound*

w'gee biguski-indibaewaun he/she slapped him/her on the head with resonance
w'gee biguski-idjeeshin he/she fell with a resounding crash
odjee w'biguski-issae the fly slammed into something

---

bim; bimau; bimi; bimid; bimidj; bimidji • *by; to go by; to go by without stopping; abreast; alongside; parallel; aside; beside; next to; at the same distance and in one direction; means of motion; in such direction* • *crossways; across; to pass; crosswise; junction; intersect*

bimi-audiziwin life
w'bimi-daubaunikoh he/she is travelling by vehicle
w'bimauk-waebigae he/she passes something; hockey
w'wee bimi-izhauh he/she is going in a certain direction; going by
w'bimid-ishin he/she lies crosswise
w'bimid-ubih he/she sits sideways

bimi; bimisk; bimisko *to injure; hurt; wound; bruise*

w'bimisk-ozidaeshin he/she hurts his foot while walking
w'bimwauganee he/she has a wound
bimiwaugun a wounded person

binauh; bini; binu; binuh *or* **bunuh** *take down; fall down as of leaves off trees; drop*

w'gee bininaun he/she dropped
w'binu-kummee mindemoyaehn the old woman lost her footing
binung-waubeeginun k'metigiwaub undo the bow-string

biniski; biniski *to open; unfurl; undo; unfold; unwind; unroll; unravel*

w'binisk-eeginigae he/she unfolds sheets, bed-spreads, linen
biniskau-bugonee a flower opens up
biniskau-beegipissae it unravels
w'gee binisk-aubeeqinigae he/she unfolds the line

binizh; binizhi *to slice; cut; split; sever; part; cleave; knife; carve*

binizhigun a slice
w'binizhigae he/she slices
w'binizhimaugae he/she slices, carves for another

bizaun; bizauni *quiet; peaceful; tranquil; serene; placid; still; at peace; becalmed*

w'bizaun-ayauh he/she keeps quiet
bizaun-atae it is quiet
w'bizaun-ishin he/she lies quiet

bizi; bizig *get up; rise; arise; stand erect; stand; hazy (from* bizug*—stick; glue; adhere; cling; hold fast)*

w'bizi-gawee he/she rises
w'bizi-gondjissae he/she jumps to his/her feet
w'bizi-gawaewoo-inaushih he/she soars or ascends higher and higher

bizisk *well; clearly; closely*

n'biziski-aendaun I know it well
w'biziski-audizih he/she recovers his/her senses; he/she matures
n'bizisk-aenimauh I know him well

bizug; bizugi *to stick; adhere to; viscous*

bizug-waugummih the water is viscous

bood; booda; boodau *to make fire; to stoke; add wood to a blaze (from* boodau*—to blow; to blow upon)*

boodawaugun a fireplace
w'boodawae he/she makes a fire
Pottawatomi keepers of the sacred fire (*Boodawae-autumee*)

bood; boodau *to blow; emit; spout; vent; huff and puff; pant; sound; blast; blare; toot*

w'boodaudjigae he/she blows a horn
w'bauboodaudjigae he/she huffs and puffs
boodaudjigae-ininih a trumpeter, flautist, etc.

boodauk; boodauki *fall into water*

w'boodaukawae-issae he/she falls into the water
w'boodaukawaenun pineen he/she puts potatoes into the water for boiling
w'boodau-iquaenih he/she sticks his/her head into water
boodji prod; thrust
w'boodj-aubishin he/she suffers an injury by falling upon a projection or by being butted or jabbed with some obect
boodji-dayaegaewin sodomy

book; booki; boopook; baek *break; fracture; smash; rupture; breach; split; crack; rift*

PREFIXES

w'bookidih he/she farts (breaks something)
w'booki-dayaeshin he/she fractures his/her rump
book-issae it breaks, splinters
boopookishkaunoon they break repeatedly
w'baegidae he/she burps

---

boon; booni *leave it; quit; stop; desist; discontinue; hold up*

---

w'booni-moh the chicken is laying an egg (has stopped squawking)
w'gee booni-itaubun he/she had quit some time ago
booni-atoon leave it be

---

boot *beat; pound; hammer*

---

bootaugun the mortar
bootaugunauk the pestle itself

---

booz; boozau; boozi • *penetrate; get on board* • *soaked; drenched; soused; wringing wet; saturated; sopped; waterlogged*

---

w'booz-aubauwae he/she is soaked through
w'booziwuk cheemauning they get on board a boat
boozi-augimih it boils or flows over

---

booz; boozi *darker; deeper in color, hue, shade*

---

booz-aundae it is darker in color
booz-augummih a liquid that gets darker
booz-aukidae it gets darker in the flames

---

bubug; bubugi *thin; flat; diaphanous; sheer; translucent; flimsy; delicate; fine*

---

bubugauh it is thin
bubugiwiyaun a shirt, blouse; thin fabric
w'bubugizih pissugawaukoohnse the lath is thin

---

buzwae; buzwau; pusswae *to sound; resound; echo; repercussion; reverberate*

---

w'busswaewaeshin his/her voice echoes and re-echoes
w'buzwae he/she makes a resounding sound
Buzwaewae Echo-Maker

C

---

chacheeng; chacheengi; cheengi *to shake; tremble; quake; fall forward*

---

chacheengi-kummikauh the earth quakes from thunder or explosions
w'cheengi-idjissae he/she falls forward
cheengwun a meteor
w'chacheengi-initauh he/she genuflects
w'cheengidau-puwae he/she falls forward heels over head

---

chaeg; chaek *run aground; on a shoal*

---

w'chaeg-ishin he/she runs aground
w'chaek-aushih he/she sails into a reef or shoal

---

chaekauh *to go into; enter the woods, forest, bush*

---

w'chaekauk-aukawoom he/she enters the woods

---

chauchee; chaucheeb; cheechee; cheecheeb; cheecheek; cheessi *convulsions; spasms; paroxysm; throes; fit; stroke; shake up; vibrate; twitch; quiver; tremble; pulse; palpitate; quaver; quake; shudder; shiver; jiggle; joggle; back and forth sway; rock to and fro; swing; cramps*

---

w'cheecheebi-tuwug-aessee his/her ears twitch
w'chaucheeb-aukossae he/she rocks back and forth
cheessi-aki-ininih one who shakes a lodge (earth)
cheechee-bee-igun a piano; an organ

---

chaug; chaugi *spent; consumed; depleted; exhausted; wear out; file down; use up; emptied; drained; burned out; played out; beat; wearied; enfeebled*

---

chaug-idae it is burned up completely
meedjim chaug-issae the food is used up
chaugi-iboodae it is worn down
w'chaug-eewee he/she has used up his/her strength

chaun; chauni *to worry; to harry; hector; anxious; nervous; restless; frenzy; frantic*

w'chaunimi-aun w'kawissun he/she scolds his/her son
w'chaunimi-aendumook they are anxious
quae w'chaunimi-itauh the woman is working in a frenzy

chaung; chaungi; chauchaung *rising; lifting; levitate; tilting; slant; slope; grade; tip; uplift*

w'chaung-aunoowaenih he/she/it raises its tail
chaung-aukissin it stands aslant
w'chauchaungawa-ook they bob up and down in the water

cheebauk; cheebauki *to cook; boil; roast; fry; warm up; grill; sauté; braise; griddle; stew; simmer*

w'cheebaukawae he/she cooks
cheebaukawaun a kitchen; cookery

cheeby *a ghost; soul; spirit; spectre*

w'cheeby-itauk-ozidaewidjih he/she has a numb foot or feet
cheeby-autik the cross
Cheeby-kunnuh the Path of Souls
Cheeby-inaukaewin the Feast of the Dead
Cheeby-aub-ooz third son of Ae-pungishimook and Winonah; creator of music, poetry, prayer, vision and dream quests; Ogimauh of the After World

cheeg; cheegi • *near; hard by; next to; adjacent; neighboring; close; nearby; proximate; nigh* • *shave, trim, hew*

cheegi-gummig near the house
cheegi-gugun a broadaxe
cheegi-ayeehn nearby

cheek; cheecheek *poke; stoke; jab; butt; dig; nudge; thrust; prod; jolt*

w'cheecheek-kizhae-igae he/she stokes the coals
Cheekaubaewiss a little manitou (*lit.* Poked in the Eye)

cheesh; cheecheesh; cheeshi • *scrape; sweep; shovel away; whisk; clear out; swipe; rasp; skin; bark; abrade; chafe* • *scuff; grit; knead; scarred; marked; scored*

w'cheeshau-goonaegae-daubaun a snowplow
w'cheecheesh-kawaeginaun ombidjeezigunun he/she kneads the dough
n'cheeshaukawaun I scrape it
w'cheecheesh-izigaewin to burn off, singe, sear feathers
w'cheeshi-kaudae he/she has scarred legs

cheessi; cheessig; cheessigau • *blurred; bleary; unclear; dim; smear; befog; obscure; indistinct; cloud; veil; shroud; on edge* • *shake; move; tremble* • *pinch; tweak*

w'cheesi-gaubowih he/she stands on tiptoe
n'cheesi-ibinauh I pinch him/her
w'cheesi-gauwi-zeebeengawae he/she is bleary-eyed

chi; chichi *sewed slightly, just a little, not much*

w'chichi-gawauzoh he/she sews something slightly
chichibi-gawaudae it is sewn slightly apart, with wide seams

chibawauh *before; beforehand; lest; in the event (see also* bawauh; bwauh*—before)*

chibwauh before

chipp *stutter; stammer; stumble; speak badly; wrinkle; crinkle; scrunch*

W'chippawae Cree name for Anishinaubaek (*lit.* he/she stutters, mangles his/her language when he/she speaks)
chipp-waukidae it curls as it burns

chitch; chitchi *time passes, goes by; elapse; lapse*

chitchi-issae it happens (occurs); time passes by; it passes by degrees

PREFIXES

D

dae; daeb *insofar; so far as; just; in as much; so much; so far; to such a degree; to such extent (distance; size); to the ends of; to the limits*

w'daebiziwin right; due; so much as one is entitled to by worth, ability, need

daeb-awaewin truth; to cast one's knowledge according to one's perception and command of language; the highest degree of accuracy

daebin-aewiziwin a right; to be entitled to; deserve; to have a stake in Mother Earth's bounty

w'daeb-issinee he/she has eaten to fulfillment

w'daeb-aubih he/she can just see

w'daeb-awae he/she is right, accurate, truthful

dae; daewi *ache; throb; pain; smart; gnaw; twinge; sore*

w'daewi-quae he/she has a headache

daewi-aubidaewin a toothache

daess; daessau; daessi • *open (as a hand, heart); stretch; distend; extend; astride* • *cupboard; put away; dresser; store; stock; hoard; keep*

w'daessi-inindjeenih he/she opens his/her hand

w'daessi-odae-waenimaun he/she feels sorry for him/her

w'gee daessi-inaun he/she greeted him/her with open arms and heart

daessaubaun a pantry

daessi-idubiwin a saddle

dago; dagoh *there is; there are* • *to make one; whole; united; join; mix; mingle; commingle; unite; intermix; combine; blend; merge; fuse*

mee woodih aen-dagook that is where they occur, are, are to be found

w'dagooshinook they arrive; by their arrival they become united with us

dagoonigun an ingredient

w'dago-weendjigae he/she swears by someone

w'dago-waukiwaun he/she nails, affixes something to a surface

w'dago-wauk-ishkoozoh he/she is caught and squeezed between two objects

danau; danee; dani *during; while; time; abide; spend time; tarry; sojourn; profit; wealth; treasure*

aundih w'ae-danizit? where is he/she staying?

kitchi-daneewin a windfall; wealth; a great feat; possessions; estate; means; assets

mee woodih w'ae-dani-waewidung that is where he can be heard talking

maegwauh w'dani-idaemoh in the meantime she/he is crying

dasso *each; every; daily; monthly; weekly; hourly; times; frequency; per; so many times; as often as; multiplied; pressed down; crushed; trapped*

dasso-geezhig each day; every day

dasso-dubeeshkoodjigun each or per pound

dasso-ozid one foot

dasso-waewaun a pair

ahneen minik-datching how many times

dassoo-naugun a trap; a deadfall

w'dasso-ozoh he/she is trapped

daubaend *high; much*

w'daubaend-aenimaun w'kittisseemun he/she respects his/her parents, elders

n'daubaendiss I have self-respect

dauhnzh; dauhnzhi *lower; dim; turn down; bedim (from* nauzh*—downward; descending; later)*

w'gee dauhnzhaenaun waussikoonaendjigun he/she dimmed the lamp

daung; daungi; taung; taungi *to touch*

daungissitoon touch it lightly against

w'daung-inumoowaun he/she touches his/her thing(s)

daup *take up; accept; adopt; hold*

w'gee daupinaun abinoodjeehnsun he/she took the baby

daushk; daushki *split; divide; separate; rip; rive; halve; bisect; sawmill; ripsaw*

daushkiboodjigun a sawmill
w'daushk-indibaeshin he/she fractured his/her skull

daut; dauti *fast; quick*

w'dauti-ibeewuk they are quick
w'dauti-ibaun-ikittoon he/she speaks quickly; he/she has a fast mouth

daut; dauti *upward (poss. from* daumikun—*anatomy; the jaw [to look aloft one must rase the jaw])*

w'dautig-aubih he/she looks upward
w'dautig-iquaenih he/she lifts his/her head

dawau; dawauk; dawauki; dawi *openings; breach; break; rupture; cleft; split; rift; gap; hole; gulf; chasm; crevice; fissure; space*

Dawauwigunning South Bay Mouth; dredged
w'dawaushin he/she is adrift; he/she breaks through ice
dawaubaun a water hole in the ice
w'dawaugae he/she makes a hole in the ice
w'dawauwinutoon dassoonaugun he/she opens the trap
Mishi-dawudunnauh The Great Divide; space

dawiss; dawissi *room; time; accommodate (from* tawiss; dawau—*space)*

keeshpin dawissaeyin if you have time
tuguh! Dawissatoon please make room
dawissitchigun a space maker

dazhee; dazhi *now; at the present time; during; while; here; there; to while; spend time and effort; to abide*

woodih w'dazhi-anookee he/she is working there at the present time
Dazhi-Anishinaubaeg the Indians residing there
w'dazhee-akae he/she is playing, loitering there

debuss; debussi *lower; below (from* dupuss; pussu—*lower; below)*

debusheesh at a low altitude
w'debuss-atoon he/she builds it low
w'debuss-aendaugozih he/she is of little worth

dibaewau *as far as; as deep as; as high as (from* dae; daebae—*insofar; to the limits)*

w'daebaewaugi-aendum he/she thinks deeply, widely (reflects)
w'dibaewaug-anikae he/she reaches as far as he/she is able
w'dibaewaugimi-ossae he/she walks as far as he/she can walk

doong; doongi; toong; toongi *spread; widen; apart*

w'doong-dubih he/she sits with legs apart
doong-akissin it is gaping wide
w'doong-abitoon he/she pries it open

doosk; dooski; toosk; tooski *partially open; half-closed; narrowed; slitted; squint; sidewise; aslant; askew; peer; peep; peek*

w'doosk-aubi he/she looks through half-closed eyes
w'doosk-aubih he/she squints
dooskoon, dooskwoon that which can be slanted, and moved sideways; an elbow
doosk-aubindjigun a peep-sight; a telescope; a scope

dubu; dubuh • *measure; gauge; assess; evaluate; weigh; meter; rule; space; mark (off); survey; graph; balance; plumb; sound; fathom; partition; to time* • *pay*

w'dubugae he/she pays
dubugun a measure, term
ningo-dubu-geezissiwaun one hour

G

gab; gabauk; gabauki; gabi; gabo; gageeb; geebee • *stopped up; plugged up; stuffed; blocked; clog; obstruct; choke; fill; jam; pack; close; shut up; cover; cork; bung; stopple; staunch; seal; dam; constipate; strangle;*

PREFIXES

throttle; asphyxiate; suffocate; congest; trammel • close; shut; secure; padlock; lock; bolt; latch; bar; fasten

w'gabi-idjaunae he/she has a stuffed nose
gabi-aukoowigun a lock
gabaukawo-deewigummig a prison
w'gabi-iskawae he/she has strep throat
gaebauk closed off (the origin of the name of Quebec)

gaeshiwish; gaeshiwishkau *loose; come loose*

w'gaeshwishkauh nubug-issuk the board comes loose
w'gaeshwi-medaussae his/her socks (or pants) come undone

gaessi; gaessika *on time; just on time; at the right time; due; just in the nick of time; meet; chance upon; stumble upon suddenly; unexpectedly; without warning; at once; instantly; out of the blue*

gaessikunnuh w'gee niboh he/she died unexpectedly
gauwauhn w'gee gaessikoowaun he/she just barely came upon him/her
gaessikah gee izhi-waebut it happened suddenly

gagawae; gagawaed; gagawaedji; goodji; goossaub *to try; test; examine; inspect; attempt; essay; endeavor; venture; seek to; aim; experiment; analyze; assess; evaluate; sample; tax*

goossaubindjigae-ininih a seer
weeki-goodji-winaun he/she invites another to accompany him/her
w'gagawaedibaenimaun he/she tests him/her
gagawaediwaewinun questions
gagawaedaukaweewin a marksmanship contest

gagawaun; gawaun *to a great degree; much; extremely*

gawaun-issuk-kummik it is exceedingly indescribable
w'gawaun-issuk-atoo he/she is suffering severely
w'gagawaun-issuk-itaugozih he/she utters terrible (dire) threats, predictions, etc.

gageebaud; gageebaudji; geebau; geebaud *foolish; silly; irresponsible; impetuous; impulsive; short sighted; heedless; foolhardy; rash; brash; reckless; absurd; inane; senseless; ridiculous; ludicrous; asinine; crazy; featherheaded; muddled; frivolous*

w'gageebaudizih he/she is foolish, reckless
geebaudj a foolish one
w'gageebaudji-indibae he/she has foolish notions
w'gageebaud-aukinigae he/she makes ridiculous decisions

gageed; gageedi; gageedji; geedji *sore; tender; pain; sensitive; raw; ache; inflamed; bruised; painful to touch and move from bruise or strain; mumble, as in pain*

w'gageed-awae he/she wails
w'gageedji-inikae he/she has sore arms or aching arms
w'geegeedizih he/she aches all over

gageek; gageeki; gaukau; geek; geeki • *move over slightly, a little; cut off a little; slice; pare; fall over* • *numb; benumbed; insensate; no feeling; senseless; deadened; paralyzed*

geeki-idubin move your chair over
geeki-idub-inaessih a downy woodpecker or a sap-sucker
Kitchi-gaugeedjiwung Niagara Falls
Gaukau-peekauh Kakapekah Falls; a falls
w'geekee-pungooshih he/she is sleepy
w'geekau-widum he/she is quarreling
w'gageedji-kaudae he/she has a numb leg

gageem; gageemi; geem; geemi *complain; murmur; grumble; crab; gripe; squawk; beef; find fault; criticize; censure*

w'gageemi-doon he/she complains

gageep; gauk; gaukau; gaup; gaupau; geepi *brittle; delicate; thin; breakable; fragile; cracked due to brittleness or state; crunch*

gaup-aubikut the metal is brittle
w'gaup-izih he/she is fragile

w'gaup-doon he/she has chapped lips
w'gaup-ozhae his/her skin is delicate
gaukauwindjigun gristle

gageewi; gaween; gaweeniwi; geewau; geewi *around; round and round; circuitous; crooked; wind; uncertain; circumlocution; circular; round about; ambiguous; meander; turn; deceitful; illogical; indirect; rambling; mislead; lead astray; dupe; trick; fool; outwit; double-cross; zig-zag; beat around the bush; vague; jargon; digression*

w'geewi-inaudizih he/she is crazy
w'geewi-inimoh he/she lies (talks in circles)
geewaudji-apee at an inopportune time
w'geewi-ossae he/she hunts (a deer circles back and a good hunter does the same)
w'gaweeniwi-inaendum he/she is uncertain

gagishk; gagishki; gag; gagi; gig; gigi • *to bear; carry inside; pregnant* • *to wear*

w'gee gagishkoowaun abi-anoodjeeyun she conceived
n'gagishkaun babeessikowaugun I'm wearing a coat

gan; gana *warn; forbid; prohibit; restrain; hold back; check; proscribe; disallow; veto; reject*

w'gana-maugae he/she warns against
w'gana-beendjigae he/she is patient
ganamaugaewin a veto, prohibition, forbiddance

ganaudj; ganaudji *beautiful; pretty; handsome; winsome; comely; fetching; appealing; alluring; fine; attractive; becoming; fair; good looking; glamorous; charming; winning; lovely; elegant (poss. from* gino*—long)*

w'ganaudjiwih he/she is beautiful/handsome
ganaudjiwun it is beautiful

gashk; gashki(kashk)(kashki)(kishk) (kishki) *can; to be able; capable; fit; apt*

w'gashki-aewizih; w'kishki-aewizih he/she is capable
gashki-aewiziwin; kishki-aewiziwin ability; power; authority
w'gee gashki-atoon he/she accomplished it

gaund; gaundi; gagaund; gagaundi *push; propel; set in motion; pole; thrust; goad; prod; force*

w'gaundissu-aun he/she pushes him/her violently
gaundi-keegun a push pole
w'gagaund-aenimaun he/she relishes his/her misfortune or wishes, or looks forward with delight to someone's misfortune
gaundji-naegaewin to force
gaundji-dugaewin to force, compel

gausk; gauski; gooshkau • *buzz; hum; murmur; drone* • *to smoke meat, fish (from the sizzling sound of meat or flesh of fish being smoked)*

gauskibugissin the leaves rustle
w'gaushkibauzoh he shaves
w'gaushk-gaushkibissitoon he strops
w'gauski-naubaugawae he/she is thirsty

gauss; gaussee; gaz; gazee • *to wash; to wash clean; to scour; bathe; cleanse; wash up; launder; shampoo; lather; scrub; mop; soak; shower; douse; rinse* • *erase, wipe out, purge, expunge, blot out, wipe clean, make clean by rubbing out* • *eradicate, delete, efface*

gazee-ipee-igun soap
w'gazee-ipee-igae he/she washes clothing
gazeegun a dish rag
w'gazee-ipeeg-inindjee he/she washes his/her hands

gauss; gautch; gautchi *small; diminutive; tiny; lean; spare; thin; narrow; barely*

w'gaush-isheehnih he/she is small
gaussin it is small
w'gauzoowuk they hide
w'gaussau-ibaewizih he/she is thin
Gaussau-baunikauh Kasabonika, Ontario (*lit.* It Is Narrow)
w'gautchi-dubih he/she has little room for sitting
gautch-daeyauh it is narrow
w'gautchi-daukawee he/she reaches to the limits of his/her arm

gaut; gautae *to care for; minister; look after; tend; nurse the sick*

gautawaenawae-quae a nurse
w'gautawaenimaun he/she nurses the sick person

gauwau; gawae *to long; desire; want; crave; covet; to be jealous; envy; yearn*

w'gauwaudaun he/she craves it
w'gauwamaun he/she is jealous of another person's wife or paramour

gawaek; gawaeki; geeyuk; geeyuki *straight; direct; true; right; in a line; just right; good; excellent; upright; moral; ethical; orderly; organized; flush; in the groove; plumb; exact; correct; accurate; precise; clear; plain; simple; candid; frank; undeviating*

w'gawaeki-audjimoh he/she delivers an accurate story
gawaeki-ummoh the road is straight
w'gawaeki-audizih he/she leads an upright life
w'gawaek-ishimaun he/she turns him/her over

gawaetaun; gawaetaunih • *excessive; extremely; boundless; beyond words; description; measure; incredible; inconceivable; unusual; unheard of; wonderful; extraordinary; remarkable; amazing* • *prodigious*

gawaetauni-kummik unbelievable; out of this world
w'gawaetaun-eewee his/her strength cannot be described
gawaetaun-aendaugoot it seems extraordinary
w'gagawaetaun-ishkizih he/she has a powerful voice

gawau; gawaub; gawaush; gawauss *to go; get ashore; removed from water; find; seek shelter from waters or a storm; harbor; sanctuary; liberate; free; extricate; extract; draw out; ladle out; dip out; deliver; rescue; emancipate; to land (see also* agawau*—shelter)*

gawaubi-onaugun a dip net; a scoop
gawaubigun a dipper; a ladle
w'gawauwidaussoh he/she unloads
w'gawautauh he/she comes out of the water, goes ashore

gawauk *moldy; rusty*

gawauk-assin it is moldy
w'gawauk-ozhae he/she is moldy with dirt
w'gawauk-tuwugae his/her ears are encrusted with dirt

gawaushk; gawaushki *jump; leap; spring; hop; vault; bound; buck; skip; bob; bounce; clear; hurdle over* • *nimble; quick; agile*

w'gawaushk-awaezih he/she is nimble, etc.
gawaushki-waessae it bounces
w'ombi-gawaushkinih he/she jumps up
w'bauzhidji-gawaushkinih he/she leaps over
w'gawaushk-initoowaun he/she leaps upon someone to violate, ravish, wound, or kill

gawautae *to shade; shadow (from* augawautae-oon*—a parasol)*

gawautaewoon a parasol
w'gawautaeshin he/she is shaded
gawautae-auh it is shady

gaweeshk *to whistle; whiz; hum*

w'gaweeshki-waushih he/she travels so quickly that he/she whistles
gaweeshka-waewae the robin
w'gaweeshk-izhih he/she whistles

gawo; gawish; gawiss; gawi *fall; fall down; collapse; succumb; crumple; cave in; fell; lie down; pitch; topple; fall over; keel over; slump; fall into a heap*

w'gee awo-gawishimoh he/she has gone to lie down
w'wee gawissae he/she is going to collapse
n'gee gawingiwaush I fell into a deep sleep

gazh; gazhau; gazhi; gizhi *to hurt; cut; wound; injury by some misadventure*

w'gazhi-widizoh he/she wounds himself/herself
w'gee gazhi-oowaun he/she wounds him/her
w'gee gazhikaukoon he/she was bruised or hurt by him/her

gazhee; kishee *fast; quick; haste; rapid; swift; fleet; speedy; express; brisk; accelerated; expeditious; dispatch; loud; deafening; stentorian; full throated; sonorous; booming; forte; resonant; resounding; vociferous; itchy; robust; vigorous*

owih oshki-nawae w'gazhi-ozhaewizih that young man is industrious

w'gazheebee he/she is itchy

w'gazheewae-widum he/she talks fast and loud

w'gazhee-ozhae-wizih he/she is vigorous, full of vim

geeb *much; a great deal (usually used with respect to pain)*

w'geeb-aendum he/she suffers a great deal

geeb-aendumoowin great sorrow

geemo; geemoot; geemootchi; gimo • *to steal; rob; plunder; pilfer; thieve; purloin; filch; peculate; swindle; pocket; shoplift; swipe* • *stealth; sneak; furtiveness; surreptitiousness; sly; covert; clandestine; shady; arcane*

w'geemoodizih he/she sneaks

geemoodee-ininih a robber

geemootch on the sly

w'geemoo-zaubih he/she spies

w'geemood-aendum he/she entertains arcane ideas

geen; geenau *sharp; pointed; keen; razor-edged; honed; cutting; spear edged*

geenau-bikut it is sharp

geenauh it is sharp, keen

w'geen-kuzheehn he/she is sharp nailed

geep; geepi *tip; fall; drop; plunge; keel over*

geep-issae it tips over and falls

w'geep-ingwaum he/she falls off his/her bed during sleep

w'geep-igawaushkinih he/she jumps down from a height

geeshk; geeshki *cut; tear; rip; gash; slash; slit; slice; sever; cleave; sunder; rend; rive; dissect; cut apart; shear; crop; bob; pare; abridge; shorten; abbreviate; hew; lop off; mow; amputate; snip; nip*

w'geeshk-aukawae he/she clears land of trees

w'geeshk-aukoodjin he/she tears his/her clothing on some sharp object

w'geeshki-ozidae cut foot

geeshkaubauk an escarpment

geeshp; geeshpi *to buy, purchase, secure or obtain with money* • *cut from; exact; sever*

w'geeshpi-inatoon he/she buys

w'gee geeshpi-inatoon meedjim he/she bought food

geesk; geeski; geetch; geetchi *take off; undress; disrobe; shed; remove; cast off; strip; divest*

geeskun k'medaussun take off your leggings (pants, socks)

w'geetchee he/she takes off his/her shoes

w'geesi-kooniyae he/she takes off his/her clothes

geetch-kooniyae-waezigun corn removed from the cob

gees; geessau *sadly; despondent; regret; rueful; contrite; sorry; remorseful; repentant; penitent; abject; bitter*

w'geessauz-inaugozih he/she looks despondent

w'geessau'd-aendum he/she is repentant

geessaudkummik it is to be pitied; pitiful; the earth itself is sorrowful

geess; geessi; geet; geeta; geetch; geetchi; geeti; gitchi *draw out; take off by degrees; lever off; draw out or take off with difficulty; remove; take off shoes; extract; draw out by force; pry out; wrest out; root up; lift off; pare off; husk; hull (see also* geesk*—take off)*

abi-anoodjeehn w'geetchee the child takes his shoes off

w'gageet-igawae; w'gagaetae-igae he/she draws out a splinter

geetauwi-aendum he/she is very prudent

gitchi-kinaewaezigun corn pared, taken off the cob; hulled or husked corn

PREFIXES

w'geetau'd'izih he/she seems prudent

geew; geewi; geewit; geewitau *encircle; go around; surround; circle; wheel; circuit; circumference; ring; belt; girdle; gird hem in; ring around; compass; envelop; turn; round*

w'geewi-inaudizih he/she is crazy, a lunatic
gauwundi-aupinaed one who is suffering from lunacy
w'geewi-ossae he/she hunts
w'geewishkawae-ipee he/she is drunk
n'geewau-issitowauh I misunderstand him/her

geewaushk; geewaushki; geewishk; geewishki *dupe; trick; bewilder; befuddle; fluster; stupefy; confuse; muddle; jumble; confound; rattle; baffle (see also* geew*—encircle)*

w'geenawishkih he/she tells lies (talks in circles)
w'geewi-inimoh he/she talks in circles—doesn't know what he/she is talking about
w'geewauss-itaugoozih he/she speaks indistinctly, in a confused fashion

geezh; geezhau; geezhee; geezhi • *ready; already; in advance of; already prepared; prior (to); previous; anterior; earlier; preceding* • *finished, completed, done, ended, fulfilled, realized, achieved, settled*

auzhigoh w'gee geezhau-kinigaewuk they have already made up their minds
w'geezhee-itauwuk they are ready
w'geezh-aendumoobun he/she has already made up his/her mind

geezh; geezho; gizh; gizhau • *heat; warmth; tender-hearted; kind-hearted; hot; humid; torrid; passionate; tepidity; fever; sultry; warm up; cook; liberal; generous; unselfish; big hearted; considerate; cordial* • *envy; covet; jealous; resent; grudge*

gizhautae it is hot
gizhi-inaumidae it is humid
w'gizhizi-waupinae he/she has a fever
w'geezho-kunaeshin he/she hunkers in (warms) his/her shoulders
w'gizhau-waenimaun he/she is envious of him/her
gizhaugi-imidae the water is hot

gidig; gidigi; gidisk; gidiski; geetchi; gidjik; geesk; gidiskau *to dislocate; disjoint; put out of joint; disconnect; unhinge; loosen; free; take off; divest; sprain; twist; remove; undress; break off; separate; sever; sunder; part; detach; unfasten; undo; unhook; rend; unlink; uncouple*

w'gidig-ozid-aeshin he/she dislocates his/her foot
w'gidig-ayauh he/she is out of sorts, in a sour mood, disconnected
w'gidis-akeewee he/she breaks loose
w'gidisk-issae it tears loose, breaks free
gidjik-naewaezigun the process of removing husks from corn by leaching; the product that results from leaching
w'geetchee he/she removes his/her shoes
w'gee gidiski-inikaeshin he/she dislocated his/her shoulder
w'gee gidiski-aubeeginaun he/she unfastened the line
gee-gidiski-issae it fell off
w'gidisk-dinimaungunae-kunaeshin he/she dislocates his/her collarbone or shoulder

gin; gina; gini *quick; fast; accelerate; swiftly; hurriedly; hastily; rapid; fleet; brisk; spry; speedy*

w'gini-bigih he/she grows quickly
w'gini-bee he/she is quick, fast

gindau; gindjind; gindjindau *to insert; put in; stick in; slide in; slip in; press in; thrust in; push in; wedge in; cram; inject*

w'gindjidau-ipeeginaun he/she immerses it
w'gindashkauh he/she sinks
w'gindau-inaun he/she thrusts it in

ginig; giniga; keeneeg; kineeg; kinig(ginig)(giniga) *to mix; admix; mingle; blend; commix; commingle; amalgamate; put together; compound*

ginig-ipeessaun a mixture of snow and rain
giniginigun a mixture, a blend of tobacco
ginig-waugummih a solution

n'kineeginauh I mix it (tobacco)
giniginig tobacco

gino; gagaun; gaun; gin; gina • *long; tall; extended; outstretched; lengthy; protracted; prolonged; sustained; strung out; span; reach; duration; extent; elongate* • *bear with; suffer; tolerate; put up with; abide*

w'ginozih he/she is tall
ginozhae a pike
ginowaesh for a long time
w'ginowauk-koohnzhae he/she (a bird) is long beaked
w'ginowauki-djaunae he/she has a long nose
w'gagauno-wauk-inindjee he/she has long hands/fingers
gino-waudjiwun beautiful; deserving a long look; a long river

ginug; ginugi *ticklish; tickle; titillate*

ginugi-dayae-meenuk hawthorn berries; berries that cause the posterior to itch
w'ginugi-idjeenaun he/she tickles him/her

gitau; gitauk; giti; gitik *safe; seaworthy; sound; sure; certain; stable; on an even keel; steady; fixed; staunch; balanced*

gitau-goondae it (a boat) is seaworthy

gond; goond; goondi; goondau *swallow; quaff; wolf down; ingest; engulf; sink; submerge*

gondaugun the throat (*lit.* the swallower)
w'goondau-wikoh he/she sinks
w'goondjigae he/she swallows

gonub; gonubi *tip over; keel over; capsize; overturn; upset; turn over*

w'gee gonubi-ishkauh he/she upset (a boat)
w'gonubi-daubaunikoowuk they overturn (a car or wagon)

gookawau *pride; conceit; vanity*

w'gookawaud-inaendizoh he/she is proud
gook-awaudiziwin pride; worth
gook-waud-aenimauh I respect him

gookook; gookooki *unsafe; unstable; unsound; unsure; uncertain; unsteady; keel over; topple; inclined to capsize (from* quaequaek—*back; back up; backtrack; retract; reverse; turn)*

gookook-waumoogut the canoe rolls
gookook-waushikauh the waves are such as to make travel by canoe unsafe
gookook-idjiwun the current will make a canoe pitch and roll

goop; goopi *inept; gauche; maladroit; incompetent; unskilled; unfit; ineffective; awkward; bungling; oafish; absurd; backward; dull; simple*

w'goopi-idizih he/she is incompetent
w'goopi'd'aenimaun he/she regards him/her as gauche
w'gee goopi-idji-aun he/she made him/her out to be foolish; he/she abused or mistreated him/her

goosh; gooss; gootau; gootaum *scary; frightening; frightful; dreadful; terrible; grievous; alarming; threatening; appalling; awful; horrible; hideous; ghastly; gruesome; unspeakable; indescribable; exceeding*

gootaum-igozih he/she is exceedingly industrious (hustles; tries hard; gives his/her all)
gootaum-igoot there is a violent storm
w'gootaudjih he/she is frightened
w'goossikee-audizih he/she is wary by nature
w'gooshwaeshkee he/she is timid

gotug; gotugi *suffer; endure pain; ache; hurt; agonize*

w'gotugito he/she suffers
w'gotug-inaugozih he/she appears to be in agony

gozig; gozigi; gotig *heavy; burdensome; weighty; ponderous; overweight; fat; corpulent; massive; onerous; laden; taxing; to weigh*

w'gee gotiginaun he/she weighs him/her
w'gotig-inidizoh he/she weighs himself/herself
gozigiwun it is heavy
w'gozig-oonae he/she carries/bears an onerous burden

PREFIXES

w'gozig-inih he/she is heavy
w'gozih he/she moves, transfers his/her burdens elsewhere; he/she must bear a heavy burden in relocation

I

inoo-inoowa *resemble; look like; sound like; similar; alike; related; kinship; as*

w'inoo-waengae he/she relates, feels and expresses a kinship for
w'd'inoowaun he/she resembles him, her
inoo-itaugaewin to mimic, mock, ape

ishi; ae-izhi *as; as if; mode; manner; according to; style; wise; system; approach; technique*

ahneesh w'ae-izhi-bimaudizit? how is he/she?
mee igoh w'gauh izhi-maudjaut he/she left just like that
w'gee izhi-inoogae he/she pointed out the direction
mee ae-izhi-idjeeyauk that is how it is formed

ishkau; ishkauk • *curved; crooked* • *stiff*

ishkaummoh meekunnuh the road is crooked
ishkaukoot it is stiff/crooked
ishkaukigun a curved chest
w'ishkauk-izih he has an erection; a crooked, curved projection

ishkot; ishkotae *fire; flames; conflagration; combustion; blaze; light; ball of fire*

ishkotae-waubo spirits; wine; whiskey
ishkotae-bugonae the cardinal flower
ishkotae-daubaun a train

ishkwau; ishko; iska; isko • *last; final; behind; after; end; terminal; at last; conclude; conclusion; at the end* • *drain completely, draw off, pump, withdraw, dry up, extract, take away, filter, percolate; well out*

w'ishkaukishin he/she is lying there completely drained or fatigued
ishkoonigun an Indian Reserve
ishkwaeyaung behind, to the rear
ishkwau-nawiquae afternoon

ishpau; ishpi *high; lofty; in the heights; elevated; soaring*

Ishpi-idunnauh higher ground (Spadina—a street in Toronto, Ontario)
ishpi-imming heaven; in the sky
ishpau-kunnae the blaze flames high
ishpau-kissin it is built high

iska; iski; isku • *to dry; evaporate; dissolve* • *to enkindle, kindle, set fire to, light up*

iskutae it is dry (a lake, a well)
w'iskeeg-imizigae he/she is boiling something such as sap for reduction to syrup
w'iskugae he/she drains; he/she sets ablaze
iskupeetchigun a pump

K

kab; kabi; kabik • *to pass by (through); time passes; time comes; goes and passes by* • *to go beyond the end of, limit (from* kabae—*all)*

kabik-issae it passes; time passes
w'gee kabik-aunaun he/she overtook him/her

kabae *all; entire; the whole; during; in; total (from* kab—*to go beyond the end of)*

kabae-geezhig all day
kabae-neebin all summer
w'kabae-ishih he/she spends the night
kabae-ishee-wigummig a hotel
kabaewaewin to forecast

kae; kaewi; wakae *frequently; easily; susceptibly; prone to*

w'kae-aukozih he/she is prone to sickness
w'kae-pungishin he/she falls frequently
w'kae-mawih he/she cries at the drop of a hat
w'kaewi-igidauzoh (kidauzoh) he/she is quick to anger

kaugigae; kauginik *perpetual; eternal; forever; for all time; everlasting; beyond the end of time; in perpetuity; immortal; always; ever*

kaugigae-bimaudiziwin everlasting life
kaugigae-auniquot perpetual cloud
kaugaenik forever
kaugaugeehn the raven, ever present

---

kaukau; kaukaub; kakau • *falls; waterfalls; a drop; tumble over; edge over; rim; steep (from* geek—*fall over)* • *square*

kaukau-peekauh a falls
kaukau-kamaugud it is square
kaukaub-isheehn a screech owl
kaukau-idunnauh a gorge, canyon
kakau-kummikauh a precipice

---

kaukeetcheeshk; keetcheeshk; keetcheeshki *to gnash; grind; ground*

w'dah kaukeetcheeshkau-ibidaeshinook goomau-apeetch some day they shall all gnash their teeth
w'kaukeetcheeshkau-ibidae-widjih he/she is so cold that his/her teeth are rattling
w'kaukeetcheeshkau-kunaeshin his/her bones rattle with the chills

---

kik; kiki *to duplicate; to reproduce; to mark; represent; symbolize; simulate; characterize; effect; clone; reproduce; copy; facsimile; to produce a likeness, transcript; match; correspond; similar; replica.* NOTE: The act of teaching is to transmit or is the transmission of knowledge or information from one to another. The knowledge or information may then be regarded as duplicated, reproduced or represented at least twice; to know someone or something is to perceive characteristics already or previously known and remembered.

n'kik-aenimauh I know him/her
kiki-inoomaukae-ininih a teacher (male)
kiki-inoomaugaewiss a teacher (male or female)
kiki-inawauzinaugoziwin a characteristic
kiki-inoowautchitchigauzowin vaccination
kikinooniwin a year

---

kishk; kishkau; kishkauk; kishkauki (kaushki) *parched, scorched, burned wood; wood burned; a tree or limb charred, blistered, seared by fire*

kaushkauk-idaek scorched wood
kaushkauk-idaek-weeyauss smoked meat
w'keeshkaukizaun he scorches it

---

kishk; kishkauk; kishki *tight; constricted; taut; tense; strained; power; authority; ability; clasp; squeeze*

w'kishki-aendum he/she is dejected, sad, gloomy
kishki-aewiziwin ability, authority
kishki-omauk-odoonaepitchigun a gag
w'kishi-inaumoh he/she has difficulty breathing
kishki-maugaewin to convince, persuade

---

kitchi *big; bulky; massive; old; ancient; prodigious; immense; monstrous; grand; large; voluminous; colossal; gigantic; vast; towering; great; extensive; wide; tall; ponderous; swollen; right*

kitchi-anishinaubae an elder or a great big Indian
w'kitchi-weessinih he/she eats lots
kitchi-gauming the old world (*lit.* the great other side)
Kitchi-neebeesh Great Leaf, the name of a prominent chief

---

kitim; kitimi *lazy; poor; impoverished; indolent; miserable; pitiful; idle; slothful; shiftless; destitute; poverty; indigent; penniless; needy; broke; luckless; unfortunate; wretched; sorry*

w'kitimih he/she is lazy
kitimaugoziwin poverty; the direct result of laziness
w'kitimaug-inaendaugozih he/she is considered penniless/unfortunate

---

kitug; kitugi *spotted; freckled; speckled; pock marked; blemish; mark; speck; spot; defect; sully; mar; taint; damage; impair; deface; blot; blotch*

w'kitug-eengawae he/she is freckled
kitug-eegin a kind of fabric
kitugaukoohnse a fawn, still spotted

PREFIXES

kizhae *revered; respected; esteemed; hallowed; acclaimed; well regarded; honored; admired*

Kizhae-Manitou most venerated manitou; God; another term for Kitchi-Manitou
kizhaeg-ininih an elder
kizhaeg-quae an elder
w'kizhae-waeninaun he/she respects him/her

kizhee; gazhee *hard; firm; solid; settled; packed; strong; powerful; booming*

kizheewae-goonugauh the snow is hard
w'kizhee-ozhaewizih he/she is strong
w'kizhee-wae he/she is loud

koo; kood; koosh; kooshi; kooss; koossi *to pile; accumulate (from* piko*—a bump)*

koossinoon missun the firewood is piled
w'koossi-itchigae he/she piles (things)
koodauwing-assinoon they are piled together

koob; koobi; koowaub; koowaubee *wind up; reel up; spool up (in); coil; curl; roll; crank; wreath; hoist up; turn; set*

koowaubee-un waeweeb reel it in quickly
koowaubee-igun a reel, a spool, a winder, a key
k'gee koowaubeewauh nah dubu-geezissiwaun? did you wind up the clock?
koob-atoon k'medauss pull up your socks, trousers, or pants (Western Anishinaubae)

kook; kooki *weave; knit*

kooki-medauss a knit sock
kooki-abinaugun a basket
w'kooki-waudjigae he/she weaves

koon; koonau • *drive off; repel; repulse; ward off; send away; keep at bay* • *peel; pare* • *covering; husk; peeling*

w'gee koonauzhiwaun he/she drove him/her off
koonaus a blanket, shawl, or any kind of covering; a peeling, onion skin

kooshk; kooshki; kishk; kishko • *startle; surprise; astonish; shake up; unsettle; unnerve; jolt; upset; shock; jar; stun; daunt; scare; amaze; start; jump; blink; quail* • *wake up; awaken; come to one's senses*

w'kooshkooshkiwae-ossae he/she staggers
w'kooshkoozih weebah he/she wakes up early
n'gee kooshkoo-auh I startled him/her
w'kooshki-awaetoowuk they rouse the neighbourhood with their clatter, brawling, etc.

kundo *watch; wait in ambush; hiding place; ambuscade; lurk; skulk; lie in wait; waylay*

w'kundo he/she lies in wait
kundomoon water lily (yellow)
kundeekun a buoy

kupug; kupugi(gopug) *thick; beamy*

kupug-izih mukwoom the ice is thick
kaupugau that which is thick
kupugadin it is frozen thick
kupug-eegizih he/she is strong

M

madoo; madood; madoon *steam bath; sweat lodge; steam*

madoodizoon a steam bath; sweat lodge, purification
madoon-waubik a heated stone used in purification ceremony
w'madoodizoh he/she goes to a sweat lodge
madootizaun sweat lodge, purification

maedau; maedaut; mae-adau; mae-adaut; maegawae; maegawaed *strange; foreign; alien; different; odd; peculiar; outsider; unfamiliar; exotic; immigrant; indistinct*

maedaut-ishinaubae a person of another tribe
mae-daut another North American Indian
maegwaehn a stranger; one who speaks a foreign language
maemaegawaehnse a little manitou; one whose language is different

maedauss; maedaussi; maess; maessi; meedau; meedauss; meedaussi *long;*

long for; miss; fail to catch (meet, see, hear); pine for; nostalgia; come up short; yearn for; bemoan; lament; evade

w'meedau-waendum he/she is made impatient to have more (by not having enough)
w'maessinaun he/she misses him/her
w'maeniss-aendum he/she is ashamed
w'maen-ishitooh he/she causes embarrassment, humiliation

maeg; maega; maegwae; maegi *in the middle; among; in the midst; amid; amidst; in the thick of; amongst; surrounded by; enveloped*

maegwae-eeng in the middle; amongst
maegawa-yauk in the middle of the bush
maegwauh while

maeg; maegi *strange; alien; foreign; exotic*

maeyeengun, myeengun a wolf
maega-yauk in the forest, a strange or unfamiliar locale

maen; maeniss; maess; maessi; menaez; menaezi *to want; be in need; lack; be short of; require; miss; not measure up; found wanting; insufficient*

w'gee maessinaun w'gushiwun he/she longed for or missed his/her mother
w'maendaut-issae he/she has not yet been satisfied; craves more
w'menae-puwauh he/she lacks and craves tobacco
w'menaezih he/she is in want

maeshi; meesh; meeshi *hairy; furry; fuzzy; shaggy; bearded; whiskered; unshaven*

w'meeshi-eengawae he/she has a hairy face
maeshiwae-eegin a velvety cloth
w'meeshi-adoon he/she has a beard
meeshaukoot it is hairy on its entire length

maewishki; meezhushk *grass; hay; straw*

w'meeshko-kae he/she cuts hay
maewishkoohnse small hay; grass
maewishkoohnsekauh it is grassy
meezhushk hay
maewishkoodae a prairie

makat; makatae *black; dark; swarthy; ebony; jetty; raven; pitchy; inky; dusky*

maekataewiss a person of dark complexion
makatae powder
makatae-augoom-ishkeehnzhikoom pupil of eye
makatae-eegin black cloth
makatae'w'ikooniyae a priest (*lit.* black robe)

mamaud; maud *mix; shake; mingle; churn; agitate; admix; intermix; commingle; blend by shaking*

w'mamaudji-waebinaun he/she shakes him/her/it

mamauk; mauk; mauki; mauko; meek *wound(ed); marked; injured; abrasion; lesion; gashed; scored; contusion; pox; measles; smallpox; cripple*

w'gee maukinuhnaun he/she wounded him/her
w'maukizih he/she is injured
w'mauk-eengawae he/she or his/her face is pockmarked

mamaund; mamaundau; maumee; maumikau; maund; maundau *wonderful; strange; remarkable; marvellous; extraordinary; awesome; striking; amazing; astounding; make bigger; exceedingly; exaggerate(d); hard to believe; prodigious; inspiring; unbelievable; astonishing*

maundau-meen corn; maize
w'maundau-witchigae he/she does marvellous things
w'maumikau'd'aendum he/she is astonished
w'maumeek-awaendum he/she is well-pleased, satisfied, delighted, contented, awed, overcome with wonder, enthusiastic, etc.

mamaundji; maundj; maundji *to tie; to shackle; bind; manacle; fetter; chain; handcuff; trammel; in irons; tether; truss; hogtie; crippled; lame; secure; hold; grasp; clutch; keep; retain; hold down (from* mindjim*—to hold)*

w'maumaundji-gooshkiwaun he/she presses down or bears down with his/her size and weight to prevent escape

PREFIXES

mindjikun a weir; that which keeps within a course, fence
w'mamaundji'g'oosae he/she is lame, hobbles
w'mamaundji-gobizoh he/she is manacled
mindjikoon hold him/her
mindaussiwaugun one who is kept in bondage

---

mashk; mashki *strength; power; vigour; vitality; potential; potency; firm; robust; durable; tough; healthy; wholesome; force; might; energy; dynamism; solid; soundness; hardness*

w'mashki-oowizee he/she is strong
mashk-oowaumigut it is tough
w'mashko-waendum he/she is resolute
mashko-waubikut the metal is firm
mashki-aki medicine; strength of the earth

---

matchi; mauzh; mauzhi *bad; evil; wicked; malicious; malevolent; sinful; iniquitous; foul; mean; harmful; malignant; adverse; lawless*

matchi-mashki-aki bad medicine
matchi-manitou the devil
w'matchi-kittoh he/she swears
matchi-izhi-waebut it is inclement
w'mauzhi-ayauh he/she does not feel well
mauzh-pugoot it tastes foul

---

maud; maudj; maudji *begin; start; commence; initiate; embark; actuate; instigate; set in motion; pioneer; introduce; launch; open; broach; give rise to*

w'maudjitauh he/she begins
w'maudjee he/she begins to move
w'maudjee-puwae he/she begins to run away
maud-ossaemigut it begins
Maudjee-Kawiss first son of Ae-pungishimook and Winonah; safeguardian/warrior of nation

---

maug; maugi *to press; depress; squeeze; weight upon; bear down; compress; crush; squash*

w'gee mauginaun he/she depressed it
w'gee maug-inindjee-binaun he/she squeezed his/her hand
w'gee maugishkaun he/she bore down on it

---

maugawae *lower; melt (poss. from* maug*—to press)*

maugawae-goonaeshin the snow settles, goes down
Mauginitwung where rivers converge at some lower point; Magnetwan, Ontario

---

maumee; maumowi; mauwo; mauwoon; mayau; mayaum *all together; total; everyone; all; completely; entirely; fully; thoroughly; everything; united; commingle; whole; entire; collective; combined; composite; universal; inclusive; add up; sum up; amount*

mauminaud-aendumowin pride, conceit, vanity
mauwidishiwaewin a visit; all together
maumowissi-atoonaun we shall put everything together; to total
w'maumi-weenoowuk they are all together
w'gee maumi-koobi-atoon he/she pulled out the entire object
maumowissitoodauh k'd'anamiewininaun let us unite our petitions
maumeek; maumeew-ininiwuk the united people; the people downstream (the name the Algonquin called themselves)

---

maumeeg; meeg; meegi • *to select; choose; elect; pick* • *to give*

w'gee maumee-ginauwaun they select him/her
w'meegawae he/she gives
meegwaetch thank you

---

maun; maunaud *ugly; unattractive; plain; distorted; misshapen; disagreeable; revolting; disgusting; foul; bad; offensive; faulty; defective; inferior; unfit*

maunaudut it is ugly
w'maunaudizih he/she is ugly
w'maunaud-aupinae he/she has venereal disease or some loathsome illness
maunaudiziwin ugliness
maunau-gummih the water, fluid, drink is contaminated, impure, noxious, etc.

---

maung *big; oversized; wide; broad; distended; expansive; thick; outspread; ample; capacious*

maung a loon
Maung-ozid Loon's Foot (name of former chief)
mae-maung-oshaehn a donkey (*lit.* big eared)
maung-daeyauh it is wide
w'maung-ishkum he/she leaves broad tracks in the snow

---

mausk; mauski *stunted; small; dwarf; midget; runt; shrimp; bantam; underdeveloped*

w'mausk-izih he/she/it is stunted
w'mausk-inaugoozih he/she appears stuffed
mauski-waubae a dwarf

---

mauz; mauzo *robust; sturdy; firm; strong; vigorous; hearty; hale; lusty; sound; stout; tough; staunch; rugged; stalwart; stocky; well-built; rigid; stable*

w'mauzo-gizih he/she is stocky
w'mauz-aubaewizih he/she is of stout frame, well built
mauz-aukoot; mauz-aukwoot it is rigid, tough

---

mauzh; mauhnzh *badly; bad; gauche; unskillful; clumsy; inept; bungle; bumble; awkward; maladroit; graceless*

w'mauzh-eewee he/she is gauche, inept
w'mauzh-odae-ae he/she is nauseous
w'mauzh-eengawaenih he/she grimaces
mauzhi-mautae it smells bad

---

mawi; mawin *to cry; weep; keen; sob; bawl; whimper; wail*

w'gee mawi-naewaun w'weedji-aki-waehnun he/she angrily went to confront his/her friend
w'kitchi-mawih he/she weeps, bawls
w'dah mawimaun apee w'maudjaunit she will cry for him when he leaves
w'mawi-nae-ikae geewaehn it is said that he charges, sets upon, someone

---

mayau; mayauw; mayawih *in the center; in the middle; dead on; on target; on time; just right; suitable; perfect; pleasing; accurate*

mee mayauw right on; dead center
meeyau-waussigae it shines directly
w'gee meeyau-ikunaumaun he/she struck him/her straight on
w'mayau-itauh he/she sits up, stands up, etc.

---

mazau; mazhi; mazhee; mishi *bare; denude; exposed; peeled; shear; de-limb; lop off; chop off; truncate; trim; trim off; detach; amputate; prune; dock; crop; clip; shorten; shear; pare; to wound; mutilate; maim cripple; clear; plain; open*

w'mazhee-gae he/she lops off the limbs, or clears land
mishishuh it is clear; it is plain
w'mazhi-dayae he/she is naked, bare-assed
mazautik a cudgel
n'gee mishau-aubundu-auh I made it plain to him/her

---

mazin *image; inscription; etch(ing); engraving; draw(ing); trace; make a likeness; represent; picture; carve; sculpt; impress; impression; mold; cast*

mazin-ininih a carving; an image
mazin-ishin his/her image is engraved
w'mazin-beegae a drawing
w'mazin-koodjigae he/she carves, sculpts

---

medawae; medawaewae *to sound; drum; resonate; music; tone; reverberate; groan*

medawaewae it sounds
medawaewae-igun; daewaegun drum
w'medawaewaetchigae he/she makes music
medawaewaetchigun a musical instrument
medawaessin it rings

---

meedae(medae) *aside; to one side; removed; at a little distance; nearby*

w'meedaegawaeginaun he/she puts it to one side
meedaegawaetchigun that which is set aside
w'meedae-gaubowih he/she stands nearby

---

meedaug; meedaugi *forgive; absolve; excuse; amnesty; overlook; disregard; remit; waive; dispense with pardon; reprieve; acquit; clear; bury the hatchet (from* meedae*—aside)*

meedaugawaenimishinaung keep us away from temptation

PREFIXES

meedaugawaendumowin remorse

meegaud *to fight; battle; war; contest*

w'meegauzoowuk they are fighting
n'meegaudinotchigun my fighting partner
w'meegaushki he/she is disposed to fight
meegaudi-naubo fighting spirits, liquors, wines

meek • *to hit with an object; strike; shoot; fell; drop; bring down; graze; tease (see also* mam-auk—*wound[ed])* • *to be equal; same; on par*

w'gee meekoowaun he/she struck him/her; he/she dropped him/her with a shot
w'gee meekoo-indji-aun he/she teased him/her; he/she taunted him/her
meekinidiwin equality

meekoon; meekoonoo *glad and thankful; appreciate; grateful*

w'meekoonoo-waendum he/she is grateful
w'meekoonoo-waeyaun he/she pleases someone
meekoonoo-waendumoowin gratitude

meen; meend *pout*

w'meendawae he/she pouts
meendawaewin pouting
w'meendawae-inaugozih he/she looks as if he's/she's pouting

meen; meeni *seed; of a seed; berry; nut (frequently pronounced as* min*)*

meen a seed; a berry
mishee-meen an apple (*lit.* the great seed, berry)
mino-meen wild rice (*lit.* the good seed)
meeni-kaun a seed
meenun; meenuk blueberries
w'meenkae he/she picks berries
meeniwun it is fertile, fruitful; it bears fruit; it is ready

meew; meewi • *refuse; deny; say no* • *reluctant, unwilling, disinclined, opposed to, averse, loath, hesitant, circumspect*

w'gee meewinaun w'daunissun he/she refused his/her daughter
n'meewitaun I put it out of reach
meewitowih refuse him/her
w'meewi-aendum he/she is unwilling
w'meewi-audizih he/she is circumspect by nature
w'mee-waudjimoh he/she is loath to talk

megooshk; migoshk *uneasy; disturbed; bothered; agitated; perturbed; unsettled; annoy; trouble; fret; irk; vex; provoke; peeve; nettle; chafe*

w'megooshkaud-aendum he/she is perturbed
w'megooshkaudiziwuk they are having troubles
w'megooshkau-issitaugozih he/she creates an annoyance with his/her demands

mig; mimig; mimigi *to wriggle; wiggle; squirm; writhe; twist; mix; shake*

geegoohn w'migiwee the fish wriggles
w'mimig-issatoon he/she mixes it well by shaking
w'migiwee he/she squirms

mindjim *to hold, retain, keep*

mindjiginun hold it
w'mindjim-aendaun he/she remembers it

mino; meno; maeno *good; fine; excellent; right; well; good; satisfactory; prime; virtuous; upright; presentable*

mino-geezhigut it is a good day
w'mino-ayauh he/she is well or prosperous
mino-meen wild rice (*lit.* the good seed)
mino-ossaemigut it works well
mino-quae a virtuous woman
w'mino-odae-ae he/she is generous
maeno-pugook that which is delectable

mino-audj; mino-audji *honor; respect; esteem; regard; revere; admire; have a high opinion for; venerate; worship; pay homage to*

w'mino-audji-aun w'kittisseemun he/she honors his/her parents
w'mino-audji-aun manitoun he/she venerates the deities

mishau; mishishuh; mishuh; mazau *plain; manifest; out in the wide open; clear; distinct; graphic; patent; bald; apparent; conspicuous; blatant; expose; prominent; overt; shown; evident; full view; public unhidden; showing; on the surface*

n'gee mishau-aubunduwauh I made it plain to him/her
mishishuh it is plain, open, etc.

mishee; mishi *huge; large; immense; titanic; stupendous; monstrous; gigantic; enormous; mammoth; whopping; queen/king size*

Mishi-zeepi the Great River; the Mississippi River
owih ogimauh w'misheen-atoon aki the governor increases his real estate holdings
mishee-meen an apple, the great seed
misheen-maukinaukoong at Michillimackinac
Mishi-bizheu The Great Lynx

misqua; misqui *red; crimson; cardinal; carmine; ruby; scarlet; vermilion; russet; cherry; maroon; auburn; blood; sanguine; incarnadine; gory*

misqui blood
misquee-aub an artery
misquo-meenuk raspberries
misquo-djeebik blood-root
Misqua-auniquot Red Cloud
w'misquo-ozhae he/she has measles

miss; missa; misso *like; love; be fond of; to covet; to want; long for; care for; cherish; treasure; desire; yearn for; pant for; lust after*

w'misso-waenimaun he/she yearns for him/her
misso-waendjigaewin desire, yearning, wanting

missau *dried; limbed; bare; peeled as of a stick; piece of wood or a cudgel*

missau-wimigut the snow falls off the trees

missuh *ill starred; unlucky; ill fated; unfortunate; gauche; clumsy*

w'missu-gawaudizih he/she is unlucky
missu-gawa'd'aendaugoot it is unlucky

mitau; mitch; mitchi *naked; without clothing; bare; peeled; nothing between; uncovered; undressed; unclothed; stripped; bald; exposed; unprotected; unsheltered; bleak*

w'mitchi-dayae he/she is bare-assed
w'mitauk-ozhaewuk they are nude

mitchau; mitchauh *it is big; large; great; vast; bulky; husky; beefy; burly; brawny; robust; solid; heavy; chunky; stout; corpulent; gross; paunchy*

mitchau-beegut the rope is thick
w'mitchau'b'aewizih he/she is stout, corpulent
mitchauh it is vast
mitchaukoot it is long

mitug; mitugi *vanish; disappear; dissolve; evaporate; fade; evanesce; melt away; go from sight*

w'mitug-aushih he/she flew from sight
mitug-ishkauh it disappeared
w'mitug-aubauwae he/she disappeared in the water; he/she dissolved

mizha *to arrive; get here; get there*

w'mizha-ikishin he/she arrives
w'mizha-aushinook they arrive by flight
w'mizha-ossae he/she arrives on foot

mizhee *much; bountiful; ample; lots; prolific; replete; increase (from* mishee*—huge)*

w'mizheenoowuk they are many
w'mizheen-atoon he/she has an ample supply; he/she increases it
mizheenut weeyauss there is a lot of meat
n'mizheenimin we are many, numerous

mizhi *to injure; wound; hurt; harm; bruise; maim*

w'gee mizhi-aun iniw moozoon he/she wounded the moose
mizhi-waugun a wounded person

mizi; miziwae *all over; everywhere; in all parts*

miziwae all over

PREFIXES

miziwae-kummik in every part of the earth
miziwae-gummeeng all over the sea

mook; mooki(moog)(moogi) *pare; cut; dig; peel; bark; carve; shear; score; gash; sculpt; whittle; emerge; come out of; issue; pour out; crop up; surface; reveal self (itself); become visible; show self; becomes evident*

mookomaun a knife
mook-idjiwun the water wells out of the ground
w'mook-indibaenih he/she sticks his/her head out of the ground
w'mook-idaussoh he/she whittles something
w'mooki-waudjimoh he/she reveals a secret
mook-issae it emerges, becomes visible

moon; mooni *dig up; excavate; unearth; exhume; quarry; bring to surface*

w'moon-aenimaun he/she suspects him/her
w'moon-ishkawae he/she weeds a field
w'moon-ikaewuk they unearth or excavate something
w'moona-pinee he/she digs up potatoes

mooshk; mooshki *full; replete; to capacity; to the brim; satiated; fill; brimming; packed; crammed; stuffed; crowded; glutted*

mooshkin full
w'mooshkinae he/she is full
mooshkinae-pee it is full (liquid, water)
mooshka-issae a bittern (a bird)

moossae *pustules; pimply; from worms or grubs*

moossae a grub, a worm
w'moossae-weengawae he/she has a pimply face
w'moossae-wigut it is worm-eaten

moozh; moozhi • *to feel; touch; sense; handle* • *to cut, shave, shear, clip*

w'moozhi-aun he/she feels/senses him/her
w'gee moozhitoon he/she felt/sensed it
moozhiwaugun scissors
w'moozhiwaugun-idayaew-ossae he/she walks in scissor-like fashion

moozh; moozhi; moozhig • *joyful; happy; delighted; uplifted* • *collect; gather; harvest; reap; pick up; eats up; consumes*

w'moozhi-igundjigae it harvests, eats up everything
w'moozhi-g-aendum he/she is joyful, uplifted; he/she collects his/her thoughts
n'gee moozhi-ginaun I picked it up

mud; mudj; mudji; muss; mussi *to awaken; set into motion; annoying; baneful; vexatious; irritating; disturbing; disquiet; agitate; unsettle; trouble (from* maud—*begin)*

w'mussi-itaugozih he/she has a vexatious voice that would startle the sleeping into wakefulness
w'gee mudji-aun he/she woke him/her up
kegoh mudji-aukaen don't wake him/her up
mussit-awaewae the noise or the sound would awaken the sleeping

muk; muko; mukwo *find; come upon; discover; uncover; chance upon; locate; descry; perceive; mark; detect*

mukwo a bear
k'gee mukaun nah? did you find it?
mukwo-pin bear's potato (an edible root)
mukwoss-augim a bear-paw snowshoe

muk; muku *to take from; steal; remove; plunder; appropriate; seize*

w'gee mukumaun he/she takes it from him/her
mukundawae-ininih a thief, a robber
mukum owih take it away from him/her
mukundawaewin plunder

mushkeeg; mushkeegi *swamp; marsh*

mushkeeg-wautik tamarack
mushkeeg-meen cranberry
Mushkeegoohnyuk the Cree
Mushkeeg-zeepi Marsh River

muyug; muyugi; muyeeng; myeeng *strange; make strange; bashful; backward; estranged; alienated; apart; separated; segregated; unfamiliar; foreign; timid; shy; withdrawn; evasive; suspicious*

myeengun a wolf (*lit.* one who makes strange)
w'muyug-aendjigae he/she is unfamiliar with
w'muyug-awaewuk they speak a strange language
muyug-awae a stranger, foreigner

N

nae; naeyau *a point; a point of land; an extension; a spit; a protrusion*
naeyaush a peninsula
naey-aubikauh a ledge; a projecting rock
naey-auwingauh a spit of sand; a sand bar

nae-ae; nanae *here and there; browse; collect; gather*
w'naenimoowuk they gather food

naega; naegawau; naegawauki *put in; insert; inlay; push in; force in; inject; thrust in; drive in; wedge (in); infix; implant; inject*
naegawauk-issae it sticks in
w'naegawaukinaun he/she drives it in
naegawaukissitchigun a wedge

naegauss; naegautchi; aegauss • *softly; carefully; subdued; low; faint; gently; light; quiet* • *slowly; gradual; moderate; leisurely; measured; paced; deliberate* • *economic; save; keep; conserve; spare; scrimp; frugal*
n'naegauss-itoowauh I listen to him/her with attention
naegautch igoh w'babaum-ossae he/she walks deliberately
naegautchitoon zhooniauh take care of your money

naen; naenae; naeni *each; every; every other; respectively; each and every*
nae-neezh every second one, or both
nae-neezhi-geezhik every second day
nae-neezhi-igoon every other day
w'nae-nauwinigae he/she divides

naepau; naepaud; naepautch *gauche; bungle; awkward; blunder; mix up; gaffe; botch; butcher; clumsy*
naepautchi-nikaessih a mole
w'naepautchitoon he/she puts it in the wrong place
w'naepautchi-odoon he/she says the wrong thing

naeta; naetawae; needa; needawae *sad; sorrowful; morose; unhappy; mournful; woeful*
w'needa-waewidum he/she keens, weeps
naeta-waendaugoot it is woeful
naetawae-tibikut a mournful night

naezh; naezhi; naezhau *loose; free*
naezh-auwingauh loose sand
w'naezhi-ingizih he/she is loose limbed
w'naezhi-auniquae his/her hair hangs free

nagi; nagik; nagiki *unimportant; of little value or worth; small; minor; negligible; inconsiderable; trivial; petty; paltry; niggling*
nagi-waendaugoot not worth much
w'nagi-waendaun he/she regards it as trivial
w'nagik-waenimaun he/she scorns him/her

nahee; nahi *facility; deftness; easily; quickness; adept; proficient; adroit; fluent; prone to; susceptible; readily*
w'nahi-kabitum he/she is susceptible to nose bleeds
w'nahi-kikaendjigae he/she learns quickly
w'nahi-baupih he/she laughs readily

nahi *neat; tidy; clean; orderly; trim; ship-shape; spruce; smart*
w'nahi-eenigae he/she tidies up
nahi-itae it is tidy, orderly
w'nahi-gaubowih he/she is upright

nakae *directions; direction; orientation; bearings; in relation to*
woodih nakae-yauh in that direction
nakae-ogaum on this side of the lake
akeewaedinoong w'nakae-wae-ikae he/she is bearing or steering north

nakawa; nakawae *reply; answer; respond; catch and return; retort; rejoin; return; come back; repartee; catch and throw back; receive (an object or information) and retain and then to return to source*

w'nakawaetum he/she answers
w'naukawae-pitchigaewuk they catch, or play catch
nakawae-beegun a reply letter; a written reply
w'nakawae-bitoon he/she catches it

nakawae(kawae) • *a moment; a pause; wait; hold up; in the interim; in the interval; hesitate; hiatus interruption; in the meantime; break; intermission* • *to track, follow*

w'nakawae-ishkoowaun he/she meets him
kawae! wait up!; just a moment!
w'd'kawae-aun moozoon he/she tracks a moose
w'bimi-kawae he/she leaves tracks, a trail

namautch; namautchi *upright; at attention; plumb; erect; oblong*

w'namautchi-gaubowih he/she stands erect
namautchi-gud it is oblong

namundj; namundji *left side*

namundji-anikauning on or to the left hand
w'namundjee he/she is left-handed

nanauk *to defend; fight back; resist*

w'gee nanaukaweewuk they resisted
gauh'd'nanaukaweeng where a stand was made (poss. origin of Gananoque, Ontario)

nanaund; nanaundi; naund; naundi *to treat; look after; medicate; attend to; drug; minister to; nurse; palliate*

w'nanaundiwi-aun he/she ministers (medicine) to him/her
nanaundiwitchigun a patient; medication
naundiwiwaewin medical treatment

nanauti; nanauto; nau-auk; nau-auki • *set right; reconcile; fix; repair; mend; restore; put back together; redo; remake; overhaul* • *revamp; renovate; remedy; recondition; retouch; refinish; refit; remodel*

w'gee nanau-atoon he/she repaired it
k'gah nau-auk-issatoon you will set it straight or upright
nau-auko-inun line it up; align it properly
nau-aukinigun a level; bevel

nanauzh; naunauzh; nauzh; nauzhi; neessi • *downward; descending* • *later*

nauzhau-bee-igun a violin, fiddle
neessau-idjiwun downstream
nauzhinun k'medauss! lower your pants/leggings!
neessi-kaungidae the place is untidy owing to articles having fallen down
kauween igoh nauzh not for a while yet

naneen; naneeni *sad; unhappy; dejected; depressed; crestfallen; downcast; gloomy; melancholy; blue; sorrowful; rueful; glum*

w'naneekaud-aendum he/she is depressed
w'naneen-witaugozih he/she sounds rueful
w'naneen-awaendum he/she is melancholy
naeneeniwizit an orphan; an unhappy person
n'naneebikimauh I scold him/her; I make him/her unhappy

naneen; naneeni; neen • *feeble; weak; frail; anemic; not strong; infirm; unsteady; shaky; decrepit; doddering; failing* • *to abuse*

ae-kitizidjig w'naneenimiziwuk the elderly are often frail
w'naneekaudji-aun he/she abuses him/her to such an extent as to weaken him/her
w'neen-imizih he/she is frail
naneeni-waendumoowin dismay; discouragement

naning; naningi; nanik • *tremble; quake; quiver; quaver; tremulous; shudder; trill; quail; throb; twitch; convulse* • *shimmer, twinkle, sparkle, scintillate, ripple*

w'naeningishkung he/she who makes the earth tremble
w'naning-ishkizih he/she has a vibrato voice
naning-issugauh rippling water sparkling in the sunlight
Nana'b'oozoo or **Nanabush** Tremulous Tail,

youngest son of Ae-pungishimook and Winonah; personification of humankind in its aspirations and in its follies

w'nanik-indib-aessae he/she is drowsy; his/her head keeps dropping

nap; napi; napee *cushion; protect; shield; sheath; bolster; absorb*

napishimoon; api-quaeshimoon a pillow

nap-eegineegun a tablecloth

napi-gidik-waeshimoon a mat to kneel on

naub; naubae; naubi; naubishkau; naup; naupi • *tie; lace; bind; join; string together; chain; in sequence; fasten; attach; link; hook together; connect; splice* • *to replace; substitute; deputy; stand in place of; represent; succeed*

naubi-koowaugun a tie; a neckerchief; a necklace

naubau-kissitchigun a handle

naubidoo-un weengae! lace it well!

w'gee naub-ishkoowaun he/she substituted for another

naub-ozhaewoon a nose ornament

naubae *male; a being*

naubae-ossae a rooster; one who struts like a male

Anishinaubae; Onishishi-naubae the good being from good intentions

naubae a male

naebae-assim a male dog

naug; naugi *useless; for nothing; meaningless; worthless*

n'naugeekawiss I'm good for nothing

naugeekaw-aendaugoot it is worth nothing

w'naugikaw-aenimaun he/she thinks another of little worth

nauk; nauko *something in the future; forecast; prophecy; anticipation*

w'nauko-dumaugae he/she promises

nauko-dumaugaewin a promise

n'nauko-dum I consent, agree

nauko-inaudjimo-ininih a prophet

naumae; naumi *glue; mucilage; pitch; caulking*

w'naumae-kaunikae he/she makes pitch

naumaequan glue

w'naumae-aun w'cheemaun he/she seals his/her canoe with pitch/caulking

w'naumae-widjee-aun he applies glue

naunau; naunauk *over and over; repetitive; routine; drill*

w'kitchi-naunauki-zhae-igae he/she stokes his/her fire repeatedly

w'naunaugata-waendum he/she thinks

w'naunaugata-waenimauwaun they look after him/her or them

naunau; naunauw; naunauwi; nauw; nauwi *in the middle; in the center, midst; central; focal; halfway; midpoint*

naunau-wa-eeng in the middle

naunauwi-gaum in the middle of the lake

naunauwi-kudik in the middle of the forehead

nauwitch far out in the lake

naunauwi; nauw; nauwi; nauwit • *bend; incline; bow; stoop; crouch; curtsey* • *waste* • *deficient; insufficient; wanting; lacking; not quite; not enough; short*

w'nauwitauh w'wee peendigaet he/she stoops in order to enter

nanauwi-pee the water is ebbing

nauwishkauh it bends

nauwi-oshkinae it is short of being full

n'nauwitoowauh I don't quite hear him

naung; naungi *light; not heavy*

naungun it is light

naungishkauh the canoe is light to paddle

w'naung-oonae he/she carries a light burden

naussau; nauzh; neess; neessau; nissi • *below; down below; lower down; at the foot; at the bottom; put down; dismantle; raze; break down; wreck* • *to come; pat down; caress (see also* nanauzh*—downward)*

w'naunauzhauni-quaewaun he/she brushes someone else's hair down

neesau-aki downhill
nauhaung-aubeeginun iwih suppaub lower the rope
w'naunauzhidjeenaun he/she caresses him/her

naussau; nissowau; nissowi; nissowo *in between; pointed*

naussau-ogaun a teepee
nisso-wayee in between
Nisso-idjiwunaung Walpole Island Ontario (*lit.* either three channels, or between channels)

naussaub *same; similar; alike; identical; exact; repeat; mirror; spitting image; agreeing; corresponding; matching; synonymous*

naussaub the same; like
w'naussaub-aendum he/she thinks as I do
w'naussaub-inaugoziwuk they look alike
naussaub-issae it is coincidental

nawae • *cheek; please; placate; appease; mollify; pacify; alleviate* • *related; cousin; kin*

nawaendaugun; nawaemaugun a cousin; a relative
w'gee mino-nawae-aun he/she pleased him/her
oshki-nawae a youth, a young man (poss. from *nawae-cheek*—new cheek)
matchi-nawaewin to offend; to slight

nawautin *calm; placid; still; cease; rest*

nawautin it is calm (usually said of a lake)
w'nawautauh-geezhigut a day of rest
w'nawautauh he/she takes a rest, recess

nawud; nawudi *seize; snatch; catch; clasp; grab; clutch; grasp; grip; lay hold of; snag*

ahow! nawudin! okay! grab him/her!
w'gee nawudimaun he/she grabbed him/her in his/her mouth as a dog would bite suddenly

nawug; nawugi *incline; bend; hang; bow head to one side; hunch*

w'nawugi-quaenih he/she bends his/her head to one side
nawugitaun bend down
w'nawug-ossae he/she walks hunched over
nawug-bikwunaewiss a hunchback

neb; nebae; nebau; neebau • *to sleep; slumber; repose; flake out; nap* • *at, during the night, sleep*

w'nebau-yauwae he/she yawns
nebaugun/nebaegun a bed
w'gee awoh nebauh he/she went to sleep
nebaugun-eegin bedding, sheets
neebau-tibik at night

nebunae *to one side*

nebunae-ayauh it is one-sided
nebunae-anik one hand
nebae-eehn to one side

neebau; nibo *dead; without feeling; insensitive; insensate; numb; deadened; without life; gone; left; passed away; breathed his last; departed; gone to his reward; deceased; lifeless*

w'nibo-winaezih he/she is numb
w'nibo-kaudae he/she has a numb leg
w'neebaubiwuk they hold a wake
neebau-tibik in the dead of night
w'niboo d'aewizih he/she is lonesome

neebidae *in a row; a column; file; one after another; in a line; single file*

w'neebidae-gaubowiwuk they are standing in a row, in line
Anishinaubaek neebidae-ossaewuk Indians walk in a single file
w'neebidae-ishinook they are set in a row

neebunuh; neebinuh *much; a great deal; lots; quantity*

kitchi neebunuh a great deal
neebunuh igoh as much as is possible
neebin summer; a time of plenty

neegaun *in front; front; ahead; foremost; fore; anterior; forefront*

Neegaun-geezhig a man's name; Leading Day or First Day
w'neegaunee he/she leads, is at the forefront
neeyau-ogaunizit the leader

w'neegaun-puto he/she leads the pack of runners

neegooshk; neegooshki *to rip; tear; tatter*

w'gee neegooshkaun w'd'auziyaun he/she wore out his/her loincloth
neegooshkaumigud it is torn to shreds

nee-in; nee-ina *similarity; likeness; resemblance; correlation; congruity; parallel; analogous*

w'nee-inoowaun he/she resembles him/her
w'nee-inaudiziwuk they seem alike
w'nee-initoowaun he/she sounds like him/her

neem; neemi • *dance; act out; celebrate a victory; ritualize some event; condition; a petition* • *to insult by gesture*

w'gee neemisskaungiwaun iniw quaewun he/she made vile gestures at that woman
neemishkugun a headdress worn in ritual and during festivals
neemiwin a dance
neemidiwin a dance
w'kitchi-neemiwuk they are dancing up a storm

neemae; neemau *to deliver; haul; transport; convey*

w'neemaekoonigun a wheelbarrow
neemae-daubaun a litter; a travois
neemae-inautik a carrying pole, stick

neesk; neeskau; neeski; nisk; niski • *untidy; disheveled; disorderly; unkempt; disarranged; tousled; uncombed; mussed; rumpled; messy; slovenly* • *encumber; impede; hamper; hinder; retard; cumber; cramp; constrain; bridle; trammel* • *stretch out; stretch; extend*

neeskaudut the weather is unsettled
animoosh w'neeskaubidaenih the dog bares his/her teeth
niskitchigun ruffled lace
w'neesk-eengawaenih he/she grimaces
niski-meenaes-kaudae it is embroidered with beads

neew; neewi; neewau *fade; subside; ebb; wane; dim; waste away; abate; get less; diminish; decline; taper off; shrink*

neew-aundae it fades
nee-waupitae the smoke wanes
neewi-ipeeyauh the water ebbs
neewau-oon the swelling shrinks
neewau-auhnzhae waussikonaendjigun the lamp's light is growing dim
n'gee kitchi-nau-neewunoowauh ginaebigoosh I bludgeoned the snake repeatedly until it shrunk in size

neezaun; neezauni *dangerous; risky; hazardous; perilous; chancy; unsafe; unsound; vulnerable; defenseless; precarious; threatening; dire; menacing; ominous (poss. related to* nishiwae*—to kill and* nissaun*—to kill)*

neezaunut it is dangerous
w'neezaun-itchigae he/she is reckless
w'neezaun-aupinae he/she has a contagious disease
w'neezaun-initaugozih he/she sounds threatening

neezh *two; twice; double; a pair*

neezhing twice
neezho-waewaun two pair
neezh-itunnuh twenty
neezho-waun testicles; balls; a pair
neezhing medaussowauk two thousand

nenau; nenauwi *divide; cut; split in half; distribute; give out; apportion (from* nauwi*—in the middle)*

w'nenauwinaun he/she divides it
nenauwitaugaewin division; distribution
w'nenauwiti-gindaussoh he/she does division

nenawaud; nenawautch *useless; good for nothing*

w'nenawaudizih he/she is good for nothing
w'nenawautchitoon zkooni-auh he/she wastes money

netau • *habitually; all the time; accustomed; usual; wonted; regular; routine; every day*

PREFIXES

• *skillfully; artistic; well; fine; excellent; first-rate; talented; gifted; expert; adept; proficient; adroit; deft; dexterous*

w'netau-geewi-ossae he/she is a skilled hunter

w'netau-waudjimoh he/she is a gifted storyteller

w'netau-weessinih he/she is habitually eating

owih quae w'netau-atoon that lady is proficient at it

---

netoo; netook *simple; unadorned; plain; informal; casual; ordinary; modest; basic*

w'netook-aubae he/she roasts, broils without seasonings

w'netook-imundjigae he/she eats without condiments

w'netook-ozhae he/she goes without body ornaments

---

nik; nikau; niki • *all; entire; total; whole; complete; in terms of immersion; submersion; engulfment* • *disappearance* • *vanish*

w'nikau-aubindumae he/she loses consciousness

w'gee nikae-wae he/she vanished

niki-ipeewoh a thick fog; he/she disappears in the fog

niki-ipeewun flood

---

nimbunae; nimundjee *left; left side; one side*

nimbunae-eeng to one side

nimbunae-anik one arm

---

niminau *to set out; go out; drift out; commence; start; begin; a journey by water (from* nauwitch; nawautch—*far out in the lake)*

niminauwaetchigun a dock or a wharf

n'minauwaenaun n'cheemaun I launch my canoe

w'niminauwaeshkauh he/she drifts out

---

nindo • *to seek to; attempt; endeavor; try; essay; strive; undertake; aspire; study; venture; search; look for; quest; hunt; trail; track; follow; probe; check out; investigate; inquire* • *explore*

nindo-maukumaesheehn a monkey (*lit.* looks for lice)

w'nindo-ishae he/she listens

nindo-kikaendjigaen! try to find out!

w'gee nindomaun he/she summons him/her

---

ning; ningau; ningo; ningot *bury; inter; cover over; vanish; disappear; fade; melt away; oblivion; out of sight; dissolve; thaw; unfreeze; shrink; pass; waste away; evaporate; dilute; once; one time*

weebah wee ningizoh goon the snow will melt soon

n'ningo-akeewuk they are having a funeral

ningooshkaumigut it vanishes

ningot-aemiquan one spoonful

ningot-oshkin one bagful

ningoting; aubiding once

---

ningau; ningauss; ningaussi • *brake; slow down; decelerate; retard; delay; detain; check speed; reduce speed or motion* • *to catch wind as in a sail; a wind break*

n'ningau-inaubauwae I'm held up by the rain

ningaussimoowin a sail

w'ningau-keegae he/she puts on or applies the brake(s)

ningaussae it is mired

---

ningawau *a snare; a hoop; to disappear*

ningawaugun a snare, rainbow

w'ningawaugae he/she sets snares, or snares something

waub-oozoohn w'gee ningawauzoh the rabbit was snared

---

ningodji *somewhere; someplace; anywhere*

w'ningodji-puwae he/she runs away somewhere

ningodji-igoh-nauh somewhere unknown

ningodjih w'pizoh he/she flies somewhere

---

ningu; ningud; ningut *accustomed to; familiar with; used to; acquainted with; ingrained; routine*

ningud-iziwin familiarity

w'ningud-aendjigae he/she is familiar or acquainted with

w'ningud-aenimaun iniw he/she is used to him/her/them

---

nipau; nipaud; nipaudji *immodest; indecent; shameless; improper; lewd; indelicate; coarse; gross; obscene; lusty; wanton*

w'nipaud-ubih he/she sits immodestly
nipaudiziwin gluttony
w'nipaudji-ayauh he/she is indelicate
w'nipaud-ingwaum he/she sleeps in an obscene way

---

nipee; nipeesh; nipi; nipih *water; drinking water; wet; moist*

nipi-eewishkauh the grass is wet
w'nipi-ozidae his/her feet are wet
nip-eewun it is damp/wet
nipeesh water
nipih drinking water
nipigon along the water
aupita-ipee half filled with water
Abitibi the name of a lake in northern Ontario

---

nishi; nishinaud • *corrupt; disorganized; confused; disorderly; grotesque; waste; wasteful; fumbling; every which way* • *base; venal; immoral; unscrupulous; depraved; sinful; lewd; dissolute; perverted; profligate; prostitute; taint* • *squander; fritter away; dissipate; reckless* • *sad; forlorn; distressing; despondent*

w'nishi-inaudjizih he/she is corrupt, dissolute
w'nishinaud-aunikidoon he/she speaks in a disorganized manner
w'nishinautchi-atoon zhooniauh he/she squanders money
w'nishinau-d'aupikinigae he/she fumbles things

---

nishi; nissau; nitau • *wet; soaked; saturated; drench; sopping; steeped; soused; water-logged* • *to drown* • *to kill—murder; homicide; die (see also* neezaun*—dangerous)*

w'nissau-bauwae he/she drowns; he/she gets drenched
w'nissaun he/she kills him/her
w'nitaugae he/she kills (an animal)
w'gee nissaun mukwoon he/she kills a bear
w'dauh nishiwae igoh he/she would commit murder

---

nishk; nishki *anger; rancour; ire; wrath; passion; rage; fury; indignation; umbrage; bitterness; resentment; displeasure; annoyance; provoke; arouse; stir up; embitter*

w'nishk-audiziwuk they are angry
w'nishk-audjeengawaenih he/she has an angry countenance
w'nishkau'd'aendumook they are resentful

---

nissau; nissauk • *to open; open; unbolt; unlatch; spring; jimmy; tap; broach; break into* • *sober; temperate; abstinent; self-control; severe; serious; solemn; sedate; staid; dignified; composed; calm; level-headed; tranquil; equanimous*

nissaukinun! open it!
w'nissaudizih he/she is sober
nissautaenigun a trigger

---

nissi; nisso *three; tri-; tremble; triple; trio*

nisso-geezhigut on the third day
nissing three times
w'nissiwuk there are three; they are three

---

nissitau; nissotot; nissitoto; nissisto • *to make two ideas; facts; statements one; to understand; one mind; comprehend; coincide; recognize; discern* • *exactly; right; precisely*

k'nissitotum nah? do you understand?
nissitoto-waendaugoot it is understandable
w'nissito-waubumaun he/she recognizes him

---

nitam *first; leading; in front; the first*

w'nitam-gaubowih he/she stands first
w'nitam-ossae he/she walks first
nitam-inigum the first born
nitam-ozhaun the first born

---

nood; noodj; noodji *habituate; beleaguer; harry; hector; hound; besiege; linger; loiter*

abi-anoodjeehn a baby
w'anoodjeekae he/she habituates one place
w'anoodji-aun zheesheebun he/she is after ducks

PREFIXES

w'anoodi-quaewae to look for girls/women

noodjim *to cure; restore to health; remedy; make well; whole; healthy; treat; correct*

noodjimoo-gummig a hospital
w'gee noodjimoh he/she recovered
noodjimoowaewin healing/treatment

noog; noogi *come to a stop; to brake; retard; check speed or motion*

w'gee noogishkauh he/she stopped
w'noogi-putoowuk they cease running
noogi-waepishkigun a brake
nau-noogi-ishkauhnse a hummingbird

nook; nooki *soft; tender; silken; light; easy; lambent; butter-like; gentle; warm; tepid; benign; mild*

nooki-auh it is soft, tender
w'nookizih he/she is mild
w'nooki-odae-ae he/she is softhearted
nookizun iwih weeyauss! cook the meat tender!

noom; noomi *to rub; rub down; massage with oil; apply; anoint*

noominigun ointment; grease

noon; nooni; noonimau *rounded; oval; circular; elliptical; ovoid*

w'noonimau-sudae he/she has a pot belly
noonim-aubikut cold rolled steel
noonimaug-issuk round log

noond; noondae; noondaess *too soon; inopportune; incomplete; stopped; premature; unfinished; short; deficient; too early; advanced; anticipatory; ill-timed; untimely; unreasonable; imperfect; undeveloped; unprepared*

w'noondaessae he/she is in want of something
w'noondae-ishin he/she is short of attaining his/her goal
noondae'b'anikaewin premature birth
n'noondae-ishkawauh I do not reach him/her on time
w'noondae-datchiwuk there are too few, not enough

noozh; noozhi *strain; filter; screen; sieve*

w'noozh-iko-ipeeginigae he/she strains, filters
noozh-iko-ipeeginigun a filter

nubawae; nubug *to fold; pleat; flat; deflate*

k'dauh nubwaeginaun nah igoh nebaugun-eegin? would you fold the sheet?
w'nubwaegishin he/she lies flat
nubug-aupikauh it is composed of flat rocks
w'nubugi-idjaunae he/she is flat nosed

O

odae *heart*

odae-meen a strawberry
n'd'odaem my family—the heart of my being, or where my heart belongs; my clan; my clan symbol
ningo-d'odaewiziwin a single family; the distended family
odaenuh a town
odaenauh a nation

odauss; odaussi *come and go; ebb and flow; back and forth*

odaussigummigut nipih the tide ebbs
odaussi-beessauh the rain comes and goes

odji *head first; upside down*

w'odjid-akeessae he/she falls headlong
odjidumoo a squirrel
w'odjidau-akeessae he/she falls headlong
w'odjid-eengawaessae he/she falls on his/her face

ogimau • *count; to number; enumerate* • *lead; chief; forefront; principal; leader; foremost; captain (a derivative of* agindaussowin*—count)*

ogimau-akindaudiwin government
ogimau-quae a female chief
ogimau-binaesih the foremost bird

oji; ojib; odji; odjib *shrink; shrivel; draw back; constrict; cringe; wince; flinch; contract; curl up; pucker; purse; wrinkle; dry up; reduce;*

abridge; abbreviate; crease; rumple; falter; hesitate; speech impediment

ojib-gawaudae it is sewn with ruffles
ojib-waukidae it is shriveled up by the fire
ojib-waubauwae it is shrunk by water
w'ojib-anikae his/her arm is shriveled

onae; onau *smoked; made hard; packed; crusty; firm*

onaezigun a dried piece of meat/fish
onaebunut; onau the snow is hard (crusty)
onae-goonugauh the snow is hard (crusty)

onau; ondau *stir; mingle; scramble; commingle; whip; churn; agitate*

w'ondau-augummigae he/she stirs up the water
ondau-gummissae the water stirs, boils up spontaneously
onau-igun a blender
ondau-igun a stirrer

onaub; onaubi; onaush; onaushi *flat; level; plane; even; smooth; unbroken*

onaushkiwaeyaumigut it is even
onaubikaumigut the rock or something is even, smooth
onaubunut it is level, unbroken

onaud; onauk; onauki *press; knead; flatten; level*

w'onaudinaun oombigjeezigunun he/she kneads the dough
w'onaudimutoon meekun he/she grades/levels the highway
onaukummikauh the ground is flat/level
onaukummikautchigun a grader

onaun; onauni *joyful*

w'onaunig-waendum he/she is joyful
w'onaunig-atoonauwaun they make it a joyful occasion
onaunig-waendumoowin joy, happiness

ond; ondj; ondji; ohnz *because; because of; the reason; reason for; purpose; justification; cause; origin; occasion; source; why; rationale; explanation; basis; grounds*

ahneen gauh awo-abi-ohnz-ikauyin? for what purpose did you come?
aundi abi-ondji-bauyin (ondjee-yin)? where are you from?
w'gee ondu-goodjin he/she fell down
w'ond-inigae he/she gets his/her supplies from a particular source
w'ondizih he/she has a source; he/she yearns for
ondubaun a source of drinking water; a well

ondauss; ondaussi *here; in this place; come here; on this side*

ondaushitah on this side
ondauss come here
ondaushimae on the nearer side
ondaussi-oonug on this side of the boat

ondum; ondumi; nindum *busy; occupied; preoccupied; engaged; intent; distract; divert; digress; put out; burden; at work; on duty; engrossed; industrious; diligent; studious; persevering, etc.*

w'ondum-ozhae she is burdened with children
w'ondum-izih (ondum-izih) he/she is busy
ondumiziwin preoccupation

oomb; oombi *upward; up; uplift; rise; raise; aloft; alight; ascend; soar higher; elevation; heave; lift; hoist; draw up; boost; upthrust; upheave; heighten*

w'oombuzhee-koowaun he/she pesters him/her
oombaubee-ishkoodjigun a pulley
w'oombishkauh he/she rises upward
w'oombeegizih he/she is loud/noisy
oombaukinae the flames flare up (poss. origin of *pukinae*—grasshopper)

onishishi *good; excellent; beautiful; of merit; quality; moral; noble; satisfactory; sound; superior; proper; fitting; meet; upstanding; commendable; praiseworthy; creditable*

onishishin it is good
Onishishi-naubae; Anishinaubae The Good Being; The Being that Means Well
w'onishishih he/she is handsome/beautiful

PREFIXES

onushk; onushki • *to load; to fill up* • *to bother; pester; harry; hector; distract; annoy*

w'onushkinutoon baushkizigun he/she loads the gun
w'onushkawaeyaun w'okomissun he/she distracts his/her grandmother
w'onushka-awaewizih he/she is distracted

oshkau *green; raw; uncooked; new; untried (see also* oshki—*new)*

oshk-autik green wood
oshki-weeyauss raw meat, new meat
oshki-noodae it is half cooked
oshkatayaub untreated webbing, cord

oshki *new; novel; young; youthful; fresh; just made; modern; vernal; budding; fledgling; immature; natal; starting; beginning*

oshki-neegish a youth
oshki-nawae a young man
oshki-bug a new leaf
oshki-igin new growth
oshki-neegi-quae a young woman

ottauwuhnshk *a kind of a reed that grows in a river and in lakes used in the making of mats and door flaps*

Ottauwau an Ottawa Indian
ottauwuhnshk a river or water reed

ozau; ozauwau(zau)(sauwau) *gold; yellow; brown; butter; primrose; saffron; daffodil; topaz; buff; flaxen; blond; sandy; straw; bay; chestnut; roan; rust; chocolate; puce; mahogany; auburn; brunette; fawn beige; tan; copper*

ozauw-aundae it is yellow colored
ozau-amik brown beaver
ozauwau-bugonee yellow flower
ozau-beekoom a brass man of the mountain, a yellow streak of lightning
ozau-indib a blonde

ozaum; zaum *too much; extreme; excessive; extravagant; beyond all bounds; over the limit; super-abundant; overfull; superfluous*

ozaum-eeniwuk they are (too) many
w'ozaum-itchigae he/she is extravagant
w'ozaum-ingawaum he/she overslept
w'ozaum-odoon he/she talks too much

ozhae *of the body; corporal; corporeal*

n'd'ozhaeg-imaugooss I smell of sweat
pekaun w'inauss-ozhaewuk they are of a different pigment
w'gazeepeeg-ozhaewoh he/she takes a bath
gin-ozhae-maeg pike, the long body
n'weed'ozhaun my kin, of the same stock, issue

P

pagid; pagidi • *let go; set free; liberate; loose; acquit; dismiss; fired; discharge; let out; unbridle; unyoke; unchain; unshackle; extricate* • *accuse; throw (at); impute; insinuate; charge*

pagidinigaewin a funeral
w'pagidinigae he/she lets it go
w'pagidau-beeginigae he/she releases the line
pagidinishin! let me go; release me!
pagid-issae it lets loose suddenly
w'pagid-atoon throw it
w'pagid-audjimoh he/she releases a report

paguk; paugauk; pauguk *thin; lean; spare; skinny; scrawny; slender; slim; gaunt; twig; lank; fleshless; scraggy; emaciated; plain; clear*

pauguk the flying skeleton
w'paugaukidozoh he/she is emaciated

pagwish; pagwishi *to gain; profit; win*

w'pagwishitoon he/she profits
pagwishitoowin profit
pagwishitoo-waendaugoot it seems profitable

papuss; papussee; papussi; puss; pussi; pussee *blink; clap; wink; flutter; flicker; slap; strike together; applause*

w'gee puss-eengawaewaun he/she slapped him/her in the face
anungook pussi-kaukinaessaewuk the stars are twinkling
w'pussi-inindjeewidiziwuk they clap their hands

patchish; patchishk; patchishki • *cut; notch; whittle; carve to a point* • *to sting; prick (poss. from* piduk; poodjaub—*to stick)*

amooyun w'gee patchishkaukoon he/she was stung by bees
patchishkigud it is pointed
patchishkiwinae tibik-geezis the moon is crescented

pauss; paussau; paussaugi *open; unclenched*

w'paussaug-inindjeeshin he/she has his/her hands open
paussau-beekauh a pass or a gap in the rock
w'pauss-igugae he/she splits wood

pawau; pawauwi; bawau; bawauwi *to conjure; dream up; dream; call; summon; invoke; enchant; awaken; rouse; invite; welcome*

w'pauwae he/she rouses another from sleep
w'pawaudjigae he/she dreams; invites and welcomes spirits into his/her presence (poss. in the World of Dream)
pawaugun a pipe that is said to conjure up spirits from the Wold of Dream and to bring peace of mind and heart
w'pawauwaudjigae conjuring a manitou in the Shake the Earth Ritual
pawauwauh another expression for the Shake the Earth Ritual

pawaushaugid; pingawaushaugid *naked; bare; nude; unclothed*

ae-pawaushaugididjig the naked ones
w'pawaushaugidih he/she is naked
w'pawaushauk-anikae his/her arm is bare

peend; peendi; peendj; peendji; peenissi *inside; in; interior; inner; indoors; in the house; intestinally*

peendig inside
peendaugun a pocket
peendae it is in a bag
w'peendaukawae he/she takes snuff
peendoonug in the boat

pekae *a different direction; aside; to one side; take another route; separate; different directions; diverge(nt); branch off; part; split; divorce; tack; yaw; bear off; switch; shunt; deviate; digress; stray*

pekae-ummoh the road branches off
w'pekae-idiwuk they separate
pekae-kunnuh to one side of the road
w'gee pekae-winaun he/she took him/her to one side
pekae-tigiwaeyauh the river divides into two branches

pekaun *different; unlike; dissimilar; another; other; disparate; contrary; diverse; distinct; otherwise*

w'pekaunizih he/she is a different one
pekaunut it is a different one
w'pekaun-geezhiwae he/she speaks in a different tone

pidik *rumbling; roll; peal; resound; sound; echo*

w'pidik-oshae he/she perceives a rumbling sound
pidik-waukoonae fire crackles
pidik-waewae it makes a rumbling sound

pidug; pidugi • *cover; shawl; blanket; protect; shield; shelter; conceal; hide; mantle; canopy; layer; overlay* • *defend; guard; keep safe; tend; care for as birds care for their young*

w'pidug-ishkum the hen is laying/hatching
pidug-inugun a cover
pidug-inugaudae it is covered
pidug-waeyaun a blanket

piduk; piduki *to stick; pierce; puncture; sting; spear; stab; prick; lance; spike; impale*

piduki-idjeegun a fork
aumooyun w'gee pidukookoon he/she was stung by bees
pidukibitchigun a grappling hook
w'pidukitchin he/she is impaled, caught
pidukidae it sticks out of the ground (as a plant)
piduk-abiniwaewoon a roach (an ornament)

pigik; pigiki; pigiw; pigiwi *of pitch; gum; resin; bitumen; tar; gummy*

pigiw pitch

PREFIXES

pigiw-waussiwaugun a torch

pik; pika; piki; pikiwae; puk; puka; puki; pukiwae *break off; sunder; snap; cleaver; disjoint; pound; strike; hit; smite; slap; cuff; buffet; punch; knock; box; belt; sock; beat; batter; jolt; jar*

gee pikishkauh it (a rope) broke
w'gee pikibitoon he/she broke it off (tears it)
dah pikissae it will break
w'wee pikitaewaun he/she is going to strike him/her
pikitaegun a hammer, mallet
piki-waezhigun a bread
Pukawiss second son of Ae-pungishimook and Winonah, disowned by his father for not living up to parents' expectations, hence the name

piko; pikowau • *a bump; clump; a rise; elevation; swelling; pointed; lump; contusion; protuberance; node; bulge; over; go over; over the top (crest, crown); surmount; climb over* • *a ball; a fist* • *to enter; fall into or jump into water*

piko-idjeessin it protrudes
pikowauk-inindj a fist
pikowaukoot a ball
w'gee piko'd'aundawae he/she climbed over the top
w'piko-jaunae his/her nose sticks out like a lump
w'piko-pee-putoh he/she runs into water

pimae *aside; to one side; beside the road*

pimae to one side
w'pimae-ishin he/she lies to one side

pishi • *impure; dirty; erotic; carnal; wanton; debauched; obscene; sensuous; lust; lecherous; sexual; corrupt; unchaste; prodigal* • *slip; lose grip; handle; hold* • *to like; respect; fond*

w'pishig-awaudizih he/she is debauched
w'gee pishi-ganamaukoowee he/she lost his hold
w'pishig-aenimaun he/she is fond of him/her

pishi; pishib; pishibau; kishi; kishib; kishibau *in circles; spinning; twirling; cyclonic*

pishibaubeewoon the snow blows in circles
pishibaubee-aunimut a cyclone; a whirlwind
pishibaubeegun a top
w'pishibaubee-aushih he/she flies in circles

pishk; pishko *(related to* **pushkwo***)* • *to take fur or pelt off; to skin; to flay* • *to gash; tear; lacerate; bruise with a shot; nick; nip; scrape; scratch; chip; score*

pishko-waegin a pelt
w'gee pishko-noowaun he/she just nicked the animal with a shot

pishuh *whip; punish; penalize; lash; switch; birch; scourge; flog; strap; flail; belt; thrash; trim; castigate; correct; discipline; chastise*

w'pishuh-ozhaegauzoowuk they are punished
pishu-ozhae-goonaub a whip, a narrow thong
w'gee pishuh-ozhaegauzoh he/she was whipped/punished

piss; pissau *to lengthen; stretch; to increase (poss. from* beessau*—small)*

w'pissau-beeginaun he/she stretches it
w'pissau-igonaun he/she uses it wisely

pissi; pissih • *frivolous; unthinking; trivial; trifling; niggling; unimportant; insignificant; shallow; inane; vacuous* • *to strike, hit, collide, crash into, bump, jolt someone or something unintentionally* • *bind; wind around*

w'piss-inaudizih he/she is frivolous/thoughtless
w'pissi-taugozih owih minissinoh that warrior utters insulting words
w'gee pissi-koowaun he/she collided with him/her
pissi-quaendibae-oon a head-band

pissikau; pissikaub; pissiki; pissau; pissaub *return; come back; go back; revert; recede; retreat; recur; rebound; send back; bend;*

flex; fold; turn about; double back; fold back; pleat; plait; crease; pucker

pissikaubee-koomaun jackknife
w'pissikaubee-putoh he/she ran back
pissiki-ataenikaudae it is folded
w'pissiki-anik-aeshin he/she folds his/her arms
pissabaugut it is springy, resilient

pissikauk; pissikauki • *enkindle; burst into flame; tinder; kindling; set aflame; ignite; torch; apply a match to* • *flicker; twinkle; sparkle; glitter; glisten; shimmer*

pissikauk-inaendjigun kindling
anungook pissikau-auhnzhaessaewuk the stars twinkle
pissika-naetoon light it
pissikanae it is aflame

pitauk; pitauki *collide; smash; crash; run into; bump; bang*

w'pitauk-ishkoodaudiwuk they collide
w'gee pitauk-indibaeshin he/she bumped his/her head on some object

pitch; pitchi; piti • *accidentally; unintentional; unplanned; unwitting; unpremeditated; unexpected; chance; unthinking; random; stray; inadvertent* • *impatient; anxious; irritable; short; rude; snappish; waspish*

aki-waehnzee w'pitchi-nawaezhih the old man was made very short tempered by something
w'gee pitchi-anoowaun zheesheebun he/she accidentally shot the duck(s)
w'gee pitchi-doonaessae mindimooyaehn the old woman inadvertently disclosed the news
n'gee pitu-indaun assineehnse I accidentally bit on a stone
pitukinaundjigaewin to strike accidentally

pizung; pizungi *flutter open and shut (eyes); blink*

ininih w'pizungi-waubih the man flutters his eyes, or closes them
w'pizungi-waubissae he/she blinks

pug; pugi; pugid; pugidj; pugidji *accuse, throw at, to impute, insinuate, charge, allege, implicate, point to (poss. from* pagid*—accuse)*

w'gee abi-pugid-audjimoh he/she unfolded the story
ningodjih w'gee pugi-atoon he/she threw it somewhere
w'gee puginaun he/she overthrew him/her

pugwud; pugwudj; pugwudji; pugwoon; bugwud *ignorant; bare; stripped; infertile; unproductive; arid; poor; desolate; barbarous; primitive; coarse; vulgar; brutish; unlearned; raw; inexperienced*

pugwudji-ininih an ignorant man; backward
w'pugwoon-iwizih he/she is ignorant
w'pugwooniwitoon he/she makes it out of nothing (creates)

puk; pukoo *roof; cover; shelter; shield (poss. from* pukoo; piko*—a bump)*

pukwaun-audjeehn a bat
pukwaun a roof
pukoodjgun roofing

pukwae *smoke; fumes; smog; exhaust*

w'pukwae-inaezigae he/she makes fumes
pukwae-paegimih the liquid is smoky
pukwaenae-augimih the liquid is smoky

pung; pungee; pungi(bung)(bungee) (bungi) *little/small amount/portion; slight; puny; sparse; scant; meager; stinted; piddling; hardly any; jot; bit; dash; dab; crumb; drop; driplet; particle; touch*

pungeeshaehn a little
w'pungeeshaehn-wigiziwuk they are few
pungee aetah only a little
pung-igauh it is dripping
pungi-beessauh rain drops

pushko; pushkwau; pushkwo *bald; bare; barren; shriven; cut; smooth; shaven; shorn; stark; bleak; treeless; unsheltered*

w'pushkwauk-indibae he is bald
w'gee pushkoobinaun zheesheebun he/she plucked the duck
pushkwaukawauh the trees in a certain por-

tion of the forest are stripped of bark and leaves

pussu; pussaun; pussud; pissudi *trench; ditch; canal; valley; bottom; dale; dell; coulee; ravine; gully; defile; depression; hollow (see also* dupuss—*lower; below)*

pussaun-okaun a canal, trench, ditch
Pussudenauh a valley in Pasadena, California
pussu-kummikauh a ravine
pussaun-akae he/she makes a ditch

Q

quaequaek *back; back up; backtrack; retract; reverse; turn*

quaequaek-idjiwun reversing current

quae • *woman; female* • *hair*

quae-assimoosh a bitch, female dog
quae-waehn fish like a woman by torchlight
makatae-wauni-quae black-haired

S

sae; saen; saeni *outspread; spanning; stretched; extended; expand; open out; unfurl*

w'saening-gaweegunaetauh he/she (a bird) spreads its wings out
w'saen-waungae-aushih he/she (a bird) soars, wings outspread
saekawae-autik or **saekawae-bumauk** a tree with outspread branches

seem; seemi *under the weather; blah; indisposed; hung over; worn; enervated; unwell; wan; drawn*

w'seem-ayauh he/she is under the weather
w'seem-audizih he/she is sickly
w'seem-inaugozih he/she looks wan

sheeshoobi; shoosi *to paint*

w'shoossi-gugae he/she paints
shoossigun-aubo paint
shoossi-gugun a paintbrush
shoossi-gugae-ininih a painter

sheeyau *straight; true; direct; linear; lineal; dead on*

sheeyauk-ummoh the road is straight
w'sheeyau-kawae-igae he/she is on course, goes directly to his/her destination
sheeyauk-izih it is straight
sheeyauk-waubeegut the line is true

shish; shishoo; shishood; zhishoo; zhishood *next to; near; alongside; along the edge of; at the border; the rim*

w'zhishood-aukawauwae he/she walks along the edge of the forest
w'zhishood-gummee he/she walks along the shore of a lake
w'zhishood-ishkoowaun he/she leans against him/her

shooshawae; shoosh; zhaush; zhaushi *square*

shooshawaeyauh it is square
shooshawaeyau-beekitchigun a square
shooshawaetoon make it square
w'shooshi-gauboowih he/she is upright
shooshi-gauh the great blue heron

sidowae *ballast, weight, sandbag, stabilizer, filling, packing, balance, counterbalance*

sidowaeshkootchigun ballast
w'sidowaeshkootoon cheemaun ballast the boat
w'sidowaeshkootchigae he/she stabilizes the boat
sidowaendjigaewin prejudice, bias, discrimination, put down in one's esteem, mind

sikwau *spittle; snot; spit; mucous; phlegm*

w'sikwaudjigae he/she spits
sikwaudjigun spit, spittle

simee *exceedingly; very much; overmuch*

w'simeengawashih he/she is very sleepy

soossawae *scatter; broadcast; spray*

s'soossawae-waebinaunun meen-kaunaessun he/she scatters seed
soossawae-aubau-widjigun a water sprinkler
soossawae-meenuk choke cherries

soosi-igoobimeesh(maewish) a willow tree

spo; spoh *take something whole and entire into one's mouth; gulp; bolt; in one's mouth; immerse*

w'gee spo-inaendaun he/she took it whole and entire into his/her mouth

w'gee spo-goon-aessae he/she fell into the snow and was buried

sundi; sundji; suni *to bury and hide; a pit*

sundjigoon a pit

sunigoo a black squirrel (*lit.* the hoarder)

w'gee sundjigoowuk they are storing things away

supp *a net*

supp-kaesheehn a spider

suppee-kaeyaub twine for nets

suppeehnse a small net

T

tabin *shelter from a wind*

tabin-awauh it is sheltered from the wind

tabin-awauyauh it is capable of shelter

tae; taetae *to rock; sway in the waves as a boat*

taetaebi-goondae cheemaun the boat rocks gently in the swell

taetibi; titib; titibi *wheel; roll; revolve; rotate; somersault; gyrate; reel; wrap; enfold; encircle; wreathe*

w'titib-idjeeshin he/she rolls over

titibee-waeginun! wrap it up!

taetibi-issaehn a wheel

tako *step; pace*

w'tako-akee he/she steps

w'gee tako-kaudaun he/she stepped on it

tako-kaush owih manitoushi! step on the bug!

tangishk; tangishki daungi (taungi = *to touch) to kick; boot*

tangishkau-gaeshkih he/she likes to kick

tangishkun pikowaukoot! kick the ball!

w'gee tangishkaun he/she kicked it

tasso(dasso) *crush; weighted; trap; deadfall; mashed; press (down)*

tassoonaugun a trap

w'tassoozoh he/she is trapped

n'gee tassoo-inauk I trapped them

tatauga *lazy; indolent; idle; slothful; listless; shiftless; slack; lax; sluggish*

w'tataugadizih he/she is lazy

tataugadiziwin laziness

w'tatauga'd'aendaugozih he/she seems shiftless

taubishko; tibishko *like; similar; same; twin; corresponding; coinciding; alike; clone; analogous*

tibishko-issae it happens; it comes to pass, coincident

w'tibishkauh he/she has a birthday

w'tibishko-assitoon he/she fulfills it, makes it analogous

tauss; tausso *to set aside; store*

taussowin a cupboard, pantry, sideboard

taussowinning in the cupboard

taussowin-ikaudae autchiginugun the room has a cupboard

w'gee taussoh he/she stored it in a compartment

tautau; tautaug; tautaugi *stamp on; tramp on; bruise; crush; smash; squash; mash; pinch; grind; pound; stomp; flat; level*

w'tautaug-ozidae-ishkoozooh his/her feet are tramped upon

tautaugau-kummikauh the land is level

kitchi-tautaug-idugun a crusher; a pile driver

tautch; tautchi *to be lame on one side*

w'tautchi-gaudae owih mindemooyaehn that old woman is lame on one side

tautiwi *at intervals; from time to time*

tautiwi-beessauh it is raining at intervals

tautiwi-gopoh there are snow flurries

w'tautiwi-ipee he/she drinks at intervals

teem; teemau; teemi *deep; profound; abyss; far down; bottomless; deepest*

teemi-gummeeng; Timagami deep waters
teemi-tigawauyauh the river/channel is deep

tibik; tibikau *at; by; during the night; dark; unlit; lightless; dim; ill-lighted; nighttime; dusk*

tibikau-bimi-inaugoot it is dusk (twilight)
tibikut it is night
tibik-geezis the moon
tibikoong last night

tik; tikau; tiki *cold; chilled; cool; nippy; frigid; frosty; wintry; freezing; arctic; glacial; biting; sharp; crisp; numbing; refrigerated*

tikip a spring
tiki-ayauh it is cool
tik-aunimut the wind is biting
w'tik-aushih he/she is on holiday
w'tiki-wauk-ozidaewidjih he/she has cold feet

tik; tiko; tikoo • *short; not tall; not long; truncated; abridged; curtailed; contracted* • *take hold of (bite); hold; arrest; confine; imprison; seize; keep fast; hold in arms; impound; take into (and keep in) custody; lock up* • *cross; traverse; span; pass over; cut across; ford*

w'tikoo-izih he/she is short
tikoondjigun tongs, pincher
tikoowauh it is short
w'tikoowaun-iquae he/she has short hair
animoosh w'tikoongae the dog bites
w'tikum-ossae he/she takes a short cut; cut across

tipau; tipi • *through a hole; aperture* • *wet; soak; rinse through*

tipau-pitae the smoke goes right through or wafts through
w'tipau-bih he/she looks out of (through) an aperture
k'gah tipau-bauwidoon you will moisten it

tissau; tissi; titae • *to paint; color; tint; hue; tinge; shade; pigment; stain; dye* • *ripen, mature*

w'tissigae he/she paints, etc.
tissau-waesheehn cicada; the painter
titaemigut it is ripe
tissigun-aubo paint

titibau; taetibae *around; in a circle; revolution; gyration; spin; coil; vortex; whorl; rotate; revolve*

taetibissaehn a wheel
titibau-ibeeginigun a reel, bobbin
titibau-oodjigun a reel, spool, winch

took; tooki; tootook; taetae *to touch lightly; nibble; nudge; tap; joggle; pat; dab; rap*

w'tootook-gindjigae he/she nibbles food
w'took-inaun he/she taps someone to get that person's attention
w'took-waukawigae he/she raps lightly

toot; tootoo *tremble; shake; quake*

tootoogut the ground is trembling
tootoo-kummikauh the earth or the ground is quaking
tootoo-kummikissae it shakes
tootoo'k'waewae there is a rumbling sound

tutigau *a spine*

tutigaugi-meen thimble berry
tutigaugiwun the spine
tutigaugiwun-aeyaub spinal cord
tutigaugikun a disc

W

wae; waeb; waebi; waewae *throw away; cast aside; sweep away; abandon; divorce; leave; taken away; blown away; carried away; disperse; scatter; broadcast*

waebigun a broom
waebinigun a cast off; an abandoned child/woman
waeb-aussin it blows away
w'waebee he/she runs away; sneaks off
waewaeb-aussin it flutters in the wind

wae; waewae; wauwau *to wave; flutter*

wae-metik-ozhih a Frenchman; one who waves a stick (cross)

w'wauwau-tigoogae he/she waves
waewaeb-aussin it flutters in the wind
w'waewaeb-inaubee he/she is casting (angling)

---

waen; waewaen; waewaeni; weengae *carefully; skillfully; cautiously; artfully; well; completely; circumspect; wary; prudent; mindful; thoughtful; fine; nice; thorough; strict; guarded; watchful; precise; accurate; correct; fastidious; painstaking*

waeweengae carefully
waenipunut it is easy, cheap
w'weengaezih he/she is skillful, careful

---

waeweeb *quickly; fast; rapidly; haste; swift; at once; immediately*

w'waeweeb-itauh he/she hurries in his/her work
w'waeweeb-ishkauh he/she hurries in his/her mission
w'waeweeb-aendum he/she is anxious
waeweeb-inaushkowih! get him/her to hurry!

---

wanuk *top; crest; pinnacle; crown*

wanukizit metik the top of the tree
wanukoong at the top of the tree
wanuk-oonuk at the prow of the boat

---

wau; wauwi; wauweezh; wawau; weewi • *round; oval; circular; cycloid; disc; ring; hoop; cylindrical; sphere; globe; orb; bulb; balloon; curved; rounded; arched; vaulted* • *roundabout; amused; funny; comical; humorous; merry; mirthful; jocular; jovial; absurd; witty; silly; droll*

w'wauwi-inaezih he/she is at a loss as to what to do (in a quandary)
wawautum a whirlpool
w'gee weewiquaeginaun he/she wrapped it up
wauwiyae-beekitchigun a drawing compass
wauwun an egg
w'wauwi-inaendum he/she is amused

---

waub; waubi *to make white; to illuminate; to cast light upon; make clear; open to light; to open the eyes; dawn; to see; perceive; behold; discern; notice; observe; regard; hold in view; espy; make out; sight; survey; stare; gaze; watch; bear an eye on*

waub-oozoo a rabbit
k'waubundaun nah? do you see it?
waubunoong in the east
waubumoowin a mirror
waubun-anung morning star
waubugonae a white flower
waubizee a swan

---

waug; waugau; waukau; waushkau; waushki; wauwaug *curved; bent; crooked; arch; vault; bowed; cambered; hook; cheat; sly; tricky; guileful; false; crafty; cunning*

waugoosh a fox
waukau-igun a round lodge or wigwaum; a log house
washkaukoozih metik the tree is crooked
waugaukoot an axe
waugunogaun a dome shaped lodge
wauwaushkaesh a deer; curved antlers

---

wauk; waukae • *resolute; fortitude; long suffering; inured; harden; accustomed; used to; able to bear; tolerance; tenacity* • *to settle* • *clear; lucid; transparent; limpid; translucent* • *nearby; close; proximate; adjacent*

w'waukae-inaumozih he/she tolerates a great deal of smoke
waukae-geezhig a clear day
w'waukaug-imissitoon he/she lets the liquid settle
waukau-gummik near the house
waukau-gummeeng near the lake or clear lake

---

waun; wauni • *to befuddle someone; to bewilder; to fluster; confuse; muddle; confound; boggle; baffle; perplex; mystify; nonplus; puzzle; buffalo; stump; dumbfound; mix up; fool; trick; deceive; hoodwink; bluff; throw off track; mislead* • *dig; shovel; excavate; hollow out; scoop; gouge; basin; tunnel; burrow; channel; spade; hollow; concave (from* wini*—lose)*

w'gee waunimaun he/she bewildered him/her
w'gee waun-initoowaun he/she misunderstood him/her

PREFIXES

w'waun-inaendum quae the woman is perplexed
w'waunikae he/she digs
w'waunikaun a hole dug; a pit
waun-kummikauh the ground is depressed

waush; waushae *clear; lucid; transparent; luminous; limpid; translucent (poss. from* wauss*—shine)*

waushae-gummauh clear lake
waush-ipeeyauh the waters are lucid
Waussau-gummauh the shining waters; Georgian Bay (Lake)

waushk; waushkau *obstinate; obdurate; unbending; hard; stubborn; bull-headed*

w'waushkaudizih he/she is stubborn by nature
w'waushk-awaendaugozih he/she seems obdurate
w'waushki-waewidum he/she sounds obstinate

wauss; waussae; waussau; waussi; wautae; wauwautae *shine; bright; illuminate; reflect; brilliant; throw light on; light; radiate; beam; glow; shimmer; sparkle; glitter; gleam; glisten; shiny; glossy; lustrous; mirror; image*

waussi-bugauh the trees are beginning to bud
wautae-bugauh the leaves are growing yellow
wauwaussikonae a flower
wauwautaessih a firefly
waussikonaendjigun a lamp; a flashlight
waussaetchigun a window
waussikodjeegun polish
waussimoowin; wauwautae, wauwautum lightning

wauss; waussi; weess; weessi • *bitter; peppery; spicy; nippy; pungent; piquant; seasoned; biting; something that causes the mouth, the pores, the taste buds to open up* • *severe; exceeding; causing great suffering; agonizing; suffering; misery; excruciating; scathing; anguish; tormenting*

w'weessi-iginae he/she suffers excruciating pain
w'waussita-waendum he/she endures great sorrow
waussigung pepper
weessi-gauk black ash
weessiki-bugoohnse a small bitter leaf

waussuh *far; distant; a long way; away; off; remote; yonder; abroad; outlying*

waussu-waukowauh the forest is far; the forest is extensive
waussu-wud it is far
waussuwae-kummik to the end of the earth

wauweek *to mend; repair; fix; put together; pull; sew (from* week*—to pull; draw)*

w'wauweeki-gawaudjigae owih quae the woman is repairing clothing
w'wauweek-inaukummatoon he/she repairs the fence or the frame
wauweek-assutoon! jerk it!

wauweesh *for no reason, nothing; for nothing; without permission; frivolously; on whim*

w'wauweesh-kumaun he/she took his/her article without permission

wauzh; wauzhi *open water as on ice; a pond*

wauzhi-ipeeyauh a pond; water on ice
wauzhi-ipee-kummikauh the ground is soggy
wauzh-waukawauh an everglade, glade

weebawau *narrow; avenued; oblong; like a corridor; channelled; a pass*

weebawau-aukawauh there is a passage through the woods
weebawau-gummishkau Misqawo-gummauh the Red Sea parted
weebawau-bikauh there is a pass through the mountains
weebawauyauh it is corridored

weed; weedi; weedjee; weedji; weesso *with; accompany; go with; side by side; together; go along with; keep company; consort; help; assist; aid; give a hand; lend a hand*

n'weedji-aki-waehn my friend
w'weessookoowaun gimoodee-ininiwun

he/she aids and comforts and consorts with a thief

n'weedjee-waugun my spouse; my companion

w'gee weepaemaun he/she slept with him/her

k'gah weedoopumaumim we will eat with her/him/them

weessokoodaudiwin mutual help

---

weeg; weegi *tatters; beggared; torn; poor; pitiful; ragged*

---

weegussaehn a remnant

weeg-izih he/she is to be pitied

wee-augit it is a pity

weegwauss birch

---

week; weeki *to draw up (in); invite; pull; summon; attract; allure; lure; tempt; suck in; breathe in; inhale; ask; beckon; endeavor*

---

weekindiwin an invitation

w'gee weeki-widjiwinaun he/she invited him/her to go along

w'weekitchi-atoonauwauh they try it

w'weeki-goondjigae he/she sucks or draws it in

weekizigun dolls' eyes (a plant)

---

weekweeng *too hard; violently; uncontrollably*

---

n'weekweengi-odae-ae my heart beats fast

---

weemb; weembi *hollow; cave; empty; excavated; concave; indented; cavernous; hole; nook; niche; recess; cavity; depression*

---

weemb-aubikauh there are many rocky caves

weembinugizih metigoosh the tree is hollow

weembi-waewae it has a hollow sound

---

ween; weeni • *dirty; impure; unchaste; grubby; untidy; filthy; grimy; squalid; unclean; soiled; unwashed; foul; besmeared; polluted; sleazy; scruffy; slovenly; mess* • *obscene; immoral; smutty; off-color; salacious; raunchy; lewd; perverted; loose; wanton; carnal*

---

w'weenizih he/she is dirty

weenut it is unclean

w'weenaun-geengawae he/she has a grimy face

w'weenitchigae he/she makes a mess

---

weeng; weengi • *good; flavorful; tasty; delicious; delectable; palatable* • *fondness for; predilection; disposition; partial to; taste; fancy; sweet on; addicted to*

---

weeng-ipoogoot it has excellent taste; it is delicious

weengushk an aromatic grass; sweet grass

weengaugummih a delicious drink

w'weeng-meenae he/she is fond of berries, etc.

Weeng; Weengosh the sandman who lures people to sleep, dreamland

---

weequaeyauh-weequae *at the end of; the terminus; the end; the limit of; the boundary; so (as) far as it goes (extends)*

---

weequaedoong at the bay

weequaed a bay

weequae-yauh the terminus

weequaek-ummook at the end of the road

Weequaedamikoong; Wikwemikong Bay of Beavers

---

weessook; weessooki *abet and aid; encourage; prompt; urge; spur; goad; incite; instigate; provoke; animate; arouse; support; assist; advocate; approve; back; sanction; countenance; further; advance; sustain; succor (from* weedji—*with)*

---

w'weessookiwaun he/she provokes him/her

weessookidaudiwin a fraternity; a gang

w'weessookidaudiwuk they help or assist one another

---

weeyau *different; various; varied; varieties; kinds; species*

---

w'weeyaugawae-issitaugozih he/she utters many different notes, sounds; he/she warbles

w'weeyaugawaukozih metigoosh the old tree is warped, deformed in shape and growth

w'weeyaugaw-aendum he/she has all sorts of matters on her mind

dasso-weeyoowigiziwin a species

PREFIXES

weeyaushi; weeyaussi; weeyowi *flesh; meat; corpse; body; the remains*

weeyaushish a deer
w'weeyowih he/she has sexual intercourse; he/she fleshes
w'weewun his/her flesh; a derogatory term for a spouse

win; wini *lose; forget; overlook; slip from mind; unable to recall; miss; omit; neglect; misplace; mislay*

w'wini-issae he/she makes a mistake
w'wini-ishinook they are lost
w'wini-gaudoon he/she hid it so well that he/she cannot find it
w'win-aendum he/she forgets
n'gee win-eekae I forgot it; I left it behind

winushk; winushki *bother; disturb; distract; disrupt; divert; digress; draw away; sidetrack; avert; switch; change; annoy; harass; put out; unsettle (from* wini*—lose)*

w'winushki-waeyaun he/she disturbs him/her
w'winushki-waewaendum he/she has unsettling thoughts
w'winushki-itauh he/she is disruptive

wiyaezh; wiyaezhi *cheat; fool; beguile; trick; deceive; cozen; hoodwink; bluff; mislead; give a bum steer*

w'wiyaezhingae he/she cheats
wiyaezhingaewin cheating, bluff, deception
n'gee wiyaezhimauh I hoodwinked him

wizhee; wizhi *make ready; prepare; prime; groom; arrange; take steps; set*

w'wizhee-itauh he/she is ready
w'wizhigae he/she builds a house
w'wizhi-atoon he/she makes it
wizhigin it is formed; a fetus

wizhi; wizhig; wizhigi *to make; manufacture; construct; make a house; a building; to build; set up; fabricate; form; fashion*

w'wizhigae he/she manufactures
wizhigun a skull
wizhigae-ininih; wizhigaewiss a carpenter
w'gee wizhi-atoonauwauh they made it

wizhush; wizhushki *mud; muck; sludge; mire; ooze; silt; bog (poss. from* wizhush + aki*—earth; land; soil)*

wizhush-aki mud
wizhushk muskrat; a mud rat
w'wizhushkum he/she walks in mud
wizhushkawaedo mushroom

Z

zaeg; zaegi; zaess; zaessi • *fear; dread; scare; terror; apprehension; fright; horror; alarm; trepidation; dismay; misgiving; qualm; anxiety; timidity; forebode; cower; daunt; worry* • *ornament; embellish; beautify; enhance; adorn; showy; gaudy; decorate; frill; spangle; bauble; trinket; medals; brooches*

w'zaeg-aendum he/she has some misgivings
zaegaudi-kummik it is frightful, dreadful
zaegiziwin fear
w'zaegi-audjimoh he/she tells an alarming story
zaenbauhn a ribbon
zaessaegawaudjigun an embroidered article; embroidery
zaessaegawau-bidae-igwin a brooch

zaub; zaubau *strength; power; willingness; ready*

w'zaubi-izih he/she is willing/strong
kauween w'zaubi-izissee he/she is not willing
w'zaub-kunae he/she is strong-boned

zaug; zaugau; zaugi; zausaugau • *out; outlet; outside; external; out of doors; in the open; vent; opening; river mouth; exterior; outer; beyond the pale; left out; excluded* • *to love; to like; to cherish; to care for; fond; attract to; crush on; infatuate; romance; esteem; hold dear*

zaugeeng; saugeen at the outlet
Zaugeek Sauk
zaugidji-idjiwun it flows out
w'zaugeengawaenih he/she sticks his/her face out

w'zaugizih he/she is stingy
w'zaugi-aun he/she loves him/her
w'zaukum she urinates

---

zauss; zauski; zeen; zeend; zeenzi; zeen-zo • *squeeze; bind; press together; compact; tighten; contract; wring; extract juice from; dry out; press; wedge; put under one's arm; ram; force; bandage; compress* • *to fry*

w'zeenizikaun he/she can hardly fit the garment
w'zeeninikae he/she is milking
w'zauzeenikogipee he/she is soused, thoroughly drunk
zaussikookiwaun a frying pan
zeendaukishkoodjigun a wedge
zeendipizoon a corset

---

zaussau • *magic; sorcery; witchcraft; wizardry; necromancy; fortune telling; soothsaying; divining* • *to be blinded, dazzled*

zaussaugo'd'aendaugozih he/she looks (seems) like a person who practices sorcery
w'zaussau-geengawae he/she is dazzled
zaussaubindjigaewin sorcery

---

zeeg; zeegi; zeeseeg; zeeseegi • *pour; splash; spell; rain; overflow; brim over; slosh; slop* • *wrinkled*

zeeseegi-oobimeesh the willow
zeesseegi-beessauh a deluge
zeeginigae-gummik a tavern
zeegiwun spring

---

zeep; zeepi *river; stream; creek (from* nipi—*water)* • *squeak; grate; squeal; squawk; scrape; creak; screech*

zeepeengawiyh a tear
zeepi a river
zeepeehnse a creek
zeepi-waewaeshkauh it squeaks

---

zeew; zeewi; zheew; zheewi *sour; bitter; acid; tart; acerbic; vinegary; unpleasant; turned back; unsweet; caustic; pungent*

zeewun it is sour
zeewi-poogoot it tastes bitter
zeewitaugun salt
zeewaugi-midae a syrup

---

zeez; zeezi *sweet; sugar; honeyed; candied; nectar; saccharine; perfumed*

zeezi-baukoot sugar
zeezi-baukoot-aubo sap
aumoohn-zeezi-baukoot honey

---

zhae *backward; retreat; go back; to the rear; behind; withdraw; back away; step back; recoil; make off; decamp; take refuge*

zhaemook! zhaemook! go back! go back!
w'zhae-abwiyae he/she rows
w'zhae-issae he/she suffers a relapse
w'zhae-itauh he/she leans back
w'zhae-putoh he/she runs backward

---

zhaeg; zhaegwau; zhaugwau; zhaug; zhaugi • *not sharp; dull; unhoned; blunt* • *a span of some kind; a long, thin, narrow geographic feature; oblong; long; extended*

Zhaegwau-aumikoong the long point in Ashland, Wisconson
zhaegwau-mookoomaun the knife is dull
w'gee zhaegwau-assitoon he/she blunted it

---

zhaek; zhaeki; zhaeg; zhaegi; shaek; shaeki *base; bottom*

zhaek-adin at the bottom of a hill or mountain
zhaek-audjiwun at the bottom of a river, downstream
zhaek-aubikauk at the bottom, base of rocks

---

zhaesh; zhaeshi *smooth; slippery; slick (see also [poss. from]* zhoosh; zhooshi*)*

zhaesh-waubikauh the rocks are slippery
zhaeshi-weegut the fabric is smooth
zhaeshi-waukoot it is smooth along its entire length

---

zhaezhawishk *flexible; pliant; bendable; malleable; adjustable*

n'zhaezhawishkauh I am flexible (supple)
zhaezhawishk-aubikut the metal is malleable
w'zhaezhawishk-auwizih he/she is pliant
zhaezhawish-koonigut the length of the boat is bendable

PREFIXES

zhaub; zhaubo; zhazheeb; zhazheebi; zheeb; zheebi *through; to go or to see through; narrows; to pass through; strait or straits; channel; conduit; isthmus; passage; stretch out; extend; elongate; straight through; transparent; unblocked; slightly; lightly*

Zheebau-nauning Killarney, Ontario
zheebau-aubundjigun(un) telescope; binoculars
zhazheebi-tuwugae he/she is stubborn
w'zheeb-pungooshih he/she sleeps lightly
w'zhashaubo-waubeeginigae mindemooy-aehn the old woman spins
zhauboowaupikissing it is sticking through (a plant)
zhaezhauboowaukissing it is sticking through (a plant)

zhaug; zhazheeg; zheeg; zheego; zhiga; zhigo • *pruned; pared; waste; ruin; despoil; violate; ravage* • *disgusting; disgraceful; repelling; offended; turned off; displeased* • *to go through; drain; piss; dreg* • *salty; briny*

zheegau-quae a widow
zheegau-ikwauh a lightly timbered bush
zhee-goopoh the fall of wet snow
w'gee zhigad-aenimaun he/she tires or is displeased with him/her owing to familiarity
zheegaushkoo-beetae it is tepid
w'zheesheegih he pisses

zhaugoo; zhaugootch *to be overcome; to overcome; beat; vanquish; overwhelm; defeat; conquer; subdue; crush; overthrow; trim; trounce; thrash; whip; drub; master; overpower; control; dominate; bring down*

w'zhaugo-odae-ae he/she is cowardly
w'zhaug-eewee he/she is spent
w'zhaugo-d-aenimaun he/she is convinced that he/she can dominate him/her
w'gee zhaugoodinaun he/she overcame him/her

zhaukae *soft; powdery*

zhaukae-goonugauh the snow is soft
zhaukae-kummikauh the earth is soft
w'zhaukae'k'ozhae he/she has a pliant body

zhaushau; zhaushaugi; zhausheeng • *crush; step on; stamp on; squash; mash; press down; bruise; trample; stomp; crush underfoot* • *chew; masticate; jaw; chomp; mandicate; munch; grind; gnaw; ruminate* • *emaciated; gaunt; drawn; shrivelled; withered; scraggy; lanky; atrophied*

zhaushau-gawaushkigizih a kind of green frog
w'zhaushau-goondjigae he/she chews
w'zhaushau-wigizih he/she is emaciated
w'zhaushaukishkoozoh he/she is crushed
w'zhaushau-g-inindjeeshkoozoh his/her hand is crushed
zhaushau-g-idu-pineeg mashed potatoes

zhaushoo; zhaushoob; zhaushoobau; zhoob; zhoobau *bind; bent; droop; wave; bow; arched; stoop; nod; rock*

zhaushoobaukishkauh ininautik the maple bends
n'zhoobi-auh ogimauh I tempt to try to persuade the leader
w'zhauzhoob-auginaun metigwaub he/she bends the bow back and forth
zhaushoobauk-issae it wavers back and forth

zhauwun; zhauwushk *green; blue; indigo; purple; aquamarine; turquoise*

zhauwun-inungossae a bluebird
Zhauwuni-geezhig Blue Sky (a man's name)
zhauwun-inoodin the south wind
zhauwunoong to the south

zhawae *kind; generous; pity; compassion; altruistic; tenderness; lenience; mercy; gentleness; sympathy; consolation; concern; benignity; charity; benevolence; forgiving; considerate*

zhawaenimishin have pity on me
w'zhawaen'd'augozih he/she is/appears to be considerate or fortunate, favored, blessed
zhawaendaugoziwin mercy, good fortune, compassion
zhawaendaugoot it is blessed

zhawaeg; zhawaegi; zhawaeshk; dazhawae; dazhawaegi; dazhawau *flatten; iron or smooth out; level out*

zhawaeginun iwih waubooyaun spread the blanket out
w'd'zhawaebeekinaun he/she stretches it
w'zhawaeshkawae-igae; zhooshkawae-igae he/she irons or presses
zhawaeshkawae-igun an iron

zhawaug; zhawaugi *bend; crooked; drooped; warped (from* waug; waugi*—curved)*

zhawauginun iwih metigwaub! bend the bow!
w'zhawaugishkauh he/she or it is drooped
w'zhawaug-anikae he/she has a crooked arm
w'zhawaug-iboodoon he/she cuts or saws it at an angle

zheeb; zheebau; zheesheeb • *stretch; elongate; extend; draw out; lengthen; expand; distend* • *fortitude; endurance; long suffering; durable* • *to shrink; distend*

w'zheeb-aendum he/she is long suffering
zheesheeb a duck
w'zheebi-tuwugae stubborn
w'zheesheeb-anikaenih he/she stretches his arms
w'zheesheeb-issugizih he/she shrinks

zheeng; zheengi • *loose; relaxed; extended; slack; hanging; drooping; sagging; dangling; free; unconfined; free and easy; casual; loose as a goose; to level; flatten out* • *hate; dislike; abhor; loathe; abominate; despise; detest; odium; rancour; hostility; enmity; ill-will; revulsion; repugnance*

w'zheengaudae-inaun he/she spreads it
w'zheengaend-augozih he/she is hateful
w'zheesheeng-anikaessae he/she dangles his/her arms
zheengau-kummikauh the land is level

zheeshee; zheesheeg • *bald; naked; without hair; hairless; smooth* • *pass water, piss* • *rattle*

w'zheesheegau-indibae he/she is hairless
w'zheesheeg-anikae his/her arms are hairless
w'zheesheegi-odoonae he/she is without a moustache
w'zheesheegih he urinates
zheesheegiwun a rattle
zheesheegawae a rattlesnake
zheesheegawauning a place of rattlesnakes

zhigud; zhigudji *wearing; tired of; bored with; inured; impatient*

w'zhigudji-abeewoh he/she is weary of waiting
w'zhigud-aendjigae he/she had too much familiarity to want more
w'zhigud-aendaugoozih he/she is a bore, seems too wearisome

zhingish; zhingishi *recline; lie down; supine; lounge*

w'zhingishinook anauma-eeng they are lying underneath
w'zhingishin nebaugunning he/she is lying on the bed

zhiwa; zhiwau *dull; blunt; not sharp; pointless; edgeless*

zhiwau-bikut it is blunt
w'zhiwau-koohnzhae he/she is dull beaked
w'zhiwauk-inukizih the tree is not sharply crowned (does not come to a point)

zhoog; zhoogi *to bring to liquid state; to melt, smelt*

w'zhoogummizigae he/she boils
w'geezhoogummizaun he/she warmed up the liquid
zhoogummizikaun a smelter
zhooqummidae it melts

zhooniauh *silver; money; means of exchange; coins; paper money; dollars; worth; value*

zhooniauh money or silver; a shiny metal; sparkling, bright
w'zhooniaukae he/she makes money
zhooniauwun it is valuable
zhooniau-gummik a bank
zhooniau-gummauh Lake Simcoe

zhooshki; zhooshki; zhooshau • *smooth; slippery; slide; slick; sleek; glassy; skiddy; icy; waxed* • *skate; slide (see also* zhaeshi*—smooth)*

zhooshkiwau-daugunun skates

PREFIXES

zhooshkoowauh it is slippery
zhooshki'd'ummoh the road is slippery
zhooshki-abooz-inautik a ski
zhooshki-wae-igun an iron
zhooshi-koodjigun a plane

---

zhugushk; zhugushki • *bend low; bow low; crouch; stoop; hunker (down); hunch (over)* • *crush*

---

w'zhugushk-itauh he/she crouches
zhugushk-aundawae a flying squirrel
w'zhugushk-pugizoh he/she throws himself/herself down flat

---

zigi; zigini *hand to hand; tied; related; touching; link; bind; clasp; connect; coupling; bond; knot; join; chain; clamp; latch to; unite; splice; conjoin; attach; span; affix to*

---

w'zigin-inindjeenindiwuk they shake hands; they join hands
w'zigi-dayae-odaubaunikoh he/she tailgates
w'zig-aubeeginaun he/she leads him/her around by a leash
zigugun a nail
w'zigaukoowaun he/she nails it

---

ziguk; ziguki(zuguk)(zuguki) • *tidy; put away; store; neat; trim; clean; order(ly); spick and span; organized* • *gather; collect; mass; assemble; supply; store up; stock up; preserve; reserve; put aside; save; hoard; deposit; conserve*

---

w'zugukinigae he/she puts it away
zuguk-atae it is tidy
w'ziguk-kummikizih he/she is tidy

---

zinig; zinigi *rub; massage; knead; apply; rub down*

---

w'zinig-idjeenaun he/she rubs him/her down
ziniginun apply it
zinigigun ointment
w'gee zinig-ozhaewaun he/she applied ointment to his/her body

---

zizug; zug; zugau; zugi *thick; brambly; dense; impenetrable; impassable; tight; impermeable; tangled; snarled; entangled; thorny; impassable*

---

zug-auh it is dense
zug-aukawauh the forest is impassable
Zugaundawae-w-ininiwuk dwellers of a thick tangled woods in Wisconsin
w'zugaun-quae his/her hair is matted, hard to comb
w'zug-izih he/she/it tangled
zuzugauh it is dense

---

zoob; zoobi; zoosoob *to suck*

---

w'gee zoobindaun zeezibaukootoohnse he/she sucked an all-day sucker
zoobinoyigun a sucker; a soother

---

zoong; zoongi • *strong; firm; healthy; durable; immovable; resolute; solid; fixed; fast; secure; stationary; rooted; steady; stable; constant; steadfast; convinced; true; determined; staunch* • *brave; courageous*

---

zoong-kummik Strong Earth
w'zoongi-odae-ae he/she is courageous
zoongun it is firm
w'zoong-kummee he/she takes resolute steps

Glossary

A Few Common Verb Roots

A

aenimoowin refers to an operation, function of the mind; some opinion, view of self

ae'poogook refers to quality of flavor

aewin refers to being; possession of certain traits or characteristics, virtues, cupidities

aeyaugidinoowin refers to the similarity or dissimilarity of persons, beings, places, features or objects

akeessaewin refers to motion toward the earth, ground, soil

akeewin refers to an act, performed by, in, on, at, for, upon, or with the earth; steps, strides

anikaeniwin refers to an arm; the shape, motion, color of an arm

anoodaugaewin refers to hire, employment, service; the purpose and duration of service

assineegaewin refers to stone throwing; to the force and direction of pitching stones

aubindukawaewin refers to reading of signs; to forecast, predict

auboo refers to the kind or character of a soup or beverage

auboonoowin refers to drifting; the pace, direction, and locale of the drift generated by a current

audjigaewin refers to the application of force, tool, instrument in the course of work or play

audjiwaeniwin refers to a perpetration of deed, beneficial or otherwise, upon a person, another being, place, or thing

audjiwaewin refers to treatment of another; to attitude, opinion, feeling, impression of others

augauwin refers to the shape, form of thing, place, being, feature; to flexibility, curvature, warp, bend, malleability

aundawaewin refers to changing place, moving

aundizoowin refers to speech; to brag, crow, sing one's own praise, to talk about oneself

aunigaewin refers to manipulation, handling

aushoowin; aussoowin refers to the manner, form, rate, character, etc. of wind-generated flight

aussoowin; inaussoowin refers to the effect of sunlight upon complexion

autaugaewin refers to motion, to or away from another person, place or thing

autikawae'igaewin refers to stick throwing

autumaewin; autumoowin refers to the outcome, result, effect, issue, aftermath, reaction, influence of news, a message, event, occurrence or happening

auwaewin; iwaewin refers to an act, deed performed by one person upon another, a place, or a thing

auwissoowin refers to the unaided performance of a deed, act for one's own benefit but not to the exclusion of others

GLOSSARY

auwiwin; auwaeyauwin denotes being, becoming, presence, existence, life
auzoowin refers to the performance of a deed, act for one's own benefit; to pretend, dissimulate
awaengaewin; aenigaewin refers to a relationship, kinship; to the administration, management and care of others
awaessaewin; aessaewin to perform an involuntary act; to suffer an accident
awigaewin refers to an action, performance, doing
ayubiwin refers to prostration

B

beeg refers to breaking
beewoowin refers to waiting; to the purpose, duration, manner of waiting
beewunaewin refers to fur, animal hair; to the change, color, condition, quality of fur
bidjigaewin refers to binding, trussing, tying, wrapping, casing, dressing, compressing; handling, assembling, fabricating, forming, casting, framing, dismantling, breaking down, alteration
bugoonaewin; bugooneewin; bugauwin refers to a flower, a blossom; to the color, purpose, character, nature, and appearance of a flower, petal, or leaf
bugoowin; boogoowin refers to drifting; to the pace, direction, and place on the river or lake; to the drifting caused by waves and wind

E

eeginaewin refers to a pelt, skin; to the treatment of a pelt
eeginigaewin; waeginigaewin refers to the handling, manipulation, arrangement of fabrics, textiles, cloth, skins
eegoomaewin; eegoomoowin refers to the nose; to the condition, state of the nose and respiration
eengawaeniwin refers to changing the expression of one's face
eengawaewin refers to the face; to the appearance, shape, profile, complexion, frame, character of a face
eenoowin; eeniwin refers to numbers, crowds, assemblies, gatherings, many, numerous
eewaewin refers to accompaniment, company, association
eeweewin; awaewoowin refers to exertion; force expended in motion, exercise, attempt, and labor
eewin; eewaewin denotes act, deed, action, commission
equaewin refers to the head; to the condition, state, mood, awareness, sense, consciousness

G

gauboowin; inigauboowiwin refers to stance, standing; to the style, manner, posture of standing
gawaushkiniwin refers to jumping, leaping, bounce, bound; to the manner, purpose, extent, pace, of jumping
geezhiwaewin refers to diction, syntax; to the nature and character of remarks
goon refers to the quality, character, nature, texture of snow
goonaebiwin refers to a feather; to the change in appearance and form of feathers, featherings
goondjigaewin refers to marinating, soaking, steeping, immersing, putting in water
goondjigaewin refers to swallowing, ingesting
goonugauwin refers to snow, fallen snow; to the character, nature, quality, state, and depth of fallen snow
goonugauwin refers to the quality, character, nature, texture, depth, kind of snow
gummauwin; gummeewin; gummoowin; gummeeng; gummeek; agaumming refers to a body of water, a lake; to the nature, quality, and character of water

I

ibeegaewin refers to the manufacture, production, drawing, tracing of lines; to the purpose, character, form, direction, extent, quality of lines traced or set down

ibidjigaewin refers to the manner and form of pulling something apart, asunder

ibigaewin refers to a thrusting motion

ibinigaewin; ibinigoowin refers to seizure, capture, taking hold of, grasping, clasping, holding, possessing, manipulating

ibinikaewin to find; to break; to defeather

ibitchigaewin refers to manipulation, handling, managing, engineering, maneuvering

idaubeewin refers to drawing, hauling, dragging; to the manner, direction of the operation, and to the nature and character of the object drawn

idoonaewin refers to the mouth; to the shape, form, condition, appearance of the mouth

idumoowin refers to definition, connotation, meaning

igaewin; ikaewin; itchigaewin; autchigaewin; ootchigaewin refers to making, causing, generating, effecting, originating, producing, inspiring, initiating, instituting

igidugaewin refers to form, frame, shape, mold, cast

iginaewin refers to pain; to the cause, nature and quality of pain

igooziwin refers to state, condition, character of a person or thing

igummaewin refers to walking, passage, progress along waterways

ikaugaewin; itaugaewin; initawaugaewin denotes going toward, forward, advancing upon, approaching; to the purpose, manner, pace, and character of the advance

ikauwin refers to motion, movement; to the direction, purpose, nature, character, quality of the motion

ikishinoowin refers to strides, steps; to the direction, length of strides

ikoodjigaewin refers to carving, sculpting, paring, peeling; to the purpose, form, shape and designs carved or sculpted

ikoonigaewin refers to flaying; to the manner, shape, design of flaying

ikoonigaewin refers to touch, caress, stroking of a person, being, or object

ikuzhiwaewin refers to a contest, meet, competition; race, run, move quickly

imaugootiwin refers to the kind of odor given off by an insensate object

imaugooziwin refers to the kind of odor given off by a sensate being

imaugooziwin; imaugootiwin refers to odor, smell; to the source, nature, character of an odor

imaundjigaewin refers to the quality, character of smell

imaussoowin; imautaewin refers to odor, smell; to the odor of smoke; to the smell of something burning

imoowin refers to language, utterance, call, usage

inaebawaewin refers to inflation, deflation; to the purpose, manner, and degree of inflation

inaegaewin refers to direction of search, quest; to the purpose, pace and course of pursuit, mission, and pass

inaendaugooziwin refers to aspect, image, presence, character, semblance, impression

inaendiwin; indaendiwin refers to absence, being elsewhere, being abroad; to the duration of absence

inaendjigaewin refers to the operation, function of the mind, perception, opinion, impression of the mind

inaendumoowin refers to an operation, activity, function of the mind; to think, imagine, will

inaendumoowin refers to thinking, imagination, will

inaewin refers to pain, ache, injury; to the tolerance, reaction, attitude, endurance to pain, discomfort, injury, slight, sickness, misfortune

inaeziwin refers to health, feeling, condition, state of being

inaubae-wiziwin refers to the human figure

inaubauwaedjigaewin; inaubauwidjigaewin; inaubauwaewin; inaubauwitchigaewin refers to wetting, dampening, watering, moisturizing; to the manner, degree, purpose and character of an act

GLOSSARY

inaubeessitchigaewin; inaubeessinoowin; inaubeewin refers to a line, string, rope, mark; to the purpose, form, extent, character of a line

inaubeewin refers to the direction, angle, contour of a line, stripe, strip, string, margin, etc.

inaubikauwin refers to rock; to the topography, nature, quality, structure, appearance, and formation of rocks, mountains, and metal

inaubindumoowin refers to imagination

inaubindumoowin refers to perception

inaubindumoowin refers to perception, imagination, view, impression; to the quality, character and nature of the being or object perceived

inaubiwin refers to looking

inaubiwin refers to looking; to the direction, manner, and purpose of looking

inaudigaewin refers to swimming, or passage by swimming; to the purpose, manner, direction, course, duration, and sound produced by swimming

inaudigaewin refers to the form, style of swimming

inaudigaukoowin refers to trek or passage by foot on ice; to the purpose, manner, direction, course, duration, and sound produced by traveling on foot on ice

inaudigauwin; inaudigauzeewin refers to trek or passage on foot in water; to the purpose, manner, direction, course, duration, and sound of trekking by water

inaudiziwin refers to state, condition, temperament, character, personality, disposition

inaudjimoowin refers to speech, narration; to the flavor, nature, character of a narration or report, as well as to its theme or subject

inaugaewin refers to confrontation, contest, face-off, encounter, counteraction, meeting; to the cause and outcome of confrontation; to the manufacture, construction, fashioning of a tool, instrument, dish, etc.

inaugaewin refers to the direction of a missile at a target, object; to the quality of a discharge

inaugooziwin denotes appearance, semblance, demeanor, cast, look, aspect, image, carriage

inaugooziwin refers to appearance, resemblance, seeming

inau-gummidaewin refers to the manner of boiling

inaugummiwin refers to the state, quality, taste, character of water

inaugummizigaewin; inaugummidaewin denotes boiling; refers to the rate and state of boiling

inaukawae'igaewin refers to hewing, chopping, felling; to the purpose, direction, and manner of felling trees or structures

inaukawaeyauwin; inaukawaeyauh refers to woods, forests, groves; to the nature, character, density of a forest

inaukawigaewin; inaukiwigaewin refers to affixing, attaching to; to connect, adjoin, join, conjoin, fasten, unite, tack, nail, seal, close

inaukidaewin refers to the cause, character, and nature of a blaze

inaukidjiwin refers to the nature, character and quality and intensity of a chill or freeze

inaukinaewin refers to light; to the quality, density of light, flame, or blaze

inaukinaewin refers to the nature, quality, character of fire and light produced by fire or blaze

inaukinigaewin refers to judgment, decision, measurement; to the character and nature of making a decision

inaukizigaewin; inaukizoowin; inaukidaewin refers to fire, a blaze; to the cause, nature, course, direction, character, pace of a fire; to the pattern and extent of damage and burns caused and suffered

inaukiziwin; inaukooziwin refers to the contour of an extended body, object, elongated thing

inaukummoowin refers to direction and pitch, angle of a stick, bar, rod, timber

inaumindaewin refers to barometric pressure; to the quality and changes in the atmosphere

inaumindaewin refers to the density and quality and temperature of smoke

inaumoowin refers to breathing, respiration; to the rate, sound, nature and character of breathing

inaunawaewin refers to a tail; to the motion, dimensions, and cast of an animal tail

inaundaewin refers to color, shade, hue, tone, pigment

inaundawaewin; aundawaewin refers to ascending, descending, changing places at an altitude; to the direction, pace, sound, duration of ascension, descension, change of position at upper levels

inaundjigaewin refers to a blow, strike; to the nature, character, and consequence, effect of a blow delivered

inaundumoowin refers to hunger; to the cause, nature, character, degree, and consequence of hunger

inaungaewin; inawaungaewin refers to flight; the flight of birds; to the direction, pace, altitude, character, style, and manner of the flight of birds

inaungizoowin; inaungidaewin refers to the posture and articulation of a prostrate or collapsed body

inaunikaewin refers to excavation, digging; to the pace, depth, purpose and manner of burrowing, digging

inaunikittooniwin; dinaunikittooniwin refers to speech, talk; to modulation, tone, pitch, pace of speech

inaunimut refers to the wind; to the force, direction, character, and sound of wind

inauniquot refers to clouds; to the shape, formation, motion, color, condition, direction, and pace of clouds; to the state of clouds, cloudiness

inaupinaewin refers to the cause, nature, character, and form of an illness, sickness, disease

inaup-inunigaewin refers to conflict, battle; to the extent, range, character, kind, and nature of damages and wounds inflicted and suffered

inaupitaewin; inaupissauwaewin refers to smoke, fumes; to the direction, color, odor, and pace of smoke; to the pattern, texture, tone of smoke

inaushiwin refers to the direction, pace, manner of being driven by the wind

inaushiwin; aushiwin; aushoowin; inaussiwin; aussin denotes movement generated by wind (flight, sailing); refers to the pace, manner, direction, course, sound, duration of the flight or sailing of people, beings, objects, and things

inaushkaugaewin refers to the purpose, manner, pace, sound, and locale of the act of pursuit

inaushkauwin refers to waves, billows; to the pace, course, action, color, and sound of waves, breakers

inaussaeyauwin; inautaeyauwin refers to light; to the source, direction, density, and nature of light

inauss-igaewin refers to light; sunlight; sunshine; sunrise; sunset

inauss-igaewin; inautigaewin; inauhnzhaewin refers to sunlight; to the creation or provision of light; to the density and quality of light

inaussinoowin refers to the direction, pace, manner of being driven by the wind

inaussitchigaewin refers to causing or influencing the course and direction of flight, navigation

inaussitchigaewin refers to flight; to the course, pattern, velocity, altitude of flight generated by the act of launching an object

inaussitchigaewin refers to the rate, direction and force of flight

inautaeshinoowin refers to the shape, contour, form of a shadow, outline

inautaewin refers to moonlight, the cast and density of such light; the heat of the sun and to the hue of plants and flowers

inautigaewin refers to moonlight

inauwaewin refers to the form, shape, structure of the human body

inauwinidiwin refers to a group walking in a body

inauzhaewin refers to light other than that of the sun or moon; to the density, color, character of light

inauzhigaewin; inauzhiwaewin denotes driving, guiding, conducting, propelling, or directing the course and pace of a vehicle or vessel

inawaewaessinoowin refers to ringing; to the sound and resonance produced by the clash of metal

inawaewaetoowin refers to commotion, disturbance made by a human or an animal

inawaewaewin refers to the production of sound

inawaewaezigaewin refers to cooking corn; to the sound and manner of cooking corn

inawaewidumoowin refers to the origin, direction, and character of articulation, enunciation, pronunciation, call, diction; to pitch, volume of voice, call

inawaewin refers to language

inaweewin refers to malleability of form

indaugaewin refers to kinship; to being of the same household

indaunigaewin to deal; to mix; to manipulate

indauwin refers to residence, domicile where one and one's family may grow and develop, conduct affairs in private, exercise beliefs and pastimes in seclusion, and where all sense of right and wrong originates and all culpability lies

indiwin refers to an act; to the purpose, quality, nature, character of an act

indjigaewin refers to taking into the mouth

indjitchigaewin denotes collecting, putting away (aside), saving, storing, preserving, stocking

indoonigaewin; indaunigaewin refers to collection, gathering, amassing, dealing

indooshkigaewin to reap, heap, collect

ineegiwin refers to growth; to the rate, quality, and character of growth

ingaewin; oongaewin; aungaewin; eengaewin refers to the use of speech in influencing, counseling, advising, urging, inciting others

iniboodjigaewin refers to scoring, furrowing, fluting, etching

inidjeenigaewin refers to the manner of handling a body; to touch, caress, stroking, manipulation of another's body

inidjeeyauwin refers to the shape, form, contour of a berry, seed, fruit, vegetable, body

inidjiwun refers to the flow of water, rivers, streams; to the direction, pace, sound, color, character, and nature of running, flowing water

inigaumoowin refers to the degree and aspect of corpulence

inigawaudjigaewin refers to form, design of sewing, stitching

inigawaussoowin; inigawaudaewin refers to sewing; the purpose, manner, style, nature of sewing

inigidauzoowin refers to the disposition for, duration of, susceptibility to, and the character of anger

iniginigaewin; inigaewin; inaegaewin; oonaegaewin; inugaewin; inaugaewin refers to an operation, function, execution, manipulation, handling

iniginoowin refers to size, mass, bulk

inigoodaewin refers to the form, state, nature of suspension of a hung article

inigoowin refers to consequences, results suffered, endured, incurred by a person at the hands of another person or by an event

inikaugaewin refers to the form and quality of fit; to the injury or injuries inflicted by collision

inikaugaewin; inishkaugaewin; inikoodaewin; inikaugoowin; inishkaugoowin refers to the nature, character, and extent of damage, injury, discomfort, harm, destruction, loss, inflicted or incurred as a result of some act, deliberate or accidental; to match, fit, correlation, correspondence, adaptation, suitability

inikaugoowin refers to the kind, nature, character of mark, injury inflicted

inikauwin refers to journey, travel, destination; to the course, bearings, purpose, pace of a trek, process, journey, movement, travel; to the direction, pace and stage of motion

inikauzoowin refers to a name; to the origin, quality of a name

inikawaewin refers to tracks, prints; to the quality, pattern, direction of tracks; to the character, aspect of trail left behind

inikingaewin refers to form and quality of fit

inindjeetauwin refers to the hand; to the forms and shapes made by the hand

iningawaumiwin; iningawaumoowin refers to sleep; to the depth, duration, nature, quality, and character of sleep

ininidiwin; oondjinidiwin denotes fighting, battle, contest; refers to the cause, location, extent, outcome, and effects of battle

ininigaewin refers to handing over, passing on to

ininigaewin refers to handling, managing

ininimaukaewin; oonimaukaewin; ininikaewin; aenimaukaewin; aussikaewin; imaugaewin denotes handing over or to, transmitting, transferring, giving, distributing, bequeathing

ini'oonaewin; iwi'oonaewin; oonaewin refers to carrying, bearing, toting; to the weight and manner of carrying a burden on a shoulder

inipidjigaewin; inipoodjigaewin refers to taste, flavor; to the taste and flavor of a meal

iniquae-ishinoowin refers to the angle and direction of reclining head

inishaewin refers to hearing, the perception of sound

inishinoowin refers to a wound, injury suffered; to the extent, character, quality and nature of a wound, injury suffered or incurred

inishinoowin refers to the angle and direction of a reclining body

inishinoowin; izhishinoowin refers to the articulation, form, lie, position, layout of a reclining body

inishkinaewin refers to the manner, mode of filling a container

inishkiniwaewin refers to the form, manner, degree of fullness, fit

inishkum refers to the state, quality of tracks left behind

inishkumoowin refers to tracks, prints

inissaewin; issaewin refers to spontaneous, involuntary motion; to the pace, direction, manner, duration, time, and sound of a spontaneous act, motion, or movement

initagawaewauyin refers to a river and its bed, course, depth, width, character

initaugooziwin refers to call, voice; to the pitch, tone, volume, effect of speech, utterance, or call

initauwin refers to shaping, flexing, contorting, twisting oneself

initauwin; itauwin; itawauwin; ootauwin refers to stance, position, posture, bearing, body language, attitude, carriage, motion, movement, disposition, belief, creed, affiliation, political and religious tenets

initauwingauwin refers to the sand; to the topography, nature, quality, formation of sandy soil

initumoowin refers to hearing; to the perception of a voice, call, message, subject matter

inizhauzoowin refers to urination; to the place, manner of urination

inizhigaewin; inoozhigaewin; izhigaewin refers to the style, manner, angle, extent of a slice, cut

inizhoowaewin denotes sending, dispatching, transmitting, communicating

inizigaewin; inoozigaewin; inaezigaewin; inoohnzaekawaewin refers to cooking; to the style, manner, technique of cooking; to a recipe

inoodaewin refers to cooking; to the way in which the meat or dish turned out

inoodaewin refers to crawling; to the pace, direction, and style of crawling

inoodaewiziwin refers to a family; to the character, size, quality, condition, and movement of a family

inoodiniwin refers to wind; to the source, direction of a wind

inoodjuzoowin refers to girth, frame

inoogaewin; inoo-igaewin; inoomaugaewin denotes direction, way, point, bearings, indication, aim

inoomaugaewin refers to emotion; to longing for, craving, pining, missing

inootaugaewin refers to imitation, copying, reproduction; to the reproduction of what is heard and seen as accurately as perception and fluency allow

inootaugaewin refers to imitating, interpreting

GLOSSARY

inoowaengaewin; inoowaewin refers to kinship, relationship; to semblance, resemblance, correlation, matching

inoowaezhiwaewin refers to conducting, guiding, leading, showing the way

inossaewin refers to the pace, direction, manner of walking

inossaewin; ossaewin refers to walking; to the pace, sound, style, purpose, direction, duration, location, manner of walking

inubiwin refers to the place, form, and manner of sitting

inudaemoowin refers to crying, weeping; to the cause, tone, pitch, volume, and sound of crying

inudauwaewin refers to selling; to the amount and quality sold, traded, exchanged

inudinoowin refers to the tone, degree of freezing, ice, snow

inudinoowin refers to freezing; to the nature, character, form, and extent of freezing

inudjigaewin refers to the manner, rate, and extent of packing, filling

inudjiwin; inaukidjiwin refers to the intensity, severity, degree, extent of cold, chilly, freezing temperatures

inudoowin refers to a trail; to following and leaving a trail

inudunnauwin refers to the altitude, elevation, depth of the structure and topography of the earth's landforms

inugaumoowin refers to plumpness; to the state, degree, and condition of plumpness

inugauwin refers to a dance, performance; to the meaning, point, sense, theme of a dance

inugigaewin; ingugaewin refers to hewing, chopping, hacking, slashing, felling

inuginaundjigaewin refers to a blow, strike, hit; to the manner, nature, character, direction, force, and result of a blow

inugindaewin refers to worth, value, price, totaling

inuginigaewin; waungawigaewin refers to scattering, spreading, covering

inugoodjigaewin; inugoodaewin refers to suspension, hanging, slinging, drape, dangle; to the style, form, and character of a hang, suspension

inukidoodaewin refers to the state, condition, degree of finish or "doneness" of a dish, flesh, meat or vegetables

inukissitchigaewin refers to construction, erecting, putting up

inukizhoowaewin refers to rowing; to the direction, pace, manner, and pattern of rowing

inuk-koodjigaewin refers to carving in a certain manner, style

inukooniyaewaewin refers to dress, attire; to the manner, style, character, quality, color, and condition of clothing

inukummeewin; ummeewin refers to step, stride; to the manner, pace, length, direction of strides

inukummikut; aen-kummikuk refers to an event, happening, occurrence

inumauzoowin refers to chanting, singing; to the tone, text, content, purpose of a chant, chanting; to the tone, pitch, purpose, content of a song

inumindjiwoowin refers to the sense or feeling of one's state of health or being

inummoh refers to the direction of a trail, path, road, route, course

inundjigaewin refers to eating; to the manner, quality, and character of eating; to a meal

inuniwin refers to a result, condition, state, consequence, brought on or produced by natural action

inu'oodjigaewin refers to firing at, discharging

inupidjigaewin refers to the manner and character of fastening

inupidjigaewin; inupizoowin; inupidaewin refers to dress, attire, habit, costume, outfitting; to the manner, style, color, character of dress, attire, drape, caparison, adornment, trim

inupizoowin refers to the manner, style and type of dress or binding

inushkauwin refers to the collapse, cave in, breakdown, destruction of shape or structure

inutiniwin; inutiwin refers to solidity; to the state or condition of a mass

inutumaugaewin refers to an act performed for another (such as setting or placing some object before another person)
ipeeginigaewin refers to immersion and taking out of water; to the purpose, manner, and duration of the immersion
ipeessauwin refers to rain; to the direction, character, nature, and quality of rainfall
ipeewin refers to water; to relationship to water; to the use of water; to distance and motion toward, away from, and upon water
ipidjigaewin; ipoodjigaewin refers to taste, flavor; to the quality of taste
ipoowin refers to snowfall; to the rate, character, nature, and quality of a snowfall
ishimoowin refers to sleep; to the quality, nature, and character of wakefulness and drowsiness, repose
ishkaugaewin; iskaugaewin; iskaugeewin refers to succession, following, anteceding, preceding, procession
ishkauwin denotes motion, movement, action, progress, flux, course; refers to the pace, direction, force of motion, advance; to passage by canoe; to the direction, pace, course, route of canoe travel
ishkauwin refers to travel by canoe, rowboat, sailboat
ishkeehnzhigawaeniwin refers to an eye; to the size, shape, movement, structure, and luster of the eye
ishkeewin refers to endurance, lasting, remaining, survival
ishkikauwin refers to an alteration, change, diversion, deflection in the direction of a course taken or intended, or in the direction of a road or route
ishkinaewin; inushkinaewin refers to filling, fullness; to the stage of fullness
ishkoodjigaewin denotes burden, ballast, weighing down, loading with, lading
ishkummeewin refers to step, stride; to footprints, tracks
ishkummoowin refers to travel, trekking, journey by land
ishkumoowin refers to putting in the mouth
iskugaewin; iskidaewin refers to an act of setting afire, ablaze; to drying up; to the nature and character of a blaze, fire
issaewin refers to the manner, form, rate, character, etc. of involuntary motion
isseewaewin refers to change; fluid, liquid; to stirring up, mixing up; to a natural change in condition
issitchigaewin; oossitchigaewin; eessitchigaewin; aussitchigaewin; aessitchigaewin refers to arrangement, order, place, preparation, setting, design, disposition, alignment, organization, classification, setting up, allocation, system, assignment, marshalling
issutchigaewin refers to a sudden thrust, force
issutchigaewin refers to jerking, shoving
itaussoowin; initaussoowin refers to storage, stockage, massing, heaping
itauwin refers to action, inclination, disposition, preference
itauwin refers to being in motion, moving
itawauwauwin denotes an invocation for the good or evil, blessing or curse upon someone or something
iwaewin denotes flight, bolting, making off, stealing away; refers to the manner, pace, sound, and direction of flight; to starting, bolting away
iwaewin refers to seeking, tracking down, and flushing
iwaewin refers to tracking down, hunting, pursuing, flushing out
izhau'd'iwin denotes going, traveling, proceeding, advancing; refers to the purpose, pace, direction, manner, course, and sound produced in travel
izheewin refers to the character and style of an act, performance
izheewin; izheeweewin refers to the manner, style, technique, approach, aptitude, disposition for undertaking and carrying out some task
izhi-eengawaewin refers to the form, shape of the face
izhi-gummaewin refers to progress by foot along waterway
izhi-ishkeehnzhig-awaewin refers to the tone, shade and luster of the eye
izhinumoowin refers to perception

GLOSSARY

izhiwaebut(iwin) refers to an event, occurrence, happening
iziwin refers to character, trait
izoowin refers to the manner, form, rate, character, etc. of conducted, voluntary motion—spontaneous

K

kawaewin refers to tracking, trailing, tailing
keewaewin refers to articulation, enunciation, pronunciation
kittoowin refers to saying, uttering
koodjitchigewin; gadjitchigaewin refers to trying, attempting, testing, endeavoring
kummeewin refers to a step, footing
kundawaewin refers to a contest, meet, competition; to racing, running, moving quickly

M

meegawaewin refers to giving
meegwunaewin refers to a feather; to the change in appearance and form of feathers, featherings
meenaewin refers to disposition; to fruit, berries

N

nakaewae'igaewin; ikawae'igaewin refers to direction, destination, bearing, way, route, course; to going toward, making for, steering toward
neegiwin refers to growing
noodiniwin refers to blowing wind

O

odae'aewin refers to character, fiber, mettle, make-up, mold, temper
odaenawin refers to a village, town, city, a gathering of families; to the size, location, character, quality of a town, nation, state
onawaeziwin refers to luck
ondji refers to origin, reason for; to purpose, cause, source
oogoowin refers to waves; to the direction, and character of waves
oohnzaekawaewin refers to steaming, scalding, scouring
oomoowin; oomaewin refers to calls, utterances, diction, language, syntax
oondaewin denotes boiling; refers to the state and rate of boiling
oondaunawaewin refers to eating, tasting, swallowing
oondjeewin refers to an origin, source, cause, beginning, issue, start
oondjininidiwin refers to the cause of a battle, fight, war
oondu-ipeewin refers to the source of water
oondumeewin refers to business, diligence, occupation, industriousness
oonoowin refers to howling
oowaewin refers to firing at, discharging a missile
oowidizoowin refers to an act that is intended to be of benefit to oneself; to a self-inflicted accidental injury
ozhaewin refers to the body, flesh, issue; to some act performed upon the body; to the changes wrought upon the body
ozhauwaewin refers to treatment, disposition, incision of a body and skin

P

pizoowin refers to flight, flying, locomotion; to the direction, pace, purpose, and character of flight
putoowin refers to running; to the direction, pace, manner, sound, character, and nature of running
puwaewin refers to flight, retreat, running away; to the direction, pace, manner, sound, character, and nature of flight, retreat, running away

Q

quaewiwoon refers to hair; to the management, care, maintenance, treatment, and styling of hair

T

towugaewin refers to the ear; to the shape, size, movement of the ear; to the quality of hearing; to the attention of the listener

U

uhmeewin refers to the pace, direction, manner of steps
uhmoowin refers to walking on an established trail, road, path
umaugaewin denotes demands, importunities, requests, solicitation
ummeewin refers to the manner, character of pace, step
umoowin refers to water; to the surface of water

W

wadauneewin; idauneewin refers to cover, blanket, covering; to matting, filming, coating; to the character, nature, quality, appearance, and condition of a coating (such as snow, dew, frost)
waewaeshkauwin refers to sound made, produced by friction
waewaewin refers to sound, call, utterance, speech; to the nature, volume, source, tone, pitch, quality, and character of sound, call, utterance, speech
waewaewin refers to the outcome, result, effect, issue, aftermath, reaction, influence of news, a message, event, occurrence, or happening
waub refers to lightening, clearing, whitening
waubiwin; aubiwin refers to sight; to the character and quality of sight (from *waub*—white)
waugaewin denotes emission, expulsion, discharge, excretion, emanation, exuding, purging; refers to making, fashioning, forming, flexing
waussaeyauwin; wautaeyauwin refers to light; to the source, direction, character of light
wauwaetaugaewin refers to repayment, recompense, return in kind, requital, getting even, reciprocation
weendumaewin refers to articulation, pronunciation
widjiwaewin refers to the ascent and descent of a mountain

GLOSSARY